PRESIDENT CLINTON'S NEW BEGINNING

PRESIDENT CLINTON'S NEW BEGINNING

THE COMPLETE TEXT, WITH ILLUSTRATIONS,
OF THE HISTORIC CLINTON-GORE
ECONOMIC CONFERENCE
LITTLE ROCK, ARKANSAS,
DECEMBER 14–15, 1992

Conducted by
President Bill Clinton

DONALD I. FINE, INC.
New York

By exclusive arrangement the transcripts of the testimony of the Clinton Economic Summit were provided by Federal News Service, 620 National Press Building, Washington, D.C. 20045

What follows is a complete transcript of the Clinton-Gore Economic Conference without excerpt or alteration. Some names used by panelists at the conference were unidentifiable. We regret any unavoidable inconvenience this may cause the reader.

Selected photographs on pp. xiii–xvi by AP/Wide World Photos.

Library of Congress Cataloging-in-Publication Data

Economic Conference (1992 : Little Rock, Ark.)
President Clinton's new beginning : the complete text, with illustrations, of the historic Economic Conference conducted by President Bill Clinton and Vice President Al Gore in Little Rock, Arkansas, December 14-15, 1992 / conducted by President Bill Clinton.
p. cm.
ISBN 1-55611-368-4 (hard). — ISBN 1-55611-367-6 (paper)
1. United States—Economic policy—1981—Congresses.
I. Clinton, Bill, 1946-   . II. Title.
HC106.8.E2747   1992
338.973—dc20   92-59972
                                                          CIP

Manufactured in the United States of America

10 9 8 7 6 5 4 3 2 1

CONTENTS

MONDAY, DECEMBER 14, 1992, OPENING SESSION

(Note: page numbers reflect when participants first spoke at conference)

THE NATIONAL ECONOMY

MONDAY, DECEMBER 14, 1992,
AFTERNOON SESSION

THE INTERNATIONAL ECONOMY

MACROECONOMIC OVERVIEW

Education and Job Training

TUESDAY, DECEMBER 15, 1992,
MORNING SESSION

NATIONAL ECONOMIC POLICY

MACROECONOMIC OVERVIEW

SHORT-TERM AND LONG-TERM STRATEGIES

PANEL DISCUSSION

ECONOMIC GROWTH AND DEFICIT REDUCTION

PANEL DISCUSSION

TUESDAY, DECEMBER 15, 1992,
AFTERNOON SESSION

ENVIRONMENT AND TECHNOLOGY

ENVIRONMENTAL POLICY

PANEL DISCUSSION

JOBS AND THE ENVIRONMENT

PRESIDENT-ELECT CLINTON'S
POST-ECONOMIC CONFERENCE
NEWS CONFERENCE

p. 405

AT THE CONFERENCE . . .

Robert Reich, Labor Secretary.

Lloyd Bentsen, Treasury Secretary.

Donna Shalala, Secretary of Health
and Human Services.

Laura D'Andrea Tyson, Chairman of
the Council of Economic Advisers.

Robert Solow, Massachusetts Insititue
of Technology professor and 1987
winner of the Nobel Prize in Economics.

Robert E. Rubin, Chairman, National
Economic Council, and former Vice
President of Goldman Sachs & Co.

First Lady Hillary Clinton with U.S. Trade Representative Mickey Kantor *(left);* Felix Rohatyn, Sr. Partner, Lazard Freres & Co. *(below).*

John Sculley, CEO, Apple Computers.

Marian Wright Edelman, founder and President of the Children's Defense Fund.

Alice Rivlin, Deputy-Director, Office of
Management and Budget.

Leon Panetta, Director, Office of
Management and Budget.

Harold Poling, CEO, Ford Motor Co.

Ron Brown, Secretary of Commerce.

Chief Wilma Mankiller of the Cherokee
Nation.

Carol Browner, Director of the
Environmental Protection Agency.

Economic Conference Opening Session Monday, December 14, 1992

PRESIDENT-ELECT CLINTON: Good morning and thank you all for being here. I want to welcome you to Little Rock and to this economic conference. Some of you I'm meeting for the first time today, some of you I've known for years. I want to thank each and every one of you for coming to my home town and for joining people from all across America who are determined to change our country for the better.

I can tell you that while this may well be the most distinguished and diverse group of Americans ever to meet to discuss our economic promise as well as our economic problems, as you all know there were many thousands more outstanding Americans who very much wanted to come here. Today we are working not only for ourselves and for them, but for the rest of this country as well.

I appreciate your presence and I thank all of those who are looking at us on television who wanted to be here today. I think as the conference unfolds there will be a general consensus that we have made the right decision about the size as well as the composition of the meeting and I am very excited about it.

Over the course of the last 14 months as Senator Gore and I, and our families and supporters, took our campaign across America, we met many people who are determined to change this country. This campaign was about them and overwhelmingly about a long-term problem in the American economy as well as this prolonged recession, which threatened to deny them the chance that they deserve for a better future.

I met one of those people I'd like to tell you about. Benjamin Edwards is a 52-year-old, unemployed man who lives in Germantown, Pennsylvania. The night of the first presidential debate he had a viewing party at his house. Neighbors had to bring over television sets and lamps, and run extension cords from a nearby apartment because his own electricity along with his gas had been cut off. About 100 people watched the debate at his place. The next day, Benjamin Edwards took a bus 15 miles to attend one of my campaign rallies. As I came down the line he grabbed my hand and told me I had to win the election because he said, "I need a job." "I will," I said.

Now that the election is over I need your help to fulfill my commitment to Benjamin Edwards.

The economy is why we started down this road. The economy is why the American people gave me a chance along with Vice President-elect Gore and all the others who will be a part of this administration to turn this country around. And the economy is why we are here today.

I called this economic conference for three reasons, first so that all of us can hear and give an assessment of where our economy is today and what has been happening to it over the last two decades. Second, so that we could bring together a diverse and talented group of Americans who make this economy work, and get your ideas and your input on how we should implement our economic plan. Third, to begin through this very public process to reconnect the American people to their government and to ask for their help too in making economic progress. I need your help and the help of every American to do what together we have to do to fulfill our obligations to ourselves and to the future.

We are here because our nation and our people must prepare for global competition. We must revitalize and rebuild our economy. A thriving economy is the floor on which every citizen stands. A thriving economy is the legacy left by our parents and an endowment we must leave to our children. It is the precondition for all Americans having a real shot at the American dream.

Our strength is our diversity. Social mobility here is still unequaled elsewhere. Our will to innovate and compete, the determination of our workers, the creativity of our entrepreneurs are still the envy of the world. But for all these strengths we clearly face structural problems that today threaten our ability to harness the energies of all of our people and to guarantee the future we want for our children.

In the years following the Second World War our economy was in every respect the envy of the world. Our corporations, our labor force, our government worked together to ensure rising productivity, rising wages and increasing incomes in a stable, global economy. But over the last 20 years our country has been caught up in the crosscurrents of increasing global change and competition, and I think every one of us would admit that we have not fully adapted.

Just ten years ago we had the highest wages in the world; today we're 13th. We've had declining productivity growth rates, increasing income inequality and poverty, especially among our youngest children. For most Americans the average work week, which begins today, will entail more working hours than it did 20 years ago, for lower real wages than they were earning ten years ago. We spend far too much money on health care for too little in return, and we have to bring health costs in line with inflation.

As many people here who've worked on the government budget will tell you, fully 50 percent of the projected deficit growth over the next five years—50 percent is in inflated health care costs alone, not in new health care services, more money for the same health care.

We spend too much money paying yesterday's bills because the government debt is so high. The debt and interest on it now consume 15 cents of every tax dollar you pay.

4

Over the past month we've seen a number of encouraging signs about the economy's short-term health. We've heard good things about the unemployment rate, the inflation rate, housing starts, even consumer confidence, and, finally, the employment rate which, as all of you know, is often different from the unemployment rate. But it's far too early to assume that the change in these short-term measures really indicates that we're out of the woods even in this prolonged business cycle recession. The real measure of a recovery will be when many people are moving back into those hundreds of thousands of lost manufacturing jobs and when 100,000 Americans a month are no longer losing their health insurance. The real measure will be when encouraging numbers of people read in the newspapers—when the encouraging numbers people read in the newspapers are actually matched by their own personal experiences in paychecks and savings. We must never let a blizzard of statistics blind us to the real people and the real lives behind them.

And as we address short-term business cycle issues, we must never forget that the most profound problems of our economy are longer-term and structural. If we intend to fix things for the long term, we must invest for the long term. As I've said many times before, many of the problems we will be discussing here did not develop overnight. We cannot expect to solve them overnight. But I am convinced that we can do so if we change course. And with a national economic strategy, we can create jobs, raise income, reduce inequality, restore hope, and lead our country back to sustained economic greatness. I think we all agree that our short-sighted approach to many of the fundamental issues form the core of the weakness in our economic picture today: the failure to invest in our human resources; insufficient public and private sector investment in infrastructure, plant and equipment, critical research and development; a misplaced emphasis on short-term consumption rather than long-term investment spending; a lack of attention to our global competitiveness; spiralling health care costs; and a largely ignored exploding structural national debt.

Our new direction must rest on an understanding of the new realities of global competition. The world we face today is a world where what you earn depends on what you can learn. There's a direct relationship between high skills and high wages, and therefore we have to educate our people better to compete. We will be as rich and strong and rife with opportunity as we are skilled and talented and trained. I do have a plan which I have pushed all across America for economic revitalization, and I intend to do my best to put it into action.

The slightly improved short-term picture does not change the core elements of what we have to do over the long run. There are, it seems

5

to me, at least five key areas that must be explored in order to lay the proper foundation for long-term economic strength.

First, we must invest in our people—their education, their training, and their skills—and take whatever steps we need to make sure every American has a chance to benefit. There must be a lifetime investment of education from preschool to college, supporting not just those who choose to go on to four-year colleges, but also those who would build their skills through apprenticeships and other means. Investments in job training and retraining are the only way to ensure Americans have the changing skills to compete in a changing world, a world in which the average 18-year-old will change the nature of work seven or eight times in a lifetime.

Second, we must increase investment, both public and private, to create jobs: investment in technology, investment in infrastructure, investment in plant and equipment, investment in research and development.

Third, we must stop the cycle of borrow and spend economics. We've always borrowed in our country, but we used to borrow to invest the way people do in their businesses and in their personal lives. Today, we're borrowing to spend, and there is a huge difference. Our national debt is an economic ball and chain dragging us down, keeping longer-term interest rates high in spite of the actions of the Federal Reserve in bringing down short-term rates. Soon interest payments on the debt will add up to more than we spend on the national defense. We can't have that, which means we're going to have to make some tough decisions and some hard choices. We can't leave our children saddled with the cost of our neglect. And at the same time, we cannot ignore the strategic investments in our future which have also been allowed to fall into deficit in the last decade.

Fourth, we need a new approach to energy and to the environment. Half of our trade deficit, after all, is due to our increasing reliance on foreign oil. Many of our environmental problems grow directly out of our energy practices. It seems to me we have a real opportunity to revitalize major sectors of the American economy without throwing it into major dislocation, with a sustained long-term commitment to a new energy and environmental policy, one which recognizes that sustainable economic growth and environmental protection are compatible and, indeed, interlocked instead of in conflict. Senator Gore and I have never accepted the idea that there is a long-term conflict between economic growth and environmental responsibility.

And finally, we must each make a personal commitment to our government. I don't mean a financial payment, and I don't mean an agreement with every policy that I or any other person would implement, but I mean a very personal commitment to change: an investment of time, in spirit, a willingness to give something back to the country, and to challenge the way the government does its business so that we are not wasting so much money and not wasting so much of our future.

Over the past week, I've begun to appoint the economic team which will help me to translate our plans into action. They are here today, at least those who have been named are. There may be some here who have not been named. (Laughter.) Their strength and diversity should underscore the importance I give to this issue. I believe they are America's best.

I want to introduce them, although I know you've seen them as they have come in. Treasury Secretary designee, Senator Lloyd Bentsen of Texas. Deputy Secretary designee, Roger Altman. Where's Roger? He's here somewhere. There he is. Office of Management Budget Director, Leon Panetta. Deputy Director, Alice Rivlin. Economic Policy Adviser, Robert Rubin. Chair of the Council of Economic Advisers, Laura Tyson. Labor Secretary designee, Robert Reich, who said he had been on my short list for the entire campaign. (Laughter.) Commerce Secretary designee Ron Brown. And I believe that earlier two other people who are on every team I play on now, my Chief of Staff designee, Mack McLardy, and my wife, Hillary, I hope were both introduced, but they're both here.

Guided by experts who served so well during the campaign and the transition, this economic team has already begun to work to turn the campaign commitments we made into specific proposals. We need your advice and energy on them, too. We are here because we have a common stake in our economic future. You know, if you've looked at the participants here, you know you represent small and large businesses. You come from university halls and labor halls, from every corner of America, from the 50 states, the District of Columbia, and Puerto Rico. You range from Kathleen Piper, the owner of Pied Piper Flower Shop in Yankton, South Dakota, to John Sculley, the CEO of Apple Computer, to Bill Gray of the United Negro College Fund.

I expect that all of us will benefit from each other's suggestions, revisions, criticisms and new ideas as we consider our options. I want my administration to celebrate ideas from the first day to the last, and I want and need your ideas. We are in this, all of us, together.

And let's not kid ourselves; these are hard questions. As you look at the difficulties faced not only by the United States but the difficulties now facing Germany and the rest of Europe, the difficulties now facing Japan and other nations, there are hard questions. How do we restore higher rates of productivity? How can we reduce income inequality, a problem that has affected other nations as well as our own? How can we reduce this terrible burden of the large underclass in America and the incredible, the incredible restriction it is putting on the future of millions of our children?

How much growth can we have without worrying about inflation? What in the world can you really do, in reducing the defense budget as much as we have to, to avoid losing that magnificent industrial base and to do something with not only the men and women who are coming out of the service but all those gifted scientists and engineers and technicians who now lie idle or are drastically underutilized from California to Connecticut? How much could you reduce the deficit in the short run without prolonging the recession and compounding all the other problems that I just mentioned?

If this were easy, anybody could do it, but I think we can do it. Let's go to work.

Thank you very much. (Applause.)

I'd like to begin by introducing our first speaker, who will give us a macroeconomic overview of the American economy. His name is Dr. Robert Solow, and he is just opposite me here, going to the podium.

He is the 1987 winner of the Nobel Prize in Economics. He's been a professor at MIT since 1950, specializing in theories of capital and economic growth.

He received his academic degrees from Harvard, and was among the first six Nobel Prize winners to endorse "Putting People First" upon its release, something for which I am very grateful.

Good morning Dr. Solow, the floor is yours.

MR. ROBERT SOLOW (MIT): Good morning. Thank you, Mr. President-elect, Mr. Vice President-elect, ladies and gentlemen. I'm used to teaching large classes, but this is ridiculous. (Laughter.)

We wouldn't be sitting here today if most American voters didn't feel in their bones that something was very wrong with the economy and that the people in charge either weren't aware or didn't care or didn't know what to do in any case.

A PFC I knew long ago once said something to me about one of our company officers that's stuck in my mind for the last 50 years. He said, "Lieutenant X, he knows a lot but he don't realize nothing." (Laughter.) And the time has come to start realizing, and the place to begin is with where we are now.

We're living with the results of four years of near stagnation, waiting for the end of a recession that doesn't seem to want to go away. Everybody is out there looking for signs of recovery like dirt farmers in the dust bowl looking for signs of rain.

The first slide that's up there on the screen now shows how anemic the recovery has been, how less well we have done than the usual

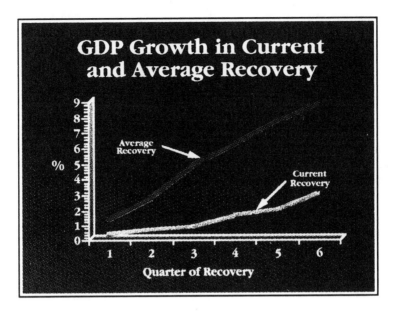

Figure 1

bounce-back from a recession. (Fig. 1) The gap you see between GDP growth in this recovery, such as it is, and in GDP growth in the average recovery is just a number, but it means lost sales, lost profits and, above all, lost jobs.

If you look at the employment picture directly in the second slide, you will see that gap in much more human terms. (Fig. 2) Private employment has not gained an inch in the past 18 months. American industry is not creating jobs because it's not selling goods. Major companies are still laying off workers and downsizing. The November figure, that last sign of recovery that President-elect Clinton talked about, showed that there had been a gain of about 100,000 jobs in the whole US economy. A hundred thousand jobs in a month is 1,200,000 in a year, and that's not enough to reduce the number of unemployed workers. We add more than 1,200,000 workers in a year to the American labor force.

This is not just a short-term glitch. Without a strong recovery, it will be a lot harder to solve the long-run problems of the economy. I'll come in a minute—and Mike Porter will come a little bit later—to a point that Mr. Clinton made again and again and again in the campaign. The only solution to the long-run problem is more investment of all kinds.

Now, there's nothing more deadening to business investment than an economy that's not going anywhere and not using the productive

9

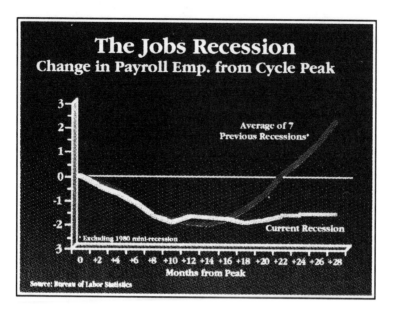

Figure 2

capacity it already has. If there had been a normal recovery in 1991 and 1992, American industry would have added at least $100 billion in new plant and equipment to what they have actually done, and we would be at least $100 billion closer to having an efficient, technologically up-to-date industrial base.

A strong 1993 and after is also important for its own sake. Three or four years from now, we will see only the beginnings of a revitalized economy from the structural point of view, but our success in creating jobs for the unemployed and for new workers who come into the labor force will be very visible. That will be the immediate legacy of the first 1,461 days of the Clinton-Gore administration.

Now, the 25 years from the end of the Second World War to the early 1970s were a genuine golden age for productivity growth in the US. The slide that's up there now shows that output per hour in the US economy grew at something between 2.5 and 3 percent a year during that quarter century. (Fig. 3) Early in the 1970s there was a slowdown in productivity growth worldwide, not only in the US. Since then, as you can see, the improvement in productivity has been much slower and very irregular. The underlying rate is not more than 1 percent a year. I've had that trend continued so you can see the gap in output per worker had we been able to continue increasing productivity as we did in the early period. The biggest part, the single biggest part of the

10

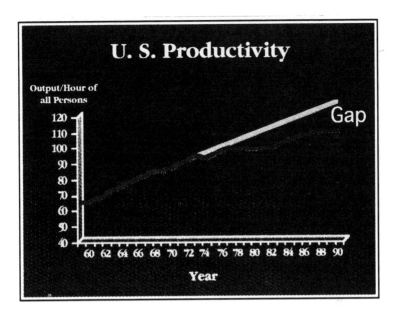

Figure 3

long-run problem of the US economy is finding a way to get that green curve moving up smartly again.

Now, productivity is an abstraction, but raising productivity is the only permanent source of a rising standard of living in any country, and that's a real thing.

The next slide that I want you to see shows what has been happening to median family income, corrected for inflation. (Fig. 4) In the 1950s and the 1960s, the early part of the period, family income was rising fast enough to double in just about 30 years. On the average, the children of those years could look forward to being twice as well off as their parents. When the productivity trend slowed to a walk in the 1970s and 1980s, it slowed to a pace at which it takes roughly 200 years to double family income. That's a very different sort of picture.

The US standard of living is very good; it's staggeringly good compared with most of the rest of the world. But people are more optimistic, more generous, more confident when family income is rising at a decent pace. When incomes stagnate, there's always fear of trouble around the corner. It's harder to save; it's harder to take the environment seriously; the loss of a job is a trauma, not an episode. But the only way to get incomes rising again is to do something about the productivity trend. The chart shows how rapidly family income could have risen if only we had been lucky or skillful enough to keep the productivity trend rising at the earlier rate.

11

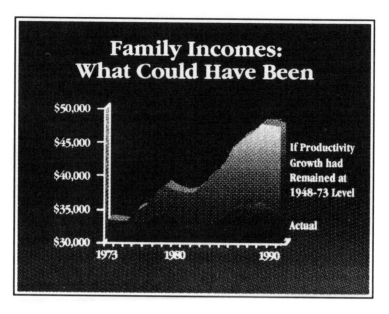

Figure 4

But the only way to restore the productivity trend is primarily a matter of investment, a matter of investment in capital equipment and in the education and skills of our people. Both are fundamental, but human investment has a second role to play. If you look behind the averages, not all families do equally well. Some families are advantaged and others are disadvantaged in terms of native ability or inherited wealth or childhood experience, or the quality and quantity of education, or the chances of health and health care, or just sheer good and bad luck. Incomes are unequal.

Now an important thing has happened in the US economy in the past 15 years and Mr. Clinton alluded to it in his talk. The gap between the rich and the poor has got bigger than it used to be. This last chart that I want to show you shows what has happened since 1977. (Fig. 5) The 20 percent of families with the lowest incomes in 1977 had absolutely lower incomes than the lowest 20 percent of families in 1977. The next few percent just about held their own. Then there are about 40 percent of families that had moderate gains between 1977 and 1992, but only the upper 20 percent of families gained big time.

We had a substantial increase in national income during those 15 years, more than—less than nothing of it went to the lowest 20 percent of families, more than all of it went to the upper 50 or 60 percent of families. That's not a cheerful picture. There is slower progress overall and fewer people are sharing in it. But there is an opportunity here

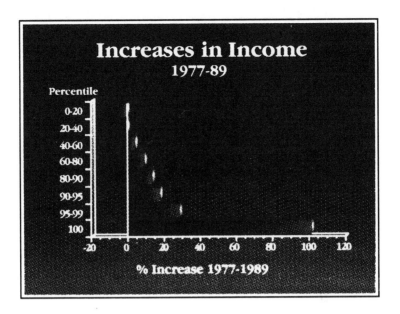

Figure 5

that falls right in with the Clinton-Gore program. The best way, probably the only way, to narrow that inequality is to improve the earning power of the poor, who are predominately, as you will see later, badly educated and unskilled.

Raising the average level of training and education would improve productivity nationwide and raise the average standard of living. And the only sure way to reverse that sad drift toward inequality that you see in that chart is to focus on the skills and human capital of those who now do so badly in the labor market.

Like any good teacher, I am going to try to summarize what I had to say in a few sentences.

The two basic long-run problems of our economy are weak productivity growth, which means that the average family's life can improve only slowly, and increasing inequality, which means that for many families life gets worse, not better. The only solution to the productivity problem is investment in modern industrial equipment, in research and development, in transportation and communication infrastructure, and in educating and training our people.

The education and training part is doubly important. It serves two purposes because it is the only realistic chance we have to improve the earning power of the poor so that they can share fully in rising incomes.

Finally, the immediate task is to create a strong recovery. That's essential not only because it's the only thing we can do that will show results in the next three or four years, but also because without a strong recovery we will not get the investment we need and the long-run problems will be harder and harder to fix.

Thank you.

PRESIDENT-ELECT CLINTON: Thank you very much. (Applause)

Let me say, Dr. Solow, I think Senator Gore has a question but I wanted to just say to the audience what the format is this morning.

We're going to have a series of presentations which we hope will complete the assessment of the American economy. If some big thing seems to be left out of the presentation, then I may, or Senator Gore may ask some question about the assessment. Then, we're going to have a brief break and then we're going to have about an hour of roundtable discussion, during which time the other panelists who don't make presentations may feel free to say whatever they wish to say or to ask whatever questions they want to ask, but I think the most important thing we can do is to flesh out this picture and then have as much time for roundtable discussion as possible. And I'm going to do my best to keep us on schedule so that we can do that.

VICE PRESIDENT-ELECT GORE: Dr. Solow, thank you so much. What I heard you saying among other things was that the signs of recovery in our economy, as encouraging as they might be, should not mislead us or distract us from the longer-term trends that we should really be focusing on. Secondly, you seem to be saying that the growing disparity in incomes ought to lead us to focus more on increasing the earning power and the skills of those in the bottom 20 percent and that we should focus on productivity. But in describing the slowdown in our productivity growth, you didn't talk about the overall levels of productivity here in the United States as compared to other countries. Isn't it true that in our assessment of our economy, it's also true that we still have the highest overall level of productivity in the entire world?

MR. SOLOW: Oh, absolutely. International comparisons like that are very inexact, so the figure I'm going to give you now can't be taken as literally true. But as far as anyone can tell, either in manufacturing or in services, or in everything taken together, we are still about 20 percent more productive than Germany and Japan. They have been closing the gap, or closed the gap, rather rapidly in the 1960s and 1970s. In the last ten years we have been more or less holding our own not because we're doing so great but because they're having their share of troubles as well. But we are still—if this were a National Football League game, I could say we're number one. (Laughter)

VICE PRESIDENT-ELECT GORE: Thank you.

PRESIDENT-ELECT CLINTON: Even though some of our players have less lucrative contracts than their counterparts. (Laughter) Thank you very much, Dr. Solow.

Our next presenter is John Sculley, the very distinguished Chairman and CEO of Apple Computers, formerly president and CEO of Pepsi-Cola, and I might add a—I believe a registered Republican. I'm glad to have him here and I want to say a special word of thanks before John begins to talk, for the incredible help we received from the Apple people on the graphics that all of us are benefitting from. Some of their people have not slept in the last two days, so I want to tell you, John, the folks that you sent to Little Rock did a great job and they need a couple of days off after this conference is over. Thank you very much.

MR. JOHN SCULLEY (APPLE COMPUTERS): Well, thank you very much, Governor Clinton, for the opportunity to bring us together to talk about some of these important structural changes. (Figs. 6–11)

I believe that we're at a turning point in the world economy today, not unlike what we saw at the time we had a transformation from the agricultural economy in the 19th century to the industrial economy that we've had for most of this century. The hallmark of this industrial economy has been mass production and mass consumption, and the mass production/mass consumption model was pioneered in the early 20th century by Frederick Taylor, who was an industrial engineer, and Henry Ford.

The model that they chose assumed that decisions would be centralized and that a small managerial elite would be managing those decisions. They broke thinking apart from the doing, and work was broken down into repetitive tasks, and they consciously eliminated much of the decisionmaking from the jobs of the workers. Quality was defined around rigid standardization and there was little flexibility in the work process.

But perhaps the biggest change in this decade is going to be the reorganization of work itself. This means the re-engineering of the way that work actually gets done to be more productive in the new economy. But there's a major problem. And that is that most Americans

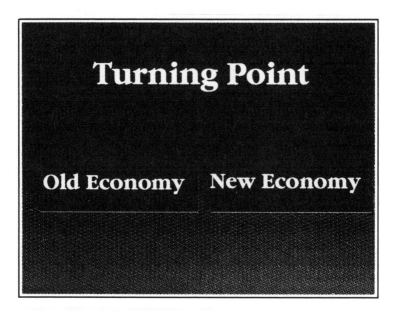

Figure 6

don't know what this new economy is and they don't realize how much of an impact it's going to have on their lives in the years ahead.

Today, we measure economic health in terms of comparisons like GDP growth and unemployment rates, but in the new global economy, the key indicator is going to be standard of living, and that's measured by external measurements like productivity rates, as we've heard Dr. Solow talk about just a few moments ago. Our high standard of living requires that we have a higher standard of living than others in the world, and we are still ahead, but we're losing ground. Our real income is down, and it's only the people who are better educated with higher incomes that have been able to hold their own.

In this new economy, that old industrial model is being replaced by a rapid move toward the customization of goods and services and the decentralization of work. Today, new products can be put together in much less time than it took in the past. We're seeing that it's possible to even custom build to order. The quality is dramatically improving. Costs are going down. And a lot of this is because of the use of new technologies, everything from computer systems to robotics to measurement systems.

The new economy is also a global economy, and it's one which depends on high skills. Workers on the front line are interacting with customers. We've seen workers on the factory floor; they're being empowered to make decisions. In fact, this is the only way that you can

16

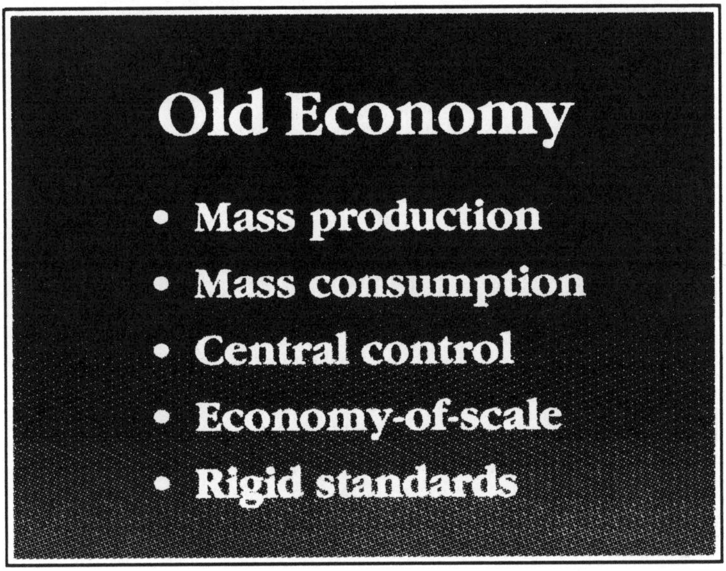

Figure 7

get customized goods and services created quickly, with the highest quality, the lowest cost, and the maximum amount of flexibility.

In the old economy, America had a real advantage because we were rich with natural resources, we had a large domestic marketplace, and this gave us the basis for economies of scale. In this new economy, the strategic resources are no longer just the ones that come out of the ground, like oil and wheat and coal, but they are ideas and information that come out of our mind.

The result is that as a nation, we have gone from being resource rich to resource poor almost overnight, and that's because our public education system has not successfully made the shift from a system that focused on memorizing facts to one that has to move toward achieving the learning of critical thinking skills. We're still trapped in a K-12 public education system which is preparing our young people for jobs that just don't exist anymore.

This new economy is also a global economy, and yet America is no longer alone at the top. In fact, the United States is underprepared to compete with many other industrialized trading regions around the world. Students in other industrialized countries are learning math; they're learning science; they're learning critical judgment skills that are more relevant to this new economy. Other industrialized countries have an alternative path for the non-college bound, including vocational study and school-to-work transition that's linked to apprentice-

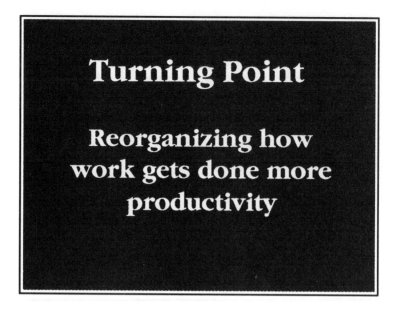

Turning Point

Reorganizing how work gets done more productivity

Figure 8

ships and worker training. In America, we have few alternatives for the non-college bound students so that they can participate productively in the high-skilled work of this new economy.

But the greatest uncertainty about the new economy—or certainty about the new economy is the pace of change. We know that people are going to have maybe five or six or seven different careers during their working lifetime. We know that the skills are going to constantly need to be upgraded. Education, therefore, must become a lifelong pursuit, not just an institutional experience early in one's life, but education, training, retraining must become as much a part of one's experience in our lives as exercise and vacations are today.

Most Americans see our largest corporations going through massive restructuring, layoffs, and downsizing. And people know that something has changed, and they're scared because they don't fully understand it and they see people that they know personally losing their jobs. They also see their neighbors buying high-quality, lower-priced products from abroad, and they ask, "Why can't we build these same products or better ones here at home?"

And the answer is that we can, but only if we have a public education system that will turn out a world class product. We need an education system that will educate all of our students, not just the top 15 or 20 percent. A highly skilled workforce must begin with a world class

Figure 9

education system because eventually the new economy will touch every industry in our nation. There is no place to hide.

In this new economy, low-skilled manual work will be paid less. The United States cannot afford, therefore, to have the high-skilled work being done somewhere else in the world and us ending up with just the low-wage work. But this is not an issue about protectionism. It's an issue about an education system that's aligned with the new economy and a broad educational opportunity open to everyone.

I believe that the reorganization of work into decentralized, higher-skilled jobs is the systemic key to a vital American economy in the future. We're talking about a standard of living that we and our children and our children's children are going to be looking forward to in the 21st century. So it's America's choice. Do we want high skills, or do we want low wages?

PRESIDENT-ELECT CLINTON: Thank you very much. (Applause.)

I want to ask just one question, and it's one that we really don't have time to resolve, but I just want to put it on the table for everyone to be thinking about, and I'll give John a chance to respond to it.

As you know, I basically share your analysis of this problem. But in view of the comment you made about the level of education in the workforce and the other issues—the decentralization of work, the

19

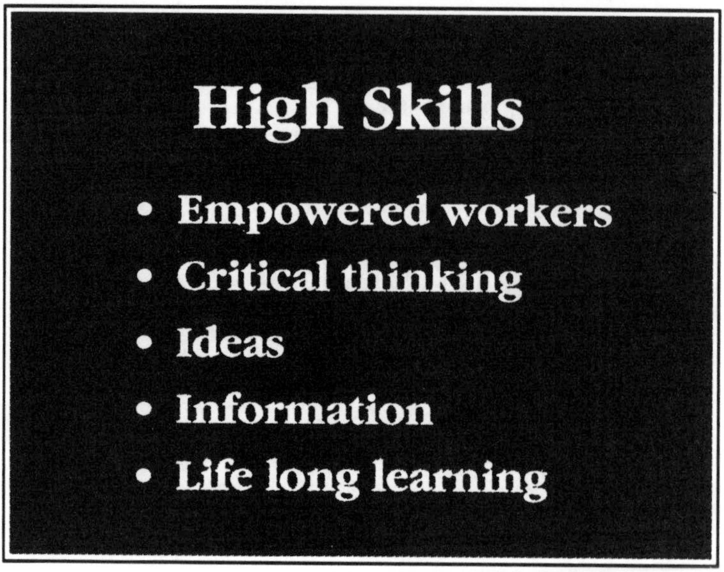

High Skills

- **Empowered workers**
- **Critical thinking**
- **Ideas**
- **Information**
- **Life long learning**

Figure 10

need for a whole new way of thinking and organizing work, and the fact that you said that it's not a matter of trade policy or protectionism which determines the health of the country—I just want to ask you the question flat out, do you believe, therefore, that the fact that in the last few years Germany and Japan have had higher productivity growth rates than we have is totally unrelated to the fact that their economies have been more closed, at least certain critical sectors of their economy have been more closed than ours?

MR. SCULLEY: I think the major reason is that they have had a greater systemic link between their education systems and the kind of work that needs to get done in those economies, and there is a more proactive role of government. For example, in Germany, their economy is built around small- and medium-sized business, and their government helps them to get the contacts to be able to build an export market. Germany is an export-based economy. Japan is also an export-based economy.

So I think that we need to keep markets open. There may have been some closed markets. We've seen them in Japan to some degree. But I think there is a better opportunity for us to stay with free trade, but get more proactive in terms of the relationship between industry and gov-

20

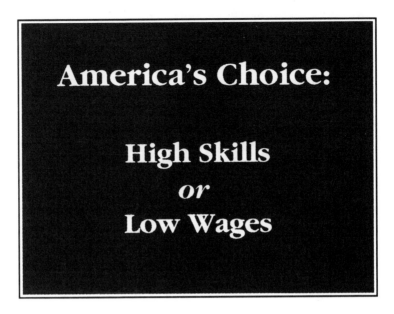

America's Choice:

High Skills
or
Low Wages

Figure 11

ernment than we've had in the past, and this means how do we get the systemic linkage to get America prepared for this new economy?

PRESIDENT-ELECT CLINTON: Let me just ask one more follow-up question, then. If the future world of work will be characterized more by decentralized workplaces and customized products and rapid change, does it necessarily follow, then, that government will have to give more attention to whether or not there is a ready availability of capital and other supports for new business and small business than has been the case in the past in this country?

MR. SCULLEY: Absolutely. We get 80 percent of our job growth from small business, and I believe that one of the greatest inhibitors of small business is they just can't get access to capital. They're high risk by the very nature of being entrepreneurial in many cases, and therefore without being able to collateralize loans, banks just don't want to lend to them. We've got to open up the banking system so small business can get good capital. Investment is key to the growth of this economy.

PRESIDENT-ELECT CLINTON: Thank you very much.

The next presenter is Alan Blinder, the Gordon Rentschler Memorial Professor of Economics at Princeton, and formerly Deputy Assistant Director of the Congressional Budget Office.

Mr. Blinder, the floor is yours.

MR. ALAN BLINDER (PRINCETON UNIVERSITY): Thank you, Mr. President-elect, Mr. Vice President-elect, ladies and gentlemen.

Albert Einstein, among other clever things he said, once said that everything should be made as simple as possible, but not more so. (Laughter.) And so I want to sound a very simple theme here this morning, which is that inadequate investment in our people, in the quality of our workforce, has been a big part of the problem we've been hearing about, and that correcting that should be a big part of the solution. That's why I think the campaign document was called "Putting People First," and I think that emphasis was quite appropriate.

So, what is this problem? Well, Bob Solow ran over it, and I'll be very brief. There are, in fact, two problems. The first is the absolutely frightening drop in productivity growth, which this chart shows in a slightly different way. (Fig. 12) You see on the left-hand side the golden age from '59 to '73 of high productivity growth matched by high real wage growth. The second two break the productivity slow-

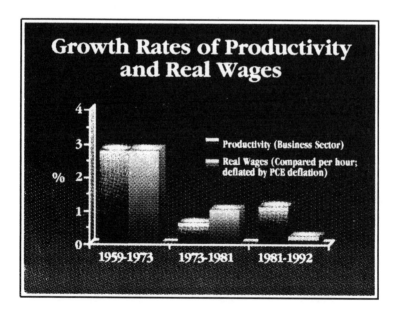

Figure 12

22

down period into two pieces, before and after supply side economics, and you can see a small acceleration in productivity growth, the sort of pink bar, but actually a deterioration in real wage growth to almost nothing. I'm going to come back to that point in a second.

The second part of the problem is shown on the next slide, which is the unconscionable rise in income inequality. (Fig. 13) The fact that these bars go uphill—that is, as we go from the lowest to the second to the middle and up to the highest—means very simply that those that were doing the best in 1973 did the best between '73 and '89.

Now, America's first response to the productivity slowdown problem actually worsened the inequality program (sic), and I refer, of course, to supply side economics, or trickle-down economics, whatever you'd like to call it. I'd like to emphasize that the logic behind that program was perfectly sound. There was nothing fallacious about the thinking. Tax incentives for saving and for investment, if they work, will give the country more capital, and workers that have more capital are more productive, and workers that have higher productivity earn higher wages. That was the logic.

Unfortunately, when you fill the bare bones of the logic with numbers, based on research findings and, indeed, on common sense, it doesn't really add up to very much trickle down. In fact, if we could look at that first slide again, you can see how little trickled down. (Fig. 12) I'd like to call your attention to the right-most bar, which shows

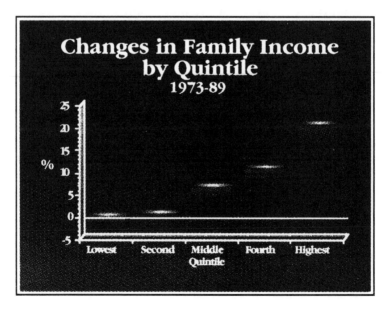

Figure 13

23

that real wages during the supply side period grew at about a quarter of a percent a year over an 11-year period. That's a national tragedy. That is the national tragedy.

Fortunately, there's an alternative strategy to trickle down, and I call it percolate up. The logic is exactly parallel to the sound logic of trickle down. That is, if you work to raise the quality of the workforce, and if you succeed, then the productivity of capital in our economy will be higher, the returns earned by the owners of capital will be higher, and there is nothing that will boost investment more than higher returns to capital.

I'd like to emphasize, because there's often confusion on this point, that the issue here is not an either/or question, but rather which is going to be the engine of growth and which will be the caboose. There's no doubt that both the engine and the caboose have to move if the train is going to leave the station.

I'd like now just to take a few minutes in concluding to address the question: Why emphasize labor quality as the engine rather than the caboose; why put people first, as opposed to, say, putting capital first? And I'll make four very brief points.

The first is a simple piece of arithmetic, which is a statement—Einstein probably said this, also—that 75 percent is bigger than 25 percent. (Laughter.) Why do I pick those two numbers? Very simply. In terms of factor inputs, labor is 75 percent of the inputs to this economy, the whole economy, and capital is roughly 25 percent. So the potential returns to a successful labor-first strategy are three times as great as the potential returns to a capital-first strategy.

Secondly, I made the point that the evidence is, in fact, very much against the trickle-down approach, and, in fact, is quite favorable to the percolate-up approach. I don't nearly have the time to go into that evidence. I just put one slide up on the screen now to illustrate the tremendous increase in the ratio of the wage rates of college graduates to high school graduates. (Fig. 14) That's a measure of the return to a college education, and you can see it's risen from about 45 percent in the late '70s up to about 90 percent. That means, roughly speaking, the financial returns to getting a high school education have doubled over that decade. And there's a lot more evidence in that regard.

The third point is a very simple one also, which is that the benefits that we put into our workforce stay in the United States. Capital and technology, as we know, flit around the globe, and there's no keeping them in any country, not just ours. The Japanese have exactly the same position. American labor does not move to Japan or Korea or anywhere else but stays in America.

And finally, last but I don't think least, the labor-based strategy, the percolate-up strategy, is a naturally equalizing strategy rather than a

24

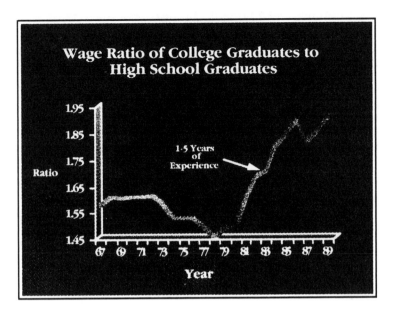

Figure 14

naturally disequalizing strategy, which trickle down is even if it works. It holds out the promise to turn growth into a participant sport instead of the spectator sport that it's been for the last almost two decades now and that this slide again illustrates, and it seemed to me that that's what this country voted for in November.

Thank you, sir. (Applause.)

PRESIDENT-ELECT CLINTON: Thank you very much, Mr. Blinder. As you know, you're sort of preaching to the choir when you make this argument to me, but I think in fairness I need to sort of try to turn it around and ask one or two questions, very quickly.

Only about 15 percent of the employers of this country report difficulty in finding workers with appropriate occupational skills. Now, some report severe difficulty, but in the aggregate, only about 15 percent do. Does that mean the employers don't know what they're talking about, or that we're wrong?

MR. BLINDER: I rather think the employers probably do know what they're talking about, but I don't think we're wrong. We've had an extremely weak job market, as you well know, and in that case, labor has been in surplus all over the map. It wasn't that way in 1989 in a buoyant economy, and I hope in the next few years it won't be that way again in another buoyant economy. As we look at the long pull for reasons that John Sculley said, skills are going to be in short supply in this country.

PRESIDENT-ELECT CLINTON: And if we were creating more jobs then we'd have to get more out of each worker, wouldn't we? I mean employers would because there'd be a tighter market.

MR. BLINDER: That's right. We ought to do both. In fact that's right, productivity naturally pops up as the economy expands. It's just beginning to happen now. The good news is that we've made a considerable gain in output in recent quarters with no increase in labor inputs, so that's good news on the productivity front. The bad news on that of course is that there aren't any additional jobs, barely any additional jobs over the last six or seven quarters of quote, "recovery."

PRESIDENT-ELECT CLINTON: Let me ask you just one other sort of structural question if I might.

The chart you had was very moving showing the ratio of income of college educated workers to high school educated workers and in fact in the decade of the '80s alone the earnings gap in the very first year of work between high school and college graduates more than doubled. But there's some reason to believe in the last two years, maybe just the length of the recession, that that trend may be moderating. Do you believe there is—is that an unlimited trend? That is, could we almost go to 100 percent of the workforce with college degrees and the income would still be spiraling? What are the inherent limits on that argument that you made there?

MR. BLINDER: I think there's something—if we could see the slide again, there is some sense in which it's definitely a limiting trend and indeed got limited. That actually went up to a peak about 1985 and then stopped. If we sent more people—thank you—if we sent more people to college, the upper part of that would start shrinking, and if we did a better job of educating the non-college bound through better K-12 education and apprenticeship programs and things like that, the bottom part would rise up. That's indeed what we'd like to do. So I don't think—this is not going to go to 500 percent.

PRESIDENT-ELECT CLINTON: Senator Gore.

VICE PRESIDENT-ELECT GORE: Dr. Blinder, a lot of people who are already in the workforce hear a presentation like this and it causes a little despair. They think, "Well, I'm already in the workforce, it's real hard for me to go back to school and finish college." Statistics indicate, if I'm not mistaken, that in the year 2000, more than 90 percent of the people in the workforce will be people who are already in the workforce right now. Therefore—is therefore an implication of what you're saying that we need to put a lot more emphasis on new approaches to job training and learning within the workplace?

MR. BLINDER: Yes, very much so. I emphasize what I did emphasize because that's in some sense the traditional role of government—before people leave the school system—state, local and federal government. Once they've left the school system and in the workplace, it's largely the job of the private sector. Now international comparisons are always difficult. One of the places they're worse is in on-the-job training. But as best we can tell, America's only investing about half the percent of payroll in on-the-job training as our leading industrial competitors are. And if there's going to be a solution for that 90 percent, that's where it must come.

PRESIDENT-ELECT CLINTON: I know we have to go on, I just want to close the gap here, to leave the one question on the table that I think is still on the table. You made a very compelling argument that we could deal with our two great difficulties, lagging productivity growth rates and increasing income inequalities, by having a people-based investment strategy. However, we still have to do some other things to create large numbers of new jobs. You would concede that just reinvesting in the workers in and of itself doesn't create jobs. There are countries where everybody in the workforce is as literate as could be and they have other lousy policies and don't generate any jobs.

MR. BLINDER: I couldn't agree more. I was only given five minutes and tried to hold to my point.

PRESIDENT-ELECT CLINTON: No, I understand that. (Laughter) I want to just—I don't want either you or, since I agree so strongly with what

27

you said, I don't want us to be left with the accusation that we don't recognize there's a whole lot of other things that have to be done, but that this is the best approach to dealing with the productivity, income, and equality problems that you outlined.

MR. BLINDER: That's right. What I was trying to emphasize is, which is going to be the engine to pull the rest along. There is no doubt that there's a lot more in the train.

PRESIDENT-ELECT CLINTON: Thank you very much.

MR. BLINDER: Thank you.

PRESIDENT-ELECT CLINTON: The next speaker is Marian Wright Edelman, the founder and president of the Children's Defense Fund, I'm sure well-known to virtually everyone in this audience, especially important to me because she gave Hillary her first job out of law school. Marian.

MS. MARIAN WRIGHT EDELMAN (CHILDREN'S DEFENSE FUND): Thank you, Mr. President-elect. I want to thank you very much for recognizing that children are a bottom-line economic issue and that preventive investment in all of our children is not only a moral imperative, but also essential to saving our national economic skin, our key to our future productivity and workforce development. And preventive investment is also crucial in reducing escalating dependency, remediation, and crime costs.

As communism is collapsing all around the world, the American dream is collapsing all around America for millions of families, youths, and children in all races and classes. We are in danger of becoming two nations, one of first world privilege and another of third world deprivation, struggling against increasing odds to coexist peacefully, as a beleaguered middle class barely holds on.

While the middle class lost ground over the last decade and a half, the already poor became poorer and more desperate, hungry, homeless, and hopeless. Today, every seventh American is poor, as is every sixth family with a child under 18. Every fifth child is poor and every fourth preschooler is poor. And if you're a black and brown child in America today, one in every three is poor.

There are more poor children in America today than in any year since 1965, despite the net 88 percent growth in our GNP during this period. (Fig. 15) And contrary to popular myth, the majority of them are not black, not on welfare, don't live in inner cities, but live in working families and outside inner cities in small town, rural, and suburban America.

Between 1989 and '92, nearly one-quarter of the 1.7 million children who fell into poverty lived in two-parent, white families, many of whom thought they'd never be out of work, need food stamps, or face homelessness or hunger. New Hampshire reported the highest rate of food stamp participation in the last—rate of growth in food stamp participation in the nation over the past three years.

I think it's a great human and moral tragedy that thousands of children and adults are starving to death in war-torn, poor Somalia, with an estimated GNP of $1.6 billion. But it is a human and moral travesty that 14.3 million children are poor in the richest land on earth, that an estimated five million go hungry sometimes during the month, and eight million lack health care in a country that has a gross national product of $5.9 trillion.

We need to ask ourselves whether this is the best that America can do and why there are more poor children in rich America than there are citizens in famine-stricken Somalia, more poor children in Los Angeles and New York City than there are in the so-called developing

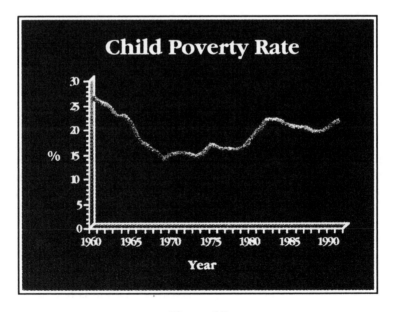

Figure 15

29

nation of Botswana. What are the true values of a wealthy, democratic nation that lets infants and toddlers be the poorest Americans when we know that poverty makes children more likely to be born too small, to die, to be sick, hungry, and malnourished and to fall behind in school and drop out and to cost their families immeasurable suffering and taxpayers billions in later remedial costs and lost productivity? How does one reconcile rampant child neglect and underinvestment and preventable suffering with the biblical warning that to those to whom much is given, much is expected?

Our extraordinarily high child poverty rates are not some unavoidable attribute of modern, urbanized societies or acts of God. They are highly unusual and conscious value and political choices. Our children are two to 14 times more likely to be poor than children in Australia, Canada, Sweden, Germany, the Netherlands, France, and the United States (sic). (Fig. 16)

And I want to highlight particularly the plight of young families with children, those headed by someone under 30. (Fig. 17) Of all kinds; white, black, rich, and poor, in all parts of the country. They have seen their incomes plummet by 32 percent since 1973, even though they're working harder. But the shift in jobs from manufacturing to the service sector and from America to abroad have made their plight very difficult. We must begin to invest in all of our children, with particular attention on young families.

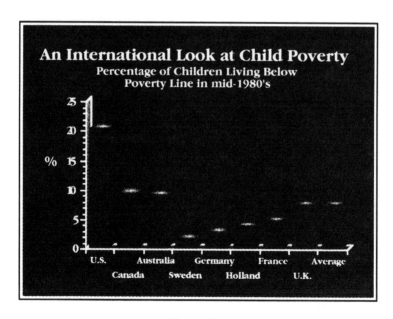

Figure 16

30

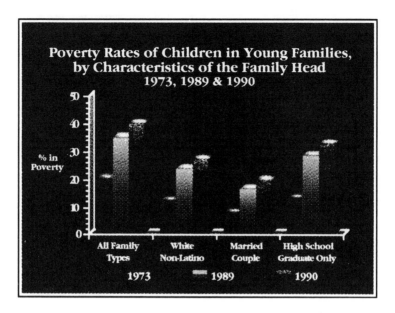

Figure 17

I hope that every American, led by you, this new administration that brings us such hope, and by our new Congress, will personally and collectively struggle to reclaim our nation's soul and give our children back their hope, their sense of security, their belief in America's fairness, and their ability to dream about, envisage, and work toward a future that is attainable and real.

And let me suggest two things that I know this great country can do in 1993 under your leadership. (Fig. 18) The first thing we can do is to make sure that every one of our children is born healthy and is immunized against preventable diseases. It is a scandal that fewer than 60 percent of our preschool children are fully immunized in most of our states. If China, one of the 20 poorest nations in the world, can immunize 95 percent of its children, surely America can do as well when we know that every dollar we invest in immunization saves $10 on the other end.

The other thing that I know that this country can do, and you have committed to doing this in your campaign, is to see that every child gets ready for school. And a down payment on that is to see that every one of our children gets a head start by fully funding Head Start, making it full-day, full-year, taking it down to earlier ages. Every dollar we invest will save almost three dollars on the other end. Unless we achieve the school readiness goal, we're not going to be able to achieve the educated workforce that is crucial to long-range productivity. Ev-

31

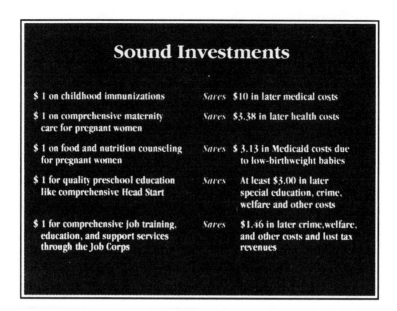

Sound Investments

$ 1 on childhood immunizations	*Saves*	$10 in later medical costs
$ 1 on comprehensive maternity care for pregnant women	*Saves*	$3.38 in later health costs
$ 1 on food and nutrition counseling for pregnant women	*Saves*	$ 3.13 in Medicaid costs due to low-birthweight babies
$ 1 for quality preschool education like comprehensive Head Start	*Saves*	At least $3.00 in later special education, crime, welfare and other costs
$ 1 for comprehensive job training, education, and support services through the Job Corps	*Saves*	$1.46 in later crime, welfare, and other costs and lost tax revenues

Figure 18

erybody says they're for Head Start, Republicans and Democrats. We know it works. And now, 1993, is the time to just do it.

Thank you for letting me come. (Applause.)

PRESIDENT-ELECT CLINTON: Thank you.

I would like—I want to ask one follow-up question, but before I do, let me just make a comment on the immunization issue. And when we come back after we break to the roundtable, perhaps Dr. Vagelos among others will address this, but I would very much like to reverse the alarming trend of actual reductions in immunization rates in several areas.

As I'm sure, and I know Marian knows this, but there are big differences in the United States between what people actually pay for vaccines, depending on whether they're private sector or medical people, state governments, federal governments. In our state now and in the public health department, our health clinics are doing about 85 percent of all the immunizations in our state. We're actually immunizing a lot of middle class, even some upper middle class folks because of the cost to the doctors, the risks, the liability, and all of that. I'd like to invite, when we come back to the roundtable, both Dr. Vagelos and anyone else who'd like to address this to discuss what the most cost-effective mechanism we could adopt to reverse this alarming immunization trend, turn it around and deal with it, as Marian has suggested. This may be something that there are external factors, other factors the government just has to do both in terms of providing the money but actually in the delivery system.

Now, let me just ask you to address one thing before you sit down. It's not anything we can resolve here, but I'd like to put it in everyone's mind. As you know, this is a conversation which has gone on between you and many Americans for more than 20 years now.

A lot of the disturbing trends that you put up, which we know we're all partly responsible for, are also partly explicable by the fact that we have higher rates of teen pregnancy, of out-of-wedlock births, of births to people who themselves are already poorer than many other countries that are in a comparable situation. And in order to deal with a lot of these issues that you talked about, we have to find ways of changing the culture, the values, and the possibilities of the parents, both as parents and for their own benefit. And I wonder if you could say just a word or two about what you think we ought to do on that score, about the roles of the parents of these children, and how we might through the government or through partnerships change that in some systematic way. I mean, the immunization and the Head Start thing are systematic responses that will help everybody. But I think we need to focus on that issue, too.

Ms. Edelman: Oh, I think parents are the most important people in children's lives, and we must foster personal responsibility and begin to have parents put children first and really make a new call to values and real family values in our country. Our religious congregations, our community leaders, our White House and Congress must all call for stronger parent values and family values. But again, you know, family values is how we live, not what we say. And so we really need to begin to make sure that we in our personal lives are reflecting the kind of values that we want our children to do.

But secondly, as we call on parents and try to educate parents and support parents in the kind of HIPPY program that you have here in Arkansas, in the parents as teachers programs that many states are adopting—these things don't cost a lot of money—it's a way of affirming the importance of family values. And so I hope that we can see a lot more attention to family support and to parent education and support. But secondly, you know, public policies have to also reflect family values, and you can't ask parents to do things and encourage their children to work and to have a work ethic unless they have the opportunity to work. And so we've got to make sure that private val-

33

ues and public values reinforce each other rather than undermine each other.

PRESIDENT-ELECT CLINTON: I just want to, you know, point out something she said. I don't want this to escape public notice here.

You mentioned a home instruction program for preschool youngsters which we do here, and the parents as teachers program in Missouri and other states. There are low-cost systematic responses to the problem of parents who are not as good as they might want to be, or as functional as the society might want them to be.

A few years ago, Marian put out a study—which you didn't mention —of single parents which showed that—then they followed groups of young women who had given birth out of wedlock, and they found that the single most effective deterrent to someone having a second child out of wedlock was the acquisition of a strong background of basic learning skills: change self-image, change the whole concept of the future, and all that. I just want to make a point here that this ought to be a part of our strategy, and there are systematic things you can do so that we're not all just standing in pulpits spouting words, that we can actually respond in an appropriate way.

Senator Gore has one question, I think.

VICE PRESIDENT-ELECT GORE: I heard something else, too, in what you were saying that reminded me of some of the earlier presentations.

Your figures indicate that one dollar on childhood immunizations saves $10 in later medical costs. You have a whole series of numbers that are exactly the same. It makes good economic sense for our country. It's not just a question of compassion—I don't like that word "just" in that sentence—but it's consistent with strong economic moves. But what I want to ask you is, do you think there is a common denominator in the oft-noted unwillingness of some US corporations to focus on longer-term growth and focus too much on the quarterly report and the short-term performance and the tendency in our country to ignore the long-term benefits, economically as well as socially, of the investments that we ought to be making in children now? In other words, as part of our assessment this morning, should we take note of the fact that part of our problem may be the mindset that we have in focusing on the short term and not being willing to pay enough attention to the sound investments that will only pay off a little bit later on, for children and for corporations?

34

Ms. Edelman: I agree with you. I think we have been penny-wise and pound-foolish. If we don't invest preventively in healthy children, in getting every child ready for school and educating children today, we are not going to have a workforce that can compete in the new century and support a strong social security system for those of us in the 50s who really look forward—(laughter)—to making sure that we are taken care of. We have got to begin to invest in prevention and in our children so that they can all be healthy and ready for school and well-educated.

And I just want to reinforce what the President-elect has said about the importance of preventing teenage pregnancy and the crucial importance of basic skills to that. The best contraceptive is hope, it's opportunity, it's a sense of a future. And if we want our children not to have children, and if we want to deal with the drug problem that is really blanketing our cities, and if we want to step down on crime rates, we have got to put positive alternatives in place, and that means a decent school and the hope of a job that can lift them out of poverty and help them raise the next generation of families.

Thank you.

President-elect Clinton: Thank you. (Applause.)

Our next presenter is Alicia Munnell, the Senior Vice President, Director of Research for the Federal Reserve Bank of Boston. She has served on advisory boards for the World Bank, MIT, The Economic Policy Institute, and the American Enterprise Institute. Let me say she's here to discuss infrastructure, something that every governor loves, but that every candidate for President is supposed to never talk about. I don't know how many times my advisers said, "Bill, don't go out there and talk about infrastructure, that's an ugly word, nobody knows what it means, and if you talk about water and sewer projects it'll be awful." (Laughs)

So all of us who believe in this have had difficulty figuring out a way to turn it into political currency, but I think people—I think all of us believe that it's an important part of our economic future. So the floor is yours.

Ms. Alicia Haydock Munnell (Federal Reserve Bank of Boston): With that introduction, thank you, Mr. President-elect, Mr. Vice President-elect, ladies and gentlemen.

Investment in the nation's infrastructure has moved to the forefront of the policy agenda. This movement has occurred for three reasons. First, for the past two decades, we have not been investing enough.

35

Second, as Bob Solow indicated, infrastructure investment, like private investment, can make our economy stronger. Third, we know profitable places to put the money.

Let's start by looking at the trends. A serious decline has occurred in both investment and in the stock of public capital, as you can see in that first slide up there. (Fig. 19) That is, airports, roads, bridges have not kept pace with the growth in economic activity. As the slide slows, investment has dropped from roughly 3 percent of GDP to 1.5 percent of GDP. As a result, congestion in our transportation system is already slowing our economy, and congestion on our roads and at our airports will increase in the future.

It is not surprising, as the second slide shows, that investment in the United States falls far below that of other developed countries. (Fig. 20) Japan for example, which is at the far left, is investing at three times the rate of the United States, which is at the far right.

The second reason we're hearing a lot about infrastructure investment is that recent research shows that public infrastructure helps increase private sector output. For example, if you look across states for any given level of private capital and labor, states with more public infrastructure produce more goods and services. Studies have also shown that infrastructure spending does not, as economists formerly believed, crowd out private investment but, rather, stimulates private investment spending. Taken together, the evidence indicates that in-

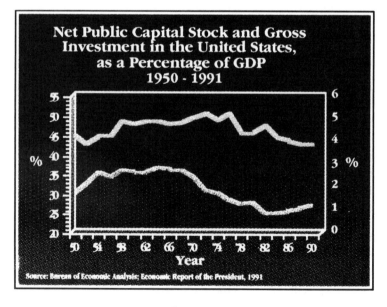

Figure 19

36

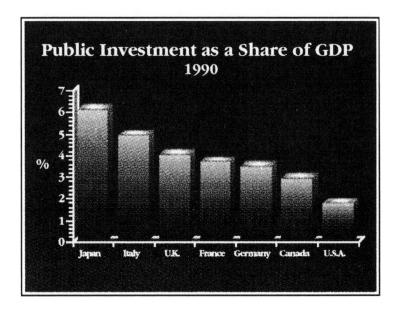

Figure 20

vesting in infrastructure can increase the size of the economic pie in the future.

The third reason that people are interested in infrastructure spending is that there are lots of projects already identified that have large potential payoffs. For example, the returns to maintaining the federal highway system can be as high as 30 to 40 percent. Big payoffs can also come from increasing outlays, both for air traffic control systems and for airport runways. The evidence also shows that people are willing to pay for more government investment. Whenever they are asked to vote on spending money for bridges, water and sewer systems, roads, or environmental projects, they generally approve the proposals, and by very large margins.

Some people argue that we don't need more infrastructure, all we need to do is use what we have more efficiently. They are right, in part. But user charges and congestion pricing alone will not solve the problem.

In short, the nation's infrastructure is not in ruins, but capital investment has declined and it is time to reverse that decline. Recent research clearly indicates that appropriate infrastructure investment can increase productivity and growth and future levels of family income. The challenge will be funneling government money to the projects with the highest payoff.

We should recall, however, that America's great public works—the

37

Erie Canal, the transcontinental railway, the interstate highway system, and the dams and water systems of the West—required great cooperation and sometimes a leap of faith. Today's technologies are not sufficient by themselves to build the 21st century counterparts. Great public works still demand large investment and broad vision.

Thank you. (Applause.)

PRESIDENT-ELECT CLINTON: I want to ask you one question which I think is very important for the next two presentations and, in the end, will be quite important, as a practical matter, for the economic judgments which this administration will have to make early on.

Let's take it for a moment as a given that you're right—I certainly think you're right. I've seen it here, I've seen it at other places. There's no question that if we increase our investment in infrastructure for tomorrow that we'll do better. We need to do it in not just roads and bridges and water and sewer systems, but in new rail systems, new air transport systems, all kinds of things that are out there for us to do. An information highway, broadly defined, is infrastructure.

You pointed out that these kinds of investments have enjoyed broad popular support, and you're right. But I must say that at the state level, as opposed to the national level, these kinds of investments are normally undertaken in two ways, not just one. You may have, for example with roads, an increase in the gas tax, and then you build the roads on a pay-as-you-go basis. But quite frequently, when voters vote in a referendum—as a matter of fact, usually when they vote in a referendum they vote for a bond issue in which tax revenues are used not on a pay-as-you-go basis, but to pay off debt over a longer period of time than the project will take to build.

I bring that up for this reason; in government accounting terms, the deficit is the deficit is the deficit. There is no distinction between different kinds of debt. When these business folks around this table make their judgments, the ones in this room, there's a difference between borrowing money to invest in the future and borrowing money to make the payroll.

When the people of Arkansas voted for a water bond issue or a sewer bond issue, they gave us permission to, in effect, borrow money to build more water and sewer projects today to pay it off for the future, but they wouldn't hear of us borrowing money to make payroll for state employees.

Should we—you made one point explicitly; I want to just restate something you said. Public investment in infrastructure crowds in rather than crowds out private investment. The reverse is normally true in the sloganeering about the deficit. If you increase the deficit at

38

the federal level, it crowds out rather than crowds in investment because it dries up capital for the private sector.

Should we reexamine this premise at the national level? Should we draw a distinction between borrowing money for investment in our future and borrowing money to pay for today's health care costs? And if so, should we try to have some responsible sort of body of economic support for drawing that kind of distinction in the future?

Ms. Munnell: My opinion—if you're going to undertake a major capital investment initiative and you're also going to undertake a major deficit reduction initiative, it's very important to start thinking about having a capital budget at the federal level. Basically, economists believe that you should pay for things that you use today today, and you should pay for things that you're going to use over a long period of time over a long period of time. So I think that you would want a budget that made it acceptable to pay for infrastructure investment over time.

President-elect Clinton: Well, let me just say, this is not a—as Mr. Panetta can tell you—this is a matter of no small moment. Ask Senator Bentsen or Congressman Panetta. This is a major issue in the politics and government of your country. The spending ceilings, the caps, everything the federal government does and everything most economists who talk about the federal budget say do not make these distinctions. And if there is a broad consensus coming out of this meeting, especially among the corporate leaders who are here, especially among those of you who may be not only in the business sector but on both sides of the political aisle, this is something we need to think about and talk about. This may seem self-evident to you based on the business decisions you make. This is a huge political point for the day-to-day operations of what we will go through when we get into deficit reduction. Isn't that right, Mr. Panetta?

So I think that—I just wanted to bring this home. This is something I hope you'll discuss at the break. I hope it will come up again and again. This is a big deal for the kinds of decisions we'll have to make about this deficit.

Senator Gore?

Vice President-elect Gore: President-elect Clinton made reference to the need for a broader definition of infrastructure. I want to draw you out on that just a little bit because earlier John Sculley made the point that the key resources we used to be rich in, that used to make all the difference, were natural resources like coal and timber and all the rest, but now the key strategic resource is knowledge. A lot of the infrastructure investment we've made over the last 200 years has been in infrastructure that makes it easier for us to move around the resources that used to be even more important. They're still important, but if the key resource is knowledge today, shouldn't we be giving a lot more emphasis to the kind of national infrastructure we need to share information and create and share knowledge, like the information superhighways referred to earlier—digital libraries, the software and the programs that make it possible for children to come home after school and plug into the Library of Congress? Do you define infrastructure not only that broadly but in a way that places more emphasis on that kind of infrastructure?

Ms. Munnell: Yes, Senator. I didn't mean to dwell on water and sewer systems. Of course educational systems and information systems are very important. I think the most important thing, though, is to get a mindset that involves thinking about ways that the government can facilitate the development of such systems.

Vice President-elect Gore: Well, since there is a broad agreement across the ideological spectrum on the need for roads and bridges and water lines and sewer lines and those things are so important, I think that part of our challenge here may be to broaden that public consensus to support more public investment in an information infrastructure.

Thank you.

Ms. Munnell: Thank you.

President-elect Clinton: Good point. Thank you very much.

The next speaker is Michael Porter, professor of business at Harvard Business School since 1973, a leading authority on competitive strategy who served on President Reagan's Commission on Industrial Competitiveness. He directed a pro bono study of the Massachusetts economy in 1991 and has led studies on the economies for the governments of New Zealand, Canada, and the Basque region of Spain. He has written widely, including a remarkable book entitled *The Competitive Advantage of Nations*. Mr. Porter.

Mr. Michael Porter (Harvard): Thank you, Governor and Senator. And thank you for the opportunity to hopefully contribute to my own country, in addition to those others you just mentioned.

I'd like to return our attention from sewers and roads and bridges to the firing line, the firing line of international competition. And I'd like to build on some of the things that John Sculley said earlier. The paradigm that's governing international competition and competitiveness has shifted dramatically in the last three decades, and American companies are struggling with keeping up.

The old paradigm was one where success was based on access to natural resources, pools of labor, scientific knowledge. The old paradigm was one where companies that could enjoy a large home market gained economies of scale and prospered. We did well at this old paradigm. But this old paradigm has been superseded. It's been superseded by the globalization of competition and by the advance of technology.

Today, natural resources are freely available on global markets. Today, companies can locate labor-intensive activities anywhere in the world to tap into low labor costs. Today, scientific knowledge is easy to get. You just send somebody—I should say MIT—but you should send somebody to Harvard to get the scientific knowledge. That moves freely today.

Today, that old paradigm has been superseded. There's a new paradigm of international competition, and that paradigm is based on dynamism, on the capacity of firms to innovate and to upgrade the sophistication of how they compete. This new paradigm means that what were disadvantages can be turned into advantages. Japan has very high energy costs and very high costs of space. Through innovation, they've turned those disadvantages into energy-saving products and space-saving production techniques such as "just in time."

In the new paradigm, economies of scale are obsoleted by more dynamic rivals. General Motors is the world's largest automobile company, by a considerable margin. It's not, unfortunately, today the most competitive because its competitors have been more dynamic.

Now, in this new paradigm, success depends on relentless investment by companies. (Fig. 21) In "Putting People First," you highlighted the role of private sector investment. You were so right. Investment today is not just in physical assets. It's not just in smokestacks and machines. Investment today is also in less tangible assets such as research and development, training, supplier relationships, and the losses required to gain access to foreign markets.

Ironically, many of these newer forms of investment or softer forms of investment are not even counted as investment on corporate books. (Fig. 22) That's interesting, isn't it? They're not even called assets. Yet

41

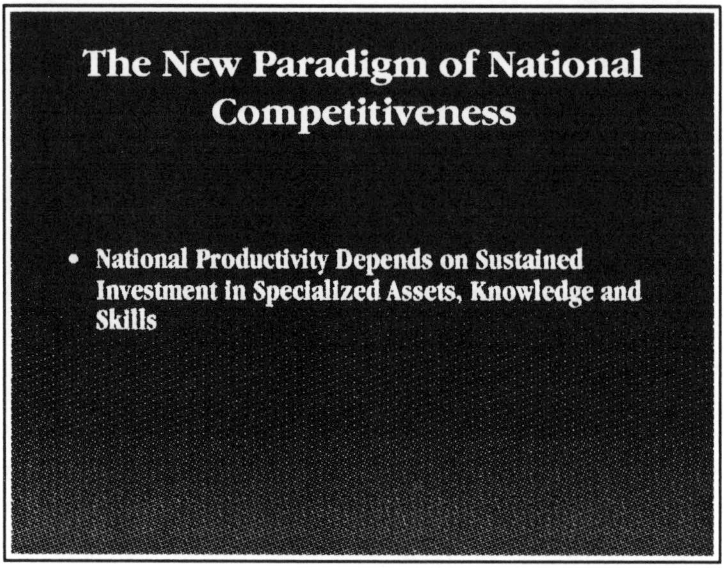

Figure 21

they're increasingly important to competitive success. They increasingly define the margin between victory and defeat.

We cannot look at these forms of investment as separate. The payoff to making one form of investment depends on making investments in other forms at the same time. You can have the shiniest new plant in America, but you're not going to get the payoff unless you also invest in training your employees to use that new equipment, unless you also invest in redesigning your product to make it more manufacturable, using the new technology and so on.

Now, how well are we doing at this new investment game? Well, we're doing pretty well in one dimension. We're doing pretty well at starting new companies. Our venture capital community represented here, our entrepreneurial spirit, allows us to get a lot of new companies started.

The problem is what happens when companies grow up or begin to grow up. And here, American industry as a whole is simply being out-invested, dramatically. As this chart shows, we're being out-invested in plant and equipment. We invest at a significantly lower rate in plant and equipment than our major international rivals. As the next slide shows, we're also being out-invested in civilian research and development, where we also invest at a significantly lower rate. And based on the best available data, these same things, this same pattern holds true for training, as Alan Blinder said a minute ago, for supplier relation-

42

Forms of Investment

- **Physical Assets**
- **Intangible Assets**
  - R&D
  - Advertising and Marketing
  - Employee Training / Skills Development
  - Information Systems
  - Organizational Development
  - Development of Supplier Relationships
- **Market Positions**

Figure 22

ships, for taking losses to gain market position. For all the forms of corporate investment we can measure, we are simply being out-invested.

Now, to put these differences in investment rates in context, I think the next chart is interesting. (Fig. 23) You may have thought that the lines on my earlier graphs were pretty close together; yeah, we were being out-invested a little bit, but that couldn't make a big difference. Well, if you look at this chart, you will see something, I think, that's very dramatic.

You will see that because Japan invests at a higher rate than we do, as a percentage of GDP, they actually invest more in absolute terms than all of US industry, despite the fact that we have a much larger economy. This chart looks only at plant and equipment and industry-funded R&D. (Fig. 24) What it shows is that in order to match the Japanese rates of investment, we would have to increase our private sector investment by more than $500 billion a year. If we cannot change this state of affairs, if we can't start winning instead of falling behind in the investment race, our companies are going to lose market position, we're not going to grow productivity, we're not going to grow our economy, and we're not going to create jobs.

Now, what is the problem? Why are we being out-invested? Well, there's two broad reasons. The first is our overall macroeconomic environment, the overall environment in which business works. We simply

43

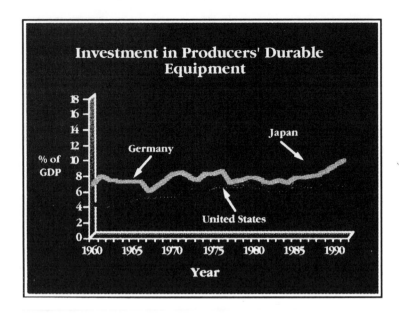

Figure 23

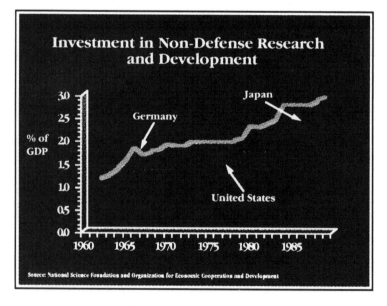

Figure 24

44

don't have a large enough pool of investment capital. We're not saving enough, either in households or in government—government saving is an interesting concept these days. In addition to this inadequate pool of capital, our policies are too erratic. We keep changing the tax code. We keep changing the rules. And that instability causes companies to waver, to hold back from investment. We've got to change these things, and I know you want to do that.

But it's not just the pool of capital. It's also how we use the capital we have. We have a system for allocating capital in the United States that is biased against investment, especially in the softer forms of investment like R&D and training. (Fig. 25)

This is not only the capital markets, but it's also the processes we use within companies to allocate capital. We don't have real owners of companies in the United States. Our average share of stock in the United States is held for two years only. Two years. Our investors are too concerned with guessing what stock is going to appreciate in the next six months or a year rather than in understanding the fundamental health of the company.

Inside companies, we have a process that pours billions of dollars into unrelated acquisitions, but yet doesn't have enough money for R&D and training. We have a system in which companies are short of capital and they're asking for government help, but yet they're buying back their own shares, spending their capital on their own shares.

Comparative Private Sector Investment, 1990
($ Billions)

	U. S.	% GNP	Japan	% GNP
Physical Capital	$524	9.5%	$586	18.9%
Industry-funded R&D	74	1.3%	80	2.6%
	$598	10.8%	$666	21.5%

Figure 25

45

We're going to need to rethink our system for investment in the United States. We're going to have to better align the goals of owners and managers and employees. We're going to have to create greater incentives for investment, as you've proposed in "Putting People First." And we're going to have to dismantle a whole array of regulations that grew up since the '30s that are constraining and biasing our capital investment system.

Let me conclude with one final note. We cannot solve our private investment problem in the United States with greater government investment. Our deficit is simply too big. There's no way that the federal government, even if we got our wildest dreams satisfied in terms of flexibility from Mr. Panetta, could ever put enough money into the system to offset the private investment deficit.

What does this mean? It means two things. One, we've got to deal with the problems in our private investment system directly. (Fig. 26) We've got to fix them directly. Secondly, when we think about using our scarce federal resources, we've got to use them in a way not for their own sake, but in a way that will provide incentives and trigger greater investments in the private sector. Federal investment can't be a substitute for private investment; it's got to trigger and complement it. Thank you. (Applause.)

PRESIDENT-ELECT CLINTON: Thank you very much.

I'd just like to ask one question. First, let me make one point. If you go back to the chart that he put up, that all of you have in your books, showing the fact that Japan is investing absolutely more money, private sector investment, than we are, it makes a point I want to make.

We will—this administration will be under great pressure, maybe from our own impulses, in the next six months to a year, to respond to the fact that our neighbors in Japan and Germany have some economic problems of their own to deal with. And they do. They will say, well, maybe this—all the troubles of the last decade are about to go away. I keep saying that we are dealing with very long-term issues. This is an example of that. There may be a real estate collapse in Japan, and it may put the banks in a lot of trouble, but as long as they can keep doing this over the long run, the consequences for what we should do cannot be changed by some difficulties they have. Everybody has problems.

Now, against that backdrop, you made a very important point that I agree with 100 percent. There's not enough government money— even if we didn't have a deficit, there wouldn't be enough government money to supplant the investment patterns we have to have in the private sector. And you pointed out what we spend less on than our

Causes of Lower U. S. Private Investment

- The Macroeconomic Environment
  - Pool of Investment Capital
  - Policy Stability
- The Allocation of Capital

Figure 26

competitors, research and development, investment in people, and all of that. What would the reverse chart be, very briefly before you go? What things does the private sector spend more on in America than our competitors?

MR. PORTER: Well, we spend more on real estate. We spend more on acquisitions, buying and selling companies. And we spend more on— those are the principal forms of investment in which we are out-investing our foreign rivals. Unfortunately, neither of those forms of investment seems to have the bang for the buck in terms of productivity and competitive advantage.

PRESIDENT-ELECT CLINTON: We also spend a whole lot more on health care, and a lot of our older companies spend more on the health care of their retirees, which is a problem you can't put at the foot of the health care providers exactly. That's a very serious problem in America for industries that have done major restructuring. We're going to hear from Mr. Poling in a minute, but one of the things that really plagues me about the problems of the auto industry and the steel industry, if you have a big restructuring and you're making more cars with fewer people, you're still paying for the health care costs of all your retirees.

And I think that is a significant economic issue that we at least—I hope we get a chance to bat around in some cases here.

MR. PORTER: It is, but unfortunately that health care spending isn't an investment. Too often, it's spending, and it prevents us from being able to make the investments required to be competitive.

PRESIDENT-ELECT CLINTON: Thank you.

The next presentation is on the federal deficit, and it will be made by John White, who was just named Director of the Center for Business and Government at the Harvard Kennedy School of Government. Between '88 and '91 he was corporate Vice President of Eastman Kodak, the Chairman of the Board and CEO of Interactive Systems Corporation before that in the decade of the '80s. Between 1978 and 1980 he was the Deputy Director of the Office of Management and Budget. He drafted the Ross Perot economic plan, and later, much to my delight, endorsed the Clinton-Gore ticket for President.

Mr. White.

MR. JOHN WHITE (HARVARD): Thank you.

PRESIDENT-ELECT CLINTON: The floor is yours.

MR. WHITE: We've heard a lot this morning about investment, about productivity, and about economic growth. And I want to spend a few minutes now to talk about those issues and put them in the context of the federal budget and the federal deficit, because the huge federal deficit, in fact, is a specific drag on our ability to have the kind of growth that we all desire.

If we look at the first chart, we have here a review of the debt as a ratio with the GDP. (Fig. 27) Coming out of the war in Korea, of course, we had huge debts. But continually over the '60s and '70s we drew those down as the economy grew faster than did our debts. Unfortunately, in the '80s it turned around. What we would like to see in the future, of course, is a continual decline, or at least a flat curve so that in fact increased indebtedness is not taking resources out of our economy.

And of course, as shown in the red line, things got much worse in

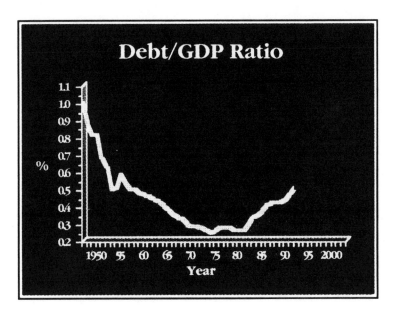

Figure 27

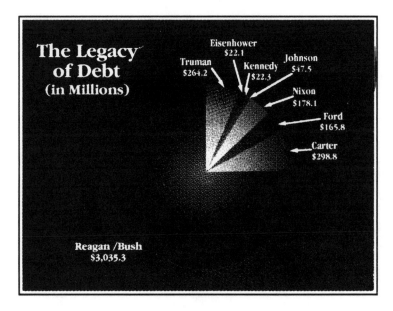

Figure 28

49

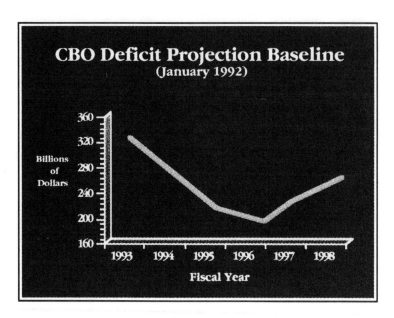

Figure 29

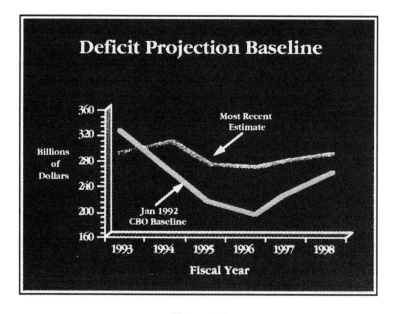

Figure 30

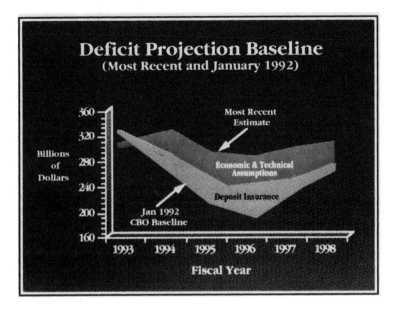

Figure 31

the last ten years. In fact, 75 percent of our debt, as shown in the next chart, was accumulated in the Reagan-Bush era. (Fig. 28)

Now, let me turn to the immediate future. The next chart shows the CBO estimates that were given in January, and they showed us some relief in the middle '90s. (Fig. 29) The dip in the deficit allowed those of us working on these problems in the summer to have some optimism regarding a lower deficit. And in fact, it looked like we could work on the deficit while still reordering our priorities in terms of public investment. And, in fact, I also thought at that time that we would be in a position to work on the out years once we got through this period. We had time to solve this problem.

Unfortunately, President-elect Clinton and Vice President-elect Gore, I have to report to you today that the more recent forecasts show a significant deterioration of this situation. The new forecasts erase the deficit declines in the '90s and add about $300 billion in new debt over this period. (Fig. 30) The flat of the curve in the middle of the decade shows that rather than recover in terms of the deficit, that our economic recovery gives us nothing but—not a decline in the deficit. In other words, things are not improving, and the fact, once again, in the latter part of the decade, we end up with a growing deficit.

Now, as shown in the next chart, I have to stress that these deficit changes are not the result of policy changes, they're not the result of new initiatives, they are simply the result of a new estimate with re-

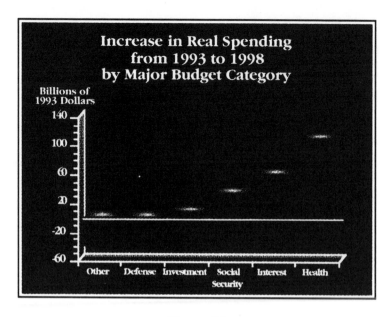

Figure 32

spect to new economic assumptions that show lower economic growth over this period and therefore a worsening situation. (Fig. 31) In addition to that, they show so-called technical adjustments, principally that our deposit insurance problem in fact continues to get worse in these years. It was not resolved on the schedule that has been forecast. In fact, that schedule has been moved several times, and we're paying the price in this era. There are also assumptions about increased entitlement costs that add to this difficult picture.

So the problem is compounded. We have a more severe illness in a weakened patient. If we simply look at 1996, we show $100 billion more deficit in this forecast than in the January forecast.

The plans that we developed in the summer took advantage of that difference. Now, with $100 billion added to it, I would not suggest for a moment that we ought to make $100 billion more cuts in 1996 programs in order to achieve previously-stated goals. But while the larger deficits make it harder to solve the problem, they in fact highlight the imperative of beginning to solve this problem now.

On my last chart, if we look at the budget trends, we again see how difficult it is going to be. (Fig. 32) The only areas that are really growing are investment—an area obviously we don't want to cut, but in fact increase—Social Security, interest, and health costs. Interest we cannot operate on directly. The others are part of our growing entitlement problem. So I would submit that given the magnitude of these problems, we have to look at every category in the federal budget, and this will be an increasingly difficult task.

In summary, in my view, the deficit problem is growing worse and must be dealt with through a multi-year specific deficit reduction program with real targets, one that is published now and shows significant progress in this decade.

Thank you. (Applause.)

PRESIDENT-ELECT CLINTON: Thank you very much. I just want to try to make more—somewhat slightly more explicit the elements that have led to the revised forecasts, so you might see the elements that would allow us to revise it the other way if we changed our behavior and got some different consequences.

First of all, this forecast reflects the consequences of lower growth rates, which means two things: number one, lower tax revenues; number two, more people at low income levels qualify for entitlements. We now have one in ten Americans on foodstamps.

MR. WHITE: Right.

PRESIDENT-ELECT CLINTON: Secondly, even higher than previously projected health care costs. This year, we're at just under $13^{1}/_{2}$ percent of our GDP going to health care. This projection reflects an estimated 18 percent GDP going to health care in the year 2000. This year, we are the only advanced industrial nation at over 10 percent. The others are at 9.5—between—roughly between 8.5 and 9.5, except for Britain; they're still under 7, but they have a system that's not analogous to ours and we're not about to go to it.

Thirdly, the S&L costs have been somewhat larger than projected. But it is also true, I think—I just want to make sure that I understood you properly—that some of the costs that were estimated to go into this budget year have been pushed into the next budget year. Is that correct?

MR. WHITE: That is correct. That is correct, yes. Much of that is reflected in that shift to the right of those costs.

PRESIDENT-ELECT CLINTON: And as you put it off, it becomes more expensive?

MR. WHITE: Yes, it does. Yes, sir.

PRESIDENT-ELECT CLINTON: All right. Now, if you go back to what he said, you go back to the chart on what's increasing and what's decreasing, investment is showing an anemic increase. Other discretionary, non-defense spending is being reduced rather dramatically.

MR. WHITE: Yes.

PRESIDENT-ELECT CLINTON: Defense spending is being reduced and will continue to be reduced. Social Security has gone up. Interest on the debt has gone up, and you can't control that now except either to reduce the debt or reduce interest rates long term. And you see where health care is basically the same as the other three items together. Health care is 50 percent of the projected increase.

And let me complicate this one step further by making sure everybody knows this. The Social Security tax itself produces an annual surplus, as against annual Social Security expenses, of something on the order of—Leon, if I'm wrong, or Senator Bentsen, correct me—I think it's something on the order of $70 billion this year. Is that about right? That doesn't mean you can't—you shouldn't reduce the rate of growth in Social Security expenses, but I do want you to understand that there used to be some sort of connection between the tax and the expenditures. And because of the bipartisan commission which solved the Social Security funding crisis in the early '80s, they did a great job of solving it, but it's now producing an annual surplus which is being used to make the debt look smaller than it otherwise would be. And that's fine now, but when the baby boomers, like me, retire, it's going to mean instead of maintaining a constant Social Security tax or a lower one, it, like health care, will become unacceptably high unless we do something about the structural deficit between now and roughly the year 2009 or 2010, 2011, when the baby boomers begin to retire.

MR. WHITE: And no matter how much money we put away, unless we solve these productivity and growth problems, we're not going to have the resources in the economy to provide you with an adequate retirement.

PRESIDENT-ELECT CLINTON: The point I want to make is, if you look at this, there is a clear connection—and that's what makes these policy choices so tough—there is a clear connection between all of these things. You have to get some more growth, or you don't get enough revenues and you don't get enough people off of government entitlements to bring the structural deficit down. You may have to raise some more money, but there's a limit to how much money you can raise without putting a burden on the economy. And you plainly have to cut spending, but your options are plainly in the last three categories; and the middle category, interest, you may not be able to cut that unless you reduce the deficit.

So the thorny interrelationships of these things, it's very, very complex. And we want to make the right calls, but I just want to make it clear that these are not self-evident. Because if you go for one hard strategy over another, you may wind up aggravating some of these other issues. And, of course, I hope, especially tomorrow, we'll really be able to begin to get some opinions about how to unpack these policy options before us.

Thank you very much. It was a terrific job.

MR. WHITE: Thank you. (Applause.)

PRESIDENT-ELECT CLINTON: Nobody wants to clap for the deficit, but give him a hand. He did a good job with it. (Applause.)

The next presentation is by Stuart Altman, Professor of National Health Policy at the Heller Graduate School at Brandeis. He is coordinating the development of health reform policy options for our transition health policy group, and I appreciate your presence here today.

MR. STUART ALTMAN (BRANDEIS UNIVERSITY): Well, Governor, thank you. This is a unique experience for me. Usually I get the opportunity to talk about the health care cost problem to individuals that may know a little less than I do. This is the first time I'm speaking to someone that really should be up at this podium making the speech. But since you invited me, and if I don't make the speech I can't get my plane fare paid, I hope you'll let me go through these numbers.

On the first chart that is presented above, you will see the fact that 20 years ago President Nixon indicated that we had a crisis in health care costs. (Fig. 33) We were spending $75 billion; it was about 7.5 percent of our GNP, and it was considered a crisis. If you look at those numbers, we have clearly failed in these last 20 years to do anything

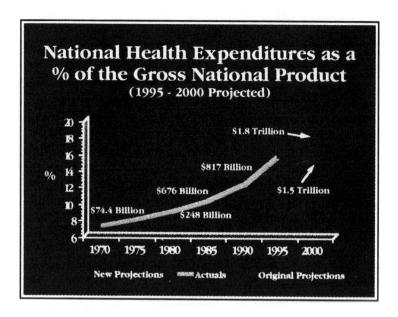

Figure 33

about this crisis. We sit here in 1992 spending over $800 billion. We've doubled that percentage to 14 percent.

I want to make another interesting point. During that same period of time, spending in this country for education, which used to be exactly the same—we were spending 7 percent for both education and health in 1970—today we spend less than 7 percent on education; health care has doubled to 14 percent.

Maybe things will get better. If you look at that chart, two years ago, I and a few others in the federal government predicted that we might be spending $1.5 trillion, 15 percent of our GNP, by the turn of the century. Our new numbers suggest it could reach 18 percent and, as you indicated, $1.8 trillion.

Now, this is a lot of money for one sector of our economy. But the problem gets deeper. As you can see in the next slide, what's happened in our system is that this health care cost, which is shown on that red line, is actually leading to more Americans becoming uninsured. (Fig. 34) It seems rather strange, we spend more and we get less. How is that happening? Well, we depend upon our private sector to provide health care for most of our workers. It used to be a fringe benefit—half a percent of payroll, one percent of payroll. Back in the 1970s it was averaged around 3 and 4 percent. Today the average American company spends between 8 and 10 percent of payroll for health care. And as Harold Poling will tell you in the next presentation, the Ford Motor

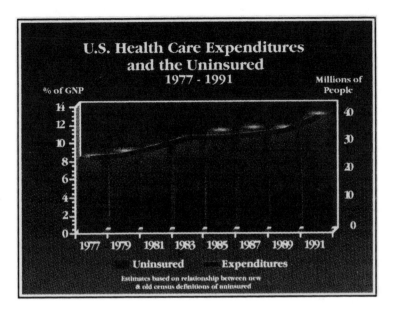

Figure 34

Company is approaching 20 percent of payroll for health care—one item. And so we have a problem that as our spending goes up, the number of Americans insured goes down.

But the problem even gets more complicated, as you see in the next chart. (Fig. 35) We have been putting a damper, interestingly enough, even though those deficit numbers show that health care is your largest growth item, we're actually doing something about it in the Medicare and Medicaid programs. And we had hoped that hospitals would respond by keeping their costs down. But, as you can see in that chart, even though hospitals received $22.5 billion, in 1990 alone, less than they said their costs were, a new tooth fairy has emerged in the American scene to keep hospital profits at the rates they had been in the early 1980s. These new tooth fairies are a very strange group. They happen to be our corporations.

Increasingly, what is happening is that we've created a gigantic Ponzi game in this country. Everybody's trying to figure out how not to pay the bill. And increasingly these dollars are being shifted from public programs and the uninsured onto the private sector. If you'll look at the bottom of that chart, they spent an extra $22.5 billion in 1990 alone to make up for these costs.

As you'll see in the next slide, fully 27 percent of the increase in premiums in 1990 for privately-insured individuals was simply to pay

Payments for Hospital Care by Payer Group in 1990

Payer Group	Payment to Cost Ratio	Payment Under or Over Costs (Billions)
Below-cost Payments		
Medicare	89.6%	($8.2)
Medicaid	80.1%	($4.6)
Uncompensated Care	21.0%	($9.6)
Total		($22.4)
Above-cost Payments		
Private Insurers	127.6%	$22.5
Other Govt. Payers	106.4%	$0.2
Total		($22.7)

[1] Operating subsidies from state & local govt. included as payments

Note: Includes all inpatient & outpatient services

Figure 35

for this cost shift. (Fig. 36) Who pays for it? It's increasingly small business and individuals, as well as our large corporations.

And so what's happening is that we lack a structure in our system. We have more uninsured than any other country. And as you can see in my last slide, a rather complicated arithmetic has arisen. (Fig. 37) If you look at the United States in comparison to Germany and Canada, in 1970, the US, which is in that fuchsia line, was spending about the same percentage of its GNP on health care as Canada, which is in the gold line. Canada actually introduced universal coverage for all of its citizens, but also developed a national policy to control health care costs. What's happened? They control—and if you look at the numbers, everyone in Canada is insured, and yet they have brought their health care costs in line with the growth in the national income. And you'll see the gap keeps getting wider and wider.

Look what happened to Germany. Germany, too, has a system that covers all its citizens. It saw a rather rapid growth and its spending began to approach our fuchsia line back around 1976. It brought together the leaders of its country and it said, "No more. No more. We have to control health care costs while we insure all our citizens." And they've done it.

So in conclusion, Governor, I think we need to do three things, and we need to do them quickly. First, we need to cover all Americans. We badly need to cover all Americans. Second, we need to provide secu-

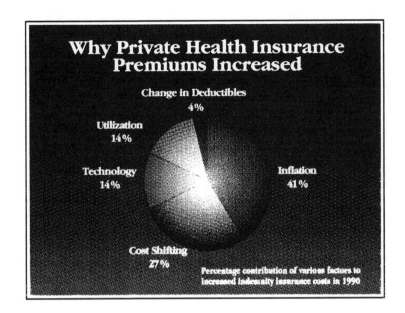

Figure 36

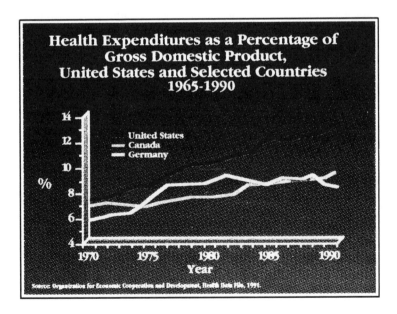

Figure 37

59

rity, that every American knows if they get sick there will be some mechanism to pay their bills. Third, we need to level the playing field so that all payers of care pay in proportion to their use. And most importantly, we need an economic policy that sits over this country with respect to health care that provides an economic discipline; restructuring the market, yes, but having a governmental presence that changes the rules of the game.

Thank you very much. (Applause.)

PRESIDENT-ELECT CLINTON: Thank you. Let me say, I just want to reinforce one point he made so that you get some sense of what an incredible downward spiral we're in, from the chart that you showed on the 27 percent cost shift to 41 percent inflation, and all that.

Because more costs keep being shifted to the private sector, more private sector people stop insuring their employees. We are literally now up to 100,000 Americans a month, just under that, losing their health insurance. An enormous percentage of them then qualify for state Medicaid benefits. Then, as soon as they trigger that in, that aggravates the federal deficit. And since states can't run a deficit, they all go out and either under-fund education, which is what we've been talking about, or underfund children's investment programs, or raise taxes, which takes money away from other kinds of investments.

Our state legislature is meeting today on a tax package to pay for Medicaid costs which are exploding because of federally-imposed mandates and huge increases in enrollment—breathtaking increases in enrollment. I've got a memo from the governor of Texas saying that it's the biggest budget problem they've ever had. We've got to fix it there. The state of Oklahoma is facing the prospect of turning thousands of people out of nursing homes if they can't raise taxes. I mean, this whole thing—the point I want to make is that pie chart is only going to get worse and worse and worse.

This is an irreversible thing unless we find a way to address the cost and coverage problems—not through government micromanagement of government programs, which is what we've been doing, but through an umbrella system that addresses what's going on for private employers, too. You can't get there otherwise. There is no way. I—we tried this thing for 12 years, and it just gets worse. And that's the central point that he made. We cannot have any kind of national response which does not deal with the private employment in the workplace there and the costs there.

Mr. Altman: I couldn't agree with you more. We need a policy that really puts both private and public spendings in a new economic discipline with some overarching controls.

President-elect Clinton: Thank you very much.

Mr. Altman: Thank you.

President-elect Clinton: The next speaker is the chairman and the CEO of Ford Motor Company, who has worked for Ford for over 40 years now. He went to work there when he was 12 years old. (Laughter.) Mr. Harold Poling, we're delighted to have you here. Thank you very much for coming.

Mr. Harold Poling (Ford Motor Company): Thank you, Mr. President-elect.

You might wonder why a car guy is being asked to talk about health care reform. And there are three very important reasons from my perspective.

First, as a citizen. I believe, along with other businessmen and women, that it's unacceptable that 37 million Americans have no health care coverage. As you, President-elect Clinton, have said, many Americans live in fear that they will fall ill and lose everything.

Second, as an employer. I want to say Ford is proud to offer extensive health care coverage for its employees, dependents, and retirees. But as we all know, there are thousands of people who do not receive the same care because they're either too poor or do not have health insurance.

Third, speaking as the chief executive officer of a company as big and solid as Ford. We have reached the point where we cannot afford double digit cost increases. Our health care costs jeopardize our ability to compete, to preserve just the existing jobs, and create additional jobs. Ford, like other businesses both large and small, has faced major and persistent increases in health care costs.

As the first chart shows, Ford's health care costs tripled as a percentage of payroll from a level of 6 percent in 1970 to nearly 20 percent in 1991. (Fig. 38) During this same period, Ford's health care costs increased at double digit annual rates, from $144 million in 1970 to about $1.3 billion in 1991. That's a jump of nearly 800 percent. Ford

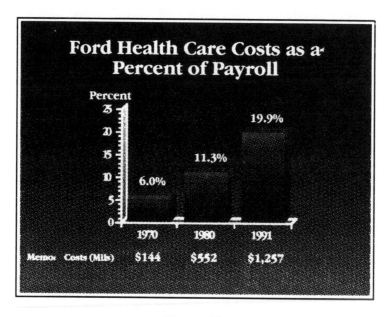

Figure 38

spends as much on health care as it does on steel. Health care providers are our largest supplier.

These spiraling health care cost increases have occurred despite working in cooperation with our union, insurance carriers, and providers to develop numerous cost containment programs, including the introduction of managed care programs, HMOs and PPOs; the use of co-payments and deductibles—people pay more attention when they participate in the cost of the care—the implementation of mail order drug prescription programs; wellness programs designed to deal with the preventive aspects of health care; and working with providers on costs and quality improvements. With costs continuing to rise despite these efforts, a national solution is required.

Health care costs also are an important factor in international competitiveness because US health care costs are out of line with the rest of the world. (Fig. 39) On a per capita basis, US health care expenditures far exceed those of other major trading partners. For example, as you can see on the chart, US costs are double those in West Germany and Japan. Ford has operations around the world, and as you can see at the bottom of the chart, our health care costs in these countries are about a third of our costs in the United States. As the next chart indicates, studies comparing health care costs on a per-vehicle basis estimate that US costs are about $500 more than Japan's. (Fig. 40)

Ford believes that business, labor, and all elements of the health care

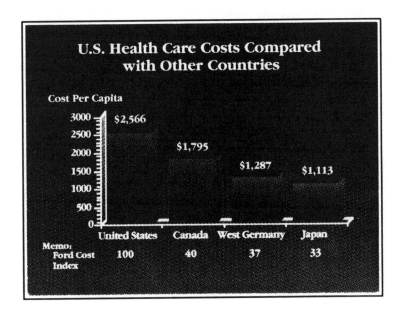

Figure 39

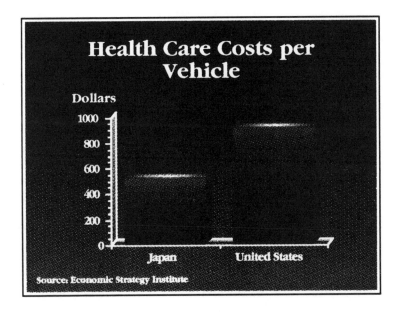

Figure 40

system can work together to solve the problem. As you, Mr. Clinton, have said on your bus tours, the goal is clear: high quality, affordable health care for all Americans. To accomplish effective reform, we must address the following five principles shown on the next chart. (Fig. 41)

Universal coverage. I'm sure everyone here today agrees that health care coverage should be afforded to every American.

Quality assurance. Studies have indicated that unnecessary operations and procedures are running as high as 30 percent.

Administrative simplicity. There are more than 1,000 insurance companies with 1,000 different claim forms. Can you believe that over four billion insurance claims were processed last year?

Cost containment. With health care costs in the United States approaching $3,000 for every man, woman, and child, neither large nor small companies nor individuals can afford to continue their health care. Purchasers, providers, and government must cooperate to develop a plan to contain these growing costs.

Inequitable financing. Costs should be spread fairly among all participants in the health care system, and cost shifting must be eliminated.

Reform needs to address all of these principles and all at the same time. We must not make the mistake of addressing this issue one part at a time and lose sight of the key objectives, universal access and cost containment.

In Michigan, along with the governor, I am co-chair of Michigan Leaders Health Care Group, which includes leaders of business, labor, insurance companies, providers, and government. This group recently reached agreement on broad national health care reform principles, despite the varying interests represented.

President-elect Clinton, Vice President-elect Gore, I recognize the great challenge facing us in achieving a national consensus. However, we can no longer delay in assuring that Americans have access to affordable health care and we must attack this serious problem impacting US industry's ability to compete globally. I believe all affected parties are willing to work with you and your administration on this problem. The time is now. It's up to us. (Applause.)

PRESIDENT-ELECT CLINTON: Thank you very much. I just want to emphasize something you said, if I might, and something that I should have acknowledged earlier in one of the earlier presentations.

One of the reasons real wages have gone down is that more money is going to health care. One of the reasons productivity goes down is if you spend more money on this, you can't spend it on research and development and plant and equipment. One of the concerns that I

Principles For Reform

- **Universal Coverage**
- **Quality Assurance**
- **Administrative Simplicity**
- **Cost Containment**
- **Equitable Financing**

Figure 41

think we all have—I know I, as you know, have been a supporter of the North American Free Trade approach of trying to expand trade with Mexico, but it is an unusual agreement in that no other advanced country has negotiated a trade agreement in which we tried to facilitate investment in another country for the purpose of making manufacturing goods to come back into ours.

And we already are now below 17 percent of our workforce in manufacturing, as compared with 28 percent in Japan and 33 percent in Germany. And it's going to become more and more difficult for us even to keep that 16.8 percent or whatever it is if we can't be more competitive in health care costs. I mean, these are the decisions that he has to make every day when he decides where we're going to produce Ford automobiles. So, I just want to—this is a major issue. If you want America to maintain a manufacturing base, we have to do it.

Let me ask you one factual question. How big a cost in this percentage you showed us, up to almost 20 percent now, is retiree health benefits? Is that a big part of your costs?

MR. POLING: It's a very substantial portion. For example, last year, the cost per contract for active employees was $4,600. The total cost for all employees, including retirees, was over $10,000 per active employee.

65

PRESIDENT-ELECT CLINTON: You see what I mean. If you look at autos and steel, two areas where productivity per employee is way up, the productivity edge is eviscerated to some extent by what they have to pay for retiree health care costs.

Now, here's why that's important. If you go back to that earlier chart in the earlier presentation by Mr. Altman, if you remember, just to remember it, it said—you saw that the Canadian cost as a percentage of GNP was way below ours, but the German cost percentage of GNP is now well below the Canadian cost. Canada has a single-payer system, which is the most efficient administratively, but because it then becomes more political, it's not as good at controlling costs as the German system, which continues to have private sector insurance, but real disciplined partnerships between business and labor and government and consumers at controlling costs.

The problem that we have, and again this is not the time to discuss this, but I want to put it in everybody's mind, is any system other than single-payer which I have seen at least continues to leave on each company the burden of the retirees' health costs, which is a big issue if you're trying to keep the percentage of the workforce in manufacturing from going even lower. I just ask you all to think about that. That is a significant problem we have to face.

Senator Gore, I think, has a question.

VICE PRESIDENT-ELECT GORE: Well, one thing I hear you saying is that the old idea that a national approach to health care would cost us more than we can afford is pretty out of date now because you're finding in your company, as many business people are, that our current system is likely to be the most expensive approach we could possibly take, and we have to have a national approach not only to provide access, but also to control costs. When you try to control costs, how have you dealt with that startling category you referred to, 30 percent of the money that may go to completely unnecessary, even counterproductive, procedures? How has Ford approached that category of costs?

MR. POLING: One of the approaches that we've taken is to develop statistical information, for example, for all of our southeastern Michigan hospitals. We provide those hospitals with comparative information for all of the services performed for patients. And that way they can compare and rate their performance relative to the others in the same area. It's been beneficial to us, but there's still a wide spread amongst the hospitals, and much work needs to be done.

PRESIDENT-ELECT CLINTON: Thank you very much.

Before I call up the next question, let me just put one other thing on the table. What we are trying to do is to get our costs in line with inflation, to slow the growth rate. I do not believe that any time in the near future we can hope to bring the percentage of GNP we devote to health care down to even that of our next nearest competitor for several reasons. One is a cultural one. We are more diverse, we have too many poor people, we have much higher levels of violence, much higher levels of people who are showing up at emergency rooms on Friday and Saturday night. We have a lot of internal elements in this country that raise health care costs.

We also spend more of our money on research and development, which is good, and more on high technology medicine near the end of life, which we are not prepared, I don't think, to give up now except in the most obvious areas.

So what we're talking about here today is not necessarily bringing America down to the level of GNP of Germany or Japan, but just getting a hold of it so that we don't have any future increases that outstrip real economic growth.

The next presenter dealing with small business in the entrepreneurial sector is Alan Patricof, the founder and President of Patricof and Company Ventures, who is the chair of a distinguished group called Entrepreneurs for Clinton-Gore.

Mr. Patricof?

MR. ALAN PATRICOF (PATRICOF AND COMPANY VENTURES): Thank you, Mr. President. Thank you, Mr. President-elect—Vice President-elect.

I was pleased to hear everyone today referring to small business and entrepreneurship. I think it's a subject that's in everybody's mind, and certainly is a very important part of the fabric of our life.

The vitality of the start-up spirit in this country is one of the essential ingredients which fuels our economy and actually distinguishes us as an entrepreneurial nation. Consider the fact that Apple Computer, which is represented on this panel today, was operating in a garage in 1977 and today is one of the fastest-growing and one of the largest companies in the country.

Could I have the first slide, please? (Fig. 42)

As Governor Clinton has stated so often, small business and entrepreneurship is the engine for job growth in the '90s. There are today over 20 million small businesses in this country, and actually only 7,000 companies in this country with over 500 employees. From 1977 to 1987, these same small companies accounted for 68 percent of the new job growth. And from 1988 to 1990, it represented 100 percent of

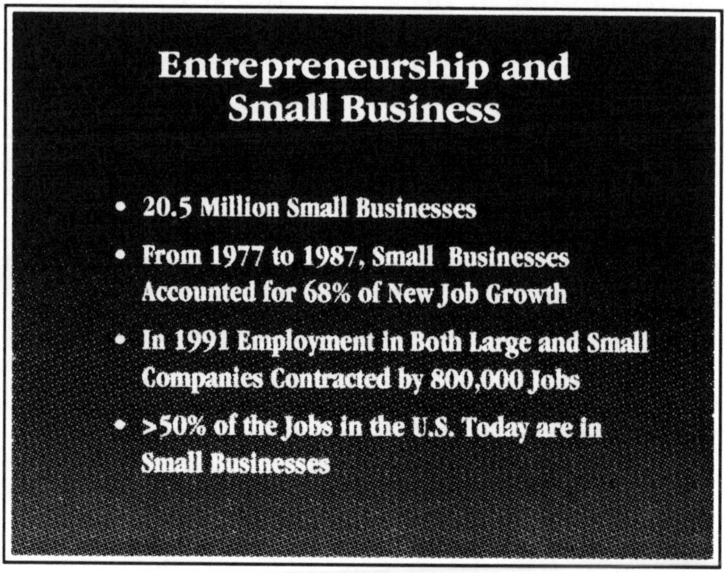

Figure 42

the job growth in the country. In 1991, as we know, both sectors declined for the first time in many years. Much of the growth in the '80s was in companies with under 20 employees, reflecting the dynamic start-up period that we went through during that early '80s.

Today, in excess of 50 percent of the jobs in this country are in small businesses. But when we look at the classification, we must recognize, and it's important that all of you leave with the thought that there are two parts of small business: one is the microcompany, which is the under-20 employees, and the other is the 20 and over.

May I have the next slide? (Fig. 43)

The microcompanies, those with under 20 employees, are usually family-owned or very narrowly owned on a local basis. They have limited credit needs for computers, for office equipment, and for small production aspect and on a local basis. They have a limited number of job growth because they are small in size, and usually many of them stay that way. They are local and play a very important part in the fabric of the local community. This is by far the largest segment of our employment in small business.

Growth companies, on the other hand, in the 20 to 500 category are fewer in number, but these companies start out with the anticipation of exponential growth. They have broad public and private ownership, and thus they must constantly look to the idea of raising debt and raising equity on a regular basis. They are national in scope. At least

68

Characteristics of Micro Companies

- Under 20 Employees
- Limited Capital Requirements
- Important Factor in the Community Fabric
- Comprises the Majority of Companies in the Small Business Sector

Characteristics of Growth Companies

- 20 - 500 Employees
- Large Capital Requirements
- Exponential Job Growth Potential
- High R&D Component

Figure 43

their objective is to become national in scope. And many of them become international. They engage in research and development, and they spend significant dollars on plant and equipment.

Next slide, please. (Fig. 44)

The concerns are very different. In a recent study done by the—one of the associations in small businesses, the microbusinesses, it was determined that the major cause of concern, not surprisingly, was health care costs—something we've heard enough of today, but we can't say it enough times. And in their case, it's not just the cost of health care which is escalating, but also their inability in many cases to provide it.

Taxes, of course, are always a concern to small businesses, and another area is workman's compensation costs. Cash flow, which really means meeting this week's payroll, is a constant problem that small businesses have to live with, government regulations and, of course, liability insurance, which is something that is difficult for a small company to struggle with.

Next slide. (Fig. 45)

Growth companies, on the other hand, are worried about what Governor Clinton pointed out these past months, that small- and medium-sized businesses were involved in a very serious credit crunch, as illustrated by the next slide. (Fig. 46) Following the new bank capital rules which went into effect in March 1989, total bank assets increased consistently while loan volumes for commercial and industrial loans

69

Concerns Of Micro Companies

- Cost of Health Insurance
- Federal Taxes
- Workers Compensation Costs
- Cash Flow
- Government Regulations
- Federal Paperwork
- Cost and Availability of Liability Insurance

Source: National Foundation of Independent Businesses, October/November 1991

Figure 44

Concerns of Growth Companies

- Availability of Credit
- Government Regulations
- Availability of Long Term Equity Capital
- Health Insurance Costs
- Workers Compensation Cost
- Sensitivity to Stock Options
- R&D and ITC Incentives

Figure 45

70

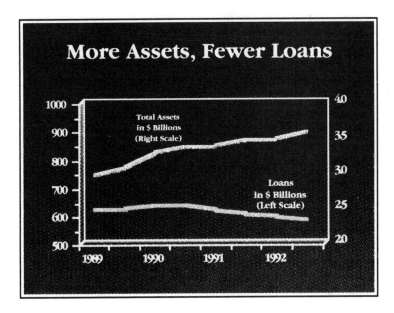

Figure 46

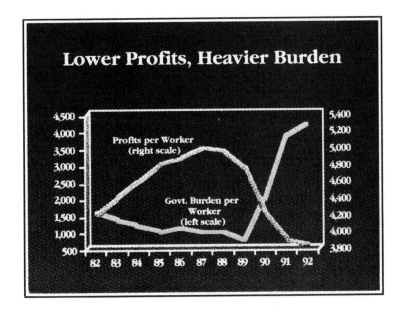

Figure 47

71

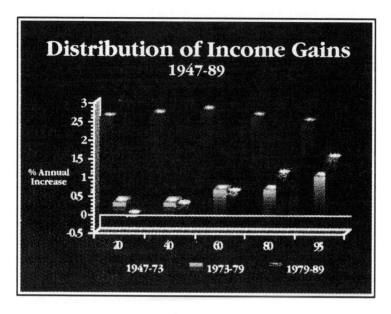

Distribution of Income Gains
1947-89

% Annual Increase

1947-73   1973-79   1979-89

Figure 48

trended downwards. This was during a period when new bank hold-ings of—excuse me, when net bank holdings of government securities went up by 68 percent. Large companies during this period were rela-tively unaffected by the credit crunch, as they could look to non-—to other sources in terms of raising corporate bonds in the corporate mar-ket, and in this case, corporate bonds increased by $200 billion out-standing. It was the small- and medium-sized businesses that were squeezed in the credit crunch.

Next slide. (Fig. 47)

Another problem that has been facing these businesses that are in the dynamic growing phase is the impact of government regulations, which is highlighted here. After seven years of trending in the right direction, suddenly we are experiencing a complete reversal, where, as the result of increased regulatory burdens which have accelerated over the past three years, profit per worker took a nosedive.

Next slide. (Fig. 48)

Not surprisingly, availability of capital is another major concern which you've heard here several times today. The growth company always has to look to the capital markets and has to have access to risk capital. And since the Tax Reform Act of 1986, we have seen a dra-matic trend in the willingness, particularly of individual investors, to take that differential and go into long-term risk investments. Health insurance appears also as a concern for the growth companies as well as workman's compensation. Of recent importance has become the subject of stock options, which play a critical role in the long-term incentive compensation scheme for young companies. And finally, most growing companies look on research and development and capital investment as a natural fuel for their development and to establish their competitiveness.

I'd like to leave you with this thought: in 1970, there was no biotech industry. There were a hundred—under a hundred small, privately owned companies who were just beginning to do research in their laboratories. In 1980, there were 300 companies, as the industry started to take form.

In 1992, there are over 1,200 biotechnology companies, many of them public. Today they employ over 78,000 people, and we are leaders in the world in this field. And the growth is only just beginning. Product sales last year crossed the $5 billion mark, and interestingly, research and development expenditures by these same companies was over $4.5 billion of that $5 billion. And invested capital from shareholders during the past ten years has been over $35 billion which has been invested into these growing companies. Who can question the job growth and quality of life that these companies have fostered, and what other achievements can be expected from them in the future?

There are other similar success stories out there, and many more starting out as we meet here today. Who knows what the next decade will bring?

Thank you.

PRESIDENT-ELECT CLINTON: Thank you very much. (Applause.)

I want to say that in the roundtable, I hope Mr. McColl from Nations Bank and others will perhaps address the whole issue of the changing pattern of what banks are doing with their money.

And let me just ask you one thing, Alan, because the chart didn't show it. How could the government regulation per worker cost have tripled in three years? What did that?

MR. PATRICOF: That was a study done, I think you'll see, by actually— I think it was called the Joint Republican Committee, and I gather it had to do with not just—well, first of all, it was passing several acts that have just emerged in the last few years which have added these costs, plus there were indirect taxes involved, as I understand, during that period of time.

PRESIDENT-ELECT CLINTON: Well, maybe the staff could unpack that for us. That seems a little (kind of rich?) to me. That's quintupled. I said tripled.

Thank you very much.

We'll talk some more, especially tomorrow, about some of Alan and other people's prescriptions for what we should do to increase the small business growth.

We're running about 30 minutes late. I'm going to get half the time back by declaring that the recess will be five minutes instead of 20.

So hurry, we're having a five minute break.

(RECESS)

PRESIDENT-ELECT CLINTON: I know of two or three folks who want to make comments, so keep in mind, just in order to hear from everybody around the table, there may not be any logical order but I'm sure that most of what will be said will be relevant to the general topic, which is the assessment of the economy.

I'd like to ask Hugh McColl to begin and to address the issue raised by Mr. Patricof about the changes in lending practices of the nation's banks and whether there are reasonably any other sources of credit for small businesses.

Hugh, you want to start?

MR. HUGH McCOLL (NATIONS BANK): Yes, sir.

Well first, what I would say is that the—what we have seen as a drying up of credit has quite clearly happened. I believe it's been an overreaction on the part of the examiners and subsequently by the bankers themselves to the S&L crisis. That is, that the S&L debacle caused a response by Congress, putting on a lot of regulation, the examiners are carrying it out to a fault, and the bankers, seeing no reward for reaching out on the risk curve, have pulled back. I think that's very serious.

I believe that money will always flow to where it is incented to flow. And so then, I think the carrot works better than the stick as one looks at how to get money to flow to small business or into community development or wherever you wish it to go.

As I look at the things that are in the way of the recovery, the free flow of credit is the number one. That is, nothing the White House can do will work unless credit flows to support the growth in the economy. What we need is a lifting of so many regulations that are trying to micromanage the banks, and let them go back to serving their communities and working with the borrower that is in trouble, or the bor-

74

rower who has a good idea but who can't possibly provide the information that is now being required. Very few small businesses can do that. So really, relaxation of regulation is what we need.

Secondly, I believe that it is quite clear that the banking industry has recovered, but that recovery is spotty and we should do whatever it takes to allow the continued consolidation of the industry and let the strong take over the weak so that we can go forward.

PRESIDENT-ELECT CLINTON: We have at least two business owners on your side of the table. I'd like to give them a chance to comment on this credit issue or anything else, Kathryn Thompson from Orange County, and Frank Brooks.

MS. KATHRYN THOMPSON (THOMPSON DEVELOPMENT CO.): Thank you, Mr. President-elect. I would like to say first that I think this conference was a bold move and certainly demonstrates your administration's desire to hear from all sectors.

Americans took a leap of faith when they voted this election, and I believe they're hopeful, they're optimistic with the prospects of change. However, I do believe there are two things that are affecting the economy. One, we heard earlier from Mr. Solow about staggering along and in some areas like in California, we're paralyzed. And one of those things is the credit crunch that Mr. McColl just spoke about. We must free up credit or the entrepreneur will become an endangered species.

Regulations must be modified for banks or we might consider two types of banks. Maybe it's time that we have an insured and an uninsured bank, the uninsured bank being able to take the risk that the banks that now have the FDIC insurance cannot do. Or, we go back to the lending policies of the '50s and '60s where the banks could make a decision based on character and based on the community good that the loan would create. I am not advocating that we go back to the "go-go '80s" but there certainly has to be a modification of the current regulations.

I can't build houses for first-time home buyers if I can't get a loan.

Second, I think Americans want to know what the rules are. Mr. Sculley alluded to it in his comments. We have indecision. It's because people aren't certain about what's going to happen, and I'll give you an example. A first-time home buyer is not going to buy a house today while there is discussion going on about a first-time buyer's credit. I don't believe a business is going to invest in equipment if they're worried about if an investment tax credit is going to take place.

What targeted capital gains? I think we have a paralysis right now that we need to make a list of all of the potential incentives or tax credits that are going to be offered. We need to make a time table and commitment to those dates so that people, consumers and businesses, can make a decision. Otherwise they are going to hold back and wait to see what is going to happen.

Finally, I would be remiss, as I'm a home builder, not to say that please don't forget shelter as a part of infrastructure. Adequate shelter in the broadest sense of the word is essential to ensure the health, welfare and economic vitality of our very population and it should be a component of any domestic policy.

Thank you.

PRESIDENT-ELECT CLINTON: Thank you. Let me just make one response to what you said that I think is a very good cautionary note for this administration. When we talk about changing the tax code, we may actually undermine the very activity in the short run we seek to promote.

Senator Bentsen, in his present position as Chair of the Senate Finance Committee, sent me a letter along with Congressman Rostenkowski, pointing out that if we were going to have an investment tax credit we need to all agree on what the effective date was, just to remove that disincentive you mentioned.

Frank?

MR. FRANK BROOKS (BROOKS SAUSAGE COMPANY): Mr. President, when I met you a little over a year ago and you came to Chicago to talk about your programs, one of the things that you talked about strongly at that time was the economic package. And I just want to encourage you to stick with that. I know there's a lot of temptation and a lot of pressures now to look at the budget and work on that. I do think that economic package of stimulus is important. I think, in using Bob Reich's contention though, that minority and small businesses can play an important role in this whole effort though.

I think if you look at where those jobs and where that stimuli is going to occur, it's probably going to be in the inner cities. And I contend that minority firms and small firms will be the ones to do the hiring. I think if you look at all the numbers—you say jobs are being created by small firms. I think though, that minority firms can play a vital role in this economy and I want to just take a brief moment to talk about my firm which had corporate support.

McDonald's, six years ago, came up with the idea that they wanted to establish minority suppliers with some presence. My company was formed. It was a start-up company. I had support from an existing supplier, so I was able to get credit basically because of the relationship with McDonald's and because of the relationship I had with a partner.

The company grew five million the first year, 10 million the second year. Over a six year period the company has grown to 30 million. The asset base is about 15 million. It's a viable entity. It's a major supplier to McDonald's. They came out and put this together and made it happen.

I am now being courted by an audience I never would have been courted [by] before. I have about 200 employees. I have the opportunity, in my mind, to grow to about 1,500.

The venture capital firms are now looking at me. They are willing to put money at me. They think I can grow to a $200 million company and even go public. I never would have gotten that audience before.

Now let me give you one quick example of how the government took a good program and it's not working though.

Two companies that I am very close to were doing government work, one with the Air Force, one with the Defense Department. Those companies employed over 800 persons. But they were in the 8-A program and so those companies grew up to about 60 million between the two of them.

President-elect Clinton: Frank, tell the people here what the 8-A program is.

Mr. Brooks: The 8-A program is a set aside program, what they call a sole source program, which is administered by the Small Business Administration.

These companies grew, they hired people, but they were forced to graduate out of the program and say "you've been in it for five or seven years and you ought to be able to do it on your own, we want new people in it."

To me, a better incentive than that would be to put more emphasis on incentives to hire more people. Instead of zeroing them in and out, they should be staying in that program. They then had to compete against a Boeing, a Northrop, and they couldn't get the contract. They then became competitive in a market they really couldn't compete in.

I say that to say I think some programs within the government really have to be looked at. I am encouraged to see your new Secretary of Commerce, because I think he'll be looking at not only that, although he won't be related to SBA, but I think he will be involved in making sure that small firms get heard.

Just in closing, I think there are two areas that you really ought to look at in addition to stimulating that economy. One would be to reduce the capital gains tax to 15 percent on small capitalized companies in order that—well, at least that are held for five years or longer in order to stimulate investment in small firms. The venture capital firms will not put money in the front end of companies like that, nor are the banks too excited about it.

The other thing we talked about, in my case I've invested about seven-and-a-half million in plant and equipment in the last year. You really ought to look at the capital gains tax for investment in order that companies like this and larger companies have a chance to get some gains for making that investment, and I know that's been talked about but I would encourage that also.

PRESIDENT-ELECT CLINTON: Thank you.

I'd like to shift the discussion for a moment to one issue that received only passing treatment in the early morning assessment, but one that I think is very important, and that is whether all these defense cuts are going to have a net positive or negative impact on the technology base of America and our capacity to generate jobs in areas that are quite important to our future.

One of the people around this table today, Ann Markusen, has written a book called, "Dismantling the Cold War Economy." And one of the things—Kathryn Thompson is from Orange County—one of the things that is hurting Orange County is not just the credit crunch and real estate, but also the fact that there are 200,000 unemployed defense industry workers in southern California alone. So I'd like to talk a little bit about that and what we might do about it.

ANN MARKUSEN (RUTGERS UNIVERSITY): Yes, thanks.

Well, Governor Clinton, as you have said over and over in your election campaign and on the night of your victory, this is one of the biggest challenges we face. I think it's important for us to remember that in the 1980s the defense budget went up by over 50 percent in real terms, from around $200 billion to $300 billion a year. And that means that now, with the end of the Cold War, we really have an unprecedented opportunity to use—to lower the defense budget and to use those funds to invest in America.

Now it's difficult to make these cuts and I think one of the reasons the Congress has shown some reluctance to make the cuts is that there is very serious fear that in an economy that already has nine-and-a-half million people unemployed, and where manufacturing job loss has continued for the last decade, that we will have much greater problems if we dump another two-and-a-half million people on the market, which is essentially the number of people that would be unemployed over the next five to seven years if we made defense cuts up to 50 percent—and 50 percent is what the experts more or less tell us we can afford.

So that's why we have to have a strong, coherent conversion strategy in this country, and I think there are two really important elements to that. One is that on the demand side we need to set out some new missions in the economy that will do what the Cold War did for us over 40 years, that is be the organizing principle for the economy. And I was so glad to hear you talk about energy and environment earlier. I think in addition to those, transportation, housing and education, infrastructure could be added.

We need to make these commitments not only to research and development in these new areas, but also to some market creation for some initial period of time. Remember that our very strong computer and semiconductor industries came out of the spending, particularly in the '50s and '60s, that we invested in those industries not just through R&D but also by creating markets.

If we created markets of these sorts, it would be much easier for the General Dynamics and the Boeings of this country and the smaller firms to see opportunities in new areas to which they could shift their skills, their creativity, and their plant and equipment.

And on the other side, the supply side, there are the adjustment programs that we need in this country. Right now we have 26 categorical programs spread across a number of different agencies that are supposed to be for conversion. The director of the Massachusetts Industrial Services program told me recently that she had to write seven grants to five agencies to get a rather modest amount of money this year for their transition program. So we need to really have transition programs for firms, for workers and communities that will move resources fast out of the military area of the economy and into civilian work. This is an efficiency question, how can we do this with efficiency? And I think what we need there is some advance planning. We need to encourage firms to do advance planning. We need some capital for firms to retool, something like an enterprise development bank, and we need worker retraining and education programs that are linked up to job creation, perhaps in these new mission areas.

And let me just close by saying that I think this is an issue not just for the defense industries but for manufacturing generally, that we have to remember that part of what happened to auto and steel and consumer electronics and machine tools and so on in this country was that the best of our resources, our industrial policy, really was narrowly focused on aerospace communications and electronics for several decades. And now it's really important to take into account the fact that those industries also deserve a shot at the best science and engineering talent we have in this country, which has more or less been hoarded by the defense industries, and an opportunity also to get the capital and trade protection when they need it for short periods of time, to really get going again.

We have 20 million people in manufacturing in this country and they are at risk. And most of them do not work in high tech industries and all the high tech job creation of the 1980s has not provided jobs for most of those who have been shut out of basic manufacturing.

High technology and free trade are not adequate solutions to the problems of these industries because they do not take into account the deeper problems of worker retraining, of changing the management and labor cultures in firms, in providing capital for the retooling process, and to really get us going again. We need to have good basic industries in this country, and shifting defense—from defense into civilian activity is one way of strengthening that commitment to basic manufacturing.

PRESIDENT-ELECT CLINTON: Let me just make one statement sort of— and support this.

It is estimated that even under the present administration's defense cuts, projected defense cuts, you could have a dislocation of around two million jobs, I think in the next five to six years. And if you don't want those people to move out of a rather high wage, high productive sector, we've got to have a much more disciplined strategy than we've had.

Ann mentioned one thing, we've got too many agencies with a little bitty piece of this and nobody coordinating all of it. Another problem is that the Congress has appropriated money that hasn't even been spent yet. So—would anyone like to say anything else about this issue? This defense transition issue?

If not, I'd like to move on, starting with Mr. Allen, if I might, and ask the people who are here—we have Delano Lewis here from C&P Telephone Company, we have Mr. Hurst there from Michigan Bell. I'd like to ask if the people who are here in communications would like to say anything about the role of telecommunications policy in our economic future.

Mr. Robert Allen (AT&T): Thank you. I'd like to make two points and they may seem somewhat disconnected to some, but I think in the context of what we've been discussing here today, I think you will find the connection.

The first has to do with what I consider to be the medium of exchange for the '90s. It is information. Senator Gore has spent a good deal of his career focusing on that issue, and so I do believe with all due respect to Hugh McColl and others who move money around the system, that information is really the coin of the realm in the coming years. And so, I think a focus on infrastructure including information networks, commercial networks which are interconnected, interoperable, national and global, needs to be encouraged, and I believe—I have some points to make about who should do what in that respect.

I think the government should not build and/or operate such networks. I believe the private sector can be and will be incented to build these networks, to enhance them and make it possible for people to connect with people and people with information anyplace in the world.

I do think, however, that the government role can be strong in the sense of first increasing investment in civilian research and precompetitive technologies, and that's not unrelated to the prior subject as we redirect the national laboratory efforts which have been heretofore focused primarily on defense, toward commercial technology.

Secondly, supporting the effective transfer of that technology to the private sector. Thirdly, establishing and promulgating technical standards which are so important, to be sure the networks and devices play together, work together so that we have the most efficient system in the world, and incentives for investment and research and development, job training, many of the issues that we've been talking about here before, I think are proper roles in this connection.

Let me just switch now and make my second point and try to be as brief as I can, and that is that I think among all the things we have discussed here today, perhaps one of the most important is what Marian Wright Edelman spoke about today. This is the beginning of the pipeline. If we're talking about long-term investment in America, we have to make a long-term investment in our children, in prenatal care, in immunization, in Head Start, in nutrition counseling and all of the issues which she supports. I think it has the highest payback in the long term. We spend a good deal of our philanthropic effort and time in that area. We intend to do more and I just wanted to support, Marian, some of the very important things you have said.

Thank you.

VICE PRESIDENT-ELECT GORE: I'd like to briefly clarify one point that you made, in talking about the need for information infrastructure and networks.

I fully agree when it comes to conventional networks and the new networks that your industry is now in the process of building, but with the advanced high capacity network like the National Research and Education Network, it does seem to me that government ought to play a role in putting in place that backbone, just as no private investor was willing to build the interstate highway system, but once it was built then a lot of other roads connected to it.

This new, very broad band high capacity network ought to—most people think ought to be built by the federal government and then transitioned into private industry. You didn't mean to disagree with that view when you said government shouldn't play a role, did you?

MR. ALLEN: Yes, I may disagree. (Laughter) That is to say that the use of that network today and the network that is supported by the National Science Foundation is not being used today in the manner in which it was originally prescribed. That is to say, there are commercial users to a network that I think was provided to connect libraries and science research laboratories and that sort of thing. And the subsidies inherent therein are subsidizing some commercial companies today, as opposed to the end users, which I think ought to be subsidized to be sure that every library and research laboratory can get on the network, so that we can all connect and benefit. That's the only distinction I make.

VICE PRESIDENT-ELECT GORE: It bears further discussion. Not now.

PRESIDENT-ELECT CLINTON: I was hoping we'd have one disagreement. (Laughter)
 Mr. Hurst.

MR. ROBERT HURST (MICHIGAN BELL TELEPHONE): Yes, President-elect Clinton, I tend to agree with the position that Bob has just taken, that the nation clearly needs an advanced telecommunications network infrastructure. It can mean millions of jobs for us, and it can go a long way in advancing our country in terms of its global competitiveness.

I think it can do wonders in terms of education. In my state we have trials of interactive video where young people are in one location, instructors in another location, tremendous opportunities there. I think it can also affect health care, including the opportunity to reduce health care.

I do believe, however, that the role of government should be that of bringing the key players together. The role of government should be in helping to create an enabling regulatory climate, a climate that would encourage investment, a climate that would encourage full competition. All of the players should be able to enter all markets and compete fully. In fact, I commented to Vice President-elect Gore last night that it would seem to me that with his interest in this subject, and his obvious knowledge of this subject, that perhaps this issue of a national network infrastructure could be assigned to him, and a task force could be put together to work with him, made up of people from the private sector and other places to move this issue because we are falling behind as a nation. There are other nations who are already at work developing this kind of infrastructure and developing it in ways that would include fiber to the home.

And so, I think it's imperative that we get on with it. A way to start that, a way to start the dialogue to get on with it, I think might be to—given Vice President-elect Gore's interest—assign it to him and put some of us together to work with him.

PRESIDENT-ELECT CLINTON: Thank you.
Delano.

MR. DELANO LEWIS (C&P TELEPHONE): Mr. President-elect and Vice President-elect Gore, I thank you for this opportunity to participate. I'd just like to say as C&P Telephone Company in Washington, we look forward to providing your information and telecommunication needs when you move to the nation's capital. (Laughter)

Let me say that there are some very specific—

PRESIDENT-ELECT CLINTON: I'm not going to bring my own set.

MR. LEWIS: (Laughter) All right, we're glad. (Laughter)

That brings up the whole issue of competition and one of the things I want to talk about is opening that door. My colleagues had mentioned it indirectly and I want to be very specific, that I represent what we call a Regional Bell Operating Company, some known as the Baby Bells.

We firmly believe that the restrictions should be lifted on the local operating companies. From this date we are precluded from getting into manufacturing. We are precluded from getting into interstate long distance, and we're precluded, although we've made some gains, in certain information services.

We think that that modified final judgment, or known as the consent decree, should be lifted because when we talk about competitiveness and competing around the world, we're going to need to have all the talent of all the companies and we represent that talent.

My second point is—and you've heard it already—less regulation would be certainly to our advantage, to enhance the economic fabric of this country. You will be making appointments to the Federal Communications Commission and other regulatory agencies. It's going to be key that that become less burdensome and less bureaucratic. And I'd certainly like to endorse the support of the infrastructure because that is going to be—if incentive's an offer, we certainly would be in line to provide incentives in developing plant and equipment and technology. So we would encourage that.

And our company has a strong emphasis on education and Marian Wright Edelman and others know that we are strongly behind the Children's Defense Fund and many other organizations in Washington, to promote our employee base because these are places we are going to get our future employees.

And my last point is that it hasn't been mentioned, but I firmly believe that labor and management must have a shared vision. We have a lot of work to do to understand the issues of labor and labor unions, and for them to understand our issues in management. And if we're going to compete fully, our companies and all the companies around this table are going to have to work closely with our labor unions. In our company it's Communication Workers of America and the International Brotherhood of Electrical Workers. And I stand ready and I know my company, Bell Atlantic, stands ready to develop that shared vision in order to move forward.

I really appreciate this opportunity to participate. Thank you.

PRESIDENT-ELECT CLINTON: Thank you very much.

One of the points Michael Porter made this morning is that we have to somehow find a way to more carefully and clearly align the goals of investors, managers and employees in America. I'd like to ask two people at least in general to comment on that and other things, beginning with David Glass, who is the President of the number one retailer in America, it happens to be an Arkansas company, Wal-Mart. And I'd like to ask Beth Renge also, who's done a lot of work on the Japan-America issues, if she'd like to say anything about that as it relates to our relationships with Japan and the kind of corporate culture we ought to have. But David, would you make a few comments?

MR. DAVID GLASS (WAL-MART): Thank you. I'm delighted to have the opportunity.

On a rather general approach, looking at what we are doing here this morning, I think if you look at the economy and what's happening, there are some very good signs in the economy and there are some good things that are happening, but I don't—from our viewpoint at least, nothing that would be conclusive in saying that we have a recovery that any of us would be pleased with. And so, I think that it's particularly appropriate that this conference is being held at this time, where some of that could be discussed.

I think with the good signs that we see in the economy, we believe that there are a lot of negatives still hanging out there that will influence the coming year, which is upon us. In the business community you've got a lot of outstanding companies in this country that are downsizing and that's been mentioned a couple of times today. That will put pressures on employment and many other areas. I think it's interesting to note, though, that I believe those companies are downsizing not because of an absence of opportunity, but because that's what's going to be required to compete in a global environment. And although we talk about it a lot at meetings like this, or the government talks about it, most of us are more protectionist or isolationist by nature or by our exposure than we would like to believe. And I don't think that most Americans fully realize how important it will be to compete effectively in a global environment going forward, or what it actually means or how quickly that will be upon us.

I think we can do it and I think that we can do it rather well, and I think that the American worker is still the most productive worker in the world and capable of doing more than anyone else in that regard.

But I think we have to look carefully at whether we have a short-term strategy or a long-term strategy, and business in general tends to be driven more by short-term strategy, but the government's not immune to that either.

I remember when we had the oil embargo and all of us focused our attention and worked very hard on an energy policy that we quickly lost interest in when the oil embargo went away. It's only been a few years ago that most business people that I came in contact with, and most Americans I think, believed that the greatest single enemy that the country faced today was inflation. And now, with low, single-digit inflation, almost an absence of inflation in our business, there's rarely a mention of inflation and I think short-term strategies bring the danger of inflationary pressures returning.

But the point that I want to make, actually, is that short-term is the view we've tended to take, the problem that's at hand, how do we fix it today? And I would be hopeful that in this measured, considered approach that all of you are taking, that we would take a longer-term view, not just to the strategy but whether it's a public or—better done in the public arena or the private arena. I think that if we look to our neighbors at the south, they are doing some very exciting things in the private arena that were always given to government there, and having some great success with it.

But to the point that you asked me to speak to, it will take in this country, I believe, an alliance between capital, between management, between labor, between shareholders, between everyone involved to form a coalition with common objectives and common goals. That's done rather effectively in pieces in parts of the economy but not to the extent or on as broad a scope as it should. But most of all I think what we need is a vision that is commonly understood and is shared by everyone.

One of the problems that I have had and I think others have had as well, is not knowing where we are going, where we can all be doing the same things at the same time and making the right things happen. It's the floundering that has caused the problem. But with a common vision there's no question but we can do whatever we want to do.

PRESIDENT-ELECT CLINTON: Thank you.
Beth.

MS. BETH RENGE (RENGE SECURITIES & CO.): I have been very involved in Japan-US relations, but truly I can probably yield it to some of my colleagues and the discussion of the international economy. I have more of a focus—(inaudible)—municipal securities firm and I would like to bring up that ugly word again, infrastructure. But infrastructure are the better, more efficient transportation systems, they're the better environment for us by building pollution control facilities, they're projects for facilities for our education and health care systems.

We've heard from Alicia why all the important reasons of rebuilding our infrastructure here in America, which you know helps productivity. But really, the good news is we really don't have to have more direct investment in these types of projects. We have all the right factors to publicly finance these types of projects. We have the voter approval of a vast amount of projects throughout the country. We've got talented people and government officers that are local and know the issues and can transact these issues. We have the lowest interest rates in a decade to borrow.

What we don't have because of the credit crunch and you know, in California it stems from the layoff of defense jobs, the decrease in foreign investment, as well as the state budget deficit. So to look at that as the sole problem of public financing these projects, I think we need to look at creative venues for that type of credit guarantee. What the Japanese and US banks did for us in the '80s, we have to look for something different.

And I have a proposal, we can look at something like General Electric Credit Corporation that backs their own financing projects. What we can do here in the United States is to get a consortium of corporations as well as pensions to look at this not as just rebuilding America, which is vitally important, but to also—it's an incredible business opportunity right now. If you're not directly involved in municipal finance, the demand far exceeds the supply and we have to present it that way as what it really is, but a different creative venue.

But that is the sole problem of trying to finance these projects.

President-elect Clinton: Dr. Vagelos, I have to let you talk before we go to the audience because we put so much on you in the primary session there. Go ahead.

Dr. Roy Vagelos (Merck & Co.): Thank you. Two comments, one concerning the vaccine issue that Ms. Edelman focused on, and that is, it is absolutely the fact that preventive medicine is the best kind of medicine. And preventing a disease is what you do with vaccines.

The US industry has been the most productive in the world in doing that, and the 10-to-one ratio of benefits to cost that was quoted in some instances is 14-to-one when one looks at mumps, measles and rubella vaccine in the United States. It is absolutely critical to get children vaccinated, and over the last few years there have been epidemics of measles around the United States in some of our major cities. And the reason for that is that the children have just not been vaccinated.

Lucy Hackney (sp) carried out a program in the city of Philadelphia where she actually had the vaccine, which was available free, and spent a good long time advertising and trying to get people to bring their children to be vaccinated, and then on a big weekend they had a big program where they vaccinated all the children that showed up and it was a great success. But the end result was really a rather small portion of those children that were unvaccinated, had never received vaccine on that weekend.

Well, what I'm saying is that I think the industry has been very productive and will continue to be productive in coming out with new preventive medicines, that we will continue to invest.

For instance, Hepatitis B, Hemophilus influenza, Meningitis vaccines have been introduced recently. Very shortly there will be a vaccine for chicken pox, next year I hope, if we have a new FDA active in approval of this thing and other ones coming in the near future.

If we're to have a vaccine for AIDS, that will come from the industry as well. So there is great hope. And what we need to do is have a government program that helps encourage the children to get to the vaccines.

Now another sort of related comment and that is on the health care cost issue, and the health care in the United States, which is clearly the best in the world for those people who can afford it.

I would say we absolutely favor a program to give access to those people who don't have it, high quality health care, and of course containment of costs. In the long run the containment of costs can be helped the most by important new medicines. If we had a drug for Alzheimer's Disease, for AIDS, for cancer, we would put a huge hole in the growth of health care costs. And why has the US industry been so much in the leadership position? Because we have had strong long-term investment not only by the industry but by government and the National Science Foundation and the National Institutes of Health. They do the basic research, our industry does the applied research and it has been enormously effective. Overall they invest about 16 percent of sales into research and development, long-term. It takes 12 years to develop a drug from the time it's first invented in the laboratory and these drugs are incredibly effective when they get on the market.

Now the future depends on continued productivity in those laboratories and that future depends on continued growth of the NIH, the NSF and most importantly, something that everyone else has touched on, the science and math education of our children. And investment there is what we have to do if the US is to continue competitively, globally in this wonderful industry.

PRESIDENT-ELECT CLINTON: Thank you very much. I just want to make one brief point and then I think Betsy Henley-Cohn has a comment and then Andrew Shapiro has a comment.

You made a point in referring to Lucy Hackney's (sp) experiment—their effort in Philadelphia—I wanted to make when Mr. Poling talked. I agree with the five points you said about what we have to do with the health care system, but it's also very important to point out that we have to really make sure we've got a delivery system for primary and preventive care out there, which means people who speak different languages in a lot of places in America, and it means a lot of store front, basic primary care operations. That would cut a huge amount of the cost.

For example, the National Health Service Corps doctor concept has not only been eviscerated in this administration, which makes it hard to have public health clinics, but Manhattan—because there are a lot of doctors in parts of Manhattan, as a group—as an island or as a borough was declared ineligible for National Health Service Corps docs, even though that also includes Harlem. So then, you've got more people showing up at Harlem Hospital in the emergency room and helping the hospital to go broke. It's a very important point and I'm glad you brought it up.

Betsy and then Andrew.

Ms. Betsy Henley-Cohn (Joseph Cohn & Sons): I have just three short points. Our business, we're construction subcontractors in New England, but we're also a business that has grown and tried to stay as a corporate citizen in the inner city. And one of the things no one—or we haven't talked about here is that in good economic times it's easy to be a good corporate citizen. When the economy is a lot tougher, my first responsibility is to cut costs to keep my employees working. What that means is that being in the city is really not the right place for me to be. It's much more expensive to operate out of the city.

When businesses—we're the last line of employment in the city. When the remaining businesses leave the city it's going to be very, very tough. It's hard to address all the social issues when there's no tax base. And I've read a lot about the ideas about enterprise zones, but in business you don't wait until you've lost all your market share before you think about how you're going to get new customers.

I'd like to have people think about taking whole, small cities and making them enterprise zones. It's a lot tougher to get people to come back to the city after they've already left. I think people should be focusing on also keeping businesses in the city, that's point one.

Point two, as a business operating in New England, New England is not out of the recession. We have many states that still have negative employment growth. And one of the things that is contributing to this, and I have a little different focus on this, the credit crunch in New England is a little bit different because we've had so many banks that have collapsed. What happens when a bank collapses, the successor institution that comes in has the right to look at the loans and decide what they're going to take. If a business has lost money in the last year or two, the new institution doesn't take it and the loan ends up in an FDIC pool.

Many businesses in New England have lost money in the last two years, so there are many operating businesses whose loans are being administered out of these FDIC pools which have no ability to deal with an operating business. And most of those companies will be liquidated.

Now I think that is a specific issue that can be looked at and addressed, that will help greatly in New England. If you look at New Hampshire and Connecticut, we've had so many business failures, and I think a lot of it is due to that issue. And I know you're under pressure so I'll—

PRESIDENT-ELECT CLINTON: Thanks. Let me ask you a specific. I saw this a lot and you know, I spent a little time in New Hampshire this year. (Laughter) I saw it a lot and I would like to ask you, as I invited everyone earlier, or last night—those of you who weren't here last night, I want everybody who's here to feel free—and I'd like for you to feel the obligation, to present us a very brief written statement after this is over, of specific things you think need to be done. I'd like for you to send me a page or two on that.

Andrew.

MR. ANDREW SHAPIRO (YALE LAW STUDENT): Thank you. I just wanted to add the young American's perspective. First, thank you for inviting me to the conference and to serve on this panel. I am neither a business leader, nor truly an economist. I'm a 24-year-old student although I was in the workforce for two years writing and teaching.

I guess I just wanted to add the young American's perspective and say a few points. I think it shows your respect for age diversity in addition to racial and gender diversity to include people of different ages here. There are really four points I wanted to make.

First, jobs are a major concern for young individuals. Of course college graduates are coming out, can't find good jobs, many of them are taking internships, they're working for less pay or no pay at all. Many of them are working and living at home after returning from college. I did that.

The second point is education and that's obviously linked directly to jobs. I think the outlook of young Americans when they are assessing the state of the economy is directly related to education and how we're going to pay for education and I think that's why a lot of young people enthusiastically got behind the Clinton-Gore campaign, thinking about the National Service Trust Fund and the opportunity for all young Americans who want to go to school to do so.

The other side of that obviously is exciting, in that the National Service job opportunities of teaching, peer counseling, health care and the police corps could be a wonderful introduction into the economy for some of those people coming out of college.

The third thing I wanted to mention is a lot of people talk about the deficit burden for young Americans. We're going to be the first generation not to live as well as our parents did, and that's a sort of truism that we hear a lot and I think it's a major concern, but I think it's less important than the direct stimulus that is needed for education loans and for jobs.

And the fourth point has to do with fairness, economic fairness. I think this relates directly to what Marian Wright Edelman said before, we are increasingly a two-tier nation, striated in different directions. And Dr. Solow said that in terms of productivity we're still number one. In fact, that's the title of a book that I published—wrote earlier this year, called *We're Number One*. But I mention more ironically that we're number one in a lot of good ways like we have the most billionaires and the highest GDP per capita and the highest corporate executive salaries. But we're also number one in a lot of more embarrassing ways like the highest percentage of children living in poverty in the industrialized world, the largest wage gap between CEOs and average manufacturing workers.

So I just wanted to contribute those four points from a young American's perspective and say thanks.

PRESIDENT-ELECT CLINTON: Thank you.

MS. MARION SANDLER (WORLD SAVINGS): Excuse me.

PRESIDENT-ELECT CLINTON: Go ahead.

MS. SANDLER: I just wonder if I could interrupt because—

PRESIDENT-ELECT CLINTON: I was going to plug you.

Since you interrupted let me plug you now. Here is a woman who actually made an S&L work in the '80s. We ought to give her a hand. (Laughter, applause) An unusual person.

Didn't cost the taxpayers a dime. (Laughs) Go ahead, Marion.

Ms. Sandler: Thank you.

I'm sort of sitting here a little bit frustrated because I think we're in some senses nibbling around the edges of the problem. And just as infrastructure is an ugly word, I think there are other ugly words that we haven't addressed and those are entitlements and I want to commend Ann for talking about defense. Because if you look at John White's material, and I thought he did a very nice job, but that's where the money is. And taxes will contribute something but we have to face up to the problem of entitlements.

Now entitlements can be divided into actually two categories. There is the safety net part of it and there is what we call the entitlements. Now the safety net we need for our citizens who are needy. But the other part, we have to be courageous and that's more than just Social Security and it is Medicare and some other kinds of items. But if you look at John's numbers, that is 49 percent of the budget this year, and if nothing happens it's going to be 55 percent in the year 2000. That's not news. I mean everybody knows it but nobody talks about it, and certainly nobody has done anything about it.

The defense, I am pleased that Ann has taken an aggressive kind of stand on that, which is that we can cut that budget in half. That is more than certainly the current administration had in mind, but that is kind of touchy also. And then, the non-defense, I mean that's where the money is coming from for all these programs and that's going down from 16 percent to 13 percent in the year 2000. So we're in trouble unless we face up to entitlements and to the defense budget.

It's not politically attractive. We have to demonstrate some courage in doing that, but all these other things can't be done. All these other things are a piece of this. But we have to focus and be disciplined and face up to the real problems that we have here.

President-elect Clinton: Anyone else want to be heard?

Ms. Lacey Norvis: Yes, I'm Lacey Norvis from the state of Florida, and I do agree with you as far as the entitlements, and I believe that there are a lot of people in the United States that would like to work but they cannot. They have children at home and in order to work they would lose their food stamps and their welfare, and I believe that the children probably should go to day-care, and the women can go to work the same as the men. That way there would be a lot more workers in the United States and the entitlements would go down, and then the children would be raised in an atmosphere of other children in day-care where they're working, so they're not sitting home with their parents who are not working. And I think that would help.

PRESIDENT-ELECT CLINTON: Let me make two points, if I might. I don't disagree with the entitlements argument, except if you look at the numbers, that the number one cost in entitlements is Medicare and Medicaid. And secondly, that as the economy goes down, entitlements go up; when the economy goes up, entitlements go down, there are fewer people on food stamps and on Medicaid, and on AFDC, on welfare.

Secondly, as to your point, the whole purpose of the Welfare Reform Act which was signed right before President Reagan left office in 1988, which I helped work on, was to begin to set up a system in which there would never be an incentive for anyone to stay home on welfare, by requiring people to enroll in education and job placement work, and to take jobs when offered. We have to do more in that. There are still some significant disincentives, but you also have to be able to create the jobs. You can't make people take jobs that aren't there. So I think it's very important that we do exactly what you said, but it's also important that there be something there for them to do.

It works. I mean, in our state, our welfare load grew at about one-third of the national average after we fully implemented this welfare initiative. But the point is it still grew because there was no growth in private sector jobs, to go back to Mr. Solow's comments. So I think we have to do both. I think that's a point well made.

Who else around the table? Jessica?

MS. JESSICA TUCHMAN-MATHEWS (WORLD RESOURCES INSTITUTE): I also wanted to add a word on something that hasn't gotten a lot of attention today, and that is revenues. I think if we're going to do what's been talked about to stimulate this economy and to reduce the deficit, that we will need additional revenues and that we ought to therefore spend some time thinking about what's the most constructive way to find them. And I'd like to offer a simple idea, which is that we shift some of our tax burden from things we want to encourage, namely work and capital accumulation and investment, to things we'd like to discourage, namely for example energy use, congestion, pollution, waste and excessive resource use.

These sorts of taxes, in addition to lifting the burden on investment and savings, share a couple of other powerful attractions. For every dollar that we collect in these we lower costs that we would otherwise be paying in cleaning up pollution, in oil imports, in the productivity losses from congestion, which now cost about $100 billion a year to the economy, two percent of GDP. We improve the environment and we offer something the existing tax structure doesn't offer, at least legally, and that is choice, both to individuals and businesses. If they want to reduce their tax burden, individuals can change their behavior. They can drive in off-peak hours to avoid a congestion tax. Businesses can redirect their R&D toward products and processes that lower their pollution.

So in short, I think this set of taxes both can give us the additional revenues we need—can do it in a way that substitutes an attack on an existing distortion in the economy for taxes that distort it—that would lower costs that we're otherwise paying, and potentially reduce the environmental regulatory burden, Mr. President, that you talked about the other day, that would improve the environment and that would also offer choice. It's a very powerful set, I think, of attractions and one that I hope gets some attention.

PRESIDENT-ELECT CLINTON: You want to react to that, Mr. Poling?

MR. POLING: I agree. I think that the present tax system will not provide the funds necessary to accomplish all the objectives we have. I think either a VAT or a tax designed to reduce consumption, encourage savings is the direction to go. Relative to taxes to address some of the issues related to the environment, I've been supportive of that for some time. When the present administration first went in I met with them and discussed two major concerns, the budget deficit and the trade deficit. And on the budget deficit we were prepared to support a tax of 25 cents a gallon on gasoline, phased in over a five—three to five years, would not impact the economy or hurt individuals unnecessarily, but it would raise substantial sums of money and would cause a trend toward purchasing more fuel efficient vehicles. We still support a tax on gasoline.

PRESIDENT-ELECT CLINTON: Mr. Donahue and then Mr. King.

Mr. Thomas Donahue (AFL-CIO): Mr. President-elect, I've listened all morning to people talking high policy and I'm reminded—there's a story told about Robert Benchley when he was at Harvard, was asked to write an essay on the Bering Sea Fisheries Treaty, and he wrote, "I don't know much about the Bering Sea Fisheries Treaty but let me put in a few words for the fish." (Laughter)

And in that spirit, since you've spent the morning talking about workers, I'd like to speak on their behalf.

You said during the campaign that people—and you've said continuously—people are working harder and longer for less, and I can't think of a better summation of the current state of how workers see the economy and what their hopes are for your administration. What they see is unemployment. They see 17 million people either unemployed or partially unemployed and looking for full-time employment. They see an unemployment insurance system that is broken, badly broken, that paid benefits to 33 percent of the unemployed at the depth of the recession, and now pays only marginally above 50 percent of the unemployed. They see a minimum wage that's a buck an hour below any standard of decency that we've adhered to in the past. They see the continuing loss of manufacturing jobs—of good manufacturing jobs, not unskilled work.

If they're listening to this program they hear talk about a global economy which they understand very well to be an economy that nobody controls. It's only controlled by the players and therefore it'll be controlled by the multinational corporations or by those nations which are willing to offer the lowest wages in order to attract jobs.

They see a trade deficit and they think the trade policies under which we operate aren't fair, and they see now what you styled as an unusual agreement which will encourage Americans to invest in Mexico, to import products back into the United States.

They see a system of labor law which simply doesn't work, which is destructive of their rights, which frustrates any of their efforts to organize together and to work together, and they see that if they are forced to go out on strike they will be replaced and the law will say that that's a fine result. Most of all, they see insecurity. And they're asked now to participate in an experiment to make the nation more competitive and nobody's offering them a great deal of a stake in that because nobody is offering them any assurances of security.

Everybody talked here about the need to improve our competitiveness by increasing productivity. Nobody's talked about sharing the gains of that productivity increase with the people. And we haven't talked—we've talked about improving their productivity as if that was the only way to improve the conditions of life of people. We need to talk about changing investment patterns to accomplish that, we need

95

to talk about changing tax ratios in order to do that. There are obviously a variety of ways quite beyond improving productivity that we could assure some better distribution of the income and the wealth of this country.

One of the charts we saw cited the real wage growth—on the subject of real wage growth, showed the continuing productivity growth through the '80s with no sharing of that in terms of real wage growth. I was intrigued with Delano Lewis' comment and certainly share the view that you need to enunciate and the administration needs to enunciate a shared vision of the workplace and of the workforce, a vision in which hopefully you will talk about government, labor and management working together, creating that kind of partnership so that people can have productive work, so that we can move toward some sort of full employment economy, and so that the people in that workforce might have hope of stability, might have their own sense of empowerment, might see some hope of the likelihood of gain sharing as productivity increases, and most of all see some job security.

We heard the figure cited of the biotech industry which added some 78,000 jobs. General Motors will cut 76,000 in the next few years. The Postal Service will cut 42,000 and the list of course goes on and on. The elimination of employment has become kind of the weapon of choice for solving all corporate problems. I think you need to try to engender a new spirit of cooperation—labor, management and government—and to engender a kind of economic patriotism that talks about creating American jobs and keeping jobs in America by balance, both of the creation of communications networks and someone else of the railroad improvements that we need, and the infrastructure improvements of that type.

If we improve those by buying trains in Sweden and importing them, or if we improve them by importing European aircraft, we're not going to improve the job situation of people in the United States and I think that ought to be a principal focus. I know it is a principal focus of yours and of Senator Gore's that we have the effort to improve things for the plain people of this country.

PRESIDENT-ELECT CLINTON: One of the things I hope we can discuss maybe later today or tomorrow is whether—how we will define security for people who are willing to work hard in this country. Given the inevitable downsizing of some of these companies, given the churning of the global economy, the increasing—to go back to John Sculley's comment about customization of work, we may—I think that this is a challenge that was largely ignored in the 1980s because so many firms themselves were insecure that a lot of people, real people, got lost between the cracks. On the other hand, if we—I think when we define security in the 1990s and beyond, it will probably never be the way it was in the '50s. We'll have to figure out a different definition of what it means to be a secure American, if you're willing to work hard and work smart, and I hope we can spend some more time on that.

Calvin.

MR. CALVIN KING (ARKANSAS LAND AND FARM DEVELOPMENT): Thank you, President-elect Clinton, Vice President-elect Gore. I have a very brief comment and some concerns that I have based on the session and how it's been going so far.

I am from Arkansas, eastern portion of the state of Arkansas, one of the poorest in the state and in the country, in the rural area. And I would like to see, very much focus from this particular conference thus far on rural, what the overall needs are and initiatives for investments in rural community development.

My position right now, and I'm working with Arkansas Land and Farm Development Corporation as well as being a part-time farmer, relates back to the farm crisis and the neglect that has taken place over the years. I think that neglect has resulted in what we find now in the greenhouse effect as far as our overall environmental situation is concerned. Also when you look at the country, ultimately as a whole, you will find that out of the two million farm operations in the country, that roughly some 1.7 million of those farms are actually family farmers and make major contribution to the overall rural economic development that takes place in this country and will continue to do that.

All the same time, during the decade of the '80s, latter part of the '70s coming on into the '80s, there has been a serious neglect of family farmers in this country, a continuing decline as a result of that. And all of those things that have been said, when you talk about the urban situation, what is occurring, from the industrial side of it, is also occurring from a rural perspective and particularly with family farmers in those rural communities that are tremendously impacted by the family farm operations.

I say that because when we look at the overall land base, a very natural resource in the South, you'll find that the contribution of that land base toward industry and industry growth in this country is very major, ultimately overall.

I would like to see, and hopefully in the future particularly, from the rural and from an agricultural perspective, that there would be a lot more coordinated, I guess you would say planning in looking at our family farm situations between the labor division and between the USDA division particularly.

97

We have a serious problem when you look at retraining and retooling. From the (image ?) perspective you also have the same situation in relationship to agriculture, relationship to family farmers. Also, ultimately, the neglect of this could very easily put this country, the United States, in the same situation—the road we appear to be traveling so far—from a highly mechanized, large scale approach in agriculture—neglect of both the environment and job creation, but headed down the same road in what has been the situation with Russia.

Corporate approaches in agriculture, large investment from that perspective, and the results itself, I think speaks for itself and what the state—and what is occurring now from an agricultural standpoint.

PRESIDENT-ELECT CLINTON: Joan.

MS. JOAN CLAYBROOK (PUBLIC CITIZEN): Thank you very much.

First, I'd like to say thank you for the diversity in this conference, very much, and I'm not sure we've said that enough. I really appreciate it and particularly allowing the consumers to come to the table along with everybody else.

There are major distortions in our economy and these affect the efficiency, the effectiveness, the fairness of our economy and they are caused by subsidies and tax breaks and loan guarantees and insurance and other disbursements from the Treasury that are achieved by lobbyists that are looking out for their own clients and their own interests and these come primarily through campaign contributions, rather than having a rational public policy for the decisionmaking on our budget. And this affects our transportation systems, it affects our infrastructure investments, it favors nuclear power over energy conservation and renewables. It affects our environment, our health care and many other areas of our economy. It affects waste, whether we have leveraged buyouts that overburden companies with debt and hurt workers.

And so, our hope, number one, is that campaign finance reform, which you have endorsed, will be a major and number one remedy that is proposed early in your administration. It is the prerequisite for achieving the fairness and the proper distribution of our budget as we have talked, and how we decide where we're going to put the federal dollar. And we think it needs to be done early because the lobbyists are going to affect whether or not it gets through, and if it isn't done quickly and soon, we can see it melting away.

The second point I would say is that in reinventing government and putting people first, that we need very much to have people be a part of the decisionmaking process and they have been excluded in recent days. This requires affirmative steps. I believe in town meetings and meetings such as this. We practice them ourselves. But citizens need to be empowered, as John Kennedy said 30 years ago in his consumer message, that they need to be heard and have a right to participate and speak as you're allowing us to do today.

There are a number of tools that can achieve this. Where you have subsidy programs there should be parity for public participation funding so citizens can be there and be a part of it. And I think that the more involvement you have of citizens in that process the better decisionmaking process that comes out of it, that that in a way does not put the whole burden on the government official, but allows the government official to hear all voices and to make the best decisions. And it does put pressure, it is irritating, it is uncomfortable sometimes, but that's okay, because I think in the end you have the best that comes out of it.

In order to be a good watchdog you have to have equal rights. In order to negotiate you have to be at the table and if you're not there, if you don't have the capacity to be there, and poor people in this country do not have the capacity to be at that table, it's one of the reasons why they don't have equal rights.

Everyone loves Uncle Sugar, but Uncle Sam is a very important balance for all of our decisions. And so, we have to have some standards and some rules by which we govern the decisionmaking process in this country so that we will have an economy that meets the needs of the public whether it's in the health and safety standards, or false advertising, or antitrust enforcement, or product information, banking —yes, banking as well.

The S&L bailout has certainly shown us that where you have large government subsidies and you don't have the rules of the game, then you have a great loss to our society and we're all paying for that debt.

I thank you very much for letting me speak.

PRESIDENT-ELECT CLINTON: Thank you.

Let me just say that the American people are at this table too. You know we have—we are hooked in to not only television but also to National Public Radio and there are some listeners there who are going to be able to ask a couple of questions in I think each of our sessions. But before we do that and before we break for lunch we have time—if there are a couple of people in the audience who would like to make comments, out here—anybody over here want to say anything?

Yes.

Karen Nussbaum: Thank you very much Governor Clinton, Senator Gore. My name is Karen Nussbaum. I work with Nine-to-Five, a national organization of working women and with the Service Employees Union.

The economic strategy of the last 20 years depended on the huge influx of the cheap labor of working women. And in fact, if we hadn't flooded into the labor force family income would have been even lower. Now some of the recurring themes of this morning have been infrastructure and productivity and I would say that in a world where women work, if we're investing in infrastructure that means we also have to invest in dependent care that's affordable for all women who work, and we also have to have paid family leave so that women can be productive in the workforce while their families are being taken care of. And if we're talking about productivity, then we also have to talk about making investments in training and doing the kinds of reorganization of jobs that John Sculley talked about, where women work, in the offices and in the service industries, not just in the manufacturing plants.

So I would just add that to the discussion as well.

President-elect Clinton: Let me just make a point here for you and for everybody else who is interested in this issue. We've tried to do some work here in state government on flex time and we've had some interesting successes and some frustrations, as you might imagine, as well as dealing with different options toward child care, including starting a center that didn't work economically and I think we were the first state that went to a voucher program for the people that were eligible for public benefits.

And this is something I know there have been differences of opinion among people in this room, but if any of you have specific recommendations about how the nation should best approach this in setting up a framework that would generate more activity in the private sector on the child care issue, the flex time issue, other things, I wish you would feel free to include that in your comments because that's a very big deal because there is no end in sight to the percentage of women who will be in the workforce with little children.

Yes, in the back there. Is anybody?

We may have to go back and forth here.

I wish I could cancel lunch and keep doing this but you'd never speak to me again. (Laughter)

100

Ms. JOANNE PAYNE: My name is Joanne Payne and I would like to add to the comments about the women. We had a discussion about putting people first. Those people in the workforce, half are men and half are women. And we've also talked about solving many of the problems and I agree we have to go into the infrastructure and we have to go into the construction. However, the problem with that is that half of the workforce is women and the largest group of poor in this country is women with children. But yet we're talking about solving the problems in a male dominated area, construction.

And when we're writing policy, I would hope that we would include in that policy women's needs and their responsibilities as well.

PRESIDENT-ELECT CLINTON: Thank you. One more, right here.

AUDIENCE MEMBER: Governor Clinton—(name inaudible). We've talked a lot this morning about productivity improvement and how this country is lagging behind some of our international partners around the world. It seems to me that total quality management, something that you put into this state of Arkansas back in 1991, could be one of the answers, total quality management being continuous improvement, as you all well know, in product and in service and customer satisfaction. And that can only come about by empowering the working men and women in this country who are on the line every day, in the decisionmaking process. That is what we think will increase productivity and will increase the quality of work life for those in the workplace, which has been mentioned. And we will let them be a part of a successful future for the company that they happen to work in.

Could we have a comment, please?

PRESIDENT-ELECT CLINTON: Well, as you know I agree with that and I think one of the—I just want to make one point about it. We ought to be out there advocating that, of course, but one of the things that occurs to me is that the government sector of our economy basically has been immune from those sorts of structural changes because they have a claim on people's money. And yet, when government does have to cut back, normally because there is no sort of participatory process that takes place over a long period of time, often you have wrenching layoffs and cutbacks which may be tougher than would otherwise have been the case. So we plan to do a lot of work on that in our administration.

I wonder if we could take a call or two from NPR. Are the NPR listeners here somewhere?

MODERATOR: Well, NPR is in the balcony and—

PRESIDENT-ELECT CLINTON: In the—I know they're up there. But—

MODERATOR: Here's Ken Hunt, of Santa Ana, California, Governor.

CALLER: Good day, Governor Clinton. My name is Ken, as he said, and I'm a laid-off tool maker for McDonnell Douglas in Long Beach, California. And—which, by the way, also has a plant in Melbourne, Arkansas. So—

PRESIDENT-ELECT CLINTON: I've been in it many times.

CALLER: Pardon me? You've been there?

PRESIDENT-ELECT CLINTON: I've been there many times.

CALLER: All right. Beautiful country. And I'm also a single father of six.

What bothers me are the two terms "defense cuts" and "create jobs." Those two terms seem to be mutually exclusive, at least as it affects my family and, you know, friends. And I have friends that have had small businesses, like restaurants and stuff, across the street from the plants that have gone out of business. Because of 20,000 people being laid off, their business has been hurt.

And, you know, there's a massive trickle-down effect of this thing and, quite frankly, I'm normally very optimistic person, but currently am very pessimistic. I mean, I'm an educated person. I have a trade that I thought was a good trade, a tool maker. And I don't see anything happening which will, at least in the short term, help my family out. I know there's things like rail and bullet trains and these sort of things, but those things take lead time and they take money for funding so that these companies can keep employees and not lay them off while

102

they're retooling and so forth. And instead of that, we seem to be getting in kind of a situation where we're killing the chicken and trying to increase the production of eggs. And maybe you can relate to that. You know, that doesn't work. You can't kill your chicken and get more eggs. You've got to keep the chickens going.

So I just wonder what your economy plans on doing to maybe get— on a personal level, myself back to work,and people like myself who work for aircraft corporations, or even the bus boy who works in the restaurant across the street, getting these people back on their feet. Because it's not just the rivet banger in the factory. People forget it affects everybody. The clothing manufacturer—uniforms. You cut the military service, the people that make the uniforms for the service are going to be out of a job because there's not as many soldiers to put uniforms on.

And, you know, lately—the latest status symbol in America seems to be a job. I think I've talked as long as I can.

PRESIDENT-ELECT CLINTON: I have a—I do have a response to that, but I wonder if anyone around this table would like to respond first. Does anybody else want to say anything to this man?

Ann?

MS. MARKUSEN: Well, I guess I could say something. I mean, this is really the—it seems to me, the nexus of the problem. It's very, very tough. If we don't have answers for people like you, then there's going to be enormous pressure to keep defense spending where it is, to sell more arms abroad, which I think is a very dangerous strategy for us in the long run. And it seems to me there are two really important things. One is to really do some aggressive work to help companies plan in advance for cuts in ways that might help move plants and equipment and skills like this into new activities without disbanding everybody and having workers individualized and out there on the street. And that's one very important part of it.

And the second is, I would say, well, even if we had advance planning at your plant and we had managed to put together some business plans, with some government help for funding them, that might really help your particular plant move over into some other form of metal-bending activity, then the real question is, well, what about maybe that can't absorb everybody at your plant. Well there, I think, is where the infrastructure program comes in. And why don't we have workers at your plant and workers in Groton, Connecticut where, you know, we've just funded two more Seawolfs, why not have all of you go out and rebuild the infrastructure of your cities in New England, Los Angeles, et cetera, in the short term, rather than just simply making more weapons that we don't really need.

CALLER: Perhaps I can say something to that, if I may. That is, I'm 47 years old, not in the best of health, and I can't swing a shovel and build a road, okay?

PRESIDENT-ELECT CLINTON: Yeah, but let me respond to that.

MS. MARKUSEN: You could drive a big machine.

PRESIDENT-ELECT CLINTON: Let me respond to that. But you're in aviation. Civilian aviation technology is one of the seven or eight areas that will produce the largest number of high-growth, high-wage jobs into the 21st century.

And I want to make—first of all, I'm really glad you called. You gave the problem in the most stark and personal terms it could have. And I agree with a lot of what you say. I think we've got to maintain the manufacturing base. We need people like you working in the industry, the general industry you're working in. The only thing that I would respond to you is that it can never be that our country would keep up a certain level of defense spending solely because that's the only way to keep people working in that area. Otherwise, that argument could apply to every sector of the economy and no economic change would ever occur.

We need people who do what you do, we just need them to do it in different areas of aviation. And the complaint I always had—and this is not one directed solely against the other party—but no nation should have ever undertaken as wrenching a reorganization in its defense budget as we began way back in 1988 without some general strategy about how we would redirect these resources and these people and these technologies. That is what I object to. That's not to say that no one like you would have ever been unemployed for a prolonged period of time, but it wouldn't have been nearly as bad as it has been in California, where you are.

So my answer to you, sir, is that I don't think you're going to have to change what you do, but we're going to have to have investments in civilian aviation technology that are appropriate and targeted so that people like you will be able to look forward to that in the future.

But I also have to say—you say you're 47. You're about my age. Unfortunately, we're not going to be able to guarantee the same job to people even who are 55 or 60. People are going to have to be willing to retrain and change the nature of their work for a lifetime. That's what I was saying about refining security. You ought to know that you can get a decent job at a decent income if you're prepared to change. That's the point Mr. Donahue was making, that even people who play by the rules are often getting the shaft today. But my answer to you is we need a strategy for you that develops the technologies in civilian aviation that will give you a chance to make a living in southern California and take good care of those six kids.

CALLER: Well, thank you. And if you have a job opening for me, I'm available, and you have my number. (Laughter.)

PRESIDENT-ELECT CLINTON: I may. I'll tell you what. If you could present every problem as well as you presented that one, you're a lot better than some of us are on this—(laughter).

CALLER: All right.

VICE PRESIDENT-ELECT GORE: I'd like to make a brief point on defense conversion as it relates to a topic we touched on earlier, availability of capital. During the campaign, I visited a company called Monitor Aerospace on Long Island, and the CEO of the company drove home a point that I think may apply to many defense contractors trying to make the adjustment to the civilian side of the marketplace. And that is, they have grown used to what are called progress payments and have come to rely on these payments from the Defense Department as a principal source of capital. And in making the shift to the civilian marketplace—in this case, Mr. Hunt's employer—if that company wants to try to sell into the civilian marketplace, one of the first things they face is the availability of capital from private lenders to make up for what they're losing from the Defense Department, and many of them simply cannot get over that first hurdle. And I mention it because as we think through a sensible defense conversion plan, I think it needs to pay a lot of attention to availability of capital.

PRESIDENT-ELECT CLINTON: Next question from NPR?

MODERATOR: This is from Elizabeth Cleveland, who's calling from San Antonio, Texas. Ms. Cleveland?

CALLER: Hello?

PRESIDENT-ELECT CLINTON: Hello, Elizabeth.

CALLER: Hello?

PRESIDENT-ELECT CLINTON: We can hear you. Go ahead.

CALLER: Oh, okay. I'm sorry. I was just wondering if you could tell me specifically how do you plan on creating new jobs if major companies like the one I'm working for are laying people off, laying a lot of people off to do the new downsizing or trimming or whatever they call it. How do you expect to create new jobs? You can't tell them, okay, today you're going to hire 5,000 people.

PRESIDENT-ELECT CLINTON: No, you can't. And the fact that so many non-manufacturing firms are going to follow the lead of manufacturing in the '80s and downsizing in the '90s is going to make our job even tougher. But if you watched the early part of the program when the early presentations were made, several points were made which I'd like to reemphasize. First of all, the only way you ever create a new job is that someone invests. They invest either because they're taking a chance or because there's already a preexisting demand for a product or a service. And what we are trying to do is to identify those things we can do to dramatically increase investment so that we will create enough new jobs not only to take account of the downsizing but to actually take account of the new people coming into the American workforce.

And I'm convinced that if we have the right kind of investment and the right volume, that we would create millions of new jobs in this country. This is an underemployed country with an economy that's operating at under capacity, and so we have to have the right kind of investment. And a lot of what we've been meeting about this morning are the kinds of decisions we can make, for example, to free up new money, either by changes in the Tax Code, changing the way we spend

106

money, changes in the way we allocate funds to health care, all those things designed to create money that can be invested in the economy to create new jobs for people that are going to be subject to this sort of downsizing throughout the 1990s. And that's our number one challenge, I think.

We can take one more question from NPR.

MODERATOR: All right. Thank you, Elizabeth Cleveland.

This is Morton Scott, calling from Elk City, Oklahoma. Mr. Scott?

CALLER: Mr. President-elect and Mr. Vice President-elect, one of your conferees there today once said that the United States has exported $1 trillion for imported oil since 1973 instead of using our domestic natural gas industry. If that natural gas had been used instead of imported oil, we'd have that $1 trillion in our economy now, we would have saved the 400,000 jobs that have been lost in the oil and gas industry, and we would have certainly increased the quality of our air in this country in the cheapest, quickest, and most valuable way. What are you going to do for natural gas?

PRESIDENT-ELECT CLINTON: That sounded like a paid advertisement for my campaign. (Laughter.)

I thank you for calling, and I appreciate what you said.

We have done our best in working with the gas producers to develop a position paper which would focus not on subsidies to the natural gas industry, but simply to creating new markets and moving toward greater utilization of domestic natural gas, renewable resources in energy efficiency, and away from reliance on foreign oil in a disciplined way that would minimize disruption to our economy, make us more independent and more environmentally and economically strong. And I'll just give you just one or two examples of things that I think we ought to do.

I think we ought to move toward having every government auto fleet in this country operate on compressed natural gas vehicles. I think we ought to do what we can to facilitate the development and laying of gas pipelines in this country where they're necessary and where we can do it at lower cost and with less regulatory delay.

One of the errors that the United States made in the '70s in the aftermath of the oil price explosion is that we substantially underestimated the volume of natural gas that we actually have in the continental United States. And as a consequence, decisions were made and years were lost and markets were not developed that ought to have been developed. So I can assure you of the—Al Gore and I have talked about this a lot, and we've been—and our ears have been filled by people from Oklahoma and Kansas and Texas and other places about this, but we are committed to greater utilization of gas.

It's 1:00—or, four minutes after. We were supposed to quit at 12:30, but I thought you were all terrific. Remember, we're going to have lots of other opportunities for people to be heard. I'm going to call an end to this session. We're supposed to be back here at 2:00, but since we're late, I'm going to start at 2:15. We'll make up half the time we lost that way. We will begin promptly at 2:15.

Thank you very much.

(RECESS FOR LUNCH)

Economic Conference Afternoon Session Monday, December 14, 1992

PRESIDENT-ELECT CLINTON: Thank you very much. First let me say how much I personally appreciated those who spoke this morning, and I think we did a reasonably good job of hearing both from the people who made presentations at the podium and everyone around the table, and then getting a few questions beyond that. This afternoon, after having focused on our own economy this morning and, I think, at least reaching a general consensus about what the major problems are and the need to take a long-term approach, we're going to talk about the international economy. I want to emphasize that we're going to be conducting these assessments in a way which is best served by abject candor. I think we got it this morning, and I want to continue to search for that. I expect as we go along and become even more specific we'll have more controversy, but that will be good, too.

I'd like to—several of you asked me, and I want to do this. I may have to do it again after everybody gets in, but many people asked, if you're going to respond to my requests that you actually write us between one and three pages of specifics of things you think we ought to do, where should you send the writings. Our transition office here in Little Rock is 105 West Capital, Suite 400, Little Rock, Arkansas, zip code 72201. That's 105 West Capital, Suite 400, 72201.

Now, we'll have a macrooverview of the international economy and how the United States relates to it from Rudi Dornbusch, the Ford International Professor of Economics at MIT. Rudi's taught since 1975. He's a research associate of the National Bureau of Economic Research, a member of the Brookings panel on economic activity, the advisory board of the Institute for International Economics, and the Academic Panel of the Federal Reserve Bank of New York. He's advised governments in Latin America, the European community, and the government of the Russian Federation, and also served as a very valued advisor to our campaign.

Mr. Dornbusch.

MR. RUDI DORNBUSCH (MIT): Thank you, Mr. President-elect, Mr. Vice President-elect. Thank you for the opportunity to speak about the world economy and introduce this session. You have asked for abject candor, and I'll try and give some of the bad news, but there's also some good news to put in, and that will help as we look at the US economy over the rest of the decade. Let me start with the bad news, and that is the immediate business outlook over the next 12 to 18 months for Europe, for Japan, and for the world economy except here.

The European problem is two-fold. One is Germany. The central bank is hung up about inflation: rightly, because inflation is rising; not rightly because other ways of fighting it—wage restraint, fiscal policy— might be better. But the fact is that Germany's monetary policy has put all of Europe now into a tailspin and that change there is not imminent. In Germany, the last measurement on inflation was 4.1 percent, up from 3$^1/_2$. Value-added taxes that come in January will raise inflation further. We can't expect that interest rates will come down soon.

But if they do not come down soon, then, of course, Europe's growth for the year to come is gone, and that is already a foregone conclusion. The question is how bad things can be. And there the answer is that if inflation in Germany continues to be a problem, if the rest hangs onto the deutsche mark because they can't see an alternative, then Europe certainly is going to have zero growth and maybe a recession. A European recession doesn't really help, because Eastern Europe needs markets, Eastern Europe needs to reform, and if Western Europe feels that things are getting worse, that certainly aggravates the picture for the world economy.

Beyond the immediate problem of German inflation, there is the much more serious problem that Europe is losing purpose. Maastricht, the unified Western Europe, was an extraordinary idea while communism was there and while the Wall was there, but it makes very little sense today. You might look from Germany: Poland is 60 miles from Berlin, and Portugal is extremely far away. And that, of course, is what is on Europe's mind as they're looking for an alternative model, but, unfortunately, without success and with very, very bad politics. One has to fear that that will influence business confidence and that as a result for quite a few years, Europe will do very poorly. For us that is important, because here is a market where we export traditionally. If there is little growth in Europe immediately and then only moderate recovery, that is bad news.

Japan is just as bad. In the aftermath of sharp increases in asset prices, in housing prices, the Ministry of Finance decided to burst the bubble, but they didn't ask what happens when you burst a bubble. If you do it literally, there is nothing left.

Now, there's a lot left of Japan, but the business community is stunned at the disappearance of demand, the growth of inventories, the banks are all bankrupt, and the government is basically helpless, trying to save face, saying "Everything will be all right," and saying it every quarter, but it isn't. Fiscal policy is coming on, but the package that has been passed through the Diet may by now be too late and too small to solve the Japanese problem. Very little growth for the coming year, perhaps zero growth or even a recession is a possibility in Japan. That is less serious for us, because Japan is a very, very closed economy, at least to our goods, so we won't suffer too much. But surely

112

there is an implication for us that while Japan may be reluctant to use fiscal policy, notwithstanding five years of big budget deficits, notwithstanding an extremely small public debt, certainly we should ask that they don't export their problems to us with growing trade surpluses.

If Europe and Japan are bad news, the same is true of Latin America. Growth has fallen to 1½ or 2 percent, and problems are widening in Mexico, where the currency has become overvalued to a point where the government has to cut down growth. And in Argentina, too, reforms have stalled as an overvalued currency suddenly puts in question a lot of the good things that happened over the last few years. In Venezuela, populism is the rule, and in Brazil, the new acting President looks like a populist even before one month in office. Latin America, then, that was an important market in the last few years as those economies liberalized, for the next few years may be a problem area and less of a source of growth for us.

Finally, the former Soviet Union is very bad news, indeed. It matters less for us economically, because all of Russia is smaller than Brazil, but, of course, from a security point of view, and from the point of view what will happen to Europe, the chaos in Russia, the imminent hyperinflation, the lack of progress in market reforms, the lack of political stability that is increasingly obvious as the Gaidar government is shaking and unlikely to last for more than three months. All of that means that there is less certainty in the world economy and, as a result, a less stable world economy.

What can we do about it in relation to the short-term macro-economic events? There's very little we can do. We could ask of Germany that they lower interest rates, but that has side effects. It certainly would push the dollar up, and it isn't clear we want that. We could ask them to raise taxes, and that would worsen Europe's recession, and that is perhaps not the right answer. We should ask them for wage restraint, but that's what the Central Bank is already asking for. In Japan, we might urge a strong fiscal expansion, but we're probably much better off urging them to open their markets to us, because for us that would be worth a lot more.

So coordination, then, I think does not carry a strong message for the next administration. But there's one area where we have to be very cautious. It's certainly the case that the US, in the coming year, will turn up, will show growth of 3, 3.5 percent, hopefully. And as that happens, inevitably bond markets and foreign exchange markets anticipate a stronger dollar and they anticipate higher yields. Why? Because growth always means inflation, and inflation means the Federal Reserve is about to come.

We certainly cannot afford a stronger dollar, and we have to carefully avoid the problems of '80–'85 when an enormous dollar rally ruined US manufacturing with lasting import penetration that would not have happened without, and was an erosion of real wages that we did not need. That risk is there as Europe slows down in the coming 18 months and as we move forward. And, of course, it is already happening.

I think there must be a strong message to the Federal Reserve that the big division between growth and output which we have, and growth in employment, which we do not have, suggests that inflation is far away. The Federal Reserve should be committed to not raising interest rates just because they see growth, and to let that fact be known. Only if they let it be known can we avoid an unproductive dollar rally and gain, in the long-term bond market, some reduction.

In the medium term, of course, deficit reduction is a very strong way of keeping the dollar competitive. Failure to go in that direction runs the other way and reinforces the belief that the US dollar should be going up. So I believe that our domestic strategy has very important consequences for the dollar, and the ruinous appreciation of the dollar of '80–'85 should be borne in mind as we look at domestic choices.

Let me go next to identify three problems that I think are important for the world economy as we move out to the next ten years. One is dollar policy relative to Asia. In the '60s, in the late '60s, we had a very hard time getting the dollar down relative to Europe. They had grown and modernized; we had failed. Today there is the same issue with Asia. We need a major dollar realignment over the next five, six years.

Second, 2.5 billion people are joining the world economy. We have to be sure to take advantage of it, and we have to be sure to keep an open trade system so that fragmentation is not the risk.

Third, and last, the good news. I think the new administration's policy on choice means that world population growth, that today is basically running in the direction of major risks over the next 30 years, can have a more positive answer as US institutions and multilateral institutions spend more resources on training and family planning to bring population control to those areas where we can least afford the growth.

There is a big—in conclusion—complementarity between the agenda at home, where we're looking for more productivity and for more prosperity, and what we're trying to do in the world economy. A dollar policy is important. A population policy is important. They're complements to looking at productivity and quality, which are the basic ingredients for the US to get ahead. In the US, the government must play a bigger role. In the world economy, the US government must play the central role in having harmony and prosperity.

Thank you very much. (Applause.)

PRESIDENT-ELECT CLINTON: Thank you.

Does any member of the economic team want to ask a question of Mr. Dornbusch? Senator Bentsen? Congressman Panetta?

REP. LEON PANETTA (OMB DIRECTOR-DESIGNATE): If I might, Bill?

PRESIDENT-ELECT CLINTON: Okay.

REP. PANETTA: Yeah, thank you. On the deficit issue again, what will those countries abroad be looking at in terms of the United States as far as the deficit is concerned? In other words, how fast will they be looking for us to bring down the deficit over the next five to ten years?

MR. DORNBUSCH: I would think that what John White showed this morning will be an extraordinary shock to financial markets worldwide. Essentially, he showed that the deficits are perhaps $150 billion worse per year, as far as the eye can see; something that was not known very publicly. The rest of the world will want a very substantial answer to a medium-term, five, six, seven-year budget deficit reduction. They don't want balanced budgets tomorrow morning by any means, and they wouldn't believe it. But a mechanism now, phased in over time, would reduce our long-term bond rates, it would stabilize the dollar, it would be good news for the domestic agenda and for international competitiveness. Failing that, I think we'll have always the budget on our back and won't be able to do all the things that are the real agenda of progress.

PRESIDENT-ELECT CLINTON: Senator Bentsen?

SEN. LLOYD BENTSEN (TREASURY SECRETARY-DESIGNATE): What do you think the possibilities are of getting the Japanese to open up their markets at a time that they're in serious trouble themselves and trying to continue the substantial surplus in exports to the rest of the world? What can we do different to get them to understand the necessity of opening those markets?

115

MR. DORNBUSCH: I'd like to answer two separate questions. One is, the Japanese problem is a problem of the Ministry of Finance that ought to be a little bit more Keynesian. When you have a problem, as Japan has, and you have a big budget surplus and you have no public debt, the time to cut taxes, do some spending and get your prosperity very quickly. There's no reason on earth not to do that. And I think that is starting to be understood, but perhaps too late. With that done, in a year and a half, Japan is not a problem; they're back to 4 percent growth, working eight days a week—all the things we know. (Laughter.) That's the time to say, and now we want market opening. And perhaps we'll pursue that discussion more productively than in the last 12 years, where there were hundreds and hundreds of negotiations and no progress whatsoever. I am delighted with the appointment of the chair of the Council of Economic Advisers. Surely that is a first message to Japan that we'll pursue serious trade policy, and we have not in the past.

PRESIDENT-ELECT CLINTON: Thank you very much.

MR. DORNBUSCH: Thank you.

PRESIDENT-ELECT CLINTON: Now, I'd like to introduce to discuss the European Community, Jeff Garten, Professor of Finance and Economics at Columbia University School of Business; Director of International Fellows Program at the Columbia School for International and Public Affairs, who authored a cold piece, "America, Japan, Germany and the Struggle for Supremacy." Mr. Garten.

MR. JEFFREY GARTEN (COLUMBIA UNIVERSITY): Thank you. Well, one problem in following Rudi is that he covers the waterfront so well that a lot of the points that I had wanted to make, he made. (Laughter.) And let me just say at the outset that I agree with a good deal of his global assessment, but in the end, I think that there is perhaps a larger role for the United States to play, and I would like to talk about that in the context of Europe.

But let me talk about three things here: the first, the situation in Europe in a little more detail; secondly, the implications of that situation for the United States; and third, my thoughts as to what the US can do.

As Rudi said, the economic picture in Europe is gloomy. Growth this

116

year may be about 1.5 percent, next year it's likely to be below one percent, and perhaps equally significantly, unemployment, which is below 10 percent now, is likely to rise to 11 percent or above next year. But beyond the economics is a social situation which I would say risks being out of control. The big problem is refugees, not just from Eastern Europe but also from the northern part of Africa. We're seeing a backlash throughout Europe by citizens who are worried about their jobs being taken away, worried about the cost of housing, worried about all the pressures that this large-scale influx of people brings.

The media focuses, rightfully so, on the neo-Nazi movement in Germany, but this is not the whole story. These kinds of pressures exist throughout Europe.

And on the political front, I would characterize politics in Western Europe, in the European Community, as being almost paralyzed. The spirit of cooperation which existed over the last couple of years is almost gone. The leaders are barely holding on to the dream of European unity. The domestic, economic and social agendas in each country are really overwhelming. But beyond that is an intra-European agenda which is enormous and which is causing tremendous strains throughout the continent: such issues as budgets and the need to allocate more money to the poorer European countries like Spain and Greece; or such issues as whether or not to allow new members into the community, be they Scandinavians or Eastern Europeans.

The system of currency coordination in Europe is on the verge of collapse. Not surprisingly, because of the economic conditions, protectionist sentiment in Europe is growing. I mentioned the problems of refugees, and on top of that is a tremendous conflict among the European countries when it comes to such foreign policy and security issues as Yugoslavia. As Rudi said, the dream of a united Europe, which was supposed to be almost realized or much closer by the end of 1992, seems to have been lost.

Now, what are the implications for the United States? I would put them in three categories. First, the slack economic conditions in Europe, the European economic slump, is going to be, in my view, a real drag on prospects for the American recovery. Just to give you some numbers, as everyone knows, exports have been a major force for GNP growth in the US these last few years, and Europe has played a large part. Four years ago, exports to Europe were growing at an annual rate of 16 percent. Three years ago, it dropped to 12 percent. Two years ago, it dropped to 8. Last year, it was six. And without any question, in 1992 the number will drop further.

The second implication is that with the European currency system all but collapsed, there is going to be tremendous uncertainty in the world's financial system. I think as most people know, the amount of foreign exchange trading that goes on every single day is absolutely enormous, almost $1 trillion a day, which is the equivalent of three months' trading on the New York Stock Exchange. That's every single day. And it's the equivalent of all the reserves of all the central banks in the world. Now, when you have this kind of foreign exchange activity and you have the European system in turmoil, it is not clear at all that the dollar can stay immune from that kind of instability.

And third is the issue of peacekeeping. I think one of the great assumptions, one of the right assumptions after the Cold War was that the United States was going to have partners in all manner of peacekeeping. We certainly had intended to count on Europe. But with the conditions there, I don't think that assumption is necessarily true. In fact, I would say that Europe is going to be dragged kicking and screaming as a partner and we still might not succeed.

Well, that has a security and a foreign policy implication, but there's also an economic implication, because one of the assumptions underlying continued decreases in a defense budget is the assumption of burden sharing. And to the extent that the Europeans are not sharing the burden or can't share the burden, I think it will put much more pressure on defense expenditures.

Finally, what should the US do? Here I disagree with Rudi a little bit because I think that there is an enormous leadership vacuum, and that difficult as it is, we have to try to fill it. There are, of course, great limits to what the US can do, but it doesn't mean we shouldn't try.

My first point here is that when we think about stimulus, I don't think it's enough to think about stimulus in a domestic context. I think there has to be some global stimulus, and I think we have to work as hard as we can with the Europeans and with Japan to help them follow policies, to encourage them to follow policies that are growth-oriented as opposed to deflationary, as is now the case. This is not easy, but to the extent that we can bring credible policies to the table, I think we will have a lot more influence. And as I said, there is such a leadership vacuum in countries like Germany and Japan, in my view, the politicians are swimming without direction, and I think this is a real opportunity for the US. And in any event, I think it's something we have to try.

Secondly, I think we need as swift an end to the Uruguay Round as is possible. I know this is not a perfect agreement. It will never be a perfect agreement. But a conclusion to the Uruguay Round would boost economic confidence around the world, it would be a shot of adrenaline into the trading system. And if it isn't concluded, if it is not ended quickly, I think we will see it come completely unravelled.

And third, I think we have to review with the Europeans the situation in Eastern Europe and Russia. Again, there are no easy answers here, but for sure one of their major preoccupations and one of the things that overshadows everything else is the economic instability in the East. And to the extent that we can help them to stabilize that situation, the turmoil in Europe will be much less.

I think a lot of these issues could be brought together in an early summit, one that occurs much earlier than the one scheduled for June or July in Tokyo. I think this is important because the trends are moving in the wrong direction. The patterns are being set. There is no leadership anywhere, and were the United States to provide it at an early date, I think it would be greatly welcomed.

Thank you. (Applause.)

PRESIDENT-ELECT CLINTON: I hope that when we get into the round-table we'll be able to deal with what I perceived to be was the main difference of opinion through the last two speakers, which is whether or not we can reasonably hope to have a coordinated global growth strategy. I think we'd better wait until we have a chance to hear from the rest of the speakers to make that decision.

I'm getting a little behind, so I think I'll go on now.

The next speaker on Japan, China, and the Asian Pacific region is Glen Fukushima, director of public policy and market development for AT&T in Japan, former deputy assistant US Trade Representative for Japan and China from 1988 to 1990, a former director for Japanese Affairs at the USTR office at the White House from '85 through '88. He is the author of books, including *The Politics of US Economic Friction*, a book published in Japanese in 1992, and he's just been elected in the last week to a three-year term as vice president of the American Chamber of Commerce in Japan. Mr. Fukushima.

MR. GLEN FUKUSHIMA (AT&T JAPAN): Thank you, Mr. President-elect. Vice President-elect, ladies and gentlemen.

In thinking about economic trends in Asia and their implications for the United States, I think three ideas are key. First, the opportunities that exist; secondly, the challenges that confront us; and thirdly, the strategy that we need. My first slide elaborates on these. (Fig. 49)

Number one, Asia is the fastest growing economic region in the world. Despite the current economic slowdown, which I believe is temporary, in Asia, Asia centered on Japan will gain momentum as the world's most dynamic center of economic activity.

Secondly, as far as challenges, in addition to offering a market to sell products and services to, Asia is emerging as the home of major com-

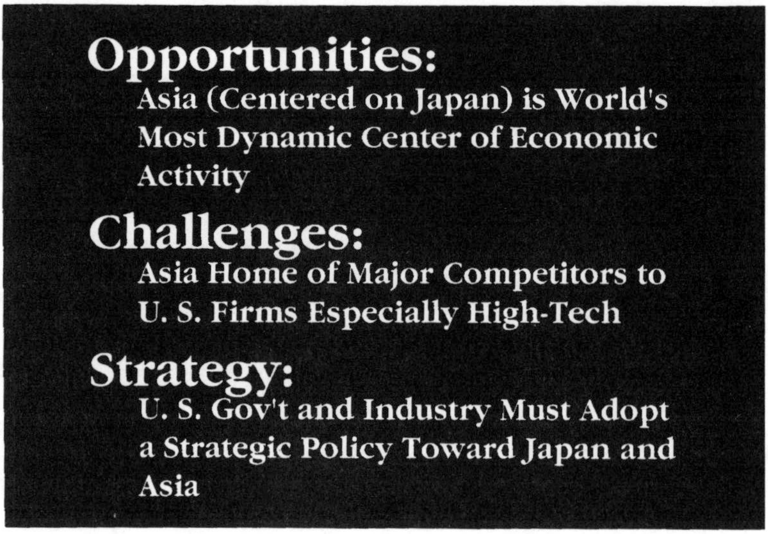

Opportunities:
Asia (Centered on Japan) is World's Most Dynamic Center of Economic Activity
Challenges:
Asia Home of Major Competitors to U. S. Firms Especially High-Tech
Strategy:
U. S. Gov't and Industry Must Adopt a Strategic Policy Toward Japan and Asia

Figure 49

Asian Economy's Share of World GNP
%
40
35
30
25
20
15
10
5
0
4%
25%
33%
1960
1990
2000 (EST)
Source: Deutsche Bank

Figure 50

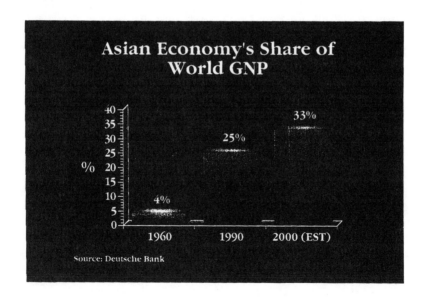

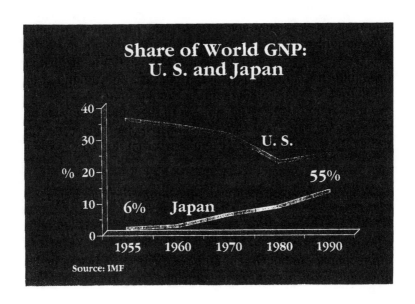

Figure 51

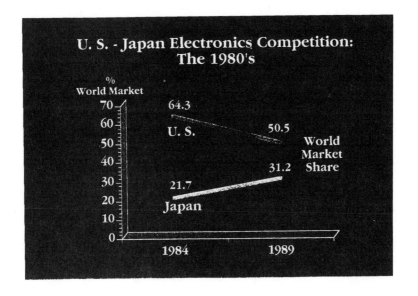

Figure 52

121

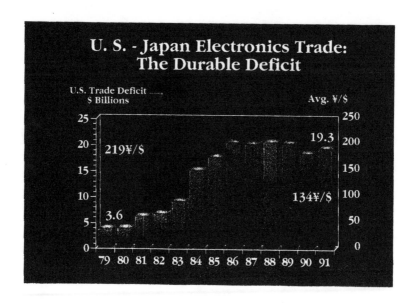

Figure 53

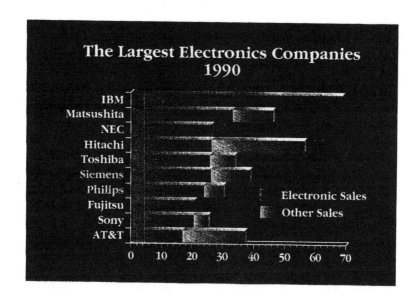

Figure 54

122

petitors to American companies, especially in the most value-added high-technology products and services.

And, thirdly, with regard to strategy, the US government and private sector cannot afford to ignore or underestimate the growing importance of Asia and its implications for the United States. For both government and industry, a systematic policy toward Asia is essential, beginning with a strategic Japan policy.

I have two slides to demonstrate the opportunities in the Asian region. (Figs. 50–1) The first slide shows the world share of GNP that is occupied by the Asian countries. In 1960, Asian countries occupied 4 percent of world GNP. By 1990, 25 percent of world GNP. And estimates are that by the year 2000 or soon thereafter, the Asian share of world GNP will approach one-third of the world total GNP.

The next slide shows, with regard to Japan in particular, in 1955, Japan's share of the world GNP was about 2 percent. By 1990, the Japanese share is about 14 percent. If you add the US and Japanese shares together, you will notice that in 1955, it was about 38 percent; 1990, 39 percent. And therefore, the two together are constant, but the Japanese share obviously has increased tremendously so that, whereas in 1955 the Japanese share of the US GNP was 6 percent, by 1990 it was 55 percent and growing.

The next three slides demonstrate what I believe to be challenges that are posed by the East Asian regions, in particular Japan. (Figs. 52–4) The electronics industry, which I am most familiar with, is a good example. Between 1984 and 1989, five short years, the US electronics share of the world market declined by 15 percent; the Japanese share increased by 10 percent.

In the next slide, we see that the US-Japan electronics trade deficit over a 13-year period rose from $3.6 billion to $19.3 billion by 1991. This is remarkable, given the fact that as you can see from the red line, the exchange rates have fluctuated considerably, from 219 yen per dollar in 1979 to 134 yen per dollar in 1991. Clearly, there is more at work here than exchange rates.

The next slide shows that of the ten largest electronics companies in the world, number one and number ten are American. I'm glad that my company, AT&T, is in there. Two are European, and six are Japanese.

Finally, with regard to strategy, I have two slides. (Figs. 55–6) Obviously, it's hard to put strategy in any kind of a quick graphic slide or a five-minute presentation. But, given the fact that Asia is such a dynamic part of the world, it's concerning to me and to other American businessmen in that area, business people in that area, that we seem to be in retreat compared to Japan.

The slide here shows that with regard to our investment in Asia, whereas in 1980, we were out-investing Japan, by 1990 Japan's investment had increased to more than 50 percent greater than the US investment. As in the United States, where speakers this morning were talking about the need to invest and to be engaged in order to reap benefits, I think the same is true with the Asian region. Unless we are investing and engaging in that region, we can't afford to reap the benefits of that growing part of the world.

The final slide shows the bilateral aid to the Asia Pacific region between 1980 and '90. Again, it shows, I think quite dramatically, that in 1980, the US and Japan were at similar levels, 1.3 and 1.4 billion. But, by 1990, Japanese aid was almost three times US aid, with clear implications economically.

So, I think it's important to understand that these developments in Asia are linked to developments economically in the United States with regard to jobs, technology, and competitive position in the world. And the automobile industry, electronics industry, and financial services are clear indications of this.

So, in summary, I want to go back to my first slide, and the speakers before me, I think, have talked more about the immediate concerns of the United States, and I agree with many of the themes that both Rudi Dornbusch and Jeff Garten have mentioned. But with regard to the longer term, I would say the five- to ten-year term, what we need to realize are the opportunities, challenges, and finally the urgent need for both government and industry in the United States to have a focused, coherent, and systematic strategy to take advantage of the opportunities and to confront the challenges posed by Asia.

Thank you very much.

PRESIDENT-ELECT CLINTON: Thank you very much. (Applause.)

I'd like to ask a question which I don't want you to answer yet, but I'm curious and I'm embarrassed that I don't know. With the big increase in Japanese assistance to other nations in the Asia Pacific region, do any of those nations that Japan assists have a trade surplus with Japan? Don't answer yet. We'll wait.

MR. FUKUSHIMA: Some of the raw materials suppliers do. For example, Indonesia and the Philippines often do.

PRESIDENT-ELECT CLINTON: Indonesia does because they—

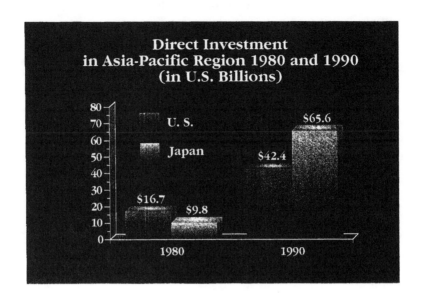

Figure 55

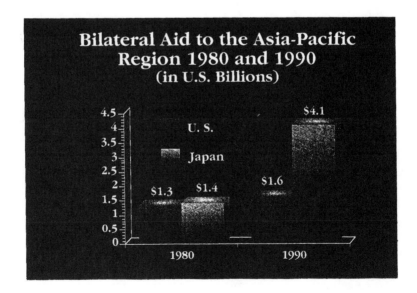

Figure 56

MR. FUKUSHIMA: Right. And Malaysia often does. The Philippines sometimes, but it's all raw materials.

PRESIDENT-ELECT CLINTON: Only raw materials though, right?

MR. FUKUSHIMA: Right. There is an increase in some manufactured exports from the East Asian countries to Japan, but a lot of that is a result of Japanese investment in those countries. For example, companies have invested—(inaudible)—materials and equipment and products that are going to be exported to Japan.

PRESIDENT-ELECT CLINTON: The next presentation, on the former Soviet Union and Eastern Europe, will be made by Larry Summers, vice president of development economics and chief economist of the World Bank, who's on leave from his position as professor of political economy at Harvard. The author of more than 100 articles and two books, *Tax Policy and the Economy,* and *Understanding Unemployment.* And I might add, someone who's been quite helpful to us in this transition period. Mr. Summers.

MR. LAWRENCE SUMMERS (WORLD BANK): Thank you very much. Governor Clinton, Senator Gore, ladies and gentlemen.

The Cold War is the third war to have ended in this century. After World War I, there was no leadership. Nations turned inward. There was no effort to rehabilitate and reintegrate the vanquished power. There followed 20 years of stagnation, depression, and ultimately the Second World War.

After World War II, things were very different. The United States led. The world economy grew together. Enlightened policies, the Marshall Plan, sought to rehabilitate and reintegrate the vanquished powers, and there followed the best 40 years of economic growth in the history of the world.

Now, the Cold War is over. Will the unhappy post–World War I experience play out or will the happier post–World War II experience play out? That is the question that will be answered in the next four years. And the answer will depend critically on the success of what is literally the greatest economic reconstruction job in the history of the world, the reform of the formerly communist economies of Eastern Europe and the Soviet Union.

I want to make three points in connection with this historic effort.

First, the former Soviet Union and Eastern Europe are history's greatest economic underachievers. These are countries that are rich in everything that should make a country rich. The former Soviet Union has the world's greatest petroleum and natural gas reserves; more doctorates in science and engineering than the United States and Japan combined; people who've proven themselves willing to work; and in the defense sector so far, critical capacity to produce and manufacture in a cutting-edge fashion.

And yet, because of a misguided economic system, the results have been nothing short of disastrous. The only thing that has fallen faster than output in Eastern Europe and the former Soviet Union is estimates of how prosperous those countries are as Western economists have had an opportunity to study what is going on. Estimates now suggest standards of living on the order of one-eighth of the standard of living that we enjoy in the United States.

And indicators of social performance are even worse. Because of environmental problems, problems in the health care sector, life expectancy in Eastern Europe and the former Soviet Union has actually declined for men by more than two years in the last 25. That is the equivalent of the damage that would be done by a doubling of cancer mortality in the United States. And it is indicative of the quality of the health and the social systems in those countries that the average woman in the former Soviet Union now has four abortions during her lifetime.

This spectacular failure has grave consequences for the rest of the world. Most relevant for today's discussion, but probably least important in a real sense, is the loss of a potential major market for American products and major source of raw materials for American, European, and Japanese producers. Forty-five Chernobyl power plants that are still operative and hundreds of coal-fired power plants are yet another reason for concern. And 30,000 still operative nuclear weapons highlight our stake in success in the Russian reform effort.

My second point, bold reform is the only answer and the only prospect for success. There are those who look at the economic distress, the very real economic distress, in Eastern Europe and the former Soviet Union and who say that this means that reform must slow and become more gradual or that they must seek a third way. That is wrong. The evidence is that the problem is the failure to reform, not the results of reform. A 50 percent reduction in trade within the former Soviet Union, a defense sector that was once one-fifth of the economy in freefall, hyperinflation caused by continuing subsidies; these are the reasons for economic decay, not efforts at reform.

Reform can and has worked around the world, but it takes time. That's what happened in Germany after World War II. That's what happened in Mexico more recently. That's what happened in Chile more recently. And that is what is starting to happen in Poland, where exports to the West have more than doubled and literally tens of thousands of new entrepreneurial businesses are not just in services, but are in manufacturing as well. Our task is to speed reform, to provide support for bold reform, that offers the only possibility of prosperity in these countries.

My third point, foreign involvement can be decisive. Look at the facts. More Chinese students studied in the United States in the last year than students from the former Soviet Union have studied in the United States since the Second World War. Imports of goods into the former Soviet Union have declined by nearly 40 percent. Think about what would happen to our economy with all that works right here if our imports were compressed by 40 percent in a two-year period. And vast technical problems in everything from dismantling weapons, to fixing nuclear power plants, to getting oilfields working again remain in the former Soviet Union and require Western expertise. And, most importantly, those who are fighting for the values we cherish, democracy, markets, and capitalism, have been promised support from the West and are looking for that promise to be redeemed.

There is a Russian proverb, "You don't want to be in the woods with a wounded bear." That points up the challenge that is involved in this economic reconstruction task. The potential gain from the kind of investments that we heard about this morning, not just in the United States, but throughout the world, point up the opportunity. If successful reform in the former communist countries can make it possible to channel several hundred billion dollars a year that have been devoted to military spending to constructive investment illustrate the opportunity that that could create.

Thank you. (Applause.)

PRESIDENT-ELECT CLINTON: Thank you very much.

We could talk about that till the cows come home. I think—I think since we have just a couple of other presentations before we get to our panel discussion, I will ask you to just go on and take your seat and let's hear from the other two and then we'll talk about all these issues at once. And I think those points are very well founded.

I might say generally on all these issues I would ask you all to think about how you would expect the administration to allocate our time and resources and energy, with the clear understanding that if we do not devote a significant amount of attention to a lot of these global issues on the theory that we've been elected to, and we have most urgently to try to, revive our own economy; number one, we may not be able to do it, and number two, when the wheel runs off abroad, we may be consumed with these matters so that we can't do anything we're supposed to do at home. This is a very important area for further discussion.

I'd like to ask Paula Stern now to come forward to discuss Mexico and Latin America. She's President of the Stern Group, an economic analysis and trade advisory firm in Washington; Senior Adviser and member of the Trade Policy Sub-council of the Competitiveness Policy Council.

For the past fourteen months she's been a senior adviser on trade and international economic affairs to us and was formerly chair of the International Trade Commission.

Paula?

Ms. PAULA STERN (STERN GROUP): Thank you so much, Mr. President-elect, Mr. Vice President-elect. I thank you for including me in this teach-in. As an aging baby boomer, it's been a long time since I've been at a teach-in, and I think that one on economics is just right for today.

Over the past year, you've drawn the tight connection between domestic and international issues, and in putting people first, you link world growth to the health of the US economy. Today I'd like to take a minute of my time to put my assigned area, Latin America, into this global context as it relates to the long-term health of the US economy. Our first order of business must now be reviving the domestic economy, and trade, trade with Latin America, in particular, is an important factor in making that recovery sustainable.

America's economic vitality depends more than ever on economic conditions abroad. In the last 20 years, trade has doubled as the percentage of our entire national product to one-fourth of the total, and we export one-fourth of all the goods we make. Exports have become crucial for American economic growth and for job creation, particularly since the effectiveness of other policy tools has been severely hampered by past economic mismanagement.

Just since 1984, export expansion added one million manufacturing jobs. About one-third of all US growth in the last six years has come from cutting the trade deficit, and in 1991, the recession would have been twice as deep in the absence of continued trade gains. However, continued strong export growth and improvement in the US trade deficit now face major challenges. The greatest threat to US export performance is the economic slowdown affecting most of the industrialized world. Japan's economy's faltering. Germany's recession is hampering economic growth throughout the European Community, as we've heard from Rudi Dornbusch and Jeff Garten. As a result, our main export markets are stagnant and a drag on the tentative domestic recovery we may be experiencing.

Additionally, the yen's current undervaluation threatens US trade performance. Now, that's the bad news. The good news is in emerging markets, particularly Latin America, developing country markets have provided nearly three-quarters of US export growth this year. Sales to Latin America alone grew by 18 percent in 1991 and are expanding almost three times as fast as US exports to the world as a whole. That's almost four times as fast as the increase to the European Community and seven times as fast as the increases to all developed countries.

Now, if you break the figures down a little further, they show that 15 percent of our exports go to Latin America now, and about half of those go to Mexico. Improvement in the trade balance with Mexico accounts for more than 70 percent of the overall improvement with Latin America since 1983. Compare the picture today to the disastrous consequences of the debt crisis of the '80s in Latin America. Then, Latin America sought relief from its crisis by cutting imports while increasing exports. Our exports, US exports to that region dropped drastically in that lost decade, costing hundreds of thousands of US jobs and creating a massive US trade deficit with the region.

During the nine years I was at the International Trade Commission, my service overlapped with this period I'm describing, and at that time I took the opportunity to note in testimony on Capitol Hill that US firms and workers were suffering grievously and were seeking relief from the surge of imports which followed in the wake of that Latin American crisis.

But today, Latin America's turning around. After the lost decade of huge resource outflows, hyperinflation, shrinking incomes, the region's gaining lost ground. In what's been likened to a silent revolution, market-oriented economic development strategies are now being adopted by Latin American countries. Governments throughout the hemisphere, shunning the statist past, have restrained budgets, cut inflation, curtailed controls on prices and on markets, privatized and deregulated economic production, and removed barriers on trade and investment.

This economic pluralism is breeder of political pluralism in that region, while fostering better relations between the United States and our southern neighbors. And as an extra dividend to these developments for the United States, Latin America is now our strong partner in efforts to achieve strengthened trading rules in such areas as services, investment, and intellectual property rights protection at the Uruguay Round of multilateral trade talks.

Freer trade and economic integration are the leading edge of these positive developments in Latin American economic policy. The peoples of that region are, of course, the greatest beneficiaries of that change, but we, too, are benefiting. Long-established market presence puts US business in a strong position to profit from renewed economic growth, from freer trade, and from expanding consumer markets. Latin America spends 50 cents of each import dollar on US goods, and for Mexico it's 70 cents. Nowhere else does the US have that kind of advantage.

Revived US exports to Latin America reversed the staggering US trade deficits of the '80s. In '84, our trade with Latin America left us $70 billion in the red, but this year we're running a surplus with exports of over $75 billion. And exports mean more jobs. It's clear, then, that Latin America is important to the economic health of our country.

However, trade with Latin America is not enough. Trade with the region is a relatively small part of our total trade. And as Rudi Dornbusch suggested, the rapid growth rate of exports to Latin America is unsustainable because of the huge external deficits that many of these countries are developing once again. Moreover, the largest economy of the region—Brazil—continues to drift, and problems loom on the horizon as disaffection grows with the slow pace of economic gains for the lower income groups in that region.

So in sum, while strong export growth to Latin America and the rest of the developing world is a welcome cushion, it can't make up for the slowdown in the developed countries, nor can it compensate for the fact that US imports—US imports here at home—are increasing once again. Latin America, and particularly its best performers Chile, Mexico, and Argentina, has shown that economic reform programs stressing fiscal discipline, freer markets, and industrial restructuring can create the conditions for recovery and sustained growth. As our experience with Latin America has shown, the pace of economic growth abroad together with the competitive exchange rate and overseas market access has a significant impact on production and jobs here at home.

The lessons we can draw have to do with the need to bring down trade barriers, to promote faster growth abroad, and to promote a competitive exchange rate for American businesses. That will mean expanding international trade not just in this hemisphere, but globally. Trade's not a cure-all for all our economic needs, but trade expansion in sync with domestic policies that strengthen us here at home as competitors in the global marketplace can play a crucial role in building a sustainable, long-term economic recovery.

Thank you.

President-elect Clinton: Thank you. (Applause.)

The last topic to be discussed before the panel discussion is Africa. Robert Brown is the former staff director of the Subcommittee on International Development, Finance Trade and Monetary Policy for the House Banking Committee, and an expert on developmental economics, particularly in Africa. He's the founder of the Black Economic Research Center, a review of the black political economy of the 21st Century Foundation, and the Emergency Land Fund.

Mr. Brown.

Mr. Robert Brown (Black Economic Research Center): Thank you very much, Governor Clinton, Senator Gore, friends, colleagues.

After being largely off the US agenda since the ending of the Cold War, Africa burst upon our agenda last week with a vengeance. And not in a very positive way, I'm sorry to say, but at least it's there. And I think it's indicative of the fact that Africa's going to play a role in our future whether we like it or not.

Somalia is there—not for economic reasons, so I won't be talking much about it. You talked today at the cost in economic terms, but I would just point out that behind Somalia there are at least three other candidates for occupying our television screens in the near future. I think now of Liberia and Sudan and Mozambique. I leave aside South Africa, but I think we're all aware that, too, is quite a tinderbox that could affect our future.

But looking at the economic situation in Africa. Very gloomy. It's hard to talk about the countries in Africa, because with 51 countries, it's impossible to talk about country by country. So, I'll speak of the continent with the caveat, that obviously, everything I say about the continent doesn't apply to every country in Africa.

But when I say that Africa has been beset during the 70s and the 80s, particularly the 80s, by serious economic stagnation and, indeed, negative economic growth. This would be true of most of the countries. There are two or three of the 51 that have escaped, but in general, that's a statement that is true for the continent.

Now, the reason for this very poor economic performance in Africa during the 80s—and Africa's not always performed so poorly. The first decade after independence—the 60s—they did rather well.

And we don't really know exactly why the situation has deteriorated so. There are many theories and ideas. I would like to point out that there are three categories of blame that I might identify.

The first and perhaps foremost, would be the Africans themselves. Liberation movements did not lead to democratic governments. That, of course, brings a number of problems in its stead.

132

Secondly, and perhaps more important than the lack of democracy, has been the fact that the African governments have been very poorly managed. This, of course, is hardly surprising in view of the fact that their colonial masters had no intention of them governing themselves and did not train them for self-government. So, if for 25 years they've floundered, this perhaps should not be too surprising. It's not an excuse, it's just a statement of fact.

I would say that there's been some change in both of these. In the last three to four years there has been great increase in more democratic government in Africa. We have had several people who actually committed themselves to election and accepted a negative outcome— peacefully. This was a great step forward for Africa. And there are several other situations that are developing, hopefully, along a similar line.

On the economic side there's been progress also. In large part, I would say, stimulated or catalyzed by the western countries through their development institutions—their principle development institutions: the World Bank, and the International Monetary Fund who have, I think I can say, forced upon the African countries the quid pro quos for getting assistance policy changes, structural reform.

Structural adjustment is the term that's being used now, which I'm not necessarily in agreement with in its entirety, because I think there's some problems with much of it. On the other hand, I think we can't deny that much of the structural reforms which the West is imposing upon Africa were things which needed to be done.

They might have been able to be done better. In fact, we cannot really evaluate the value of these programs in part, because it's been too soon. But secondly, because these kinds of programs knowingly— not intentionally, but knowingly—unavoidably impose very severe hardships on the poorest of the people in these countries.

So, it takes great courage combined with a rather generous foreign assistance for a government to go along with these kinds of programs which they know will cause disaffection and unrest. And a few heads of state have lost their presidencies because of these structural adjustments which were not accompanied by sufficient funds to pacify the people who were hurt most by it, which, of course, would be the poorest, most powerless people in these countries.

But, in any case, (let's say?) structural adjustment seems to be working. With Mr. Summers here, I'm sure he would want me to say that.

The World Bank—apparently the staff at the World Bank has great disagreements within the staff as to how successful structural adjustment is, but no one has a better alternative at the moment.

Secondly, after the Africans are as blameworthy for their problems, I would put the developed countries. I think we have created conditions

133

in Africa, and perhaps in other third world countries which are partly our responsibility. And I don't have time to go into them. I can mention some of the obvious ones.

For instance in Somalia. Most of the civil war in Somalia is being fought by munitions that we gave those people. And that's true elsewhere in Africa. Now, it's true, they accept them. You can say it's their fault. They accepted them, they bought them, got them however. But they came from us. So, I think we cannot shirk that responsibility.

There are other ways in which I think we've not been very helpful. Maybe not intentionally so. For instance, much of the technology that we've brought into Africa seems to me eminently inappropriate for them at this stage.

Africa has been victimized by—I'm sorry to say it in this room—but by excessive zeal on the part of some American salesmen. And I think they're suffering from (affecting?) much of Africa's serious debt burden and debt overhang which is really depleting their ability to recover, because of the capital outgrow when they need to have a capital inflow, because they're trying to service debt that they never should have made.

And, of course, it's their fault for incurring the debt. But, on the other hand, the western countries, plush with petrol dollars that they had to put somewhere, gave them out much too easily and now the people who were susceptible and accepted those dollars are having a hard time repaying them.

And then another thing that I would mention in this regard, because I think it has a great deal of application to what we've said earlier today is that while the western countries—including the United States —on the one hand try to assist these countries on the other hand may be viewed as a bit hypocritical, because with the other hand they sometimes undermine the very development they are proposing, allegedly, to assist.

And I will just cite one or two examples. There's something called tariff escalation. It's very common-place. And what this means is that a country like Zambia, for example, which depends mainly on copper for its foreign exchange—about 70 percent of its earnings are from copper mining—exports copper ore in raw form. If it's to develop, of course, it would like to process that copper and export higher grade, refined copper at later stages of development.

So, it would create lots of jobs for its people and get it out of being just a primary producer. But, of course, the tariff laws are written so as to allow the copper ore in its crude form to come in tariff free. But the more refining takes place, the more processing takes place then it becomes more and more difficult, because the tariff rises.

Well, from the perspective of the countries that impose those sorts of tariffs it makes sense. Of course, we're trying to keep jobs here. Everything we've been talking about this morning. That's good for us. Keep those jobs around our (continent?) to develop the copper.

MR. BROWN: But for Zambia, which is trying to develop, it needs to export processed copper, not copper ore exclusively.

But of course our tariff position does not allow them to do that.

Just one other quick example, the textile industry. Now every economist and most other people probably know that textiles is probably the industry with which it is easiest to get started for a developing country. But we, of course, have many restrictions on textiles coming in.

Why? Well again for the same reasons we talked about this morning and I'm part of it. I'm very concerned about jobs for poor black people in North Carolina, for example, where much of our textile industry is.

But on the other hand, if we are really trying to help these countries develop, we have to decide what the tradeoff is going to be.

I would hate to see black women in North Carolina pitted against black women in the Ivory Coast, for example, but, you know, these are the conundrums with which we have to deal. As Mr. Clinton said earlier this morning, if we had the answers to all of these things we wouldn't be sitting here.

And the third area in which I would put some blame, and I'm on less sure ground on this one. And that is that there may, in fact, be some bias in the global economic system which makes it very difficult for these countries to move ahead.

I'm reminded, for example, that the decade of the 60s was declared by the United Nations as being the decade of development, the target being to try to reduce this enormous gap between the capital incomes in the poorest countries and in the wealthier countries.

Well, we are now three development decades later and that gap has not diminished in any substantial way. It's true there have been a few countries that have done well, others have done worse. On average there's been very little improvement.

Now, one can quickly jump and say, well, it's the countries' fault because as long as you have a few countries that have done well then that proves that it can be done. And I suppose there is some truth in that.

The countries most frequently cited, of course, are Korea and Taiwan. I've never accepted those two countries as stellar examples of what can be done. I'm much more inclined to take Malaysia, for example.

I happen to have lived in Southeast Asia for six years—the last half of the fifties—from '55 to '61 and I was well aware what aid programs were because I was working in the AID program. First in Cambodia and then in Vietnam. This was before the war of course.

And we were very envious and watching how much money—US money and other money—but particularly US money was going into South Korea and into Taiwan.

Now these funds are not included in AID monies and so, when we talk about AID it may not show. It was primarily military money, defense money, because Syngman Rhee and Chiang Kai-shek, who were the leaders of those two countries at the time, were being challenged under Cold War framework.

And so they got unlimited money.

But that money, which may have been defense money—it built a road network and an infrastructure for both of those countries which enabled them later to take off and it did not happen immediately, let me remind you. This money went in in the '50s and early '60s. As late as the '70s there were congressmen who were referring to the Korea and Taiwan AID programs as money down a rat-hole.

It was only in the '80s that these countries began to turn around.

So we may be expecting too much of Africa too soon.

And speaking of this turnaround, let me just share with you a fear that I have. Yes, Korea and Taiwan are success stories now, in retrospect. But are they success stories that inspire the United States and Western countries that the same things are done in all other countries? Because Korea and Taiwan have already been cited as serious competitors of ours today. Do we make all the world competitors of ours? I don't know.

But it makes one wonder just how serious we might be or it give us —it's another conundrum with which we must deal.

On this question of whether the system is biased against the countries, I would just point out that during the second year of the Clinton —all right, the second year of the Clinton term will also be the 50th anniversary of the Bretton Woods conference. World Bank and the IMF were created then.

They were created in a world quite different from today's world. Most of the member countries had not even come into nationhood at that time and I would suggest that the system may have been devised for the countries which were then in existence and certainly those in power, but were not conducive to the development of poor countries that were not yet in existence.

So I would suggest to the President-elect that he might want to celebrate the 50th anniversary by a Bretton Woods II, which would look at these institutions again and look at the global monetary system again and see if perhaps there are some biases inherent in that which makes it so difficult for us to do something with development.

Well, I see my time is up and I knew this would happen. I have not yet told you why you should be interested in Africa. But I think you're interested in Africa primarily for humanitarian reasons now. But there are solid economic reasons that we should have an interest in Africa and there are also some strong environmental reasons. Unfortunately I don't have time to go into them.

Thank you very much for listening. (Applause.)

PRESIDENT-ELECT CLINTON: Thank you.

Let me say, first of all, there are a lot of environmental reasons we should be interested in Africa and maybe we can go into them.

I would like to just say in response to one thing you said that, yes, we built—we helped to build Korea and Taiwan. But I think it's also important to point out that in the last few years they have virtually abolished—both of them—their trade surpluses with us without doing any serious damage to their growth rates and that Taiwan now has something over $80 billion in cash reserves. I think, on balance, it's been a pretty positive thing for the world and we'll have to continue to work on that.

Let me make one procedural point. I hate to bring this up, but our staff did a real good job of working with everybody in the morning session, and we were more or less within the time. We have now run a total of 18 minutes over the time allotted for all those presentations. Now, I wanted to wait till the end, cause it's just like the scripture said, "All have sinned and gone astray" here. (Laughter.) And once I got started, I didn't want to cut off anybody, but in the afternoon and following tomorrow, I will have to do that. And so I would urge you to re-examine the time allotted and how much your remarks are going to take, because otherwise you're taking time away from everybody else at the table and everybody in the audience.

Having said that, I'm going to take it out of the next break. (Laughter.) So let's start around the table. We have a lot of people who have been actively engaged in exporting, and I wonder who would like to go first, and in what order. Shall we have Linda Yang first—Yang, and then we'll just go around, and anybody else who wants to speak, I'll recognize you in some order. Linda?

MS. LINDA TSAO YANG (LINDA TSAO YANG & ASSOCIATES): Yes. Thank you, President-elect Clinton, and Vice President-elect Gore. I'm from

Davis, California, originally from Shanghai, China. It certainly is an honor to be here today.

We have heard a lot about Europe, about Africa, about Latin America and Japan, but I would like to cite first a few simple facts. Number one, the United States is an Atlantic nation. We are also a Pacific nation. Our cross-Pacific trade is greater than our cross-Atlantic trade. These are facts.

Number two, having heard a description of the economic outlook in the rest of the world, all very bleak, but we have bright spots, and that is in East Asia, Southeast Asia. They have been growing 5, 6, 7 percent. Four percent growth to them is considered to be depression. And the future still looks very good—very good.

And yet, what have we been doing? We have, under the leadership of the United States, the Canada-US free trade, NAFTA; there's talk about Western Hemisphere trade zones. The perception on the other side of the Pacific is exclusionary—exclusionary. So there is a movement on the part of some politicians over there. They want to set up trade zones with Japan, but not the US.

Now, remember, we are a Pacific nation. We are still an economic superpower, and right now no one is taking leadership in that area. Sooner or later somebody's going to step in. Why not us? Why not the United States take the leadership now to set up a network of—with Asian nations, those who wish to join—those who want to wait, fine, but it's always open to them—to set up a regional network so that we can work out problems to reduce trade barriers, to open markets for product, especially US products.

And furthermore, that could also be a back channel method to work out some of our trade frictions with Japan, because certainly Japan will be a part of it. And that could also be a building block in the future for truly multilateral trade networks to reduce trade barriers and to open markets for our products.

I have another point to make. Very little [has] been touched on, on China. Without the world paying much notice, there is a de facto China-centered economic zone in the making. Today, the combination of the PRC—the People's Republic of China—and with Taiwan, as President-elect Clinton pointed out, with $80 billion of cash, and with Hong Kong, with its famous middleman's role of a trillion dollar exchange rate every day, the three of them putting together; they have developed such economic power and momentum that by some study, by the time President-elect Clinton, at the end of your second term—(laughter)—you will find there the export trade of these three, excluding their intra-trade, will be greater than the export of Japan. And that should certainly upset or change the world trade pattern, which would have enormous implications to us.

Then. Right now no one is taking the leadership. Why not us?

Thirdly, I have another point—these are the macro-policy questions I think we need to address. I have some nuts and bolts on the implementation problems. In this country many of us still have this mercantilistic notion that export is a vent for surplus, not export or die like the Germans or the Japanese, even the British. Okay, we may not want to resort to export or die, but certainly if we don't export, we're going to shrivel and wither away, that's for sure.

I think our diplomatic missions abroad should make it their primary responsibility to give hands-on experience to our smaller and medium-sized businesses to open up markets, to find niches, to bring the business people together, through trade shows, trade—talking to the chambers of commerce and so on.

And finally, I think I'd like to address Secretary of Commerce–designate Ron Brown. You need a good budget to implement those missions. Thank you. (Laughter, applause.)

PRESIDENT-ELECT CLINTON: We could have done without that last line. (Applause.) Very good.

MR. BROWN: I agree.

PRESIDENT-ELECT CLINTON: Who said I agree? (Laughter.)
Go ahead, Mr. Reed.

HOWARD CURTIS REED (CURT REED & COMPANY): There is a curious area—well, it's curious in that it has not been discussed other than what Professor Dornbusch mentioned earlier in this session, but we haven't talked very much about US dollar policy. And when we talk about a coordinated global growth strategy, my view is that it must start with the dollar policy. I am not a proponent of what was started back in 1985, and that was the lowering of the dollar for the almost exclusive purpose of increasing exports of US manufactured goods. It took roughly five years before we saw any results of that, and I think that particular policy, which is still in effect to a large extent, lacks the importance of our other global responsibilities as a nation.

For example, our banking institutions, the asset and capital positions have been impaired significantly because of that policy. It has limited those institutions in their ability to participate in the international activities throughout the world. And that, in turn, has limited our ability as a nation to have economic influence and to carry out our role as an economic leader.

This is particularly important, I think, if we look at Eastern Europe and the former Soviet Union. With the dollar at its present low levels, and it's likely to continue that way unless we take steps, I think, in the next few months to address that issue—we are not going to be able to participate in the economic development of Eastern Europe. Therefore, our industrial and banking institutions won't have influence, and it's going to impair our ability to participate in the long run in a political way.

Now, a lower dollar policy also impairs our ability to function as a military superpower, because the linkages, as has been pointed out by President-elect Clinton, are significant, in that a strong economic power in many ways diminishes our need to use—to threaten to use our military power. And if we are not going to talk about that issue, I don't see how we can accomplish an industrial policy, a quasi-industrial policy that we are talking about today.

The last point I'd like to make is that a successful industrial policy requires preferential access to capital by certain institutions and certain industries from time to time. And that, again, entails a stronger dollar. And I do not mean—I do not want to be misunderstood—I do think trade is important, but I think there are other considerations that we should put on the table, and at the very least vigorously debate what our dollar policy should be.

PRESIDENT-ELECT CLINTON: Does anybody want to disagree with what he said about the dollar policy? Susan?

SUSAN COLLINS (BROOKINGS INSTITUTION): Yes. I mean, I agree very strongly that the level of the dollar, the level of the value of the US currency must be considered in the context of a number of different objectives, and one of the objectives which I think is quite important is that the value of the dollar is, in part, one of the factors that determines global demand for US workers and other US resources.

And I would link up this discussion at this point with some of the points that were made this morning, I think, very effectively. In particular, if we think over time that a long-run policy that makes a lot of sense is one of investing in people in this country, that would support a stronger dollar over time. And it seems to me that one needs to take a longer-run perspective that brings in some of the considerations that you were mentioning earlier with the perspective as well in terms of how one facilitates the shifting of resources from one set of industries to other sets of industries. And that also links up with some of the things we talked about this morning in the context of a dynamic global economy that Michael Porter raised. It seems to me that one needs to perhaps try to balance the short-run considerations with the longer-run considerations, and therefore try to fashion a policy that brings those things together.

In that context, I'd like to just briefly answer a question that President-elect Clinton raised earlier, and that is how should we think about this issue of whether there is a role for a macroeconomic policy coordination. It seems to me that there again there are short-run issues and long-run issues. I heard that one of the main points in Rudi Dornbusch's comments in that regard to be that we should recognize that Germany and Japan in particular are dealing with structural problems in the short run and that puts some constraints on the kinds of international or coordinated policies one could put together that would directly affect US growth in the short run.

None of that, in my view, says anything about how important it is to move toward an enhanced dialogue, I would say, that recognizes the fact that first of all, objectives across different regions in the US are overlapping; and second of all, the kinds of policies that are undertaken, both macro-policies and structural policies, investment policies, have global effects. And it seems to me that in that context it's really of crucial importance to move toward a global dialogue that enhances discussion of what kinds of things might be done, even if in the short run there might not be quick fixes. Thank you.

PRESIDENT-ELECT CLINTON: Senator Bentsen, do you have a response to that? Do you want to say anything?

SEN. BENTSEN: Well, I would say certainly it's time that the United States reassert its leadership in the G-7. That has been—it's been lagging in that regard, trying to work toward some correlation in monetary policy amongst these various countries. I think that's critical for us.

PRESIDENT-ELECT CLINTON: Anybody else want to respond to the strong dollar/weak dollar argument? Jeff?

MR. GARTEN: Well, I'd just like to add one thought. I think that if the United States is going to be a high-wage economy, as you've described it, and if we're going to compete with—in the areas of high-technology where I think our future is, over time a weak dollar is not compatible with that. Over time a policy—a trade policy based on a weak dollar is a policy to compete with the Koreas or the Mexicos and not with Japan and Germany.

It's no accident that Japan and Germany have had highly-valued currencies and have been competitive in those areas where quality and skilled labor matter. And so I think I would like to add my voice to those who are saying depreciating the dollar in the interest of trade competitiveness is a quick fix, and over time our country deserves better.

PRESIDENT-ELECT CLINTON: I agree with that, but let me just make— and then I'll call on Larry in a minute, but let me, just from a non-economist point of view out here in the real world where I saw people struggling to make a living in the 1980's, let me just flip that over. One of the inevitable consequences of decisions made in 1981 to cut taxes without really cutting spending—we cut social spending, but we increased defense by more than we cut discretionary social spending— was that we had a huge debt and we—in order to avoid having inflation, we had to finance that debt with massive inflows of capital from overseas for which we had to offer very high interest rates, real interest rates at historically high levels, which gave us a very strong dollar, which under—which was overvalued relative to our real competitive position in the world so that we lost huge export markets in many critical sectors of the economy.

I agree that we ought to have a long-term strong dollar package if it is supported by the underlying reality of our economy. But we got the living daylights kicked out of us between '81 and '87 because we had a strong dollar to finance our deficit policies, not because of the underlying competitive realities of our economy.

Then a lot of—but to give the dog its due here, this other argument, after we lowered our dollar value from '87 on, we did pick up export markets, because we did it in some areas, but we made no headway, real headway in any sustainable way with—because our oil exports kept getting worse and because of our relationships with Japan. So even though our trade deficit with Mexico, Taiwan and Korea dropped precipitously, we still have a trade problem.

But I just—I have to tell you where I'm coming from, and I want you all to be free to disagree with me, but you have to know what my bias is. I'm for a strong dollar if it is supported by the competitive realities of the American economy. And I think we may have to shore it up, because we don't want to look as weak as sometimes I fear we are in some sectors, but I think that artificial strong dollar we had from '81 building up through '87 is part of the reason we're in the fix we're in today.

Larry.

Mr. Summers: Mr. President—President-elect, you spoke in the same general line that I was going to speak to. I think everybody in this room can agree that a more productive American workforce that can compete at a higher real exchange rate would be a very good thing for the country. I think however that it would be unfortunate if we were to prematurely raise interest rates and risk slowing the recovery and cutting off the process of job creation out of concern about the level of the exchange rate, and that it would be more appropriate for the primary role of our monetary and our fiscal policy to be—to speed the process of economic recovery and increases in the rate of investment. If we do that successfully, I think we will have the dollar at a healthy level that will make it possible for the world economy to grow.

President-elect Clinton: I'd like to, if I might, move just a little bit on this and go to the whole issue of what our trade policy ought to be, and call on some people, in the beginning at least, I think who favor open trading rules, even though it may not be in their immediate sector of self-interest, and then I'll call on some other folks, if I might.

I'd like to begin by asking John Bryan and Walter Elisha and John Ong to talk a little bit about their views of the trade issue, and then I'll call on a couple of other people. But I'd like for those three folks to talk first. Go ahead, John.

John Bryan (Sara Lee Corporation): Thank you very much, and congratulations on the meeting. It seems to me that what's happening here is that we're searching, or you're searching for an economic strategy, and that there are at least two things I'd like to remind us all of. They've really been said today. One is that the global marketplace, some—is an inevitable tide. And that, plus the technology, is going to change regardless of whether we want it to or not. It's going to restructure America, it's going to change the products that we manufacture, the products that we use and how they're done in industries and all of that.

This should be, in my judgment, very positive. If you look at the course of history, open markets and economic integration have really been the most important source of growth for most economies. It's been said here that this economy in the United States, manufacturing jobs have been created almost exclusively by exports. Japan is a successful export economy. Germany is also. And Asia, since the Japanese have moved in with their money and made—become a catalyst for growth in that area, they've had stunning success.

In Latin America, if those economies can commence to grow, they need exactly what we have. We've got capital goods that they do not have. We've got the sophisticated service infrastructure that they don't have. To get the contract, industrialized Latin America is politically and economically a great opportunity in my judgment.

Now, so I think a strategy that we have has to be in the context of these facts to take advantage of the global marketplace. The first thing we've got to do is to continue to be a leader in opening markets around the world. It is not easy. But because negotiation is difficult, we don't need to lose sight of the advantage that it is to us.

And the second thing we have to do is to make America a very attractive place in which business can operate and be successful.

Training the people has got to be almost number one, because education is the major problem that we have today. We have fiscal problems, 10 or 12 years of our deficits have kept real interest rates too high. The health care problem, the infrastructure problem are all very important to us.

There's one aspect of it, however, that I—of programs that I'd like to take some issue with. I've been very reluctant, in my judgment, am very reluctant for us to be subsidizing business in all of this. Investing the resources of government in business is a very risky thing to be doing. Tax preferences in my judgment distort at the very least and they usually don't work, and therefore become very wasteful. They can change the timing occasionally of business behavior, but they rarely change business behavior in the final analysis.

I think myself that business wants a very consistent and a competitive tax code. We've pretty much got one today, and I favor staying where we are with corporate taxes.

The best way generally to make business more competitive and the most effective way is to make them compete, to compete externally and to compete internally, to keep the regulations as moderate as possible, and let government concentrate on working for the people and not so much for business.

So I guess my point is that the global marketplace is a plus. It's a plus not just economically, but politically. And we very much need to take advantage of that as we fashion strategies.

President-elect Clinton: Thank you. Go ahead.

144

WALTER ELISHA (SPRINGS INDUSTRIES): Thank you, thank you, Governor. We've certainly heard some awesome descriptions of the world around us this morning. And, Bob, I'm reminded of the man who gathered his family around the Thanksgiving table and said, "I have good news: We are doing our part in helping those in other parts of the world. And I have bad news: I am no longer employed." And which really reminds me to say that I think if we look at the history of the trading policies of this country, it's really a history of only about 50 years. We have lived with the Bretton Woods agreement for the last 50 years, what I would characterize as an externally-driven trade policy to deal with the enormous economic challenges of Europe in the post–World War II period, facilitated even more by the Marshall Plan in 1948, and a way to help the defense of this country to support the defense policy in dealing with the Soviet Union.

And we find ourselves today, if we list I think what we have learned from some of that is that the acquisition of markets has become significantly more important than the acquisition of any territory. The history of civilization, I would say, up until the end of World War II, was one built wealth in their nation by acquiring territory. And from World War II on, we've learned that the acquisition of markets has been really a way for one to build wealth for their country.

We find ourselves then at a time today when while this country accounts for 25 percent of the gross national product of the world, we are buying half of the product exported from Third World countries, a trade policy—a policy, if you will, that's developed out of the old GATT–Bretton Woods discussion.

So, I would—Bob, again referring to you—support your idea of a Bretton Woods—I'd call it Bretton Woods 2000, where we develop, Mr. President-elect, a Bretton Woods internally-inspired trade policy for our country, recognizing that trade policies are enormously complex. I would liken it to probably moving a cemetery, in terms of the complexity required, and making everyone feel good about it. (Laughter.)

But we need to look at the realities, the realities of what are going on, have been going on in our country just in the last decade, when in 1975, '80 we were the world's most successful producers of airplanes, we were the world's leading low-cost producer of food, and we were the world's low-cost and most efficient producer of computers; and all three of those are in an ebb of sorts because world conditions have changed.

So my recommendation, even in the face of these learned economists who have been speaking to us, is to recommend to you a Bretton Woods 2000 where we look, we would reposture the way we feel our nation needs to be moving into the next century with our trade policy,

145

rather than living with what's an extension of a trade policy developed at the end of World War II.

I think finally one needs to say that the—we cannot have a strong nation, we cannot have strong businesses without a strong K-12 educational system. And while we have our weaknesses in business, and I certainly have made my share of errors along the way in leading a corporation, the public education system in this country, which provided the vehicle for growth through most of its early history, is no longer developing for us what we need to have. We need national standards for K-12 education. We need to fund it. We need the quality of people coming along, properly educated, teachers properly rewarded, more than 180 days in the classroom in order to have the talented people to compete with these countries who are now competing with us, and who should also be buying their share of products from Third World countries to the same extent that we are buying products from Third World countries.

So certainly anything we can do to support you in that endeavor, we will.

VICE PRESIDENT-ELECT GORE: If I could interject a brief question there, you talk about the volume of goods we're buying from Third World countries. Is it not true that last year 35 percent of our exports went to Third World countries?

MR. ELISHA: My point was not that they are not buying from us, it is that there are nations who were favored under the Bretton Woods agreement who are not buying their relative share from Third World countries. I don't think this country should be the sole supporter—or sole support is not correct—be buying half of the production of those Third World countries in order to help them develop. And we should. It's the humanitarian thing to do, and it makes for good business. But I think we should look to other countries that in 1945 were destitute, and are no longer destitute, to be picking up on some of that as well.

VICE PRESIDENT-ELECT GORE: I agree with that. I don't want to belabor the point, because obviously we are more open to their exports than many of our trading partners in Europe and Asia are, but it seems to me that we have as a nation failed to fully recognize the opportunity that the developing world represents for us. I think Paula Stern referred to the fact that 75 percent of our export growth has been into those markets, and we're filling 50 percent of that market overall. And it's more than a third of our total export market. And just as we heard about the problems in some of the areas of the world that can have an effect on our economy, I think it might make sense for us to have a little more focus on the problems that characterize the developing world, because of the impact their purchases of our products have on the US economy. But I agree with the point that you were making.

MR. ELISHA: I can't disagree with what you've said.

PRESIDENT-ELECT CLINTON: Let me—

MR. ELISHA: My starting point would be with our country and with what we should be doing rather than with those other countries in bringing it back here.

PRESIDENT-ELECT CLINTON: I just want to fix the order of speakers. I want to let Laura Tyson interject here, but after Mr. Ong, Cliff Wharton, Owen Bieber and Mr. Goizeuta, I think all had their hands up. So, go ahead, Laura.

LAURA D'ANDREA TYSON (CHAIR-DESIGNATE, COUNCIL OF ECONOMIC ADVISERS): Okay, I just wanted to make an observation and raise a question. The observation is that in talking about the benefits of US exports to developing countries and maybe the cost of US imports from developing countries, the way we get into that is by, I think, not addressing something which so far has been left out of the discussion, and that is that trade does have dislocational effects, and some people in the United States in some communities in the United States are hurt as a result of increasing imports.

That doesn't mean we shouldn't be in favor of more trade. It means that we have failed at the adjustment, retraining, support mechanism. That is, it gets back to the President-elect's question about security. We can't guarantee that people will be protected in the jobs that they currently have by closing ourselves off to imports, but we must take very seriously the fact that imports do cause pain to some people. Often those people are singularly unequipped—ill-equipped to take on the job opportunities in the export sector.

If you look at the domestic—the characteristics of workers in import-impacted industries and export industries, you'll see that in import-impacted industries, often you have disproportionately large numbers of unskilled female workers, whereas the export powerhouses of the United States have highly-skilled, often male scientific workers.

Now, we have a problem here of training and moving those who are adversely affected by the imports. And I just think if we get that out as a policy problem, then we won't have debates about whether trade is good or bad for us; it's good for us.

PRESIDENT-ELECT CLINTON: I agree with that, but I also want to put one other policy problem on the table, then I'd like to go back to the panel, and it refers to the very persuasive point my friend John Bryan made about not—the government not picking winners or losers either through tax policy or other policy. In principle I think that is fine; in practice these advanced nations that Mr. Elisha pointed to do things that, for example, affect those high-wage, high-growth jobs in Silicon Valley. Or Airbus, the European project, had a big effect on McDonnell Douglas, and that was the question we got this morning from the field there. And on Boeing; it's having a big effect on Boeing, and it may be having an effect on some other companies here represented. So I think we don't live in a world in which our own actions are the only actions which impact us, and that's something else we have to be sensitive to.
Mr. Ong.

MR. JOHN ONG (GOODRICH): Thank you, Governor Clinton, Senator Gore. I would simply, perhaps at the risk of restating the obvious, point out that probably the greatest thing we can do—foreign economic situations are what they are and they will change as they always have, but if we, going back to our discussion this morning, build the kind of long-term, sustainable, non-inflationary economic growth in this country that was being outlined by the panelists this morning, that's the single greatest thing we can do to make ourselves, to make our industries competitive around the world. And it's ultimately more important than the precise nature of our trade policy can ever be.

However, having said that, it does seem to me that we need to do a better job of integrating economic policy with all the balance of our policy outreach to the world: national security, foreign policy and the like.

I don't know about the idea of a Bretton Woods agreement. I'm not so sure that the international trading system is as broken as some think it is. We're sort of like the old farmer; we're not farming as well now as we know how. And I think we do lack integration in public policy in this area and have for a long time. I think it's very encouraging that you're thinking along the lines of trying to change that.

We have a system under which we've got a lot of leverage. The multilateral trading system I think remains important. Perhaps it should be modified. I wouldn't argue that at all, but I think that we can play in that game more effectively than we have in the past. And I certainly think that the important first step is to complete the Uruguay Round.

Likewise, I think in the real world we live in, it's important to have regional trading blocs. And again I think the completion of the NAFTA agreement would give us a very powerful tool on a regional basis to supplement our participation in the GATT.

The next line of defense is obviously bilateral discussions, where specific trade policies can be addressed. And finally as the last line of defense, we have our own trade laws, which permit us to react in a variety of situations. And I think that probably some of the activities that you made reference to just a moment ago on the part of some of our trading partner countries can perhaps best be addressed not by picking winners and losers within our own economy, but by vigorously exerting our position both in bilateral negotiations and a very vigorous enforcement of our trade laws.

A final point. It does seem to me that there is a lot of merit in trying to reorganize the whole structure through which our international economic policy is carried out. All of us who have been, whether in business or government, involved in this area over the years, recognize that the organization is fragmented, there is no responsibility and less accountability than there ought to be. And while I have no prescription for it, I think that an early priority of your administration should be to look at that whole structure and see whether we cannot find a reorganization that would point us in the direction of making economic policy a prime mover in our relationships with other countries around the world from this point forward.

PRESIDENT-ELECT CLINTON: Thank you. Cliff.

CLIFTON WHARTON (TIAA-CREF): President-elect Clinton and Vice President-elect Gore, it's a pleasure to be here. Before I make three observations and comments, I think it's important that I have a disclaimer. I suspect that among our 1,600,000 policyholders, undoubtedly there are some who are listening in right now, and they would have expected me to have spoken out on how to protect their pensions and how to deal with issues of quality on pensions, but I will resist that and take you up on your offer to submit a separate letter.

There are three areas that I felt have not yet been put on the agenda for at least a presentation discussion that I'd like to mention. One is relating to the question of all of the discussion about the investment in human capital which has to take place. I completely agree with regard to the K-12 in the earlier observation. However, one of the striking things in my mind is that when one asks the question of where is, in fact, that intellectual human capital developed, it is primarily within our universities and colleges, and particularly in our graduate institutions.

When you look at what in our economy has one of the largest attractors from abroad, it is our colleges and universities. We have, I suspect, between 350,000 and 400,000 foreign students. And at the graduate level, in the last 20 years, there's been a three-fold growth in foreign students at the graduate level. It's gone from 60,000 to over 180,000. Those students are here because we are able to provide that capacitation.

And then I have to ask myself the question: What has been happening to that particular educational infrastructure? And I look across the United States and I see case after case, particularly in our public universities, where massive reductions are taking place. And what those reductions threaten to do is to wipe out a great deal of the capacity that we have which took many, many years to build, because we are not paying attention to protecting what, in fact, is one of our greatest comparative advantages in the creation of intellectual capital.

So I would mention that as being very central, not only to our own domestic economy, but also in terms of how we face up to competitiveness on the world scene.

The second issue, which I think needs to be put stage center relates to what I find to be an amazing confluence between the faces of poverty in the United States and abroad, and what do we do about it. I think that your proposals with regard to how to address this domestically are right on target, but I also look at what we are doing abroad, particularly with the Third World, and some of the comments that Bob Brown made.

And I personally believe that it's about time that we took another hard look at what is being done in the area of economic assistance, security assistance, and the totality of foreign aid. I realize that right now foreign aid is not a very popular subject, particularly in Congress. Nevertheless, I think we need to watch very carefully what Mr. Fukushima talked about in terms of Japan spending three times what we are in bilateral assistance. They're not doing it just to be doing it for humanitarian reasons alone. I think once again that this is an area in

150

the long term where we need to address this because, in fact, unless we make those kinds of investments and make that kind of assistance again, we'll be back in the issue of how, in fact, are we going to generate those particular jobs and how are we going to have those export markets.

And last, which may be a bit non-traditional, I happen to think that there are major economic consequences, both domestically within the United States, as well as overseas in the foreign nations, in relationship to ethnic and religious conflict. I think there is a tremendous price that is paid within our boundaries and within the boundaries of most foreign countries. And I personally think that this is an issue where frequently leadership and symbolism plays a very important role. I believe that how we in the United States handle ethnic and religious conflicts, whether it's in Queens between blacks and Jews in New York City or between any other group in the United States, does have a role in terms of how we are perceived worldwide, and does have economic consequences.

And speaking of symbolism, I would just like to close very briefly by saying that I think just the example of this highly diverse group that you have gathered together to address these issues, coming from a tremendously diverse background, as it goes out over television, over the media, across the world, shows, in fact, the kind of leadership on dealing with this kind of diversity that I think is very, very meaningful, again, in providing leadership across the world. So I appreciate that and I think you ought to be commended for it. (Applause.)

PRESIDENT-ELECT CLINTON: Thank you very much. After Owen and Roberto, Dr. Whitman and Karen Horn will be next.

Let me just respond to two things you said. I think Senator Gore and I both agree with your comments about foreign assistance. I agree with you that our institutions of higher education form a network that is still the finest in the world unquestionably. It is an enormous source of goodwill and foreign capital and all kinds of good things for us.

I would also point out—we don't have time to discuss this now, but of all the market basket of things which are considered essential in 1992, the cost of higher education is the only one that went up faster than health care in the last ten years. And that's something that bears some looking at also.

MR. OWEN BIEBER (UNITED AUTO WORKERS): Thank you very much, President-elect Clinton and Vice President-elect Gore. And I want to comment—to commend both of you for putting this conference together. I think it has been superb.

I will submit letters to you on various topics, and I know that time is running short, so I'll be brief. As the discussion unfolded today, I came to the conclusion that either I'm the most fortunate or the most unlucky person to have—represent workers in almost all of the industries that have been enumerated here that have problems, starting of course from the auto industry, which everyone knows, but I would point out that the call from the McDonnell Douglas worker, while he may be from the—I'm not sure whether he belongs to my union or the machinists, but in any event, your point of the tremendous pressure we're under from competition such as Airbus, McDonnell Douglas Commercial is a good example of this—a company which is at a crossroads now, and it will take some real ingenuity if that company is to continue to be a player in the commercial aircraft industry in the future.

I want to also say that the people who I represent do not fear competition, and I think that over the last ten years we have demonstrated that. We are—the union that I represent, I say proudly, has always been a union that has supported open and free trade. Add to that the necessity of fair trade. And those of you who have had an opportunity to hear me speak on this issue over the last several years since I've been president of this union—1983—Senator Gore certainly has had that opportunity and Senator Bentsen—that has always been our position.

I couldn't help but feel when the discussion took place about the weak dollar, I sort of said, in the absence of other trade policies, thank God that we got to that weak dollar when we did. Otherwise the domestic auto industry, as we know it today, would probably be much smaller than what we observe today. I couldn't help but remember that during the time that the Japanese yen was—its value so high in relationship to the dollar, in the heavy earth-moving equipment business where I also represent workers—everything being equal, meaning wages, the cost of raw material, everything equal, the imbalance of the yen and the dollar meant that in those earth-moving pieces of equipment that retailed for $250,000, $260,000, there was built in a $60,000 competitive disadvantage. And no one can compete against that. Workers can't compete against that.

On the question of the GATT, I would urge you, as you have certainly clearly said you were going to take a hard look at NAFTA, I would urge you to do the same thing on the GATT agreement. I heard John Young make the point that we have our own protective, so to speak, but from what I have observed, the Dunkel draft would weaken our ability, and I think in terms of 301 treatment, I think it weakens that; I think it moves into GATT procedures the resolve of some disputes that we today have an opportunity perhaps to do through our own laws.

I repeat again that—and some of the things that were said this morning—the whole question of health care costs. That has to be addressed, and I would be remiss if I did not point out that one of the things that specifically wasn't announced this morning or wasn't talked about and has great negative effect upon the domestic auto industry is the whole question of the application of FASB and what that means to not only the domestic auto companies, but for that matter, in all of the (old line ?) industries in our country today. In the case of General Motors, as an example, if the total of that FASB potential was claimed now, you would be coming close to two-thirds—

PRESIDENT-ELECT CLINTON: Could you tell the participants what FASB is, for the ones who don't know?

MR. BIEBER: Well, this means that they now have to show, on their bottom line, the cost of retiree insurance and what that cost will be spread out over the term or the lifetime of those retirees. You're talking about a potential of $24 billion as the maximum in the case of General Motors, being written off on that bottom line. And I took the time to take a look the other day what stockholder equity is. It's about $33 billion, so that gives you some feel of the various problems that we face.

Again, I say to you, Mr. President-to-be in a very short time, and I'm happy for that, I ask you to look at these things, and I think we have to recognize that all the things that were talked about this morning as well as this afternoon really dovetail, and I would urge that the American workers and the American populace in general not be the victims. I think we've been the victims in the last 12 years far too often.

MR. ROBERTO GOIZEUTA (COCA-COLA COMPANY): Well, first of all, let me thank you, Governor and Senator, for the opportunity to be here. You have been commended for the diversity of this group, and I want to add my words of commendation because it gives me a wonderful opportunity to practice my Spanish—(laughter)—during the breaks and social hours. I have spoken more Spanish today and last evening than I've done in a long time, other than being in Spain or in Latin America.

I think it's become obvious through all the discussions today that the tenor of our foreign policy must now change from that dealing with political and military matters to one dealing with political as well as economic matters. We have heard time and again that unless the economies of the rest of the world progress, it will be very difficult for the economy of this country to really move ahead. And from the perspective of my company—and we don't export from this country. We are not multinational in the sense that is widely known. We call ourselves multi-local because Coca-Cola is produced locally in close to 200 countries of the world in which our product is sold. And I think we see a number of trends that favor investment in these international markets.

First of all is the fact that most of the people of this world are now realizing that government is not their provider, and they are no longer looking to government as the institution that mostly determines their standard of living. Most people of the world are now looking to private enterprise to supply the products and services they need and want, and they look to private enterprise to create the real jobs and be the engine of sustained economic growth. The role of government, they view it as providing the climate in which business can carry out its role.

Then thirdly is this development of natural economic and trade alliances. We talked about—we mentioned China, mainland China, Taiwan, and Hong Kong. Those alliances were first created to spark growth through trade among themselves. We had the Latin American Free Trade Association, and we have had it for a long time. We don't know what it has done, but we have had it for a long time. But now they are being created by nations really fearful of not fitting into the new global trade puzzle. And you were so absolutely right, that we should look across the Pacific. After all, that is one of our borders, and you were right on target.

And then, the last trend that we see around the world is that the institutions that best understand and satisfy what people want are the ones that will thrive and prosper. And I think that augurs very well for business in the international marketplace because as businessmen and -women, we know that those who do not serve the needs of their customers and consumers are not going to do very well for very long. So I think it augurs well for business, but means that business must step forward and go hand in hand with governments in order to improve the standard of living around the world.

Thank you.

PRESIDENT-ELECT CLINTON: Thank you.

Dr. Whitman is next, I think. I want to hear—and then Karen Horn, and then Mr. Roberts, and then Sandy. And I want to hear from everybody we haven't heard from, but we can only talk about 12, 15 more minutes, then we got to have a little break. So we got to accelerate it, so go ahead.

Ms. Mariana Whitman (University of Michigan): Thank you, sir. I'd like to just try to pull together some of the things that we were talking about both at the end of the morning and this afternoon, with all the stress on competition in the global marketplace, which obviously means a need for increased productivity, which means by definition that the same work is going to be done by fewer people. That's the only way you can be competitive and have high wages.

The problem—and this has been referred to by several people, Mr. Donahue, Mr. Bieber, and others—is how do you preserve and increase good jobs while having this increase in productivity? There are really two alternative routes.

One is, there's a real human temptation to sort of try to freeze the situation where it is to avoid or minimize job loss—and you talked about that, Mr. Clinton, toward the end of the morning—through trade protection or restrictive regulation or something. In the long run, that's not going to be viable. In the end, the cost—if you just look at the—what happened with the British coal mining industry. The longer you try to do that, the worse the distortion builds up and the more awful the dislocation is when you finally have to adjust.

The other route is to facilitate transition to new processes and new products both by workers and by firms. And again, most of the burden for that is the responsibility of the firms and the workers. But there are things, I think, that government can do to help facilitate transition by making both people and companies more flexible. One is, of course, the obvious, that a sustainably growing domestic economy is critical because it's always easier to make change in the context of growth than the context of decline. A second one, which again has been referred to, is to maximize export opportunities for our goods, which means completing the GATT and the NAFTA as quickly as possible, because we have to remember that the barriers that will be gotten rid of by the NAFTA are not largely barriers to imports into the United States, they're barriers to exports out of the United States into a fast-growing market like Mexico.

At the same time, though, we need to find effective ways to make sure that other countries carry out their obligations under international agreements in terms of giving access for our goods and so forth, and at the same time don't shoot ourselves in the foot.

There are two other things, though, which I think haven't been touched on so much. And one is that we need some kind of change in the social compact with which we came out of World War II, where in

155

this country, American business, and particularly large corporations, took on obligations for certain kinds of things which in other countries were government, that is, obligations of all the taxpayers, be it pensions, health care, and so forth. Now that we have this great increase in global competition, that becomes more and more of a competitive disadvantage for our so-called traditional firms. We've already talked about the health care burden, the pension burden.

And it also means that if there is a shift in production from traditional firms to new firms producing in this country, you may have a severe tearing of that social compact, such as, for instance, if some major traditional US corporation went belly up, it would bankrupt the Pension Benefit Guaranty Corporation, even if the production were picked up in this country by somebody else. There would be that danger.

So, we have to find some way, I think, of relieving, both on the health care side and the pension side, some of that—the non-competitive aspects of the way we've chosen to do that financing. And that was referred to by Mr. Altman this morning when he talked about the private sector overpaying.

And then, finally, I think we have to find ways to deal with the social or environmental demands, things like, again, health care, pensions, environment, where again a lot of that has been carried by large companies. The whole issue of, for instance, how the electric car will be financed. There are many others. Can we find ways to get effective cooperation among firms and between firms and governments without picking winners and losers, without interfering with competition, but finding some effective way of financing these things in a way that doesn't make us uncompetitive, particularly when some other companies, of course, are doing that for things which have a great social advantage?

And, finally, to find market-based ways of regulating to get these social ends rather than command and control. This relates to things like what Jessica Mathews talked about this morning, using taxes to do it or tradeable permits and so forth. I think all of these things would help that flexibility.

PRESIDENT-ELECT CLINTON: I fully agree with the market-based issue, and I don't—time doesn't permit a response to every point you raise, but I think that I just want to reiterate one of the points you made. Because we have allowed this health care cost thing to rage out of control for so long, I have a serious question in my mind about whether we can find a traditional market-oriented approach, including the managed competition approach, which I favor in the health care area, which will alleviate from our traditional manufacturers the burden of carrying retiree health insurance. It is not a big problem for a lot of industries, but for autos, for steel, for some other sectors, it is a massive problem. And it seems to me, just on sheer economic terms, you know, perhaps the most powerful argument for some sort of modified single-payer plan, something which I have not favored in the past. But if we don't solve that problem, some of our sectors are going to continue to have difficulty.

Karen?

Ms. Karen Horn (Banc One): As I listen to the presenters and my fellow panelists, I'm reminded that Yogi Berra said we are faced with insurmountable opportunities. And I'm optimistic on this—on our surmounting these opportunities, in part because one of the themes I hear is coordination.

I hear it when we had the free trade discussion and we talked about the need for regional trade networks. We have coordination through GATT, which you will face very early in your administration. And, of course, one of the very early free trade issues you will face in your administration is NAFTA, the North American Free Trade Agreement.

I would argue on that front that, in fact, we do need this kind of coordination of regional trade networks and that NAFTA perhaps should be even expanded beyond Canada and Mexico, that as Mexico —that our reasons for doing this are political as well as economic, and that as we create a strong southern neighbor in Mexico, their people who have done so much for themselves in recent years now get the additional encouragement and if they can find jobs at home, they may not need to come here to find jobs so much.

But if we look to our whole southern rim, it seems to me Chile has a good government. It could be encouraged. Colombia seems to have a rather good government, and perhaps with some strength and richness, they could help deal with the drug situation in Colombia. So, it seems to me cooperation on that front in the name of free trade is certainly a very positive theme.

Also, we've talked about coordination in other parts of the discussion, as Susan said, the global dialogue as we have G-7 meetings and that sort of thing. I think we're going to be driven to it by the trade tensions that will arise as we have the problems in exporting to our traditional partners that are not growing.

And if the dollar rises, that will drive us further, because I think one —my view on the dollar is the dollar should be what the dollar should be, but what we're worried about in terms of a high dollar is that it shouldn't overshoot where it should be. Because that would, in fact, be damaging to our industries, and I think we experienced that in a previous decade.

And that if we really, through these meetings, develop a true base of understanding, I think some of the other things like that will begin to take care of themselves. I think to be really effective in those discussions, we're going to need to put our own house in order. I believe that many nations don't find us very credible lecturing to them on what they should do when they see the way we've run domestic policy at home. And we will, of course, have another level of discipline on that through the internationalization of capital markets. Those that do it right will be rewarded. Those that don't do it right will be penalized. And the United States is no longer exempt from that law.

So, I'm very excited about the idea of coordination being so important in the next administration's policies.

PRESIDENT-ELECT CLINTON: Brian and Sandy, Jill.

MR. BRIAN ROBERTS (COMCAST): Thank you, Mr. President- and Mr. Vice President-elect. I guess I represent a part of the American dream which is a successful family business, as a son following his father's footsteps. I'm even more fortunate that my father happened to get out of the men's belt business in 1962 and chose to get into cable television and telecommunications. (Laughter.) So, I have an opportunity to talk about some of these issues.

This great conference is available to all Americans on C-SPAN and CNN, not just in a 30-second soundbite, and that's a radical change of where we were a decade ago. And we should be very proud of that. And I'm not sure that all of us realize who don't get the chance to travel abroad how far ahead we are today than the rest of the world in television and telecommunications. Japan still has three or four channels of TV, and a lot of Europe the same thing.

And in this country, as we've heard from various participants, we're really on the verge of a technological explosion and the pace of the change is breathtaking. And I think you're both right to single out telecommunications as an area of great national importance. I think it can mean new jobs, and it'll be great for consumers, both at home and abroad.

So, if I could, I would just touch on at home for the moment. I think we have to push our technological lead. Listening to Glen's presentation on the electronics industry, we were at this point before with VCRs and computer chips and in other industries, and it would be a shame if we don't push to lead. So, I think you're right, and it's difficult to choose industries to encourage development on, but I think this is an important area.

If you do choose to make financial incentives, perhaps that's the solution, as opposed to the government owning the networks, then I would encourage not picking winners and losers; trying to include telecommunications in any investment tax credits; push a policy of more competition, less regulation. If you need to regulate certain industries, then it should attempt to be modest.

And I think that we represent a small company, now maybe medium-sized. We're in a world of larger companies, start-up businesses. If the policies can encourage all of the players to participate, then I think that's where you'll get the maximum growth in the years ahead.

And then, as you look abroad, there are certain markets, like the United Kingdom, where American companies are bringing CNN and MTV and the Disney Channel and other services to the UK, and telephone services, competitive telephone services. But other markets, we're completely shut out. And so, I think you need to take a look at where we're getting reciprocal treatment and where we're being discouraged.

But the Gulf War was a defining moment for our industry, with the coverage that CNN brought to all of the world and that, as I travel around, it's the kind of products that we've invented here that we should really take advantage of the lead.

And I would like to thank you for inviting all of us to participate. And regardless of how we got here, I think we probably all share the same optimism for the great economic team you put together and wish you much success.

President-elect Clinton: Sandy.

Mr. Sandy Grieve (ECOLAB, Inc.): Thank you. I want to start by answering a question that I've answered to my friends and associates back in Minnesota. And that is why did you go, or why did you accept this invitation? And I tell them, look, I realize we're not going to go down there in two days and discover the Rosetta Stone of all economic strategies. That takes a little longer. (Scattered laughter.)

But here was an historic opportunity where you have reached out and invited business to come and sit with you in council, and that could be an historic watershed where we dispense with an enormous amount of adversarial relationship that has always dogged the federal government and business. And if you can find new mechanisms to continue this process and break down these barriers, I would tell you that the one area alone that can change our economic perspective is in the area of regulation. This morning when you asked Professor Porter where are some of these high-cost areas that put us at a disadvantage, such as the health care, the other one that wasn't mentioned is regulation. Now I can't speak about regulation in every industry, but I do know a number of them, and I have included the remarks, in the interest of time, in the paper that you've asked for. I'm saving the postage and delivering it today. (Scattered laughter.) And it refers in here to the problems the telecommunication industry suffers with the modified final judgment issues on the telephone companies, what my own industry, the chemical industry, suffers from.

To illustrate, we make sanitizers that clean and sanitize the dish after it's—the soil is removed you still want the germs removed. Those sanitizers are classified as pesticides, and we're treated, then, exactly in the same way as if we were shipping ten trainloads of pesticides into the ag market, and we have to comply accordingly, which is an enormous burden on us because the regulations we live with are several from different federal agencies, all 50 states, and most of the 83,000 municipalities—all make us register and prove that those, quote, "pesticides" are all right.

Now we're happy to have uniform regulations, and that's a point I would make. I encourage you to seriously consider a special commission that would not last long, but would come into being and examine all of the regulations that have come from 60 years ago and that have just piled up to where we have to have specialists that do nothing but try and figure out what it is we're supposed to do, and then we pay a penalty every time we make a mistake. But let's examine all these regulations and go for simplicity.

Scientific support—do we really need it now? Some of these were invented in the 1930s to solve problems that long since went away. Let's eliminate all that, and above all, let's standardize it and make uniform so we don't have conflicting laws from the states and the federal government. I tell you, in that area alone, if we do that, you'll have the money for your research and development and for the re-training. And American industry would be delighted to invest every cent it benefits there back into those two areas.

In the matter of global activity, I think it's very right, and the messages we've heard about the problems with Russia and that we can't ignore them, and in Africa, and in East Europe. But in our experience in business, the place you lose market share is never where there is a static market or even a declining one because you know that market and you fight to hang on to everything. You lose market share in the growth areas, and we stand at risk—we're going to lose in Latin America and in Asia because they are growing faster than we understand,

and that's where we have to have our policies focused because we're going to lose out, because they're going to grow whether we like it or not, and we'd better figure out how to be much more proactive in working with those nations.

And to illustrate that, just in our own company, we have four manufacturing facilities that will go up in 1993. One is in Central America, and three are in Asia. None are in North America, none are in Europe, and for sure, none of them are in Russia. We just have to go where our opportunities are, but so does the United States, so—

PRESIDENT-ELECT CLINTON: Thank you. Can I just—let me make two points. First of all, we're 40 minutes late now and I want everybody else to have a chance to talk, but please remember that. I'm going to give you a little break and we're going to start. We have put the dinner tonight off by a half an hour, so I think we'll be okay.

First, you ask us to continue this, and I assure you we will. And I want to invite all of you who write in with your suggestions to also feel free to make specific suggestions about how you think we ought to continue this kind of dialogue. Should we do it in a sector-specific way, and—you know, your ideas—I've got my ideas. There's not time to discuss it, but I want yours.

The second thing, I want to assure you we've devoted a lot of time to thinking about this government regulation thing, and believe it or not, in state government, you get regulated a lot by the federal government. I know what it feels like to be governed by this country—(chuckles)—and my strong preference is for market incentives over command and control regulation, and where regulation is appropriate, for setting out clear objectives and then evaluating results rather than trying to micromanage the process at each step along the way. I will do my best to pursue both those objectives. I think there will be broad support for it.

Now obviously how you get from here to there is a complex matter, but I assure you that on both those points, having lived under this government for the last decade, I am devoted to doing what I can to that end.

Jill?

Ms. JILL BARAD (MATTELL, CO.): Yes. I will be very brief. I understand about time crunches. Christmas and Hanukkah are upon us, and being in the toy industry, I only have a few days left. (Laughter.)

We've talked about NAFTA and we've talked about GATT. What we haven't talked about is MFN—Most Favored Nation status for China.

161

And this remains the single most important trade issue affecting many industries and my industry, the American toy industry. Duties on toy products would increase from 12 percent to 70 percent if MFN status is not renewed. Obviously, consumers would be very, very affected by that increase, and we want toys to be accessible to all families and all children in the United States. And it's reflective of something that went on in 1960 when foreign competitors went to lower-cost sources while US toy companies were sourcing here in the US. Our market share was eroded dramatically and it wasn't until we went to lower-cost sources that in fact we were able to dominate the worldwide toy market, which in fact we do today. And we hire and employ thousands of US workers in high-wage, high-value jobs, the kind of jobs we want to have here in this country. So it would be very, very difficult to maintain that competitive edge if we were to withdraw the MFN status from China.

At the same time that the toy industry would be affected, the American shoe industry has 60 percent of their product produced in China. The textile industry has $4 billion in Chinese export. So, though I know, President-elect Clinton, we are all very, very concerned with the human rights situation in China, we would hope there is another way to address this situation that would not affect American industry, American competitiveness, and most importantly, American jobs.

PRESIDENT-ELECT CLINTON: I think there may be yet, but I'd like to point out, after we started raising a little sand about this, and after Congress screamed and yelled about it repeatedly—and Senator Bentsen can comment on this better than me—that the Bush administration finally began to put a little heat on the Chinese. They have a $15 billion trade surplus with the United States. It is our third-biggest trade surplus. And lo and behold, they agreed to stop sending us products made by prison labor and to open their markets to some of our products.

So I don't want to isolate China for political and economic reasons. I don't want to dislocate any industries here. But I do think in the aftermath of Tiananmen Square and in the errors that I feel that we made in the aftermath that we have an obligation to try to at least continue to be insistent about the things in which we believe. And I don't think we'll have to revoke the MFN status, and I don't favor revocation of the market-oriented private sector companies, and I don't favor the revocation of the state-owned industries' MFN status if we can achieve continued progress along these lines. I don't want to do it economically, I don't want to do it politically, but I think we've got to stick up for ourselves and for the things we believe in and how those people are treated in that country.

Senator Bentsen, you want to say anything about that?

SEN. BENTSEN: Well, I—

PRESIDENT-ELECT CLINTON: We're getting results. I mean, they're changing. They like our market. They like the 15 billion bucks a year. It'll be bigger before you know it.

SEN. BENTSEN: No question about that. That's an exploding market. And what you've seen in the escalation in the trade surplus with us is extraordinary. And yet it's one of the most protectionist markets that we run into. Remember that old saying, let that giant sleep, as was said by Napoleon. That giant is not going to sleep. It is really growing. It is a very important market for us. But they must understand early on that we expect, if we're going to have an open market for them, they must have that for us.

VICE PRESIDENT-ELECT GORE: May I also add a brief mention of the problem of proliferation with respect to the export of nuclear technology and ballistic missile technology, where behavior should also be taken into account in our assessment of future progress in the bilateral relationship.

PRESIDENT-ELECT CLINTON: Yeah. Let me reiterate something. I am very happy, basically, with the growth of market economies in China. I think on balance it's a plus for us. If you look at the—if you look out into the world 10, 20, 30 years into the future and you realize the kind of problems we're having now as a globe with transforming Russia and the former Soviet republics into market economies, the rather rapid progress being made there over the long run means a higher rate of global growth which can generate jobs in this country and real opportunity and diminish international tensions if the Chinese will deal with the issues that we put on the table here today. So the last thing in the world I want to do is isolate them, but I think that our country has other obligations that I believe we can pursue in concert with our obligation to continue to trade with the Chinese. And I think that, as I said, I want to give this administration some credit, under prodding from Congress and the recent developments here at home, some real progress has been made in the last few months, and I think it's not accidental.

Dan, would you like to say something? And then Fred and Jack. Go ahead.

MR. DAN TELLEP (LOCKHEED): Thank you. Mr. President-elect Clinton and [Vice] President-elect Gore, it's a pleasure to be here, and I echo the comments you heard earlier today about a great session, and I hope we can continue this in some other forum. I'd like to tie into some of the comments made earlier about Airbus and the aerospace industry. It came up twice, and you mentioned it yourself.

The aerospace industry is a vital part of our economic health domestically and internationally, and I think many of you are aware of the fact that last year the aerospace industry contributed $30.8 billion as a net trade surplus. Eighty-one percent of that came in the civil aircraft sector. Many of you associate McDonnell Douglas and Boeing as the big names in civil aircraft, but hundreds, thousands of other companies throughout the length and breadth of America participate in the civil aircraft industry, which brings me to my point.

I think I have the proxy of Frank Shrontz of Boeing and John McDonnell of McDonnell-Douglas to make the following point: they are not asking for subsidies, they are not asking for protectionism. What they want is a level playing field. And therein lies the problem.

As you know, the Airbus is a formidable competitor to these American giants, and it got there through 20 years and $26 billion of government investment. They've had subsidies ranging as high as 66 percent as they've developed their market share and new product lines. Recently an agreement was struck to reduce those subsidies to 33 percent. That's still hardly a level playing field. And so, I think the urging that we would have for your administration is take another look at these subsidies and take a firm position to eliminate the subsidies which the Europeans enjoy for the Airbus Consortium. That's point number one.

Point number two is that I heard this morning in this room kind of a resonant theme about let's make some investments in infrastructure and R&D. I think that the NASA budgets currently have about five percent allocated to aeronautical research. I think that component should be increased somewhat, and I know that Senator Gore is very interested in that and I urge you to take a look at that. That's consistent with the policy, I think, of Dan Goldin, the current NASA administrator, and those two things, getting a level playing field and perhaps upping the amount of R&D would greatly help our aerospace industry.

We expect to downsize. We expect lots of downsizing. We've had losses of hundreds of thousands of jobs and that will continue. But it does mean we must keep a vital civil aircraft sector.

Last point, and that is the last time we had a clear, coherent policy on defense exports was under President Carter, presidential decision memo number 13. He was unambiguous and it was against defense exports. Our industry is not taking the policy or the position that we should arm the world, far from it. But we do not have a clear policy now. Reagan revoked the Carter policy but did not put in place a new policy. And I'd heard John earlier talk about some of the fragmentation and perhaps inconsistencies among State, DOD and Commerce on exports. That's also true in Defense and I would urge your administration to take a look at defense export policy.

PRESIDENT-ELECT CLINTON: We'll do that. As you know, it's a very tough thing. A lot of this growth that has been touted for our country in the last quarter came from all the defense exports which were announced during the political season. And I don't say—I mean I agreed with a lot of them. I don't want to say they were all political, but it is a very difficult thing.

There was a meeting last year in Paris in which the major arms exporters of the world attempted to get to first base on this issue and they really got nowhere, as you know, because of the economic problems we all face. And it's a big problem for the Russians now, you know. Even though we've done a pretty good job dealing with them on nuclear non-proliferation, on the non-nuclear issues it's almost impossible not to get them to sell the whole store because they desperately need money, and it's a terribly difficult issue and I take your admonition seriously.

Fred.

MR. FREDERICK SMITH (FEDERAL EXPRESS): Governor, Senator. Let me give you, rather than a philosophical statement or two, because there are plenty of those, let me give you some statistics which I think are very important about US trade.

Federal Express today carries about two million shipments, 150,000 of those internationally. Two billion of our eight billion dollars in revenues come from international trade across the Pacific, to and from North America and Latin America and Europe. The major elements, it seems to me, that prevent us from answering the question that Dr. Brown asked over there is what do we do about competing with workers in North Carolina and the Ivory Coast is we've got to go up the same food chain, if you will, that Japan and some other people that have involved themselves in managed trade for a number of years. We've got to get into the higher value-added jobs.

Now, of the things we carry, those 150,000 international shipments, about 80, 85 percent of our revenues come from moving electronics, computers, aerospace, optics, medicines, things that Dan Tellep makes, most of the companies that are in the high value-added trades around the room.

Time and again we observe that the United States loses out in the export of this type of goods to our foreign competitors for three reasons. One, because the United States for years has sacrificed our commercial interests for geopolitical interests, and I am not going to belabor this point. There's a great article in Foreign Affairs a couple of months ago that just details it all the way since World War II.

Secondarily, our negotiators for many reasons are just not as tough as the foreign negotiators. Part of it's because of the open lobbying we have in this country. You made a big point about that in your campaign. Part of it's because the tenure of our negotiators are not as long as some of the foreign competitors. But we simply do not require our foreign trading partners to give us equal treatment. We constantly open up our market, which after all is still the largest single market at 22, 23 percent of the total world economic pie, and we let people come in here, and generally what they do is they'll come in on an export basis and then establish a foothold, and then they'll put their plants in here. Now that's very important from a service industry standpoint because about half of all of the trade internationally is intracompany, Mitsubishi to Mitsubishi, IBM to IBM, and foreign manufacturers tend to prefer to do business with foreign carriers in moving these goods.

Well why is this so important? Even though the movement of goods by air internationally is only about half of one percent of the tonnage, it's over 35 percent of the entire value of the trade to the United States internationally. If you take out commodities like oil and agriculture, it's well over half. So we and our able competitors are in essence the clipper ships of the computer age.

And then, you get down to the third element which we see over and over again, which disadvantages our US exports, and that's foreign governments using structural impediments.

You mentioned Taiwan a few moments ago. Taiwanese electronics exporters can export to the United States. Ninety-six, 98 percent of those things are cleared before they ever touch the ground here because our Customs Service is modernized. China Airlines has their own facility in US airports. In Taiwan, we've been trying for years and years, as is Delta and United and others, to get our own handling there. The government-owned warehouse there looks like something out of an old movie. The customs clearance procedures are archaic and so naturally if you are a US exporter your goods are not going to be as competitive as those products built in Taiwan, in Brazil.

Paula Stern mentioned that we'd had a tremendous increase in trade to South America. Well, the reason for that in the main is because Brazil finally was forced to relax their informatics prohibition and we were able to export electronics down there. For years, they kept our electronics out, exported commuter aircraft into the United States, a high value-added item with virtually no impediment. Our pharmaceutical industry has all of their patents taken at will by the Brazilians and what have you.

And it's not just in the manufacturers. I mean, in the service areas, American Airlines can't self-handle at Milan, Fed Ex can't handle at Milan, United Airlines gets charged a differential rate in Australia than the Australian carrier. The situation in services is just egregious.

So, if we want to solve this international trade area and about half of everything that's bought in the United States is manufactured, is built abroad and 25 percent of our manufacturers are exported, we're going to have to get serious on those three things. We're going to have to have a real focus on commercial exports, and we're going to have to make sure that we're tough, and third we're going to have to solve some of these structural impediments.

President-elect Clinton: We've got to wrap this up. Jim, Jack, Kathleen and we're going to close with Sheryl, who sells in Japan.

Mr. James Fallows (Atlantic Monthly): I'll make this as mercifully specific and brief as I can. As you know, if you look, if you compare the US with countries that have been more successful in productivity and in world trade, there are numerous differences you see, some that make the US look good, in its university structure and its openness; some that look bad, for example our abundance of hand guns. There is one that seems good, but has become bad for us. It's the one that Mr. Poling and Ms. Mathews mentioned before, which is how cheap our gasoline is. I think this has become an important foreign policy and trade problem for the US.

The environmental sideeffects of a higher gasoline tax you well know. There are also some inflationary sideeffects that are bad, that also would have to be taken into consideration. What is not so often discussed in the US is what this does to your foreign trade and foreign policy structure. I think it can be best illustrated by what Japan has done. Japan, as you know, has virtually no oil of its own. All of the oil it consumes, it must import. Nonetheless, because gasoline is so expensive in Japan, it now relies less on imported oil than we do, with our oilfields.

And it was not much known in the US that during the war in Iraq and Kuwait, one reason for the lack of enthusiasm in Japan is that they didn't need the oil as much as we did. Their gross national product had a smaller share of imported oil than our's did, even though they have no oil of their own. And so, for trade balance reasons and foreign policy flexibility reasons, I think it's worth considering this as a source of revenue.

PRESIDENT-ELECT CLINTON: Jack, Kathleen.

MR. JACK OTERO (LABOR COUNCIL FOR LATIN AMERICAN ADVANCEMENT): Thank you, Governor. I want to offer my congratulations to you and to Senator Gore for bringing together this impressive array of college professors, economists and CEOs, but also for including those of us who represent working people in America, especially Hispanic workers who have borne the brunt of the cynical results of the trickle-down policies of the last 12 years.

And so, Mr. Clinton, as you begin to assemble your policy for the future of our country, both national and economically, I ask you to take into account the startling statistics that are a national tragedy for our people.

Today, unemployment among Hispanic workers stands at double the rate for all other Americans. And when it comes to poverty, lack of medical care, infant mortality, or lack of education, it is indeed a tragedy. So we hope that as you prepare your economic policy both nationally and internationally, that you will resist the calls of those who want to deal with the deficit first before putting into effect an economic plan that promotes the rebuilding of our infrastructure, our industries which will result in immediate job creation.

We also hope and pray that you will set aside the fast-track North America Free Trade Agreement negotiated by the Bush administration. In our view, your promise to create good jobs, to promote industrial rebuilding, and emphasize exports would be negated by the approval of NAFTA. And the biggest losers will be American workers, with a special detriment to Hispanic employment.

Surely we need to trade with Japan, Europe, Canada, Mexico, Latin America, and we support a national trade policy that is fair, equitable and one which works to the benefit of workers in all the segments of our society, not only those who benefit from profit. But in our view,

NAFTA is not a trade agreement. NAFTA is an investment scheme which if applied the way it is today, it will impose a low-wage structure in the United States. The main thrust of NAFTA is to take advantage of the massive unemployment and underdevelopment in Mexico and to exploit Mexican workers, who on an average earn one-seventh of American wages.

If you look at ads that appear today in business journals in southern California and other parts of the country, you will see that they greedily proclaim that for every $10.50 job—$10.50-an-hour job that they can transport from the United States to Mexico, that represents a profit a year of $10,700, a big lure to take our jobs to Mexico to increase profits.

Frankly, in our view NAFTA is nothing but an expansion of the maquiladora program which has already cost this country 500,000 jobs, tens of thousands to Hispanic workers, with more than 2,000 American companies that have relocated to Mexico, not to talk about the increased degradation of the environment that we have watched on both sides of the border.

We cannot in good conscience allow the continued exploitation of Mexican children, young women workers by greedy American companies. The wanton violations of labor rights and standards and EPA standards here and in Mexico is a matter of conscience for all of us. And can we really say that NAFTA will help Mexican consumers when in reality the maquiladoras have proven that Mexico is an export platform and the Mexican consumers are unable to buy the products that are made there for import.

I say to you, Mr. President-elect, that NAFTA will be a very divisive issue, an issue that will be tough to pass the way it is. I believe that time is required to modify changes in the text and to provide for legislated labor and environmental protections. We should also construct proposals that attempt to help Mexico resolve its problem at the same time that we protect our interests at home.

Finally, I believe that a national industrial policy to be effective and successful must be accompanied by a trade policy consistent with the national interests, not with the profits of multinational corporations.

We live in a global economy, no question about it. We need to trade with other nations, with Japan, with EEC, and such trade must be effected on a level playing field. That's not the case today.

I hope, Mr. Clinton, that as you assemble your team that you will think of including many qualified Hispanics who understand the nuances of our culture, our language, and the idiosyncrasies of the various groups that make the Hispanic community. For too long now, our government, especially in the State Department and other US agencies, have ignored this resource that is Hispanic America. And I hope you will be the first president to prove us the other way. Thank you, Mr. President.

PRESIDENT-ELECT CLINTON: Kathleen.

Ms. KATHLEEN COOPER (EXXON): Thank you, Mr. President-elect and Mr. Vice President-elect. I'm very pleased to be here.

I have slightly different views on a couple of those issues, as you might imagine. But the bottom line that we're all here talking about today and what we care about is jobs, without question. And, in my view, especially looking at it from the point of view of why I'm here, which is that of a multinational corporation, what that means is that US businesses have to be more globally competitive. They must become more globally competitive, and I don't mean just the big companies such as the one I work for, but the small ones as well. It's not one or the other.

We've talked about a few issues today that affect the competitiveness or make it more difficult for businesses in the US to be competitive. One was health care. We've talked, as well, about another that I—this is where I take a slightly different point of view, and it's more the point of view that we really do need to move ahead even more with the open trading system that we have had for so long, that has helped us so much, that has helped the world grow so well. And we can talk for a good while longer about setting up and looking down the road at our trading system, but I think today what we need to do and do now is to get the GATT round put together and finished as soon as possible. And I would also support—we also support NAFTA. It's not an agreement that helps the oil industry, clearly, in this country because Mexico did not open up its oil industry. Nevertheless, we think it's good for the world trading system, and we definitely support it.

I get nervous, I will admit, with discussions about picking winners and losers. We've had some discussion about this already, and I'm definitely on the side that would have difficulty with doing more of that.

You mentioned earlier that we are—there are a lot of companies around this table that trade a good deal, and obviously we do. You mentioned earlier, President-elect Clinton, about oil and the amount of oil—I've heard it any number of times already today—the amount of oil that we bring into this country. But I simply would like to remind people that the amount of imports, the percentage of our imports that are oil today are a much smaller number than they were in the early 1980s. Only 10 percent of total imports today are oil versus 30 percent in 1980. So, an open trading system is very important.

The second and only other issue I would mention, and it's been talked about to some degree by others, is even-handed treatment of foreign-source income versus domestic income so that companies, no matter what size they are, will not be discouraged from doing business overseas because strong business overseas will mean generally more jobs and some very good jobs back in the United States.

So, this has been a tough decade for large companies in this country, both here and around the world. It's been a struggle to become more competitive. I don't think the struggle is over with. But I, for one, am very, very confident that US businesses and their workers can compete very, very effectively around the world.

Vice President-elect Gore: Could I ask you about that statistic you used, less as a percentage of our total imports than the early 1980s? But what would it be as a percentage of our total oil consumption?

Ms. Cooper: It is not terribly different. It's around 40 percent, between 40 and 45 percent of our total consumption that we import.

Vice President-elect Gore: So, the statistic really measures the dramatic change in the base figure, not in a reduced level of oil imports.

Ms. Cooper: Well, in prices, for one thing, but many people blame our trade deficit purely on oil, and that was what was discussed earlier. That's the reason I brought up that number. But we do import about the same percentage that we consume as before.

President-elect Clinton: Let me just put one thing out here. I think that—I don't agree with this, but I feel obliged to throw it out here, since you're here representing not only yourself, but your industry. There are a lot of people that think that the prevailing opinion, which we've heard expressed today, which is that we should become less energy-dependent on foreign sources, is wrong in the present economic context, that the United States has gotten a heck of a ride in the last ten years from ample quantities of cheap imported oil, and as long as OPEC is not capable of reconstituting itself in the form that it existed

171

in the early '70s and gouging us to death, that it ain't all bad, that we got a steady stream of cheap oil.

Now, I think it is a very risky strategy, because no matter whose angle on this statistic is right, it is clear that if you look at our trade deficit, that our trade deficit largely constitutes—is constituted today of an operating deficit with Japan, an operating deficit with China, and an operating deficit in oil. And there are all kinds of problems with it, but I do think that we ought to—this is something you can all ruminate. You just need to decide what you think, but I do think it's important to say that if you ask this outgoing administration and the previous one what they thought their major accomplishment was, they might say keeping inflation low. And one reason is we had a whole lot of cheap oil, and why should we have fooled with it? And whether it was by luck or design, we didn't have to worry about it. I don't necessarily agree with that, as you know, but I thought we ought to put it on the table.

Let me tell you what I'm going to do. We're going to close now with Sheryl Handler, who is a remarkable story, and I thought it would be good to close with her. We're going to take a very short break. I'm going to start again in five or six minutes. I'm going to implore all of you—we put the dinner off tonight to an appropriate time. We have six presenters in the next panel, three on preschool education and three on what happens after school. They are six very impressive people who have a major contribution to make. I think all of you will learn something from them. So, I urge you not to scurry off too far.

And, Sheryl, you've got the last word.

Ms. Sheryl Handler (Thinking Machine Corp.): Thank you. After lunch, I wanted to tell you that the conversation at lunch and also listening to the callers that were calling into TV were all saying the same thing, that you have a remarkable ability to listen and synthesize, and that we're very lucky to have you at the helm. But now, at 5:30, I think there's something even more astonishing. You have managed to keep a group of the most intense and energetic people sitting still for three hours in a row, both this morning and this afternoon, and that defies human nature. And if you can do that, you can accomplish anything. (Laughter.)

But, on that note, I want to just talk a little bit about the ideas of competing internationally. There is so much talk in government, amongst companies, and in the press about how we have to compete with Asia and with Europe. And while that's important, I think it actually misses another important point. That's not enough.

If we're going to be leaders, we have to set our sights much further.

172

We have to go beyond what others understand how to do. And that's fortunate, because I think imagination is what's required, and imagination is this country's long suit. And I hope that one of the things that you will do is to really set the tone that will spur this country on, and in fact you're already beginning to do that. You've got the company—the country dreaming again. And I—that was a slip because I also meant that for my company and companies I talk to. You have us dreaming again. And that's very powerful.

So, I hope you'll use the bully pulpit of the presidency to drive home some values that have to do with passion. And in business, one of the most important things, I think, is for businesses to set their sights on being proud of what they do and setting off to do things that are significant. And if they do that well, then getting the economic returns. And so setting the values that—what you do should be so important that you would do it even if you weren't paid for it, and I think you have a history of, in your career, of living that way. And you could do a lot for all of us to—

PRESIDENT-ELECT CLINTON: You know, I haven't had a raise in 12 years. (Laughter.) They finally voted the pay up when they decided I was leaving. (Laughs.) Go ahead.

MS. HANDLER: And the second thing—I can't underscore how important it is to have a passion about what you're doing. And also the issue of long-term commitment—you talked about that, it's important for the government to take a long-term position, but it's also important for companies to do the same thing, and one of the things I'm worried about is there is a lot of talk in Washington about diminishing the sort of values of stock options. And I wanted to just mention that stock options are one way for people to make—have a commitment in what they do for the long term, not just their immediate weekly salary. And I would hope that rather than diminishing stock options, that this country would, if possible, see the day where every employee had a stake in their company.

The next point I just want to make is that I hope you will drive us—drive us all to seize global leadership in three dimensions: in quality, in inventiveness, and in cost competitiveness. And if we can do all three, I have no question that we will sort of outpace our own imaginations of where we think our country is headed.

Now how could you do this? I wanted to mention something that I think you have—I think you have an awesome power, but it's rarely spoken of. The government is the largest customer in this country, and

I think you have the potential to use that power very creatively. The—on some level, if we could achieve just one simple goal, is to have all of you think about that. How can you use that power creatively? Too often, government thinks of using the power to purchase as a way of keeping costs down, and that's important but it's not enough, and I'd like to just mention why over a few minutes.

To go back to the first comment about imagination, imagination is important, but it doesn't amount to anything if there isn't a receiver, if there isn't a user. And we all need someone to satisfy, whether it's a small store or a large enterprise inventing new products, or even a service organization, you have to have someone savvy or some group that's smart in order to satisfy. Now who are American businesses going to satisfy? And if you think about it, Japan and Europe had America to satisfy. Japan in particular set out to sell in America, and they had a lot of changing to do in order to be able to be effective. They combined their—the desire to satisfy American consumers with their own cultural values and skills, such as their long-term orientation and their attention to detail. So I can't underscore enough how important it is that our country not look just to Europe and Japan in order to have a market to satisfy, but that we have our own internal drive and standards that we require our businesses to reach and look up to.

So the government, as a smart customer, is so important, and it's even more important now for two reasons—and I'll be very brief—but one is the military has played an enormous role in our economy, not only the direct ways that are obvious, but some of the speakers this morning mentioned that many of the component technologies that have been developed over the last two decades were necessary in order to meet military needs, even the integrated chip. And you have a customer, a consumer in the military that is very passionate. They have to have not only good products, they have to have very good products because lives depend on it, and we need a replacement for that.

And also, Michael Porter's comments about the dynamism in the marketplace—that is such a powerful rhythm, and the need to constantly change and update—in order to do that well, you have to have users that are willing to take what's new. And I want to also mention that Senator Gore is particularly adept at this. Not only has he been a proponent of technology, but I often think the only reason is he can't wait to use it. He has an enormous appetite to take advantage of whatever is at the leading edge and harness it to some important goal that he has. So I'm hoping that you'll use the government creatively in this way.

And I want to just suggest an idea that might be a little bit off the wall, but quite often when you think of a person who is attracted to government for a job, they certainly aren't attracted to government because the salaries are high. Maybe they're attracted because the—there is some power involved, but wouldn't it be wonderful if the reason people were attracted to government as an employee would be in part because they could take advantage of the newest, most effective tools, whatever they are—tools and services?

So whether it's the government buying food services, or recycled paper, or chairs to sit in, or computers, the government should be demanding not only what the lowest bidder provides, but what the most inventive people can produce. And I think if you do this, we will be forced to live up to your expectations, and we will win in the international marketplace.

PRESIDENT-ELECT CLINTON: Thank you very much. We're going to take a—about a five-minute break, and I'll start again in, actually, six minutes. That's when I'll start.

(RECESS)

PRESIDENT-ELECT CLINTON: Believe it or not, we may be able to have dinner on time.

We—I think we have a good idea, which I want to pursue here. We have six panelists—three on preparation for school, three on preparation for work. And what I want to try to do is to let all six people talk for somewhere between three and five minutes each. That will take somewhere between 20 and 30 minutes. Then after that we're going to open it up for a free-flowing discussion, and I'll keep up with everybody around the table, and we'll also take some calls from the radio audience. They're going to kick back in here. We will then wrap up at about ten to seven, or—just a minute. Let me look at my schedule. Ten to seven or five to seven, which means we'll quit only about 20 minutes late, and then we'll get over to the Arts Center for dinner between 7:30 and 7:45. We—I'll start—we told them to start 20 to 25 minutes late there. We were going to start at 7:30. So that's fine. Everybody—everything will be fine, and that's all adjusted. So we'll start now, and we'll do this for 20 to 30 minutes, then we'll open up to the panel and to the call-in audience.

I want to begin with the preparation for school. Let me say that this lifetime learning issue was one of the six national education goals that I helped to write in late 1989 that the governors embraced and that the President endorsed at the State of the Union address in 1990. It is something that everybody in America now recognizes as an absolute essential, but there's a lot of difference between embracing this goal in theory and figuring out what to do in practice. The big problems are at the beginning and the end of the age scale, I think, and that's why we've organized it in this way.

The first panelist is Lisbeth Schorr, a lecturer in social medicine at Harvard, a member of the Harvard University working group on early life, director of the Harvard Project on Effective Services, and a national authority on improving the future of disadvantaged children and their families. She wrote a highly influential book which I especially admired called *Within Our Reach: Breaking the Cycle of Disadvantage*, because she actually cited strategies that work.

Lisbeth.

Ms. LISBETH SCHORR (HARVARD UNIVERSITY): Thank you, Governor.

We've heard a lot this morning about how—thank you—long-range economic prosperity requires an educated workforce. And now we've returned to the beginning of the pipeline, as Mr. Allen called it this morning, the fact that an educated workforce requires investment in young children. Today we have the knowledge that we need to assure that all children will enter school ready to learn. We failed to act on that knowledge in the past, in large part, I believe, because of a lack of confidence in American institutions, especially government. I believe that those doubts that have been so prevalent in the past can now recede both because of your determination, Governor Clinton, to really make government work to meet human needs, and in the face of the new knowledge that we now have. We now know not only that early education and health and human service programs work, but we know how they work and why they work.

We know now that success in changing the lives of disadvantaged children is achieved by programs that are comprehensive and intensive and flexible. They're outcome-oriented rather than rule-bound. Whether they're in health or education or early childhood or family planning or family support, these programs establish a climate that is warm and welcoming and respectful of families and communities.

These successful programs know that strong families are the key to healthy children, so they work not just with one generation, but with two. They nurture parents so that they can better nurture their children. Successful welfare-to-work programs know that it's dangerous folly to ask mothers to engage in training or work without paying attention to the quality of care for their children.

In the early childhood arena, we have a highly successful program to build on, and that's Head Start. Among community-based programs that operate nationwide, Head Start is unique in its comprehensiveness, in its rootedness in local community, and its achievements. Head Start has shown that when three- and four-year-old children are systematically helped to think and reason and speak clearly, when they're provided with hot meals and health care, when families and communities become partners in their children's learning, then children achieve higher rates of school success and are in less trouble as adolescents. They're less likely to become pregnant early. They're less likely to be arrested. They're less likely to drop out of school. And that's why, of course, there's so much support today for the full funding of Head Start.

But now that the nation is committed to school success for all, now that more and more mothers of young children need to be free to enter the workforce, and now that we know that the fundamental building blocks of school learning have to be in place as early as infancy—now that we know all of that, full funding of today's Head Start is no longer enough. We have to now expand and enrich Head Start. We have to expand Head Start downwards, sideways, and upwards: downwards to —from preschool to prebirth to support beleaguered families not for one year, but for the whole five years of their children's development during the preschool period; sideways to make high quality services available full-day and full-year; upward to assure not only that the children are ready for school, but that the schools are ready for the children.

I visualize the Head Start of the Clinton-Gore era to include all the elements whose cost effectiveness and long-term benefits have now been established: prenatal care, immunizations, home visits, parent support, and developmentally sound child care. And, of course, many of those pieces are already in place in Success by Six, Parents as Teachers, HIPPY here in Arkansas. And most often, those are partnerships between non-profit organizations, government, and, frequently, the business sector. What's been missing is national leadership.

If the committed people who are now struggling in communities throughout this country are going to succeed, they need not only new funds, they need new thinking at the top. And it's not going to be enough to move existing boxes around. We have to break out of the boxes we've been living in. We have to think across outmoded boundaries, we have to think beyond short-term crises so that communities can respond to the untidiness of human needs and intervene early to prevent later disasters.

Most of the work has to be done locally, but it can't all be done locally. Resources and leadership have to come from every level of government, but especially from the highest levels to make it easier to put things together locally and to counteract the effects of a depleted infrastructure and a decade of thinking small and just fiddling at the margins.

You know, I think a lot of us have the sense here in Little Rock today that we really are at a golden moment that could transform our ideas of what is possible. If we invest wisely in the futures of our children, we will see the rewards in long-term cost savings, in a new sense of family and community in America, as well as in the long-term prosperity of the nation.

PRESIDENT-ELECT CLINTON: Thank you. (Applause.) Very good. Thank you.

Heather Weiss is the founder and director of the Harvard Family Research Project and a lecturer at the Harvard Graduate School of Education, a nationally recognized authority on family support initiatives. The Project's mission is to conduct and disseminate research that contributes to the development of comprehensive family support programs. She's the author of books and articles and papers on child and family policies, and we're very glad to have her here today.

Heather?

MS. HEATHER WEISS (FAMILY RESEARCH PROJECT): Thank you very much, Governor Clinton.

First of all, I'd like to thank you for including a session on lifelong learning and a discussion of young children and parents in this meeting on our economic problems and how we solve them. I think this sends an important signal that our economic future is tied to our children and how we treat them, that parents have major responsibility for raising our kids, and finally, that we—all of us here and those listening and watching—must work together to support parents because they are raising our future.

We know that children who do well in the early school years have parents who care for them and love them, who are crazy about them, who have high expectations for them, and parents who spend a lot of time with those kids, helping them, learning them (sic), picking them up when they fall, helping them move ahead. We know it's harder to be a parent now. There are more stresses and fewer supports for families. But we also know, as we have said and others as well, we know how to work with families to empower them so they can effectively help their children, and those kids will then succeed in school and hopefully in life.

We have many programs that have been developed and tested over the past 20 years that support and reinforce parenting: Parents as Teachers, the HIPPY program that you're familiar with here in Arkansas, Healthy Start. There are literally hundreds if not thousands of these programs developing in communities around the country.

What do we know about how they help families, and what do we need to do to help them? I want to talk about this in terms of this set of tables, and I want to start at a kitchen table. I want to start at a kitchen table where there's a home visitor working with a mom and maybe a dad and talking about how important that mom and dad's role is in terms of the development of that child: what they can do in terms of reading, what they can do in terms of nurturing that child so that that kid has a good chance.

Then I want to move to another table, perhaps a rocking chair in that very same home where that mom is working with that child, taking to heart and to mind some of the things that she's worked through with that home visitor that she can be doing in that home to help her child. In that process, that home visitor has reinforced, I think one is one of our—what is one of our most basic strengths, and that's parents' desire to help their kids.

Then I want to move to another table. I want to move to maybe a community center where that program is set. There's a group of moms who come out once or twice a month to meet each other, to support each other, to talk about nutrition, how to get health care—all those kinds of things, to build informal support, and to get access to other formal services in that community. At that table, moms are recognizing they can learn, too. They've gotten charged up, and now they're ready maybe to go back and get a GED, go back to a literacy program, and the program folks at that table are helping them connect with those kinds of things. They're newly empowered, they know they can help themselves and their kids. Programs like that help children. They build continuing parent involvement that we know is critical for learning. They reduce dropouts. They contribute to parents' own growth and development.

Now I want to move to another table, where the staff of that program is meeting and trying to figure out for some of the parents that have come to those programs how do we help those families connect with the other basic services that we know that they need—with health care, with high quality child care, with all the things that we know those kids need. What those program folks know, and they've learned through their experience with the families and their experience trying to access services for those families, is the wisdom of the African proverb "It takes a village to raise a child." And they're trying to connect a village, they're trying to build it to support those families so they can help their kids.

I want to move to a final table. And at that table, at the county level or at the city level, the state level, the national level, the representatives of health, human services, education, child welfare, the private sector, a lot of the people in this room, and parents. And they're all at the table, and they're talking about how do we build a village? They're asking the question how can we work together not just to develop a program, but to develop a system of formal and informal services that are going to support those parents as they try to nurture those kids. How are we going to work together, all of us, to build our village for our kids and our parents?

Thanks. (Applause.)

PRESIDENT-ELECT CLINTON: Thank you very much.

The next presenter is Arnold Hiatt, who was Chairman of the Stride Rite Corporation from 1982 to 1992, and for 20 years, from 1969 to 1989, was the CEO and President of that company. He is the Director of Business for Social Responsibility and a member of the Higher Education Coordinating Council of Massachusetts, and for many years was a model for enlightened business leaders around the country.

Mr. Hiatt, the floor is yours.

MR. ARNOLD HIATT (STRIDE RITE): Thank you, President-elect Clinton, Vice President-elect Gore and overseer of Harvard University. (Laughter.)

The well-being of our company can't be separated from the well-being of the community and its employees and especially the children of both. I've come to believe that making this kind of a connection is a necessary part of doing business; it's not incidental to it.

When I first arrived at Stride Rite 20 years ago, I could look out the window of my office in Roxbury, which was then a neighborhood in decay and worse now, and see small children playing in the streets: children at risk, children of welfare single parents who couldn't work even if they wanted to. So, it was only natural to respond to a need that wasn't being met at that time, nor today sufficiently, by opening a daycare center that provided many of these community children with support services that were missing from their lives.

We chose to invest in children because that's where the greatest opportunity was. Early intervention, as has been pointed out several times today, has meant large returns with limited resources. Our training programs for hard-core unemployed young people in the inner city had been meeting with very limited success.

A number of other initiatives over the years followed, again designed to be responsive to changes taking place in the workplace or needs of those in distress. We developed an inter-generational center to bring young people together with older people who were being neglected as more and more women went into the workplace. And

180

bringing these two constituencies together, both now deprived of extended families, children of working parents and isolated older people, was just a natural, and it really became a mutuality of enrichment.

Some other initiatives followed, like a community service program whereby 40 inner city students earn their way through college—earn their way—by performing public service in an otherwise blighted environment where there were no role models. We've developed a mentoring program, which encourages our employees on company time to work with children at risk at several inner city schools in Cambridge. Our family leave program has been around for 10 or 12 years, and is 19 weeks, not 11 weeks, as vetoed by President Bush. And a tuition assistance program has allowed many to attend college for the first time.

Now, these investments seem to be costly to some of my peers in business, but they've had a very large return, not only for thousands of people over the past 20 years, but for the company as well. They've contributed to a workplace that attracts good people and retains them, thereby reducing turnover. The savings on lost productivity, as well as recruiting and training one new employee, is estimated to be $21,000 by the National Conference Board, not insignificant in a highly competitive industry.

And the cost to our company? Well, our financial performance has been ranked in the upper one percent of all New York stock exchange companies over a very long period of time. So, we haven't neglected our stockholders; we've just made additional stockholders out of our employees and our community.

While we've been recognized as being one of the best companies in America to work for, the real reward has been a sense of community that has developed within the company. And this coming together, this kind of ownership or feeling of shared interests, has really been the wellspring of productivity and quality.

And our incoming and innovative Secretary of Labor would do well to focus not only on today's workforce, forgotten in so many ways, as Mr. Donahue pointed out this morning, but tomorrow's workforce as well. Studies have shown, our studies and other studies, that those children who've had a decent head start, at Stride Rite and elsewhere, have stayed in school longer; they've entered the workforce with more frequency; they've had fewer social problems; and they've become taxpayers instead of tax consumers.

More corporate tax dollars for investment spending in education from prenatal care through Head Start through higher education with access for all is ultimately the most cost-effective way that I know as a businessman to recover the competitive advantage that we've lost overseas. And by defining our responsibilities more broadly to include

181

communities and employees, business can provide leadership to restore vitality to this economy and to retain our soul as a nation. And the presidency, I suspect—especially after today's session, no longer a suspicion, I believe deeply—will become as never before a beacon of hope to encourage that vast reservoir of energy and good will of our citizens and our corporate leaders to help those who are less fortunate, especially those one in five children who are living below the poverty line. Thank you. (Applause.)

PRESIDENT-ELECT CLINTON: Thank you very much.

I'd like now to introduce the three presenters on preparation for work, beginning with Hilary Pennington, the director of the nonprofit organization, Jobs for the Future. She's one of the nation's leading experts in developing apprenticeship-type programs, and I can tell you that she and her organization have been involved with our state for many years. And I think the work they have done for and with us is not the only reason, but one of the reasons, that for most of the last year we've ranked number one in private sector job growth in the country, thanks in large measure to a lot of the suggestions we've implemented over the years from Jobs For the Future.

Hilary.

MS. HILARY CHALLEN PENNINGTON (JOBS FOR THE FUTURE): Thank you. That's some introduction.

I'm going to move us from talking about young people to teenagers because I believe that raising the productivity of the American workforce in a global economy is going to require us as a country to improve the transitions for young people from school to work and further learning.

And as I start, I'd like to just ask a question of all of us here. How many of you have graduated from a four-year college in this room? We are the minority in America. Three-quarters of all Americans have not. And for young people in America today who are not baccalaureate-bound, they are on a path to nowhere.

Under the guise of opportunity and free choice, we leave them largely to flounder alone in the labor market, from low-wage job to dead-end job through their 20s, until they get serious and settle down into a stable job. By comparison, 60 percent of all young Germans and Danes enter a structured school-to-work transition program that puts them—gives them a five- to ten-year head start in gaining high occupational skills in the workplace. We can do better here.

A major part of our strategies for economic renewal as a country must be building a system of diverse pathways between school and work and lifelong learning. And one important piece of that, I believe, is the youth apprenticeship program proposed by President-elect Clinton.

Youth apprenticeship uses the workplace as a learning place for young people. Generally, these are programs that involve structured work experience, starting in the last two years of high school and continuing on to the first couple of years of college. They lead to a high school diploma, to a college degree or certificate, and to an industry certificate of mastery that would be recognized by any company in an industry.

Youth apprenticeship has advantages, not only as a way of career preparation, but also as a way of learning because it values both mind and hand, and it recognizes that most of us learn best by doing. And this kind of active, contextual learning has enormous value for mainstream education reform, as well as career preparation for some kids because it addresses some of the things that I think many of our education reforms over this last decade have left untouched, which is how young people are motivated and how they learn.

Youth apprenticeship programs are springing up all over the country, in health industries, in manufacturing, and in others, and there are several thousand young people now who are earning while they're learning. They are in productive, satisfying relationships with adult mentors, and they are on the path to somewhere. Yet these programs are still small, and one of the things we need to address is what it will take to get from a series of isolated demonstration projects, which we are very good as a country at creating, to a system that offers universal access for all who want it. And I think it will take something from every person in this room to reach that.

From schools, it will take attention to the forgotten half, new ways of teaching, collaboration with employers, and making this part of mainstream educational reform.

From organized labor, it will take contributing the experience of registered apprenticeships so that youth apprenticeship and programs like it, by whatever name they come to be called, benefit from that proud tradition in this country.

From employers, it will take expanding our notions of education reform and school-business partnerships to provide learning slots for young people, to collaborate in building curriculum, and to develop industry standards and certificates that could have currency. And also, it will take linking youth apprenticeship to training strategies for adult workers. And it will take organizing work in a way that will require and demand high skills of all workers.

And then, finally, from government, building a youth apprenticeship system or a diverse system of career pathways will require us to test models, different models, to see what works, to build an infrastructure of occupational credentials and high-quality academics and access to post-secondary education, to challenge the business community to provide an adequate number of learning slots so that we can move from a few thousand young people to hundreds of thousands within a few years. And finally, to set an example by offering youth apprenticeships in government.

I think, in sum, building such a system of school-to-work transition will require a new way of governing, a new partnership between the public and private sector, between local, state, and federal governments, and between youth and their communities. And, most important, it will require of all of us some new attitudes, valuing work as a way of learning, and accepting and acting on our collective responsibility to our young people and to our economic future. Thank you. (Applause.)

PRESIDENT-ELECT CLINTON: Before we do the next two presentations, I just want to make—I want to interject two points, if I might. Because this is very, very important. Basically, the census data of 1990 shows that all of our young workers who graduate from high school and get at least two years of relevant post–high school education tend to get jobs in which their incomes grow. Those who either drop out of high school or finish high school and get less than two years of relevant post–high school education tend to get jobs where their incomes drop quite precipitously as compared with the incomes of their educational counterparts 15 years previous.

There are two reports which have come out in the last five years which ought to be required reading, at least the executive summaries ought to be required reading, for the people who are interested in this. One is the 1987 report of the Grant Commission called "The Forgotten Half." You heard Hilary use that phrase. We have at least two members of that commission here, maybe more, but William Julius Wilson for the University of Chicago and Hilary were on that commission.

The other is the report that was issued either last year or year before last, I think last year, by the Commission on the Skills of America's Workforce, called "America's Choice: High Skills or Low Wages." You heard John Sculley mention that today. John Sculley and Ira Magaziner and Hilary, among others who are here, were involved in that endeavor. The executive summary of both of those is very much worth reading and easy to get by anybody who is interested in that.

I want to just make one sort of factual clarification so that we can get the dimensions of this problem. The dropout rate in this country is somewhere between 25 and 29 percent, people who don't finish high school on time. About half of them come back and finish high school within two or three years, so the actual dropout rate that's permanent is somewhere around 15 percent. Right, Mr. Shanker?

Mr. Albert Shanker (American Federation of Teachers): Right.

President-elect Clinton: That's more or less right? Okay, so you've got those people to worry about. So, then, of the other 85 percent, approximately 55 percent of those people go on to four-year colleges, but the college dropout rate is twice the high school dropout rate. So, a lot of those folks who do a year or two don't wind up, even if they do two years, with a functionally appropriate two-year education.

The others find their way into what we're advocating. They go to a community college. They go to a vocational program. They get properly trained on the job. They go into the military service. But there is no system by which we can keep up with all these people. And most high school districts, for example, don't keep up with their graduates after they're gone, and there's nobody else to keep up with them.

Other—because of the networks that exist in our major competing countries, not nearly as many people go on to four-year colleges, so we beat them badly in that category, and they don't graduate as many people from four-year colleges, but the rest of this leaves these great, gaping holes that I thought it would be worthwhile just to fill out the factual dimensions of this issue.

The other—only other point I want to make is Hilary made a point which deserves to be hammered home over and over again. We are now learning a lot more about learning, and we know that a lot of people with very high intelligence levels learn better in practical settings. And we also know that practical skills now require a higher order of thinking, so that the old dividing line between vocational and academic is fast becoming blurred, and will become more and more meaningless as time goes on, which gives heightened importance to this discussion.

The next presentation will be by the very distinguished president of Spelman College, a universally recognized leader in higher education, and someone who grilled me on national television a few months ago, Johnnetta Cole. Thank you for being here.

Ms. Johnnetta Cole (Spelman College): Thank you. I'm really honored to offer some brief comments on the importance of college and university education for the economic strength of our nation. I would also argue that higher education is essential for the very soul of our people. And as I offer these comments, I know that there are any one of thousands of colleagues in post-secondary education who in fact could make an even more pointed and passionate plea than I for ongoing attention to and support of American higher education.

You know, the world praises our system of higher education, and I think we can say—not with arrogance but with pride—that America has one of the very best higher education systems in the world. But the best higher education system, like the very best complex machine, if it is not constantly checked out, updated, oiled, and a few parts changed every now and then, will not be the very best for very long.

So here at an economic summit one hardly needs to repeat certain facts about higher education, but it's rather like what happens when we go to church or the synagogue or the mosque or a temple, and that is we come together in part for affirmation and reaffirmation. Permit me then to launch our discussion on higher education in that spirit and to make, very quickly, three points: first, that education really is a seamless web, and so any efforts to pit K-12 versus higher education, to pit higher education against vocational education and training, or to pit any of these forms of education against professional and graduate schools does not serve any of our students well.

I, too, am thinking of an African proverb today. The one I'm thinking of says that when elephants fight, it is the grass that suffers. (Laughter.) Of course we must focus on improving K-12 education in our nation. Anyone who has read, for example, Jonathan Kozol's piercing and moving book, *Savage Inequalities*; even better, any one of us who has walked into certain of our urban schools knows that we have got to fix K-12 education in so many parts of our America, but we cannot do so at the cost of higher education. In part, that is because higher education is a powerful source for us of human knowledge, higher education is a powerful source for the invention and the development of new products and production methods. It is from our higher education system that we receive much of the flowering of the arts and the humanities, and it's our higher education system that involves and then in turn produces those individuals who search for solutions to the most critical problems in our nation and our world.

The second point is that higher education must be as accessible as possible to all American students. There must be a national goal that every student is prepared well for meaningful work or a post-secondary education. But so many in our nation, so many youth have neither the preparation for work nor for higher education. Let me share two startling realities: first, that a little African-American girl has one chance in 21,000 of ever receiving a PhD in mathematics, in the physi-

186

cal sciences, or in engineering. But she has one chance in five of dropping out of school before high school graduation. She has two chances in five of having a baby before her 20th birthday. And I think of those realities and then I think of what happens in our women's colleges around our nation, where indeed mathematicians and physical scientists and engineers are produced with great regularity.

The second stark reality that I remind us of is that today there are more college-age African-American men in the cells of our jails and prisons than in the dormitories of our colleges and universities. Clearly it must be a national goal that every American is well prepared for meaningful work or a post-secondary education.

In the spirit in which Governor Clinton has called for reuniting America, we must make our colleges and universities welcoming places to all who genuinely want that education. It's incredibly sad when an inability to pay for a college education is the only reason that a person is denied that wonderful human experience. After all, when we deny young women and men that college education, we may be shutting out that very American who could discover the cure for cancer or for AIDS, or write the next great novel, or become one of the most important people in our world—a teacher.

My next and final point follows then as night sort of follows day, and that is that we must focus on ways in which all students who want a college or university education, who have the discipline, and the motivation, and of course, the "smarts" to do it, have an honest way to fulfill their dream. My experience as the president of an historically black college tells me that without federal support, without financial aid, without government grants, and yes, without loans that young folk have a fighting chance to pay back—without that kind of support, many young African Americans would never have the extraordinary experience of a college or a university education.

I also know that we must find ways to make a college education possible for non-traditional students—those who are a little bit older than 18 years of age, women who've been involved in raising their children and now want to pick up where they left off with college.

Just before we began this afternoon, I met someone who reminded me of two students that I had at Hunter College—Anna and David Rabinowitz. And I just received their greetings and learned that they are still taking courses in their 90s.

Because so many of us in the higher education community think that access to colleges and universities must be widened, the way to do that is to attack the problem of the cost of that education. President-elect Clinton, we greeted with joy your proposal for addressing this problem. You have called for keeping Pell Grants. We applaud that and we ask you to notice that there is a $2 billion shortfall between the authorization and the appropriation level. You have called for scrapping the existing loan program and the establishment of a national student trust fund. What a mighty idea!

Your proposal says, then, that all who need the funds to attend college can borrow that money, repaying it in one of two ways. They can either serve in their communities as teachers or health care workers; in short, they can engage in community service—or they can participate in an income-guided repayment program as they go immediately into the workforce.

Your proposal has genuinely captured our hearts because so many of us are worried about the cost of education, and we appreciate that there is much concern about default rates. I deeply and passionately believe in community service. I am one of those taught as a youngster that doing for others is just the rent you pay for living on this earth. But we also know that we must be very careful to work out the details of this program. We must use our intelligence so that a very pure and wonderful idea succeeds.

I want to end, if I may, President-elect Clinton and Vice President-elect Gore, by expressing the enormous excitement I and millions of Americans feel about our new administration. I want to use the words that a campaign worker used the day after your election. Saul Benjamin put it to me this way. He said that "Governor Clinton and Senator Gore have made us fall in love again with our own possibilities."

We look to you for leadership in education—certainly in higher education. But we also know that all of us in our nation have work to do with you, and that's why we're in love again with our own possibilities.

Thank you. (Applause.)

PRESIDENT-ELECT CLINTON: Thank you very much. Thank you. Our final speaker is the chairman and CEO of Xerox Corporation, Mr. Paul Allaire. He's a member of the Council on Foreign Relations, the Business Roundtable, the Business Council, the Council on Competitiveness, and he's been a valued adviser to me and to our campaign.

I first met him about a year and a half ago in Europe when we were at a meeting together of business and political leaders from around Europe, and we got asked a lot of tough questions about this country we didn't do a very good job of answering because we didn't have the right answers. And now he's stuck with helping me find the right answers.

Mr. Allaire.

MR. PAUL ALLAIRE (EXXON): Thank you. President-elect Clinton, this morning you started by stating that America must become more competitive and more productive. You noted our increasingly intense global competitive environment, and you also noted that we hadn't done very well in responding to that environment. We've also heard this morning from a number of our eminent economists on the need to increase productivity to create jobs and wealth.

Now clearly all of this applies to our individual commercial enterprises, as well, and their ability to individually compete in this global economy. I agree, and I fully understand this. I am here as the CEO of a company, Xerox, that ten years ago was on a trajectory to go out of business. When our Japanese competition—good competition—came into our market, we were not well prepared, and we put over 100,000 jobs in jeopardy—Xerox jobs, including my own, and jobs of our vendors. Now fortunately, we did react to that. We have dramatically changed our company. We are now successful and we are growing. But in doing so, we have learned a lot about competitiveness, as have a number of our enterprises in America, from Alcoa and AT&T through the alphabet to Proctor & Gamble and Xerox.

And what I would like to do is to briefly share some of the things that we learned and some of the implications of this for our workforce and our workforce needs. So what have we learned? We've learned to create high-performance organizations focused on productiveness, and have defined productiveness as Michael Porter did, fully utilizing all of our assets—not just our physical assets, but technology, people, and our intellectual assets.

We've learned to use total quality management to focus on real customer needs and to truly involve and empower all of our employees. And we've learned also, as Michael Porter said, that speed and innovation are critical ingredients once basic quality is achieved. And most importantly, we have learned that the American worker given this environment can, in fact, successfully compete with any worker in any workforce in the world.

Now, these new approaches have significantly increased productiveness. And we're not talking 2 or 3 percent; we're talking 10, 20, or 30 percent per annum. And we've also noted a number of examples show that these approaches work in manufacturing, in basic industries as well as in high-tech industries, and for service organizations of all types. Now, what are some of the key features of these new organizations using these new approaches?

Well, the first is what we refer to as microenterprise units. These companies, these organizations, have been restructured to create small units that control a product or a service or a customer need end to end with line of sight to the customers—the things that John Sculley was talking about this morning when he was talking about decentralized organizations.

Second, are self-managed teams. These enterprises have used self-managed teams empowering workers to both redesign and manage their own work. And time and time again, we have learned that the people closest to the work are those that have the information and knowledge to improve how it is done.

Third is the removal of waste. They've involved workers in taking apart the work processing, finding the redundancies, the excess cost, and the waste that can be eliminated.

And fourth is training. They have all invested very heavily to enable workers to function as full partners in the enterprise.

And last is management and labor collaboration. Some of the most successful examples of this kind of approach have been the result of joint efforts by labor and management, recognizing that their common goals far outweigh their differences.

Now, these approaches also take advantage of the unique aspects of the American workforce. The American workforce creativities, its diversity, with the innovation that comes from managing that diversity, unlocking that creativity, its positive attitude toward work, and its natural focus on working as teams: these are advantages that our foreign competitions find hard to duplicate. And the worker in these organizations also benefits significantly. These approaches result in more meaningful jobs, higher earnings, by sharing this productivity with the workforce, as Tom Donahue indicated, was critical, and, of course, saving as well as creating new jobs, really resulting in job security.

Now, in all of this, this is obviously not without issues and not without dilemma. The issue—one, for example, is clearly that change is disruptive, and this is particularly difficult for middle management with downsizing and certainly changes in roles. This also challenges traditional labor and management attitudes and requires change and flexibilities on both parts to be successful. And, of course, the apparent dilemma is that this approach really requires more from the worker at a time of decreasing skills of people entering the workforce. We need workers capable and interested in more complex efforts, working in teams, achieving objectives, often without supervision.

Now, clearly, everything that we've heard about in our education—public education is required. We need an improvement in literacy and numeracy, but I believe we also have to change our approach to education so that we're talking about education for work as well as education for life. Our students must learn how to work in teams and particularly in diverse trends, and understand this value, this benefit of diversity. Our students must learn problem solving. They must learn to use technology, and particularly information technology, and I believe

190

they should learn what business is all about. And all of this should be done by the time they are high school graduates.

But clearly, this is going to take time, and in the short term we have a significant gap from that, and I believe it is a role of industry to fill that gap. We need to undertake massive entry-level training, and we need to undertake massive retraining of our current workforce. The latter is something that only we in industry can do. It will only be accomplished by on-the-job training, by workers learning from each other and learning from their involvement with the work. I believe the government should encourage us to do this and possibly assist in training for a redeployment, which is required beyond an individual corporation. But the main burden, obviously, relies on business and our need to be competitive.

The other point that I would make, we talked a little bit this afternoon about the military and the defense industry. There is an excellent source of training capability in the defense industry, and we should utilize that as we convert that defense industry to commercial enterprise. That's one of the skills that is absolutely first class.

In closing, I have focused on the commercial enterprise because I believe it is a core of wealth creation and job creation, but clearly these high performance organization approaches also apply to government and, I believe, also to our education entities. And I really strongly believe that if we can have all of our sectors involved—if we have business, labor, education, and government working together, we can significantly improve the competitiveness and the productiveness of our society, and we stand ready to do our part working with you.

Thank you. (Applause.)

PRESIDENT-ELECT CLINTON: Anybody around the table want to say anything? Bill?

MR. WILLIAM WILSON (UNIVERSITY OF CHICAGO DEPARTMENT OF SOCIOLOGY): Let me take about 60 seconds to pursue the problem of school-to-work transition as it relates to career counselling in high schools.

Now, one of the problems facing students attending public high schools in cities like Chicago is that in the current system, career counselling is provided mainly by guidance counsellors. However, because the education of guidance counsellors focuses on behavioral science, they tend to have had little exposure to and knowledge about businesses and careers outside of education—you know, the kinds of credentials necessary to acquire them. They tend to have little knowledge about present and future labor market requirements. And currently, they are—there are few resources available in these schools to give these guidance counsellors the time to fill this gap in their knowledge and background.

Now, some preliminary findings from the research that we're now conducting in a Chicago inner city school as part of a program to address this problem reveals that guidance counsellors neither have the time, the informational materials, nor the training to provide the students with effective career counselling. And many of the students themselves are aware of this. It's sort of depressing when we read the reports from the students about their future careers, and they expressed considerable anxiety about their career prospects. And personally, I believe that these concerns may reduce their enthusiasm for and commitment to learning. And I think that these concerns realistically reflect the weak connection between their education and post-school employment.

Now, let me just end by saying, what can be done to address this problem? Well, our program is emphasizing two simple and, I think, relatively inexpensive solutions.

One, place in each school a small but sufficient number of individuals who might be called specialized career counsellors, as distinct from the current guidance counsellors—specialized both in terms of their training and background and their specific responsibilities in the school. Now, these specialized career counsellors would work with students from their freshman through their senior years and provide them with high quality information about career and educational opportunities and how they can and should use their high school experiences to prepare for these opportunities. That's the first point.

The second proposal is to place in each public school system individuals who would prepare and annually update a report submitted to the superintendent of schools on the city's labor market needs and the quality of post-secondary institutions, both academic institutions and vocational institutions. And this report would be made available to all the specialized career counsellors for use in the planning—in planning the careers of their students.

Now, to repeat, these proposals would be easy to implement, they would be relatively inexpensive, and I believe that they would help to ease the transition from school to work for many of these students, particularly some of the students in the inner city schools.

PRESIDENT-ELECT CLINTON: Thank you very much.

Let me flack for him a minute. (Laughter.) In addition to this subject, for those of you who are interested in the whole issue of how we're going to rebuild the cities, a couple of years ago Professor Wilson wrote a book called *The Truly Disadvantaged,* which is only about 180 pages long, which is the best brief description of why the urban areas of this country are in the shape they're in that I have ever read. And it gives us some guidance about what we ought to do about it.

Kay?

Ms. Kay Koplovitz (USA Network): Yes, I'd like to address Bill's point, and also bridge the education—the educational challenges from K through 12 by giving an example of a program with which I am familiar and a participant in, the Junior Achievement Program, which is a national program. It started off as a 5-through-12 program to give students an education about how the economy works, how business works in America, and what the free enterprise system is all about.

We have 1.5 million students throughout the country in the program today. That program, though, we know is not sufficiently addressing the needs of children at risk in this country, and the only way that that can be addressed is in a K-through-6 program which has been initiated and will have 2.5 million students participating in another three years.

So I think there are ways that corporate America—this program is funded by corporate America—can help meet the objectives in schools that the government seeks to provide: that is, training and education to students, in this case from K through 12, about the free enterprise system, about work, about jobs, about what is involved in taking the responsibility for jobs in a very realistic way. And I think perhaps there are some additional ways that this program can work with Head Start to even reach a younger audience.

My point is, I think, that there are a lot of ways for the people in this room who represent corporate America to participate inside the school system providing role models, and most importantly for children at risk, providing self-confidence, assurance of success, and the kind of support they need to say that they are valuable as human beings. And that's what this program strives to do. I'd like to see more of these programs across the country.

President-elect Clinton: Thanks.

Diana, Dick, Linda, and then David. Go ahead.

Ms. Diana Meehan (UBU Productions): Thank you, Mr. President-elect. I would like to take note of something that you and Mr. Gore and Mr. Emerson and all of your team have done here, which is to unite the subjects of work and family, which women have always united. For women, it has never been two separate spheres, and we know that this is true today from a very up-to-date poll that was conducted under the auspices of the Center for Policy Alternatives and the Ms. Foundation, which showed that what women value most in our country right now is their work and family together. They don't see them as separate spheres. Public policy, however, has not always kept pace with the changes in these two arenas, and, in fact, has always viewed them as separate.

And what I like about what I've seen here today besides the diversity and the attitude of excitement and new ideas is viewing children as an investment, which I heard from Lisbeth Schorr and Marian Wright Edelman and also members of the business community, which I think is very significant, the payoff coming to society, obviously, and also the responsibility for children is shared. It is not for government to replace families, or [the] private sector to replace families, but certainly to assist families.

And a few years ago, when we got involved in trying to foster children's support in the environment of the work world through Paramount Studios, which started a child care center—the first studio to have an on-site child care center—and we went around the country and talked about our experiences, there was a man in South Carolina who told us this personal story of how he had experienced it in his own business. And he was talking to the Chamber of Commerce members, and he said "I had a small business, but I had valued employees and I did not want to lose them. And so I opened a very small daycare center."

It started with one child, a boy named Max, who came in as a baby, and he said "We saw Max cut his first tooth, and we watched him every day at lunchtime, and we saw Max take his first step, and we all felt that Max enriched our lives and made our work world a more humane place." And one day, Max's mother came and thanked him for what had—he had done, and there were now other children there. But she said her husband had been posted to a different state and she would be leaving the company. And this man said he was very understanding and he was very sorry to see her go. And then, all of sudden, he realized, and he said, "You're not taking Max!" (Laughter.)

And my point is that this collaboration is to be encouraged, because I think it's meaningful for our country and our children and our economy and also our personal selves.

PRESIDENT-ELECT CLINTON: Thank you.
    Dick.

194

MR. RICHARD JENRETTE (EQUITABLE COMPANIES): Kay just spoke about the opportunities to obtain corporate support for K-12, and that brings up one of my pet ideas. I've never been able to push it very far, but I'd like to try it out now. And I'm not going to—this gets to the whole issue of public versus private schools, and I'm not going to open Pandora's box about that except to say there may be a middle route.

I'm intrigued by raising private endowments for public high schools and elementary schools. Just as we have a principle—the state universities all have private endowments, why shouldn't the local public high school do that? Mr. President, you just mentioned that most high schools don't keep up with their alumni who get out. But I think it's possible to take on a little more of a coloration of a quasi-public/quasi-private.

We did this in my—I went to a public high school in Raleigh, North Carolina, and I was very concerned because with the research triangle there, the best teachers are being lured away by high salaries. And I set up an endowment. They had to set up a foundation to receive it, but it supplements teachers' salaries. It's an "excellence in teaching" program. And I got quite a few other people to come in on it.

But I really think it's an idea whose time has come, and that if public schools had endowment funds, private corporations and other funds would give to it. Even poor schools can also get money. There are people who want to help poor schools. But I think that we might think a little more about a middle of the road that a public school can have a private endowment.

PRESIDENT-ELECT CLINTON: Linda, and then—

MS. LINDA JOHNSON RICE (JOHNSON PUBLISHING): Thanks, Governor Clinton and Senator Gore. I am a business person, but, more important, I am the mother of a four-year-old. So, I know personally how important it is to support all of the Head Start programs. Don't brush them aside. I'm just echoing Lisbeth Schorr because it may not be just one Head Start program that helps us deal with all of the severe problems of educating our young; it's probably all of the programs together.

I also want to touch on what Dick has talked about, and the one word I haven't really heard us talk a lot about is teachers. The importance of teachers in our children's lives is tremendous. In some cases in the inner cities, teachers have more of an impact than the parents do on the kids. Let's not ever forget about that. There's got to be some way to recognize them on a state, on a local, on a national level, through corporations, through the government. I just cannot stress that point enough.

And there's one other thing that I wanted to bring up, and it's regarding the inner city schools, especially in Chicago, where I'm from. The school should be a place that is a safe haven to be in. It should be a nurturing environment. It is not. It is frightening. It is a travesty. The kids who are in school are scared to even go to school for fear of getting shot, for fear of getting stabbed. Something has to be done about that. I cannot just sit here and let that go by.

UNIDENTIFIED PANELIST: Mr. President-elect, Mr. Vice President-elect. We've talked a lot today about the classroom, we've talked about the crucial role of parents. There is another, a third force, in education. It's not one that we talk about a lot, and it is one that I know something about, and that is television.

As most of you know, that's where children spend more time than they do in school. Most of that time, in fact, is mindless or worse. What if we figured out a way to convert some of that time, more of that time, to constructive educational uses? You found that when you went to MTV, young people listened and they responded. I suspect that if leadership were given to making more of television, not just public television, which is already a leader in this field, but more of television really educational, that we could make a difference with some of those other hours. I think we could support that programming with educational materials for parents, for caregivers, and we could make a real rapid improvement in the overall productivity of education because that's what I think we're all talking about, is making educational life more productive than it is today.

PRESIDENT-ELECT CLINTON: Buzz.

UNIDENTIFIED PANELIST: Thank you, Governor Clinton. I would simply like to expand upon Paul's remarks and note that it may be that our best opportunity to increase productivity in this country may be among our existing workforce, those in the workforce today. A compelling case has been made for preschool, for student apprentices, and for higher education. I would urge us all to look at the workforce, promote training in team building, problem solving, decisionmaking techniques, because there may be more bang there than we realize. And I would urge that you consider having government policy promote that kind of training in the workplace.

196

President-elect Clinton: If I might just interject there, I think we ought—this may seem very basic compared to everything we've been talking about. I think we ought to have a goal that at least within the next five years, we'll teach everybody with a job to read and give everybody with a job a chance to get a GED so they can fully participate in these on-the-job programs. And for a relatively small amount of money, every state in this country could develop the capacity to provide on-site instruction in GED and literacy in every workplace with, say, 150 employees or more, on site, never mind other things. This can be done. We've gone from $14^{1}/_{2}$ thousand people in adult education programs to nearly 70,000 here in eight years in a workforce of approximately a million. So, I mean, it's—you can have a huge impact with a relatively small amount of money.

Candice, and Mary.

Ms. Candice Carpenter (Time/Life Video and Television): I'd also like to comment on this school-to-work transition and on John Sculley and Paul's comments on what's required in the new workplace. It seems to me that educational models or traditional models are going to be very hard-pressed to prepare kids for this workplace. If you look at the skills they've been talking about, the ability to solve problems, to work in teams, to be personally responsible, and to reinvent oneself vocationally, it's very hard to learn these by the absorption of data.

I think the only way to really learn these skills is by practicing them actively. Your comment was so great about practical training really teaches higher order skills. I've seen thousands of kids go through Outward Bound, many of them disadvantaged, and acquire profound leadership capabilities along the way by hiking through the mountains, because they have—you know, I've seen kids that are dropouts master topographical maps, which is no small feat, because they were motivated to lead their fellows.

And I just wanted to give one other example about the earlier in education, because I believe this can start very early. A group of fourth graders last year in a public school in a low-income part of LA, in an experiment funded by a corporate foundation, studied the ecology and the politics of the rainforest and then put together the money, raised the money and purchased an acre of rainforest in Brazil, and are now managing that land. And to do that, they brought in lawyers and bankers and environmentalists. And they did all of this themselves, basically. They mastered fifth-grade science in the process. The only problem the school had is that kids were coming to school sick because they didn't want to miss the action, and parents were just asking, you know, who are these kids?

And I think what that shows is that kids are very turned on by the acquisition of the very same skills that the workplace needs, and it's really getting the educational system to respond. And I agree with Kay that I think corporations can make a huge contribution in this. And I just hope that at the same time that we invest in our goals for the year 2000, which really have to do more with catching up with our competitors, that we leapfrog and really reinvent education in this way. And I think the government and corporations can really be a powerful partnership. Thanks.

PRESIDENT-ELECT CLINTON: Mary, and then Raul, and then I want to take one or two calls from our NPR callers, and then we'll come back and finish the panel and go to the audience. Go ahead.

MARY KELLEY (STRAIT, KUSHINSKY & CO.): President-elect Clinton, thank you for letting me be here today. I was very struck this morning when you talked to the gentleman who was out of a job about his need to retrain. And I think as we talk about lifetime learning, I think the only source of job security in fact comes from lifetime learning and from our commitment to lifetime learning.

The only constant is change, and as an employer and as an advocate for small business, I see two prongs that we need to look at in terms of job skills. One is general. You've talked about it in terms of reading. Certainly good employee skills, communication, flexibility.

And the other is specific skills, which we've also talked about, specific to the job, practical, on-the-job experience, both low tech and high tech. I'd like us to be very careful to remember that one size of job training doesn't fit all, and that the role of small business in lifelong learning is considerable.

Most of us got our first jobs in small businesses. Most of us, 50 percent of us, are employed by small businesses, and I'd like to look at how we can expand it and enhance the role of small business in job training and I have two specific suggestions.

One is to reinstate the jobs tax credit, similar to what we had in the mid-70s, which would provide a credit to businesses for a net increase in jobs. And the other, as we talked about infrastructure development, has to do with expanding Internal Revenue Code Section 179, which is —this is a CPA talking—which is the expensing allocation for businesses. It's currently at $10,000. I think not only will there be stimulus to the economy by expanding that to $25,000, but also it's going to provide more state-of-the-art equipment for employees to learn on, to train on, and to become more skillful.

Thank you.

PRESIDENT-ELECT CLINTON: Thank you.

Raul.

RAUL YZAGUIRRE (NATIONAL COUNCIL OF LA RAZA): Governor, first of all, let me thank you for pronouncing my name correctly. I think you're the highest official who has ever been able to pronounce it correctly. You stand among very unique company.

Let me share some thoughts with you. First of all, it's amazing to me that we talked a lot about the two sectors in our economy, the public sector and the private sector, and we haven't mentioned very much about a third sector that is enormously important in terms of our economy and in terms of the subject that we're discussing today.

I'm referring to the nonprofit sector, the third sector. I'm referring to those thousands of organizations who deliver educational programs, Head Start programs, employment-in-training programs, who run national voluntary organizations, who run think tanks that produce the ideas that we're talking about.

I mention that sector because federal policy has enormous impact on the life of that sector. By the way that we issue OMB regulations, by the way that we formulate tax policy, the way we treat charitable contributions, the amount of freedom that we give to this sector in terms of its ability to lobby makes a very big difference, and I think it's an important part of this total discussion.

We've also tended to talk a lot about macroeconomic policy and international trade policy. It seems to me that it's also important to include microeconomic policy, not only in the sense of micro enterprise and small business enterprise, but also in terms of the fact that economic development occurs at the ground level through neighborhoods, and the revitalization of neighborhoods should be an important part of any strategy.

In that context, one of the most effective vehicles that we've found over time to deal with neighborhood revitalization and the creation of jobs and integrating a variety of federal programs to make sure that they all work and that they produce not only jobs but the people from the neighborhood who are equipped to take on those jobs, is something called Community Development Corporations, CDCs.

CDCs were an important and popular program during the '60s and early '70s. Since then, in the decade of the '80s, they've been almost decimated in terms of federal support for that. Fortunately, corporate America and the foundations, particularly the Ford Foundation, has been very helpful in keeping alive a tradition and a mechanism that I think is a very useful tool.

Lastly, Mr. President-elect, we haven't talked very much about the federal role in employment and training, and the program that is our avenue, our vehicle for doing that, Job Training Partnership Act. We had a little bit of a shell game played on the American public in the '80s. We said to the American public, like we did in many other ways, that we could serve the same number of people with half the cost. And what that did essentially was to make sure that nobody got served very well.

The Job Training Partnership Act by and large has not been as effective as those who, and I'm watching my words very carefully, as many of its architects had hoped that it would be. Recent evaluations of the program done by the Department of Labor itself indicate that whole population groups are totally underserved in some cases. The Hispanic community is grossly underserved. But even population groups that are served as parts of the black community, parts of almost all the Native American community and all the Hispanic community, even when you do serve them it has no impact.

So we have a program that doesn't work, not because—and by the way, I want to make sure that I don't mean to suggest to you in any way that that means we ought to eliminate it. Quite the contrary. We need to strengthen it and we know how to strengthen it. We know, for example, that if you're talking about long-term unemployed people, you need to provide basic education. You need to provide the supportive services. You need to make training much longer.

We need to get away from the shell game of the numbers and just make the numbers look good and not provide effective education and training to the population.

I have a particular interest in this topic for a number of reasons. Hispanics are the most under-educated minority in this country. We enter the workforce earlier and leave it later than any other group. We have the lowest hourly wages, and despite all of that, education programs, federal education programs, underserve us, whether it's a Trio or whether it's Head Start program or any federal program that we looked at, we're underserved, and that leads us to having the lowest hourly wages of any group in America. Thank you very much.

PRESIDENT-ELECT CLINTON: Thank you. I want to take a couple of calls from the NPR callers and then we'll come back and begin with Mike Bailin, who had his hand up.

Moderator: We have a call for you, Mr. Clinton, from Rebecca Smith of Lynwood, California.

Caller: President-elect Clinton, I'd like to thank you for the opportunity to address your economic summit. I'm not your typical AFDC recipient parent. I'm attending a major university here in California and my major is accounting, and I'd like to relate to you my experience with my son in Head Start.

When my son started the Head Start program in the community college I attended, I thought it was wonderful at the time. But halfway through the school year the parents were questioning why our children weren't learning the alphabet and simple things like how to write their first names.

The answer was that we would never see our children sitting at a table with papers and pencils, that the center was there to give our children "experiences." I hardly consider pointing to the first letter of your child's first name an experience. Or sitting down to watch the R-rated *Batman the Movie* as an experience. Head Start did not give my child the head start I anticipated. I believe that Head Start needs to have more of a clear-cut curriculum and goal.

Another thing I'd like to address too is that the State of California has been cutting AFDC payments quite drastically. I have had an 11.5 percent cut in my cash aid. The federal level is $703 for a family of three, and currently Californians receive $625. This academic year my Cal Grant award was cut 15 percent.

The poor in California have taken the brunt of it. For those of us going to school we have been given a disincentive to continue. I feel empathy for my friends who are only sophomores or juniors because they have very little hope of continuing. As a senior, I only have to endure this for another five-and-a-half months.

I can understand a system that encourages education and employment and not sitting at home waiting for the first or the fifteenth of the month to roll around. However, the current programs are not communicated to the recipients. I took the initiative and I asked questions, I asked hard questions of people of what was available.

Others, however, live in fear that if they go and get a Stafford loan or a grant or a scholarship for college work-study that they'll be penalized or have their aid taken away.

I'd like to know what hope if any you can give to people who, like me—like I said, I only have a short while to go. But there are many behind me who hear all the talk, all the rhetoric, and yet they see no hope.

PRESIDENT-ELECT CLINTON: Well, let me say first of all, you raise three issues. Let me take them in reverse order.

It is true that there are too many people who are on public assistance who need help that would make them more independent who just don't know what's available, and that is something that the federal government should require the states who get the money and administer the programs to do more to publicize.

With regard to the cutbacks in California, I have to tell you, the hard truth is that California doesn't have the money to pay for the levels of benefits that it formerly did, or, unfortunately, to pay for the levels of access to higher education because it's got the highest unemployment rate in the country, a huge number of people going onto welfare and unemployment, and a massive number of new mandates coming from the federal government to cover—spend money on health care that formerly would have been spent on welfare and education.

So they've got less tax money to spend on people, more people who want the money, and the Congress and the president have made it worse for them in the last four years. And California's like every other state. They can't print money. They have to run on a balanced budget so there are a lot of miserable choices, none of which are good, which have confronted the people who are running the state government in California.

The best thing I can do for you is to try to get you a growing economy out there again so that there will be some money to spend on education and public assistance and so that there will be fewer people needing the help.

Now, I'd like to ask—it strikes me you have raised an issue with regard to Head Start I want some of the Head Start authorities around the table to respond to, but one thing that no one has said in this whole conference is that there are great Head Start programs, good Head Start programs, and Head Start programs that may not be so good. And there's a lot of evidence, even, that the gains that children make in Head Start tend to be more permanent in those programs where the parents are most integrally involved, which is consistent with what Heather said in the beginning of this program.

But maybe somebody else would like to respond to her criticism of the Head Start program. Lisbeth, you want to talk about it?

MS. SCHORR: Yes, I think one of the problems in that Head Start program, it sounds to me like the collaboration that you would like to see between the parents and the people who are running the Head Start program hasn't really extended to some very good communication.

Now, it's very tricky how you balance experiential learning and cognitive learning for very young children, and we do know that young kids learn by playing, they learn by having experiences that don't involve recognizing letters and numbers.

But I would hope that in that—in that program there would be some better communication and collaboration between parents and the people who run the Head Start program because, as you say, Governor Clinton, there is some variation in quality of Head Start programs today. And one of the things that I hope will happen is that, as Head Start gets funded properly, that Head Start programs will be helped to upgrade quality where they need that.

One of the strengths of Head Start has been the great variation, that there is no national curriculum, and I think we'll want to see national standards in K-through-12. I don't think we'll want to see a national curriculum for preschool education. I think that does have to very much reflect the local community and the parents whose children are in those programs.

VICE PRESIDENT-ELECT GORE: Rebecca, I just wanted to say a word of commendation. You seem to be balancing quite a lot, and in the midst of it all you're about to finish an accounting degree and hopefully get a good job, and you have the time to help us figure out some of these problems to boot, so thank you, and good luck.

CALLER: Thank you.

PRESIDENT-ELECT CLINTON: Is there another caller?

MODERATOR: There are. This is David Smith right now, who's called from St. Louis, Missouri.

CALLER: Mr. Clinton, being originally from Arkansas, I want to thank you very much for holding our state in such highlight and your economic conference there. I hope quite a bit comes out of it.

My question is, I graduated from a school, public school, just outside of Little Rock back in the mid-'70s and went on to go through the apprenticeship program through one of the unions in our country, and it served me quite well for 17 years. Obviously, with the recession and all, we've had problems in the construction industry and there are quite a few of us that are all out of work and times are real hard.

203

Where the national unemployment rate may be 7.2 or whatever they want—whatever number they want to put on it, in the construction industry we're at least double that, if not maybe even triple that. What's got me concerned is, the apprenticeship program that you're talking about, I'm wondering how exactly that's going to be implemented and what's going to keep that from overburdening fields that have already—already have too many people in there where we don't have jobs to use the people that are already in the fields will have jobs.

PRESIDENT-ELECT CLINTON: That's a good question. If you look at the two best sorts of apprenticeships today, I think the answer is clear about what we have to do. The first is, apprenticeships which involve labor and management cooperation in a specific area, presumably they wouldn't hire people or take them into an apprenticeship program unless there was going to be a job there at the end of the program, those work-based apprenticeships.

The second thing is a very good question. A lot of people get their job-related training in two-year institutions, vocational education institutions or community colleges, and increasingly the good ones are becoming more and more alike.

And I think I would go back to a point that Mr. Wilson, William Julius Wilson, made earlier about the high schools. We need to be very disciplined in getting those people good information about labor market trends in the area so they do not put people through training programs for jobs that will not exist. There's pretty good information about that if it's adequately used.

One of the biggest problems we've got in this country now with big default rates in the student loan program is a lot of these fly-by-night training programs, set up just so they can churn the student loan program, get the student loans. They train people for jobs that don't exist. They don't care what happens to the people. They got their money. And because it's a 90 percent government guarantee, the banks don't get burnt so bad, and the charade has just gone on and on and on.

In the last couple of years there have been some attempts to do something about it, but that isn't—you have given us a good caution. We have got to make sure that as we expand these apprenticeships we do it in areas for which there is a genuine demand, and we'll work very hard on that.

CALLER: Thank you very much, and I appreciate your time.

PRESIDENT-ELECT CLINTON: Thanks. Nice to hear someone call in without an accent.

(Laughter)

PRESIDENT-ELECT CLINTON: Mr. Bailin?

MR. MIKE BAILIN (PUBLIC/PRIVATE VENTURES): President-elect Clinton, Vice Presdient-elect Gore, I'm pleased and gratified to join this broadly diverse and impressive group of citizens that you've assembled for this conference, and I thank you very much for the opportunity to be here today.

I work at Public/Private Ventures, the Philadelphia-based organization that designs, tests and evaluates programs to improve the education, training, and job prospects of young people from low income communities. And from that perspective I'd like to urge that we not lose focus on that part of your human investment and economic stimulus plans that speaks to the needs of distressed communities with their concentrated numbers of low-income residents, and particularly the needs of the young people who live there, who have few resources directed their way and even less opportunity.

I'd be concerned that the apprenticeship ideas and the national service trust as they're presently developed don't go very far to meet their needs and to provide them with opportunities. The apprenticeship strategies to prepare the non-college-bound for high-wage jobs just won't be a solution early on for many youth who are lacking greatly in developmental, educational, and work skills.

In addition to all you've proposed, I guess I'd urge that some effort and ingenuity be directed to finding ways to utilize the various and abundant low-wage jobs that exist even now, jobs that perhaps can be used more creatively and more intentionally to support the wide-scale creation of highly structured work experience for young teens.

I think the idea would be to use work as a developmental vehicle here as a way to attach youth to mainstream values. Too many of the kids that I'm talking about have never had a chance to work at all by the time they're 18, so that if we combine this notion with efforts to involve the schools, but more particularly the nonprofit community-based organizations, the voluntary agencies that would provide these young people with much-needed support as they get their work experience, we might perhaps then develop the first couple of rungs on a ladder of an apprenticeship system that could include more at-risk young people. I think this actually might be a really good assignment for the Youth Opportunity Corps that you've suggested in your plan.

205

And then briefly I'd like to make one other point. It will be very brief. And that would be that you target some portion of the infrastructure projects on poor neighborhoods and ensure that some portion of that work be done by the community-based organizations and the residents of those neighborhoods themselves.

I think the Youth Conservation and Service Corps, programs like the one in Los Angeles that Martha Diepenbrock here runs, which are springing up by the dozens in many of our cities, might be one particularly effective vehicle for writing this. They accomplish very valuable work. They teach kids a good deal and they provide them with good support, and I'd urge you to consider that as you continue with your plan.

PRESIDENT-ELECT CLINTON: Thank you. I have visited the Los Angeles project and I would like to just ask you to put these two suggestions into writing as your contribution to this dialogue. I think you're absolutely right about what you said.

MR. BAILIN: All right.

PRESIDENT-ELECT CLINTON: Larry and Martha, you all want to talk?

MR. LARRY FARMER (MISSISSIPPI ACTION FOR COMMUNITY EDUCATION): Thank you, Governor Clinton, for this opportunity. Vice President-elect Gore, I feel like a neighbor. I'm from Mississippi, from Greenville. It is good to be around someone who doesn't speak with an accent for a change—(laughter)—I must admit. In the way of my organization, and my organization is Mississippi Action for Community Education and we're a 25-year-old community development corporation.

I've heard a lot of things here today I expected to hear, a lot of things I knew I would hear, and some things that I did not hear that I hoped I would hear, especially given the fact that both you and Mr. Gore, President-elect Clinton, are from rural states.

I come from an area of a state that in many respects resembles an underdeveloped nation. And quite frankly, I wish some of us have some of the problems you all have. We have not achieved that level of problem yet.

(Laughter)

I'm talking very basically about human infrastructure, about physical infrastructure, when ladies who are 90 years old who don't have indoor toilet facilities in this day and age in America, 17 kids living in a three-bedroom house. And it amazes me when I hear corporate executives, I hear people talk about the urban problem, there's no correlation drawn between the aegis of the problem and the problem.

I mean, half of my relatives and most of the black folk in this room from Chicago would admit that their folk are from Mississippi somewhere too. There's a direct pipeline, out-migration, looking for a job, a decent life. And it wasn't a matter of being a good or smart economist. You simply want a decent life, a job, a house, a toilet, and to be treated like a human being.

Today, this day, right in the South, and it's not just to the African-American community but on the Native American reservations, the Hispanic community, we have people living in subhuman conditions today. If we're going to talk about capitalization, then let's talk about it across the board. Let's start with human beings. If we're going to start with people and put people first, then that's the logical place to start.

Let's increase their capitalization. Let's build CDCs, CBOs for those people to work through to do things for themselves in their own communities. Let's stop making government a handout. Let it truly be a hand to help build something within those communities.

And our young people, we must invest in our young people in our communities. It was sad when the doctor was talking about the young black men in incarceration. We have young black men walking the delta of Anguilla, Mississippi, a town of 500 folks strung out on crack cocaine. All they got to do is lay down and stop breathing, they're dead. That's how far gone they are. But that's not an urban problem, that's an American problem. It's a rural problem, it's our problem and let's find ways to try and solve the problem.

If we're going to solve the problem, let's start dealing with the symptoms. Let's let some of the corporations that are based in this country in urban centers—people in rural areas drink Coca-Cola, they buy Bryant wienies, but you talk to those corporate executives and they only give where they have corporate facilities and you will never solve your urban problem until you help and assist us in solving our rural problem.

PRESIDENT-ELECT CLINTON: Thank you very much. (Applause.)

Just to try and reinforce what he said, if you look at the census data, the poorest part of America is still the Mississippi delta between Memphis and New Orleans, and the second poorest part of America is still south Texas, south of San Antonio. Mostly rural.

Martha?

Ms. Diepenbrock: It's hard to begin, really, after hearing that, but I am struck, too, by the connection still with what you just described and the increasing—that describes more and more of the people in Los Angeles in well, the number of people living in one house and the lack of just basic housing and so on. So I think that to understand the problems of other parts of the country through even this kind of an exchange I hope can bring us together in the solution.

I'm also, I think, struck by what we do know and what does exist, and if we can build on those examples by coming together and learning from each other, then I continue to have hope that we can move forward.

I would like to touch on a couple of things that have been mentioned. One is in terms of the policy ideas that have been put forward in the "Putting People First" paper, to connect more of them. The idea of the National Service Trust can be broadened to include non-college-bound young people and can connect, I think, with the apprenticeship idea and some of the things that Hilary talked about.

I mean, if we look at the youth opportunity centers, youth apprenticeship, national service, and also all of that engaging young people in delivering much of the domestic agenda, that while we have these immense problems that have been described so well already, we have young people who want to do something about them.

In education, in vaccination, in conservation, in environment, in health, in public works, the list goes on and on, and I would like to urge that the National Service Trust not be another program but as a way to get things done and broadened to include all young people because for the young people with whom I work, it's often their first job. It's a way to continue their education and get their GED while they're working and earning money. And for now more and more it's the entry into college.

So I think a program can be designed and I think there are models that already exist where it can go both ways, as an opportunity for young people to pay back their college experience and as an avenue for others to get there.

I think also that in listening to what Candice said and again Hilary about the importance of opportunities for young people to learn from their experience, that when we see young people engaged in service to their community, that is when the excitement of learning takes place and that's what we've seen with the junior high school kids with whom we work, that when they have an opportunity to do something about the graffiti or to do something about the homelessness, they get excited and then that stimulates them to learn more.

I think the more that we look not only at lifelong learning as a system but to connect that with lifelong service that young people, even in kindergarten, all the way through high school and into college find opportunities to serve that that can connect us with each other. And I think then that service gets young people engaged again in learning and that it continues to reinforce.

I would also just like to reemphasize the importance of building locally and strengthening the community organizations that do exist there, as has been mentioned, because I think that's where the connectedness again can come. But most of the nonprofits, or many of the nonprofits, are struggling and kind of chasing money to try and put it together, and there are some tremendous examples of organizations that have managed to put together different funding sources from the city to the federal level, to end up with comprehensive programs.

But it's unusual to be able to do that, so I think we have to figure out how to enable the money that exists to be used more creatively and more flexibly in addressing these problems because the funding streams are categorical, but the people with whom we're dealing need pieces of all of those things, and the good programs are the ones that have managed to put the pieces together.

The other thing I just want to end with is, before I left I asked the 100 or so young adults who are 18 to 23 with whom I work what they wanted me to say and what they thought the connection between young people and employment was and what they thought were some of the ideas that young people could be employed to do in service to their community.

The things that they are looking for are jobs with not even 10 or 15 dollars an hour, but to start at six dollars an hour with a scholarship at the end, child care, health care, training to get higher skilled jobs. What could they do? What could they be employed to do? They could run after-school programs, they could work with the homeless, they could provide child care, they could help keep libraries open longer. They could run after-school programs and recreation programs in the parks. They could clean up their neighborhoods, they could renovate housing and they could serve their elders.

Thank you very much.

PRESIDENT-ELECT CLINTON: Thank you. Let me say first that the program in LA is truly remarkable and I can't help noting that Mickey Kantor, who was in charge of putting this conference together, has also been very active in the birthing of the LA Conservation Corps. It's a remarkable thing.

We do plan to try to craft this national service program so it includes people who want to go to two-year schools, two-year programs as well as four-year, and I think we can organize it so you can earn the credits before you go as well as pay it after you get there. Depending on what service you do, it's probably more functional to do it before.

That's the way the City Year program works in Boston. You work in it beforehand. You earn credit and then you go. But I will say I certainly agree with everything—every program I've seen, every service program I've seen from LA to Cleveland to Boston to a program I saw in Florida, they all have the same impact and we need more of them. It's the most cost-effective thing I think that's being done for young people in this country today.

Yes, Peterson? Peterson Zah, the head of the Navajos in America wants to say something.

Mr. Peterson Zah (President, Navajo Nation): Thank you. You know, I've always wanted the opportunity to speak to a bunch of immigrants.

(Laughter, applause)

So, I thank you for the opportunity. You know, as I have been listening to all of the discussion that's taken place, there's one thing that really comes to mind that we haven't really mentioned, and that is if you look at America you still have Indian people, Indian reservations out there. We come from a minority. Yes, we are a minority, but at the same time we have a different status with United States government and that is that through all of these treaties, we really have a government that is also sovereign.

We have in this country three sovereign governments. You have the United States, you have the states, and then the ones that people normally don't know about is Indian reservation, Indian nations, Indian people. And on that land we have resources, natural resources, oil, gas, coal that I don't think is really being utilized to the fullest extent possible by our nation, but yet we look to other countries for these very same resources.

I would like to urge the incoming team of Clinton-Gore administration to work with us so that some of these could be developed. And if we do develop those with you in partnership, then we could have the jobs.

I've been listening to some statistics that are being thrown around by the various groups here. We have on the Navajo nation over 30 percent unemployment. On other Indian reservations, you have anywhere from 50 to 70, 80 percent unemployment, and we have young people that also want equal opportunities to get education, to go to school. Many of those people are now beginning to come back to those lands because that's where their home is. And they want to have meaningful participation.

210

I would suggest that in your program, make sure that we get those opportunities that we're looking for when it comes down to educating our people. Now they want jobs. Now for those of you that are business people that are attending this conference, one thing that we're always looking for is business to relocate to Indian reservations so that we can get into a partnership business with you to provide jobs to the Indian people on those lands.

So before you start looking at Mexico, keep us in mind because don't just call on us when there's a war going on, when there's a world conflict going on and tell us to go fight your battles for you. Call on us in peace, knock on our door and say, we want to help. Because we need your help. We're not asking for a handout but we're asking for a helping hand. Thank you. (Applause.)

PRESIDENT-ELECT CLINTON: Thank you very much.

Ed Artzt of Proctor & Gamble, and then Anne and then Keith Geiger.

MR. EDWIN ARTZT (PROCTOR & GAMBLE): Thank you President-elect Clinton, Vice President-elect Gore. I just want to tell you I think this has been a great event so far and it's really a privilege for me to be a part of it. I look forward to some kind of a continuing opportunity to review some of these issues on future occasions.

This morning I think we reached something of a consensus on a point relevant to the economy that relates to what we're talking here, and that is that it's going to be a national priority to restore growth in real family income, particularly in the bottom strata of the population, and I think that's a worthy and essential priority.

I might add that access to capital for small business is certainly key to job creation and I thought that case was presented very well this morning. I endorse that and our company endorses that fully, even though we're not truly a small business but we recognize that that's where the jobs are coming from.

What I wanted to talk about was just simply to support and strongly support the concept of a national apprenticeship program that Hilary Pennington talked about. This can certainly strengthen our workforce, train our non-college-bound students for higher paying jobs, which relates to that priority objective. It certainly has worked for companies like us in Germany.

And I like something you said before about the importance of the relevance of the apprenticeship to the opportunities to get jobs. In Germany where we have eight manufacturing plants, virtually 100 percent of our manufacturing workforce came through the apprentice-

211

ship program. In other words, they are the only source, not just the primary source, of our new employment.

As a result of that, we and other companies in Germany, where this has been in place for a great many years, are willing to significantly fund this program. I'll give you a little insight into how it works. The students in Germany, in German secondary schools—you explained it a bit before—follow one of two tracks from the age of 16 on. Some are prepared for university and the majority enter one of some 200 programs. This is not just for manufacturing employees. It pertains to electricians, gardeners, all kinds of skills go through this program.

The program lasts for two-and-a-half to three-and-a-half years and includes practical training, classroom work and eventual certification. And the foundation of this is the vocational training school, where the students spend 12 weeks a year for this two-and-a-half to three-and-a-half years, and the state government, not the federal government in Germany funds that part of the program. It's a big expense. In fact, it's one of the big issues in addressing apprenticeship as a major national priority is to deal with the funding side of it.

Today in Germany about 500,000 non-college-bound students go through apprenticeship and they all get hired and they all go into the workforce well trained, and in fact I can say without hesitation that we have some of the highest productivity levels of any of our manufacturing sites, 60 manufacturing plants around the world, in Germany where these students have been trained in the apprenticeship program.

If you multiply on a pop basis the program in Germany and think in terms of our getting there some day, we're talking about perhaps educating two million students this way.

Now, it costs us, just to give you the dimension of this thing, it costs us about $23,000 dollars per year per trainee, per apprentice. Now the salary is mandated by the German government and it's in that figure but that's not all extra because those people are working and they're paying their way.

The training cost is the bigger part of that figure. We today have about 2 percent of our total workforce in Germany in the apprenticeship program. It represents just under 200 apprentices in our company. It costs us about $4 million a year.

I'm mentioning this because I think that business in this country would be willing to step up and take a share of the funding of a national program. I know you mentioned that it's one of the least expensive things we can do, and it is in the form that we've tried up to this point. But if we really want to make this a national priority, I think we also need to look at what about a plan modeled more along the German lines, which has a major funding element from the private sector.

PRESIDENT-ELECT CLINTON: I want to recognize Senator Bentsen but just to follow up on that. To give you some idea of the dimensions of the numbers, 2 percent, 2 million people in America. Remember what Mr. Blinder said today? Early on he said, at present rates, even in this so-called recovery, we would be creating 1.2 million jobs a year, which is barely replacement for the new workers coming into the workforce. So about 2 million a year is about where we ought to be in the training of new workers.

Thank you.

Senator.

SEN. BENTSEN: I just want to make a one-minute comment on that. As we were having hearings before the Finance Committee, looking at international competitiveness, amongst the witnesses we had were industrialists from around the world. And I asked the German industrialist, I said, "If you just had to settle for one thing that gave you a competitive edge against the rest of the nations of the world," I said, "what would it be?" He said, "Our apprenticeship program. Educated, trained, competitive workforce to really create jobs in a country and export trade."

PRESIDENT-ELECT CLINTON: Anne? Come on up. You can borrow one of our mikes.

MS. ANNE COHN DONNELLY (CLINTON TRANSITION TEAM): Mr. President-elect, Mr. Vice President-elect, I'd like to make two comments regarding the childhood issues we've been discussing.

PRESIDENT-ELECT CLINTON: Wait a minute. This is Anne Cohn Donnelly who's a member of our transition board and she's going to be talking about something she does, I hope. Go ahead.

MS. DONNELLY: We've been talking today about making sure that children have a fair start and a head start and a healthy start, and I'd like to suggest that we expand that discussion just a little bit and include the notion of making sure that children have a safe start as well.

It's been mentioned that too many children go to school and confront violence in their own educational environment and can't learn. It's also the case that too many children live in communities where the level of violence almost resembles war zones. Those children simply cannot benefit from the educational system today.

And it's also the case that too many children grow up in homes where their own families turn on them violently. Last year alone there were over one million confirmed cases of serious child abuse, neglect. There are certainly many that weren't reported. There were over 1,300 fatalities, almost four a day, a number that increased 10 percent during the recession.

Children who are abused and neglected grow up with a wide variety of emotional and developmental problems that inhibit their ability to do well in school and inhibit their ability to be productive in the workforce unless there are some other kind of interventions along the way. So I think as we talk about making sure that young children are ready for school, as we concern ourselves with their health and their educational readiness, we also have to concern ourselves with the safety of the environments in which they're growing up.

I think as we talk about that issue and concern ourselves with preventing child abuse along with preventing childhood illnesses, the second point I'd like to make is that I think it's well to keep in mind both what Lee Schorr and Heather Weiss said to us, which is programs really need to be comprehensive. They need to be integrated.

It's certainly not sufficient to set up a single program that deals with immunizations, a single program that deals with school readiness, and yet another that looks at preventing child abuse when indeed all the research tells us and all the experiences indicate to us that both to be most effective but also maybe most significantly most efficient, we need to integrate those services together.

Heather mentioned a program in Hawaii, Hawaii's Healthy Start program, where starting at birth home visitors work intensely with new families, making sure that they get off to a good start, teaching them parenting skills so they never cross that line and become child abusers, but at the same time hooking them up to a medical home, so that they get their children to well-baby clinics and those babies do get immunized. And at the same time, working with them and hooking them up with other programs in the community that ensure that those children are ready for school.

So even as we might expand our discussion of what needs to happen to children in those early years so that they are ready for school, I think it's also important to keep in mind the need to integrate those services so they are maximally effective and efficient.

PRESIDENT-ELECT CLINTON: Thank you very much.
Keith?

214

Mr. Keith Geiger: Governor Clinton, three years ago in Charlottesville, Virginia, you were one of a few governors that stayed up all night negotiating six national education goals. I have always thought that goal number one was put there for a specific reason because of its importance.

I think children are worse off today than they were three years ago when we negotiated those six goals—or you negotiated those goals. And I simply want to add my voice to all of the other voices that were said today. You provided the leadership three years ago to write those goals and to make school readiness goal number one.

I would hope that you now provide the leadership so that we all work together. This country simply cannot continue to treat its children from before they're born until they're five years old the way we do now, and this is rural, urban and suburban, no matter where they're born, and then expect kindergarten teachers to be miracle workers.

If we don't do something for our children, for our pregnant mothers, so that children can be ready for school and so that schools can be ready for the children, we aren't going to succeed in goals two, three, four and five. So I would ask you to be the same leader today and next month and in February that you were three years ago, only this time it's not writing a goal. This time we have to all work together to make sure that those goals are reached.

President-elect Clinton: In the back there.

Mr. Ed Gardner (Soft Sheen Products): I'm Ed Gardner, of Soft Sheen Products Company, out of Chicago, Illinois.

This has been an interesting session. You addressed many issues. However, to me one of the most major issues in America today is the plight of black Americans. Black Americans as a sector of Americans have given 200 years of free goods and services to this nation, over 150 years as second-class citizens and we are still on the bottom. And there's a reason for that. It's not that we want to be there, that we want to be the drug dealers and so forth. It is the really lack of concern by leadership and particularly by corporate America. I mean, major corporate America.

We used some terms today such as job transitions. Black America has been in job transitions since 1690. This isn't anything new for us. We talked about—the economist Mr. Solow said productivity, increasing productivity. Where do you go to increase productivity? In the

215

inner city, as the gentleman over there, and the farm areas of the South where jobs are so needed.

Somehow in the past, corporate America's been allowed to escape and I'm challenging corporate America to do what our small company has been able to do. Frank Brooks mentioned this morning about the role McDonald's has played. McDonald's has been successful because they want to do it. It's just that simple. Such firms as Sara Lee and Kraft and Frito-Lay, they want to do the job.

All we're saying is, share economic opportunity, share jobs with the minority community. And you can't tell me if we could use or spend $240 million (sic) in this nation every year and less than probably one-tenth stays in the black community, that corporate America is now absorbing those dollars. Every morning they're backing their trucks up into our community, selling their products, pulling dollars out. How many of them are putting jobs, business opportunities back in our community? Very, very few.

It's just a matter of wanting to do it. I've been through the whole scenario of going to corporate chairmen and they say, oh, yes, we're going to do this, we're going to do that. And you get down to that purchasing person, it's a whole new ballgame. Oh, no, we can't do this, we can't do that. It ends up that vendors who should be supplying jobs to the inner city, they can't do it. And it's being frustrated.

We know that the situation we have in America today, particularly inner city situation and rural situation, must be accepted as a challenge by you, Mr. new President, and by corporate America realizing that those days are over. It's going to get to the point where black America is going to say, it isn't worth it. And we worked like the dickens to help you become elected and I hope we don't forget that—that you don't forget that in the future because America can solve this problem but it's not going to solve the problem if you let corporate America off the hook.

I just happened to have lunch today—out of about 400 people there I sat next to a young man who was with a company that services one of our primary components. This component, they have a monopoly. We must buy $300 (million) or $400 million worth of merchandise from them every year. I said, gosh, it's a pleasure to meet you. I said, where are your companies located?

He said, well, we bought this company from The Netherlands, but we have a factory here and one here—all of them are suburban factories. None were in areas where the people who buy their products could get the advantage of him returning dollars to them, and he wasn't even that much knowledgeable about if he had any mix. He said, "I think we've got some Hispanics out in California."

We're buying the millions of dollars, the minority, the black commu-

216

nity is spending millions and millions of dollars with major corporations. It's just too bad that they have not assumed—and they're not going to assume this responsibility, Mr. President, until you put the pressure on them consistently.

So I know what we did in the last two-and-a-half years. Our company started a bottle manufacturing company with less than $5 million and we now have 78 employees. Now, we're less than $100 million in sales. And we knew how to do this, and multi-billion dollar corporations don't know how to do this? They don't want to do it. They do not want to share the wealth of the economy of this nation and they have to be brought to the table and compelled to.

I'm not saying all. There are some who really, really want to do it, but you're frustrating black Americans until we really address this issue, and I think this is the administration to do it. Things are not going to get better. When you go to the areas of Chicago, stand on the corner of 69th and Racine, 42nd and Indiana, and see the frustration of loss of life of those good minds.

When our present governor visited our plant for the first time and he saw young black men and women intelligently handling research and development, compounding, just doing a beautiful job. I said, Governor, these are the same black men and women you have in the prisons throughout Illinois.

It's just a matter of an administration being concerned and being dedicated to making life better for the sector of America that's given more than any other sector of this nation. Thank you.

PRESIDENT-ELECT CLINTON: Thank you. (Applause.)

I'll take another couple of questions out there. Is there anybody around the table who hasn't spoken yet who wants to be heard and then I'll go out. Anybody around the table? Al? And then the gentleman back there next. Go ahead.

MR. ALBERT SHANKER (AMERICAN FEDERATION OF TEACHERS): Governor Clinton, Senator Gore, you're calling for a tremendous amount of change, change which I strongly support, I think the country needs. But I don't think the country will support the change unless they realize the seriousness of the problem. We may have this business cycle upturn and maybe quite a few people will think the problem is solved, so at least with respect to lifelong learning they ought to look at and become familiar with some of the achievement results in this country.

Youngsters who graduate high school—we can't test those who quit. We can only test those who are still there, but youngsters who are still

217

there and about to graduate, only three percent who graduate are able to write a good letter or essay. Only six percent are able to read any of the books you talked about and it's going to be great to have a president who reads good books. And only five percent of them can perform the mathematics which is required for college entry in any other industrial country in the world.

So we've got a lot of very satisfied parents out there because their kids are going to college and they don't realize that their kids are going to college and getting an education which in every other industrial country would be their high school education or their junior high school education. So we've kind of found a way to make people happy by changing the standards.

And I think that these achievement results point out that while we have very special and very difficult problems with youngsters who are in poverty, and I think everything that's been said today about the special things that need to be done for them and their communities and their families and their schools are certainly true, that this shows that we have an overall problem with almost all the kids in this country who are students.

Now what's good about what you're proposing is that it's not a magic bullet, just do this and it's going to handle all the problems. If we were businessmen and we were losing to some competitors, the first thing we'd probably do is take a look at what are they doing that we're not doing. And it seems to me that that's pretty easy to see.

Other industrial countries do not have the childhood poverty that we have in this country. These other countries have early childhood and day care systems and they're not targeted only to poor youngsters. They are for all parents. I think it's time that we had an integrated high quality early childhood system in this country, and people who can afford to pay ought to pay. I'm not saying that the whole thing ought to be a government-financed program. I think that's one of the things that education is about, is having all kinds of kids be with each other, from a very early age. And, while Head Start has been great, I think it's about time that we made it greater by getting everybody into it and having kids start with each other. Kids in these other countries don't have to worry about medical care. There are policies which don't force women especially to make the horrible choices that they have to between caring for family and work.

These are some of the things, but there are other things, too. All these countries have national standards in place so that every teacher and every youngster and every parent and every employer, they all know what you're supposed to know when you're 18 or 19 years of age.

By the way, those figures of three percent, five percent, six percent, reaching those standards in the United States, in Germany it's over 30 percent who reach that top standard. It France it's 26 percent, and they're not throwing their other kids away. These are the college entry kids. Most of those countries, except for the English-speaking countries, are really doing a good job for all the kids.

They have national high standards so that everybody works hard to achieve them. Until we deal with that—and there's a lot of talk about how we can't have national standards. I'm not talking about federally mandated standards. I'm talking about standards which as a nation we grow to accept, and I think if you put good standards out there there'll be a lot of states that accept them.

But they have assessment systems. They have teachers who have different status than our teachers do. By the way, part of that status has to do with income distribution in those countries. If you look at it in dollar terms, their teachers may make about what teachers make here, but in the United States you're looking at what other college graduates make and so that makes a difference.

They've got textbooks that are geared to the curriculum and they're able to have very good ones because they've thought about the curriculum over a period of time and textbook publishers in this country try to sell in eight or ten states so they've got to have a big fat, boring, unfocused book that corresponds to what ten different states think should happen.

The other thing they've got there is that they have got very clear and visible consequences for youngsters and teachers and others. That is, a youngster knows that if he doesn't reach a certain standard, he doesn't go to college. If he doesn't make another standard, he doesn't qualify for the apprenticeship program or he doesn't qualify for something else and that makes people work harder and makes them achieve.

What we've been doing in this country for a good many years, which is essentially fooling people and giving them pieces of paper that don't stand for anything, we're not helping the kids because eventually there's a marketplace out there that sorts the kids out in terms of what they really know and are able to do.

These other countries do have this widespread apprenticeship program and I want to say something that one or two others have said. I don't think it's going to work on a voluntary basis. I think you need something like pay or play. There's no reason why if I were an employer I should train lots of people who will then be stolen by somebody next—taken away by somebody down the road who isn't making that sort of investment. So it's the kind of thing where the whole country and all employers ought to make that sort of a contribution. And they have systems of lifelong retraining.

I'd like to just say one or two other things and conclude quickly.

John Sculley talked about a new type of workplace. Well, the school is a workplace. It's a workplace for students and it's a workplace for teachers. And if we're going to educate students to work in new types of workplaces, the school has to be a new type of workplace because the schools that we have today resemble the old-fashioned factories and if we're going to have new types of workplaces, the school has to reflect that and youngsters have to start working in a very different environment.

I too want to underline Jonathan Kozol's *Savage Inequalities*. We talk about equality of educational opportunity. I don't see what we can possibly mean by that phrase if we take the youngsters who start with the greatest handicaps, the greatest difficulties, and give them less of a chance in all sorts of ways, in how we distribute books and money and teachers and buildings and everything else. We need to do something about that.

Finally, in this audience, Ernie Boyer is here and about 20 years ago he gave a speech which he sent to me at that time. He said, we now have Medicare in this country and other countries have had these systems of caring for the body from the cradle to the grave. He said, well it's about time we had a similar notion for education because education is not something that just starts when you're five or six and ends when you're 18, and he said we need to have a concept of education which goes from the cradle to the grave, which he in that speech called Educare.

I'm sure that as he's sitting in the audience and listening to your proposals for this great new vision of what education is about, it's too bad we had to wait all these years but thank God it's finally happening.

PRESIDENT-ELECT CLINTON: Let me just say one of the things—I would invite particularly those who care about this educational equality issue, equality of funding, to give me any suggestions that they think are appropriate, for federal incentives at least, to try to get the states to equalize funding.

You know, over 90 percent of the funds for public education come from the state and local level. The federal government share used to be about 10 percent. It's now I think something just under seven. We're going to try to get it up again. Keith says it's less than that. But our leverage is a little less.

But I'll say this. It's interesting to me. A lot of the same people who will tell you that it's not a money problem all of a sudden change their opinion if you want to redistribute the way the money's spent. And it's one of my rules of politics is when somebody tells you it's not a money problem, they're talking about somebody else's problem. (Laughter.)

But it isn't entirely a money problem but there is the resource relationship. There's no question about it.

Leon, did you have a question, comment?

REP. PANETTA: No, I'm glad you said what you said, because I think a word of caution is in order. We've talked about a lot of programs and we've talked about a lot of efforts that have to be made, and most of these programs I think most of us would support strongly.

But as you do it with limited resources, it's going to be very important that we target this assistance to the programs that work and not simply think that we can shoot money at a whole sphere of other programs. We're going to have to be very targeted.

We did this last year as a matter of fact. Even as we tried to fully fund Head Start, we also recognized that in funding Head Start we wanted to transition it in because we didn't want to just throw a lot of money out there so that people assumed that they could just start a Head Start without making sure that that program worked.

So I guess just several cautionary notes here. One, it ought to be highly targeted to the programs that work. Secondly, we ought to transition some of this money in, as we see that it's able to perform according to the standards that we want, and thirdly, I would hope that people would use their imagination in terms of funding because with the kind of limited resources and the other constraints we're facing, we're going to have to use our imagination about how we approach some of these programs.

PRESIDENT-ELECT CLINTON: You know, I think we ought to quit, unless somebody else around the table who hasn't talked wants to say anything. It's 8:00, and we all have got to go over to the Arts Center and have dinner. Hillary doesn't want to talk. She already said that.

This has been a fascinating session. I'd like to give the panelists another hand. They were great.

END OF DAY ONE CONFERENCE ACTIVITIES

Economic Conference Morning Session Tuesday, December 15, 1992

President-elect Clinton: Good morning. I want to begin by thanking you all for yesterday. It was, I thought, a remarkably successful day, thanks to our participants, not only those who had a formal role, but those who spoke around the table and in the audience. And I want to thank the people who called in, too. I thought they did a very good job.

This morning, we're going to deal with a number of topics which I hope will lead us toward some options for specific policy actions, beginning with the second working session on investment for short-term growth. There will be three analysts who will begin today, and I just want to—I'll introduce them all at one time. They'll talk for a few minutes each. James Tobin, Allen Sinai, and Charles McMillion.

James Tobin was the winner of the Nobel Prize in Economics in 1981, one of the first of six Nobel winners to endorse our platform in the campaign. He's Sterling (sic) Professor of Economics Emeritus at Yale, where he has taught since 1950. He was a member of President Kennedy's Council of Economic Advisors and is a member of the National Academy of Sciences.

Allen Sinai is executive vice president and the chief economist of the Boston Company and president and CEO of the Boston Company Economic Advisors, Inc., a wholly owned subsidary. He's a well-known forecaster, educator, and econometric model builder, known for his analyses and forecasts of financial markets, and is the developer of the Sinai Boston Model of the United States economy. Before founding his company in 1988, he was the chief economist and managing director at Shearson Lehman Brothers.

Charles McMillion is the president of MBG, the Washington-based business information, analysis, and forecasting firm, former associate director and senior research fellow and associate professor at the Johns Hopkins University Policy Institute, where he researched business and economic policy in the United States and abroad. He's also served in various staff director and economist positions with the United States Congress.

Mr. Tobin, the floor is yours.

Mr. James Tobin (Yale University): Mr. President-elect, Mr. Vice President-elect, I think this is the most remarkable and memorable conference I have ever attended in my career of attending a lot of conferences. The excitement of this transition reminds me of the transition to the Kennedy administration in 1960, which I enjoyed as well.

The nation suffers from two macroeconomic maladies. It's important to keep them straight. One is a demand-side problem and the other is a supply-side problem. One is a short-run, business-cycle problem; the other is a long-run trend problem. And one of them concerns jobs, creating jobs and restoring them; the other concerns the quality of jobs and the real wages that they will earn.

The challenge to the coming administration is to provide medicines for both of those maladies at the same time, although it may seem that they, in some respects, demand exactly the opposite medicines.

Growth of the capacity of the economy is what determines the trend of real gross domestic product over the long run. Reading it across business cycles and across the decades rather than from year to year or quarter to quarter, potential gross domestic product at full employment—let's say full employment is around 5½ percent unemployment rate—the potential of the economy to produce goods and services grows at about 2½ percent per year, maybe a bit less, maybe a bit more. About half of that is due to the growth of the labor force, new workers coming on the scene, and the other half is due to the growth in productivity.

Now, yesterday, you heard from Bob Solow and others that the growth of gross domestic product over the long run is too slow and that particularly the growth of productivity is too slow, lower than it was in this country before 1973 and lower than it is in the other advanced democratic capitalist countries. And that's the long-run problem, the long-run malady. And we need to increase the rate of growth and increase potential GDP for the benefit of our kids and their children and their grandchildren and so on.

The short-run problem, short-run business cycle difficulty, is that we haven't even kept up in the last four years with the capacity that we're able to produce. And the symptom of that is excess industrial capacity to produce, and unemployment, and other symptoms of excess labor supply. So the recovery problem is to get back to the potential track to use the excess capacity, and use the idle workers that we've got today.

That 2½ percent is—call it the sustainable growth rate of the economy because it's that growth of GDP that will just absorb the new workers and the growth in productivity. Growing at the sustainable rate won't put unemployed workers back to work, and won't reduce the unemployment rate. It may do so from one month to another, but not in a longer horizon.

The par for the United States' macroeconomy is 2½ percent growth or thereabouts, not zero growth. When we have positive growth in GDP, but it's below 2 percent, it's nothing to write home about, it's a failure, and that's what we've had for the last four years, most of the time. So relative to the sustainable growth rate, the par of 2½ percent, the economy has been in recession for four years. And most of that time, GDP was growing positively, but less than 2 percent or 2¹/₂ percent, and that's why unemployment increased by 2¹/₂ or 2 points, about 2¹/₂ million people. And that—the other implication of that is by falling short for four years of our capacity to produce, we opened up a gap between the actual GDP and the potential GDP of around 5 or 6 percent. And we have to grow, in addition to our normal sustainable growth for the next four years, we have to grow, in total, another 5 or 6 percent in order to return to a decently low rate of unemployment.

The—that means that on average over four years we have to grow about 1¹/₂ points more than the sustainable rate—that means around 4, I'd say 3¹/₂ to 4 percent on average for four years, just to return to the potential track with 5¹/₂ percent unemployment. That's the speed of recovery that would be needed to create 8 or 9 million jobs in the next four years—8 or 9 million meaning approximately 5 million—a little more than that—for new workers, and let's say another 1 million for workers who have left the labor force because they know there are no jobs out there and they are discouraged, and who will return in prosperity, and 2¹/₂ million workers who are now unemployed.

And will that catch-up recovery of demand—will that occur on its own, or are we going to need some fiscal stimulus? The problem is a demand side problem; that is, there is not enough spending going on by whoever spends—that's consumers, foreigners buying our exports, governments buying goods and services, businesses making investments. So is there a case for stimulus to create the jobs we need by 1996? I think there is. The labor market is weaker than the unemployment rate suggests, for several reasons. Many workers are involuntarily working short-time when they would like to be working full-time. Most strikingly, there is a very high—a very low rate of vacancies, as measured by the help wanted index. It is unusually low for the present levels of employment—unemployment rate, and suggests there are just not jobs waiting out there for workers who are displaced.

As everybody knows, we're experiencing a serious and unusual series of layoffs by businesses—permanent layoffs, not temporary, cyclical layoffs—it's downsizing. And some of that's related to defense cutbacks, and it's inevitable in these times. Some of it is the belated adaptations of many of our firms to global competition. So despite some—the recent favorable economic news, notably the 3.9 percent growth rate on an annualized basis in the one quarter—third quarter reporting, there—we still have a big problem to reduce unemployment and catch up with potential, and we have a big problem of finding where the demand is going to come from to do that job. Rudi Dornbusch told us yesterday about the slumps in the foreign countries that represent the chief demands for our exports. And we're having very low investment these days. It's scarcely—private investment is scarcely exceeding what it was four years ago in real terms.

The one piece of good news in recent reports was the high rate of productivity growth in the third quarter of nineteen—of this year. Well, that's good news in the sense that if it is a portent of a higher rate of productivity growth that will continue to happen—and we all know that it is—that will continue to happen, then that was relieving the long-run problem of productivity growth that I referred to earlier, and that would be good news. But the flip side of that is that it means that we would need more of an increase in demand, more of an increase in production in GDP to catch up with potential, because potential would be a little higher than we estimated it to be before.

One question is, why can't the Federal Reserve do this job by itself? Well, we heard about the bank credit crunch yesterday, and we see that the Fed has more or less given up on doing anything more to stimulate demand even though it has 300 basis points left between interest rates—short-term interest rates now and zero. I think maybe the Fed did things so late and so little during the recent downturn that they let the economy and business expectations slip away from their grasp. That's why the country needs some fiscal stimulus in the short run. Almost every cyclical recovery since the Second World War has had the help of fiscal stimulus, and you recall that the one in the 1980s had the most massive fiscal stimulus that's ever been given in peace-time thanks to the Reagan tax cuts and defense build-up.

At the moment, inflation is unlikely, non-existent, and it's going to —we're a long way from having congestion in the capital markets. There's not any particular reason to hold back on expanding the economy for those reasons. You will—you of the new administration will want to get the Federal Reserve on your side so that they will accommodate a decent recovery, a prudent recovery, and I would hope that the Treasury under the new secretary will stop issuing long-term bonds at excessively high long-term interest rates.

Now, fiscal policy for recovery is bound to raise the deficit temporarily. And we're fooling ourselves if you think there's a way of having a fiscal stimulus that doesn't have that result. The thing to do, I believe, is to combine the short-run fiscal stimulus with credible deficit reduction policies that will be phased in at a later time—so far as possible, enacted so that they will come into effect at a later time, whether they are tax increases or expenditure reductions. And we know that one of the necessities of any deficit reduction plan in the longer run is a solution to the health care problem.

In today's weak economy, a fiscal austerity would be counter-productive and would actually reduce investment in plant and equipment and technology and human capital for the future. So it actually damaged the prospects of our children and grandchildren rather than improving them. In a robust economy, two or three years from now, it would help to reduce the deficit—at least reduce the deficit as it finances consumption in order to divert saving from deficit financing to productive investment. In the meanwhile, the Clinton administration has the opportunity to provide a fiscal stimulus needed for short-run recovery by borrowing and spending in ways that leave behind them permanent gains in productivity due to investments in infrastructure and education, a[n] admirable contrast with the purposes for which deficits were accumulated in the 1980s.

Thank you.

PRESIDENT-ELECT CLINTON: Thank you. (Applause.)

MR. ALLEN SINAI (THE BOSTON COMPANY): Thank you, Mr. President-elect and Vice President-elect. I want to focus—I'm tempted to say "like a laser beam"—(laughter)—on the topic of investment for short-term growth: Is the economy growing enough fast enough to create enough jobs?

The US economy is not growing fast enough to create enough permanent new jobs. The economy is growing faster than it was before, having picked up and is now in sort of recovery, but at a pace that will not generate anywhere near the usual number of permanent new jobs that occur, nor enough jobs to reduce the unemployment rate very much over the next year.

The economy looks like it's growing at about a $2^1/2$ to 3 percent pace, perhaps higher near term. But this range on average over the next year could probably only produce non-firm payroll jobs of 100,000 to 125,000 a month whereas typically 200,000 to 300,000 jobs per month are generated. A significant number of new jobs that are occurring are in health care, the cost of which holds down the economy elsewhere. Many of the jobs have been in temporary positions.

Why are so few jobs being created? One, weak economic growth is the primary reason; $3^1/2$ years of almost no growth; seven tenths of a percent per annum. Second, structural changes in the US economy are another, such as in defense, where huge numbers of jobs are being lost. Third, management practices, especially for large companies, which now keep jobs down to a minimum as a strategy for increasing profits. Fourth, skills mismatches, especially for those with only a K through 12 educational background, not enough basic skills for many of the jobs in an information, knowledge-based and highly technological US and world economy. And fifth, technological change; the substitution of machines and new technology for people in order to increase the productivity of those who are still working, and because of high employee health care costs, pension fund liabilities, and possible litigation expenses.

More rapid economic growth is the principal way to generate permanent new jobs, but this is difficult now in an economy beset by numerous long-run structural problems and a huge structural budget deficit that ultimately must be worked down and balanced. A safe rate of growth over the next year or two would be about 3.5 percent on average, given the current potential of the economy, in order to permit a gradual downward movement in the unemployment rate without reigniting inflation. This rate of growth also would permit policies to be designed and implemented to lift long-run potential output in productivity so that later, faster growth in potential supply could permit faster short-run actual growth.

How can the faster growth necessary to create the new jobs be achieved? Ultimately it is long-run potential output, the maximum or optimum growth attainable for the economy, that must be raised. This rate is only about 2 percent, by our estimates, maybe 2.5 percent a year now, down sharply from the earlier post-war trend of 3 percent-plus, and a real speed limit on growth in jobs in the short and long run.

In the short run, a modest dose of net fiscal stimulus probably is necessary to lift growth and jobs as part of the task of raising potential growth in the long run, as well as to sustain a fledgling business expansion. A $20 billion to $30 billion program of short-run fiscal stimulus, I believe, should be ready to go, legislated as needed in early 1993, although with an option to put it on hold should the current pick-up in the economy gather too much momentum.

The characteristics of the measures used in this fiscal stimulus, I think, should be—they should do double duty or be efficient in the sense of being measures that lift short-run growth and jobs, but also raise long-run potential output. Candidates for double duty or efficient measures of this sort include: infrastructure spending on roads, highways, buildings, airports, rail and telecommunications; and equipment investment tax credits, all of which can lift jobs and growth short run, but also can add to potential output longer run. Investment tax credits would produce the greatest bang for a buck if they were targeted toward productive equipment, incremental and refundable. Other possibilities are measures such as inflation indexing of capital gains, R&D tax credits, education and manpower training programs, and incentives for small business.

Short-run fiscal stimulus can be viewed as insurance to make sure that the economy permanently exits its weak state or as a down payment now on the long-run measures necessary to rebuild the nation's capital stock, raise productivity growth, improve educational capabilities, and to raise long-run potential output. To be stimulative, such measures necessarily involve a temporary planned increase in the federal budget deficit.

But a major effort should be made to find measures that can raise growth without raising the federal budget deficit. Some possibilities include: an easier bank regulatory environment for bank lending to improve growth at little cost to the budget; a shift in the composition of Treasury financing further away from long-term issues to reduce the interest costs of federal government financing; greater efficiencies and reduced costs for the provision and delivery of health care services; new financing mechanisms for infrastructure programs, such as new tax-exempt securities or financing agencies which issue securities backed by or insured through the federal government.

Would investment in short-run growth conflict with the goal of reducing the federal budget deficit in the longer run? Not necessarily. It must be noted that faster growth produces additional tax revenues and less government spending on unemployment benefits. Fiscal measures that raise deficits and growth thus will help pay for themselves, although not fully. If the measures are efficient, lifting growth and jobs near-term and raising potential output long-term, the potential of the economy to generate more tax revenues at full employment would be enhanced.

Unfortunately, there are two big macro problems for the economy now, at least on the domestic side—inadequate growth with too few jobs, and too high structural budget deficits. Both cannot be corrected at the same time in the short run. Using fiscal policy to raise growth initially means higher deficits. Reducing deficits with fiscal policy means less growth and fewer jobs. Therefore, a sequencing choice is necessary. On economic grounds, the preference should be greater growth and more jobs first, using fiscal policy measures at the cost of a temporarily higher budget deficit and then eliminating the structural budget deficit later.

So, if it is decided to use fiscal stimulus to invest in the economy short run, it is absolutely essential to legislate at the same time a multi-year program to balance the structural budget deficit with fiscal restraint to be triggered when the economy is up and running, perhaps at an unemployment rate around $6^{1}/_{2}$ percent headed toward 6, since tough measures can more easily be tolerated at better rather than bad economic times. Measures such as higher gasoline taxes and other energy or carbon taxes, increased excise taxes, greater taxation of Social Security benefits, possibly taxes on health care premiums paid by employers or health care benefits received by higher income recipients, using cost of living adjustments less a percent point, for example, for pension and entitlements, and others, could go a long way toward eliminating the structural budget deficit and be good macroeconomic policy if the economy has been growing at 3¹/₂ percent or so and the unemployment rate is down to 6¹/₂ percent or below. Very important, perhaps most important, government at all levels, as part of such a program, needs to be streamlined, much as the private sector has done, to effect savings and efficiencies to the greatest extent possible.

Thank you. (Applause.)

PRESIDENT-ELECT CLINTON: Thank you very much.

Mr. McMillion?

MR. CHARLES MCMILLION (U.S. CONGRESS COMPETITIVENESS COUNCIL): Thank you. I'm very glad to be part of this public process to rebuild business and consumer confidence in this great country of ours by facing our problems rather than by ignoring them as our government has done for far too long.

I'd like to make three quick points. First, our structural problems are far more severe than most people realize. Second, there is now no apparent economic engine capable of driving the US economy to sustained healthy growth. And finally, I'll say just a few words about why I believe that a coherent national strategy for growth and investment is urgently needed now.

First, the structural problem. The United States had real economic growth of 4 percent per year throughout the 1950s and '60s. It slowed sharply to 2.8 percent per year in the 1970s, and then slowed further to 2.6 percent in the 1980s. But even the slow growth of the 1980s came at a price that is hard to comprehend. Consider this. In Fiscal Year 1992, our entire economy—nominal GDP—grew by $250 billion, while our federal debt grew by $290 billion. We borrowed it all. It was far worse in 1991. In fact, since 1980, nominal GDP has doubled from 3 to $6 trillion—a growth of $3 trillion, at the same time our federal debt has grown from $1 trillion to $4 trillion, also a growth of $3 trillion. And there is no end in sight. Clearly, this country has to find another way to grow.

It was discussed yesterday that our rate of productivity growth has been slowing for a generation. I would also urge everyone to read the recent Cuomo Commission report that points out that at global market exchange rates, the US no longer ranks even among the world's top ten most productive economies. And it's not that Americans don't work hard, it's that we have been losing the high value-added industries and the tools to do the job. We now employ fewer people in manufacturing than in government. Private investment in plant and equipment, in research and development has fallen steadily as a percent of our economy. Japan, with half of our population and half of our economy, invests more than we do. The US is losing or has already lost our lead in major technologies of the future. We've had study after study. Since 1986, most patents issued in the United States are issued to foreign owners—that's in the United States. Our wages now rank only 13th in the world, and still we have the largest trade deficits the world has ever seen—$100 billion a year trade deficit has become normal in the United States.

Finally, and where all this is really felt, real growth of after-tax, per capita income has fallen steadily for a generation, and fallen sharply. Massive numbers of women, as was mentioned yesterday, entered the workforce in the 1970s, not because of challenging opportunities, but also, in many cases, to sustain their families' living standards. In the 1980s—in the early 1980s, still trying to sustain their living standards, Americans also went into debt as never before. And finally, in the late 1980s, Americans also spent down their savings from the already low levels of 7 to 9 percent of personal income to 4 to 5 percent. I could go on, but these are serious structural problems that will take some time to straighten out.

This brings me to my second and shorter point, that there is no apparent economic engine to drive sustained job and income growth. The good news is that the national recession is over. The bad news is that, at least technically, it has probably been over for 19 or 20 months. This may be as good as it gets for a while. This recession was badly misunderstood by those who focused on the unemployment number; but those who followed employment and income, as you did, knew what the American people and American business knew, that this was the worst recession in over 50 years. Job loss in this recession was worse than it was in 1982, and real after-tax per capita income suffered its longest period of decline in the post-war era. Even in the most recent quarter, with seemingly healthy growth of 3.9 percent, jobs declined, real after-tax incomes declined, personal savings declined in a major way, and overall business profits declined.

Let me just say that the principal sources of jobs and income, as Allen said earlier, the principal source of jobs and income growth over the last several years, aside from government deficits, have been in health care, improved net exports, and government employment. Each of these seem likely to weaken in the near term. It's very hard to find sufficient engines for sustained job and income growth as you look down the SIC listing. I challenge each of you to do that.

Which brings me to my final point, that we need a coherent strategy for growth and investment and we need it now. We cannot grow our way entirely out of this deficit, but as John White suggested so eloquently yesterday, we can certainly cause the deficit to skyrocket if growth stalls, as it very well could, in the next two years of global turmoil, unless we create jobs and income growth. Now, by a coherent strategy, I refer to a consistent set of rules and principles that will give us a government that can say "no" more often, "no" more often to wasteful spending, but can also say "yes" more often to productive measures and can effectively deliver on those commitments.

I've gone over my time without listing the types of principles that I would like to see in your strategy. Let me just—but there will be plenty of discussion, and that will probably be a better place to do that anyway.

Let me just say in summary that I believe that our structural problems are more serious than people realize. I think that there is no obvious engine to get us out of this ditch, and I think that the time is now to have a coherent economic strategy for jobs and income growth.

Mr. President-elect, as you said in opening this conference, these are hard questions, but we can do it. Yes, we can. And I believe that with Clinton-Gore leadership, we will do it.

Thank you. (Applause.)

President-elect Clinton: Thank you very much.

I want to thank Mr. Tobin, Mr. Sinai and Mr. McMillion. I thought each of them did an excellent job of presenting the real dilemmas we face in making a decision. To try to reinforce the "let's don't get too rosy" thing, I basically am positive but I just think you all ought to know, just to illustrate the points that have been made, that just this morning IBM announced they would cut their workforce by 25,000, and for the first time in history will have to use layoffs unless the economy picks up. Product development will be cut by $1 billion, the exact thing we don't want them to be cutting.

Now, let me try to frame this, and then I'll just start calling on—this is a wonderful panel this morning with a variety of different perspectives, but let me try to frame what I consider to be the dilemmas here.

I think we all understand the price we're going to pay if we continue with this deficit. I mean, I think everybody understands that if you just keep borrowing money to consume on an annual basis at the rate we've been doing it, with no necessary investment correlation, you will continue to have low growth, and the whole purpose of deficits in the past—until the last 12 years, with minor exceptions like right at the end of the second war—when we had deficits, they were either to pay for investments or to deal with the stimulus issue, the very thing Mr. Tobin started talking about, the traditional Keynesian economics.

We now have this huge structural deficit, and I take it we all agree that that's a bad thing, as big as it is, if it keeps—or certainly the rate of growth is a bad thing. On the other hand—and not only that. Obviously, it doesn't necessarily promote any kind of economic activity.

On the other hand, we plainly have a huge investment gap here, so we're not generating jobs and income growth. And if we adopt a discipline program to bring this down over the next five years, you know, we're going to get into this—this declining productivity has been going on for 20 years, so to say that we ought to have a $30 billion short-term stimulus in year one, and then from year two through six we're really going to crack it and cut this debt in half—which turns out to be $100 billion bigger than we thought it was per year, nearly—means that if you sacrifice investment, you still may not get growth. And if you don't get growth, I don't care what our budget plan says, the deficit will be bigger than we estimate because the revenues won't come in to support the new budget package. That's one of the things that happened in 1990. You can ask the members of Congress here. We had this budget deal in '90 that didn't work partly because the economy didn't pick up, number one, and health care cost more than everybody thought it would. And it's a slot machine that pays off every time. It's an entitlement. So if there's going to be a permanent increase in investment, what does that do to the debt reduction strategy?

The third thing I want to point out that McMillion pointed out, that the job growth—you got to quit looking at the unemployment rate. You got to look at the employment rate every month. My state ranked first in the country in job growth this year, and it wasn't until the middle of the year until we got our unemployment rate down below the national average because nobody ever dropped out of the unemployment pool here, and every time more jobs were created, people came home because they left in the early '80s. It didn't mean anything, are the jobs growing or not.

And if you look at the sectors of job growth, health care—that's bad for the economy, because paper workers are growing at four times the rate of nurses—paper shufflers. Government employment's growing not so much at the federal level, but at the state and local level for two reasons: federal court orders on penitentiaries because the prison population doubled in the '80s, and people working in health and human services designed to meet the staffing ratios mandated by the federal government. You can ask Mr. McEntee about that. The rest of the state and local government's not growing very much. Policemen aren't keeping up with crime, for example.

And the third area, exports, will obviously be affected if there's a recession in Europe and in Japan, which argues again for a big increase in domestic investment to increase income and growth here and domestic consumption.

This is a very tough call. This is the major economic policy decision we're going to have to make. I have and they have laid the dilemmas out well, but I'd like to know—you know, what we've got to decide to do is what to do, how much, and when. And I—you know, and I just —and as specific as you can be, if you can say "Well, if you do this, this is what I think will happen," I'd really appreciate it. I'd like to start with Adele, if you're ready to talk.

ADELE SIMMONS (MACARTHUR FOUNDATION): (Laughs.) Okay.

PRESIDENT-ELECT CLINTON: I've got an idea. You could increase by tenfold the number of MacArthur fellows, and that would help the economy. (Laughter.)

MS. SIMMONS: Well, let me thank both you, Mr. President-elect, and Mr. Vice President-elect, for putting this on and the opportunity to be here and say that I think you've already begun. Consumer confidence has gone up in the last month. I don't think that was an accident. I think it was a statement about how people feel about your leadership and the country at this point. If you are going to make things happen quickly, I hope your personnel people will look closely at the good people who are currently working in the government so the transition can be quick and we can take advantage of the strength already in place.

I side with those who do feel that we need some short-term investment, but I'm a long-term person, and I think it's critical that that short-term investment reflect your long-term goals. This country needs a strong statement about new values. We need to create new attitudes. We need to engage the public and release the energy at the local level. We also need, and I value, the people around this table who are economists who realize that economic models don't give value to future generations. Bob Solow has written about that, and as Jonas Salk says, our greatest responsibility is to be good ancestors.

Having said that, I think there are important short-term investments that fit into your long-term strategies. We talked roads and bridges, but where will they be built? In the suburbs, to attract more corporate leaders or headquarters to move out of the inner cities, or in the inner cities or the rural areas?

The environment. There are water treatment plants already under construction, and that construction timetable can be hastened. There are water treatment plants already in blueprint form that we can begin on.

High speed rail. We can't design the new system in the short term, but there are ways in which we can improve the rails immediately, laying the groundwork for energy efficiency in the long term.

Coastal and inland waterways need a lot of help, and will help those who are trying to get their goods to market more quickly. The Safe Drinking Water Act is in place. There are already things on the drawing boards that we can do to implement that more quickly. And there are already blueprints for rehabing federal buildings to improve their energy efficiency, a very strong statement of the government's commitment to provide leadership in this area.

The one area we have to avoid in the short term, unfortunately, is toxics, because the mess around the superfund is so great it will take us a while to unravel how best to spend money in the toxic area.

I think it's important, too, to make a strong public statement that investing in people is part of a short-term investment. Head Start could be kept open this summer. We could, I think, bring on line some of the immunization programs that are already on the drawing board. Summer food services for kids could be provided. And there are off-the-shelf construction projects for children and youth that we could implement already. And, finally—and if I may I'd like to turn over to my colleagues from Chicago, Mary Houghton and Vince Lane—to pick up on these issues, we can do a great deal in the area of low-income housing immediately.

Thank you very much.

President-elect Clinton: Thank you very much. I do want to recognize Mary and Vince.

Let me just kind of reinforce a point one of the first three speakers, I think Mr. Sinai, made that you made that anything we do in the short run ought to be consistent with what we want to accomplish in the long run. I guess the point I was trying to make before that I didn't make quite clearly is that even after we get into long-term deficit reduction, we must continue to increase our rate of investment. There will not be enough time elapsing. You can't go back to the former investment levels, which means that we will have to continue to be in a very vigorous attitude of cutting inessential costs or reducible costs in health care and other things for the foreseeable future because we need investment increases for a decade, I think, to overcome what's happened in the last decade. That was the point I was trying to make earlier that I didn't make very well.

Mary and Vince, would you go next.

MARY HOUGHTON (SHOREBANK CORPORATION): Thank you.

I wanted to first add to the description of the problem with one sentence by saying that another major problem that has to be kept in the short-term forefront is the debilitating and increasing problem of poverty and drugs in the inner city. But very few people realize that there are vast market opportunities to invest in inner city communities, and that the business sector, the banking sector, and the not-for-profit sector can all deliver and invest resources in the inner city now.

In terms of short-term investment opportunities, if you could get the low-income housing rehabilitation movement back in gear by making low-income tax credits permanent now, you would restore a market, a market economy of people who are trying to do low-income housing rehabilitation. If you could work with the unions or pursue the idea specifically of some partial waiver of Davis-Bacon wage requirements, you could get three times the value of low-income housing subsidy.

Today in Chicago, unskilled workers must be paid $20 an hour to work on low-income housing development, $20 an hour. We could get three times the use of that subsidy by paying what are actual prevailing wages in inner city communities of $7 to $9 an hour. So, you could get three times the bang out of subsidy now if there could be a way to work on the Davis-Bacon regulation.

Another short-term strategy would be to challenge the banking industry to use its credit knowhow to deliver more credit into distressed markets. My own very small bank makes $30 million of new loans each year into targeted inner-city communities. That's three times our capital base. If a large bank were doing the same thing, they would be generating $5 billion a year of credit into inner-city communities. So, the capacity of the banking system and the capacity of the nonprofit development system are there today to be used if they can be incented in any of a thousand ways to get to work in the inner cities. Thank you.

PRESIDENT-ELECT CLINTON: Name three.

MS. HOUGHTON: Name three?

238

President-elect Clinton: Of the thousand ways. (Laughter.)

Ms. Houghton: Offer incentives, offer higher deposit insurance to commercial banks that demonstrate delivery of resources into inner-city communities. Offer other regulatory changes to those banks in exchange for public delivery of—for a public purpose. I'm sure that there are a thousand things that the bankers have thought about. (Laughter.)

President-elect Clinton: Vince.

Vincent Lane (Chicago Housing Authority): Mr. President-elect and Vice President-elect, I know we're short on time, but I do have some things I really want to get on the table. And I guess I want to start with just a conceptual thing.

One is that we have a double standard in this country, one for normal people and another for poor and minority people. And that double standard has led to bad public policy, public policy which assumes that poor people can do nothing to help themselves. It assumes and equates poverty with being bad. We have got to address that and we've got to change those public policies. Nowhere else do we discourage savings except when it comes to poor people. We have got to now not only invoke sanctions with people, but we have to put incentives in place to change behavior.

How do we do it? How do we restore our urban communities? I think there are about five things that make for good neighborhoods, and that's what got this country where it is, strong neighborhoods.

One is public safety. Another is decent and clean housing. Economic incentives to encourage people to put into place public safety and clean and decent housing will start the rebuilding of our communities. We've got to improve education and training opportunities. And, finally, what everyone has said here today, we've got to create jobs. And we can create jobs. We can create jobs by supporting micro enterprises, supporting the people in these communities in conjunction with the private sector, both for-profit and not-for-profit.

The Progressive Policy Institute came out with a book recently called *Mandate for Change*. And the things that I'm going to talk about pretty much align with what they've suggested in *Mandate for Change*.

Public safety. We've instituted something called Operation Clean Sweep in Chicago where the worst situation exists for gangs and drugs. And we've made a positive impact. That could be expanded through-

239

out the country. Your national police corps could be utilized in truly tough places like public housing and could draw upon military personnel who are no longer used in—given the state of the Cold War. We could provide incentives for localities to encourage them to utilize community-oriented policing and to support community self-defense programs. There are a lot of localities that won't do it, so federal policy is going to have to somehow encourage localities to do it.

Drug treatment. We need drug treatment, given the situation of the drug programs of this country. In Chicago, we took—foreclosed a HUD hospital, Mary Thompson, and converted it to a place where we now bring mothers who are addicted to drugs, pregnant mothers and their below-school-age children, to get them off of drugs. We could do that by tying those two programs together, foreclosed hospitals and our drug-treatment program.

Clean and decent housing. From the public sector, public housing has to be delivered differently. What we've been doing for the last 30 years does not work. You cannot stack poor people on top of each other and expect to get anything but what we have today. We can do things like create socio-economic mix. There are programs that are out there that will provide working people as role models for families who are on welfare.

There are literally billions of dollars in the pipeline for modernization at HUD. Why is it there? It's there because of red tape and micromanagement of government. That could be—that micromanagement and red tape could be eliminated. That money could be put out there and jobs created.

We should support resident management. At LaClere Courts in Chicago, the residents there for three years have been managing a $2.5 million budget annually, and 80 percent of the jobs are held by residents.

Home ownership for public housing residents should be encouraged, but it should be encouraged in a way that we don't diminish our valuable public housing stock. And we should implement the program by again tying together family reunification, bringing those traditional family households back together and promoting work over welfare.

Funding. FHA, Ginnie Mae, Fannie Mae, Freddie Mac, and pension funds are already established vehicles for building housing. We ought to use them.

We should be promoting home ownership of first-time home buyers and we should also be promoting home ownership by families who earn less than $50,000 a year. We could do that with a two-tier, transferable tax credit. In other words, for a family that's going to buy a home in a traditional community, they get a lower tax credit. If they're going to buy a home or build a home in the inner city, then they get a higher tax credit.

We could finance down payments, because there are a lot of young families who haven't accumulated assets, but clearly if we helped them with down payments, the current income could support owning a home. We could have them repay that down payment financing out of the appreciation of the home or as the family's income increased.

The National Association of Home Builders sent me some information. They said on a $2,500 tax credit, we could create 100,000 to 150,000 homes, 200,000 to 300,000 jobs. We could create an additional 50,000 to 120,000 homes by financing down payments. The low-income tax credit that Mary spoke of. Literally, there are thousands and thousands of privately-assisted housing out there that's 20 years old or older, and they're in deplorable conditions. Nobody—this country should be ashamed of itself for permitting children to be raised in conditions that exist in some public housing and in privately-assisted government housing. We should be using the low-income tax credit in cooperation with not-for-profits to fix those places up and to eventually turn them into resident-owned cooperatives.

Economic incentives, the mixed income program. We could do it by offering to people, if we give you a good home, then let you have some responsibility and do something for yourself. One, keep your family drug free; two, participate in local educational programs that are structured with the schools; three, if you're healthy, work. Promote work, not welfare. And for that, we'll create an escrow for you to own your own—for a down payment on a home. Now, that's how we can move people from poverty to full participation in this country.

I know we're short on time. Creating jobs. We took our mod money in Chicago, and instead of contracting it out, we put to work in three months 300 residents and paid them $15 an hour. We also put to work 150 tradesmen. And that ability exists throughout public housing in this country.

To wrap up, we need to cut administrative costs at HUD and other agencies. We need to provide incentives for agencies to increase revenues and cut costs, like buying gas at the wellhead. We've saved about $30 million at Chicago in four years by implementing that program. We need to refinance existing mortgages out there that were financed years ago at today's interest rates. It would be a tremendous savings for government.

And finally, the byword, I think, in the future will be integration and coordination of all of these various federal programs in a holistic manner, both to achieve short-term goals and our long-term strategy. And I would suggest that you appoint a presidential commission to evaluate, consolidate and streamline federal programs and make sure that they function in the most productive way with state and local government.

Thank you.

PRESIDENT-ELECT CLINTON: Jim?

MR. JAMES JOHNSON (FANNIEMAE): Thank you very much for holding this conference, and thank you very much for the illustration that it provides to the American people and, I think, to people who work for government, both at the state and local and federal level, your approach to government, your willingness to listen, your willingness to pay attention to the facts, and your willingness to take action.

Let me say a few things about the housing sector. The first and most important thing to say, I think, is that building economic confidence is the best short-term housing policy. We have very favorable affordability figures today in terms of people's ability to purchase new homes. And the most important stimulation and investment strategy for the long term in housing, of course, is low interest rates, and that's true whether it's low-income housing, moderate-income housing or middle-income housing. Low interest rates is vital to all that we're going to do in the housing sector.

Let me mention a few other things quickly that I think you might want to focus on as you go forward through the next couple of months. I agree with Vince very much that we need to revitalize HUD. We particularly need to revitalize the FHA. We need to make permanent the low-income tax credit and the extension of the mortgage revenue bonds. Those are all vital steps that need to be done very quickly.

Secondly, I think there very badly needs to be a better integration of our focus on shelter and our focus on social services. Too often now, we are separating the component parts in a way that make it very difficult for people who are on the edge, who are working families or low-income families, to put together the different components of moving forward. I think that's a very important point.

Throughout the system, there's another point that we can't ignore, and it's sometimes very difficult for people to face, and that is that there's altogether too much discrimination in the home mortgage finance system at all levels. There's too little service to the inner city. There's too little focus on underserved communities. There is, in fact, discrimination in all parts of the system. I think federal leadership and presidential leadership is really vitally required in order to move forward in that area.

242

Let me also say a word about rental stock because so often people focus on home ownership and don't focus enough on maintaining affordable rental stock. We have a real crisis in this country in terms of the amount of income that people are spending on shelter. People are spending way too much income on shelter in order to make the other needs that their families have—to meet the other needs that their families have. One of the exciting things going on, and Mary talked about this and Vince talked about it, is that in community after community now around the country, there are really vital private sector/public sector partnerships that are dealing with housing issues. We have to take every possible step to revitalize and to further invigorate those structures because there's an awful lot that can be done if people work together with the federal government in these partnerships.

And finally, I do want to say a word because I think it is a problem for the homebuilders and the home construction industry, and that is that there is a real credit crunch around home construction lending, I believe, and I think as a final step, that's something that we need to focus on.

In conclusion, 1992 was really a very big year in terms of home mortgage finance. We did more originations—$800 billion of originations—by far than have ever been done before; 250 billion more than the previous record.

What that means in economic terms—Allen Sinai and I were talking this morning. What it means in economic terms is there's quite a lot of net stimulation that's coming from the refinancing of home mortgages. That's positive from an economic point of view. There's also something else going on in the economy as a result of the home mortgage finance picture. That is that people are taking shorter-term mortgages, and we now have a forced savings effect that's coming through people having 15-year and 20-year mortgages rather than 30-year mortgages. And I think that has a net positive economic benefit.

So we've got a lot of work to do. We have a home mortgage finance system that works beautifully for 80 to 85 percent of the American public, and homeownership is increasing for those people. We have another 15 or 20 percent, who Mary and Vince were talking about, who have very substantial needs, where presidential leadership and government cooperation is vitally needed.

PRESIDENT-ELECT CLINTON: Thank you.
Senator Bentsen, and then Roger Johnson.

Sen. Bentsen: Thank you, Mr. President. First, let me say I think the presenters did an excellent job of it.

Dr. Tobin, I'm looking at a situation where we're talking about a growth of around 3 percent. Not great, but not bad. A good part of that with a 2.5 percent increase in productivity, so a very low net increase in jobs. And I'm interested in what you're speaking of in the way of a short-term stimulus as to the amount and the duration.

I listened to Mr. Sinai talk about keeping an option in there in order that you can moderate that stimulus if you see this growth extending beyond 3 percent. But I couple that with a problem that I think we have to reinvigorate G-7, and that the United States has to exercise some real leadership in that, and in trying to work out a monetary policy that will avoid recession in Europe and in this country, and be productive for all of us. So it has to be credible what we do in trying to sell Germany and Japan that we've been credible on the fiscal policy at the same time.

So I'm interested in getting a feel from you as to what you're talking about in the way of the amount of that stimulus and the duration of it.

Mr. Tobin: I would be willing to see something like 1 percent of GDP stimulus which, if you—it would be about $60 billion a year, and for a couple of years. I think you could make it less in the second year if that seemed desirable as the economic returns come in in 1993. If you think of that multiplying into the secondary expenditures that result from the stimulus itself, that's about—would probably amount to 1.5 percent of GDP in a year per year. And as I said in my presentation, the gap that we're trying to close is five or six percent. So you're not doing anything that's very dangerous by that degree of stimulus, in my opinion. Now, other people may prefer a smaller amount.

The credibility about the long run I think should be obtained by announcing and, in part, enacting, so far as possible, the steps that will be taken for long-run deficit reduction. And that could include, as Allen Sinai said, tax increases scheduled for a later time—gasoline or carbon taxes, for example. And it could include whatever additional defense cuts beyond those now in the—in President Bush's proposals would be adopted by the new administration, and other things as well.

So I think that we could be credible to our own country and to foreigners as well, by that kind of dual program. They have as much interest in global expansion as we do, and avoiding a global stagnation or a global recession, which means low interest rates in Europe and Japan as well as in the United States.

SEN. BENTSEN: I would say that I'm much more sympathetic to letting the chief executive have the option, insofar as reducing that stimulus some. I find that I have become much more sympathetic to the executive side of the government recently. (Laughter, applause.)

PRESIDENT-ELECT CLINTON: If I had 400 more Cabinet positions I could pass my program! (Laughter.)

Roger Johnson, then Bob Rubin, then Bob Reich. Go ahead.

MR. JOHNSON: Thank you, Governor. Thank you, Senator Gore. I come at this, if I may, from a little different viewpoint. That's probably because I'm not an economist. In my company, you have to build things and sell things to make a living, so I come at it from that standpoint.

Our industry has made a lot of progress, and so have others, in what we call time to market—the time from design to volume production. One thing I suggest is, we might frame some of these thoughts, some of the programs that you might have in the context of time from action to jobs, because we need to create the jobs. We can do a lot of financial stimulating, but fundamentally, someone has to decide to buy something for a job to be created.

Any good salesman will tell you that a buying decision in the final analysis is an emotional decision. After all the analysis is done, after all the figures are in, whether you buy a car or a computer or a whole powerplant, you make the decision, if you're a consumer or an executive, on the basis of how you feel about tomorrow. I think, therefore, we just cannot underestimate the value of the confidence that's being built in the country. That doesn't take a lot of stimulus; that takes a continuation of the programs you started a year ago.

I think that that confidence level can now be accelerated and can be spilled over into executives who have to make the decisions to buy the inventory, add the capacity, add the jobs. We have to believe the forecasts our sales people are giving us. There's some things I think you could do to help accelerate that confidence.

One, we talked yesterday about levelling the playing field around the world. I think you can continue to give signals, as Senator Bentsen did yesterday, that we are going to do that one way or the other. So countries around the world should start right now levelling those fields, because they're going to get them levelled one way or the other.

I think we should have a quick but prudent final negotiation of NAFTA. I think that ought to be accelerated and extended into further parts of Latin America. One of the better ways to create demand is by opening new markets. I think the value of the export market incrementally to marketing companies far exceeds the risk of any job losses we have.

Thirdly, and this is not protectionism, this isn't picking winners or losers, but American companies—manufacturing companies have done a great job over the past few years in improving themselves. Our quality is better. Our performance is better. Our costs are lower. And, you know, old buying habits are very hard to break. People bought foreign cars some time ago because maybe our car industry wasn't up to snuff. Without picking winners and losers, I would suggest you ask the American public in their next buying decisions—a car for example, at least test-drive two American cars, cars built or assembled in the United States. In other purchasing decisions, at least consider American products. If they don't have the quality, if they don't have the performance, or they cost too much, don't buy them. But give them a chance. We've made a lot of improvements, and I think we could convert some things quicker.

I think if you clarified some of the times for the new programs—the ITC, the targeted capital gains tax—put a little more beef around them, put dates on them, I might suggest, Governor, that you select the date of today's conference as a retroactive date for any of these programs you go forward with. That would put a real significance to these historic gatherings, I think. I think the credit rules that many have talked about need to be investigated, need to be relaxed, and maybe could be a high priority for Senator Bentsen and the rest of your economic team.

Some federal stimulus, I think, is good—infrastructure, accelerating those programs where monies have already been spent—but I think those should be done not to stimulate jobs but because they're broken. We need to fix them anyway, right?

I think really, though, the key here in my view, and the least costly and most highly leveraged is to continue to build the confidence of consumers, business people around the world, so that we feel better about tomorrow than we do today and we're ready to take those risks and get jobs going again. So I think we need to keep our eye on the long-term programs which you've identified and on which you ran and on which we elected you.

Thank you. (Applause.)

PRESIDENT-ELECT CLINTON: Bob, and then Bob Reich, and Gerry McEntee.

That was a good statement. I liked that. (Laughter.) I hope we can do it.

ROBERT RUBIN (GOLDMAN SACHS & COMPANY AND CHAIRMAN-DESIGNATE, NATIONAL ECONOMIC COUNCIL): Jim, I want to ask you a question, if I may, and the question doesn't imply an opinion, because I don't have any opinion. This is just a question. If you undertook your $60 billion stimulus program for two years, or, I think Allen, perhaps, was talking about a somewhat lower number, I think. You were talking about a $30 billion—so you were in that range of, say, $30 to $60 billion for a year or two years. What effects would it have on the kind of confidence that Roger was just talking about, which many people think is ultimately the key to getting the economy functioning effectively again, a restoration of confidence, given how focussed people seem to be on the deficit? It's some kind of an index of our economic ills, rightly or wrongly focussed. And secondly, what effect would it have on long-term—the long-term bond market, long-term yields, and by virtue of that, on economic growth? The effect on confidence, the effect on long-term bond market, and by virtue of that effect, on the economy?

MR. TOBIN: Well, I think confidence and expectations will be consistent with a plausible and actual, real economic program. And if the program is as I stated, which is to have the stimulus when it's obviously needed and to have the fiscal austerity when it's needed, I think that should create confidence, because that is not an inflationary program, it's not a reckless program that will, in the long run, spend money as if it didn't matter, it is a—intrinsically a program that should build confidence. I think a do-nothing program that fails in the first year or two to build jobs, and where it's not evident that the government is doing anything about it in spite of the mandate it obtained at the election that would—might destroy the confidence that the election itself has created. So I don't think we can try to outguess the way these things work in psychology, and we should have a program which, if people expect that program, they will have confidence because the program is adequate to do the job.

Now I think that if you—with the help of the Federal Reserve and, of course, with the secretary—the new secretary of the Treasury, you can explain this program to the financial community, to the bond markets, to the gnomes of Zurich or of the Battery, whoever they may be and wherever they may be, and it does not justify an increase in long-term bond rates.

Also, the management of the debt can create and help to create a supply-demand situation which will not encourage higher long-term bond rates by curtailing the growth of the supply of long-term government bonds. The government is the main borrower at long term, and

247

the main source of increased supply of long-term securities. The Federal Reserve can help in that, too, by going into the long-term market on occasion. So I think they're not helpless in the face of those bond markets. And they don't like to give up yields in order to earn 3 percent at short term, and they won't do that indefinitely.

PRESIDENT-ELECT CLINTON: Bob, and Gerry.

MR. ROBERT REICH (HARVARD UNIVERSITY AND SECRETARY-DESIGNATE, LABOR DEPARTMENT): My question goes to one of timing, Jim, and Allen, and Charles—maybe you want to answer this as well. And the first question, or at least part A, has to do with the timing with regard to when a stimulus would actually take hold. Let's assume the worst scenario, let's assume that come January the job situation has not improved substantially, Jim, that we're still way below capacity with regard to what the economy could be or should be in terms of output, and that in your view, and Allen, in your view, some sort of stimulus is necessary, how soon do you think in the best of all worlds that stimulus could actually have an effect, given what government could do, given the various things you said. I think, Allen, you talked about infrastructure. Jim, I think you also talked about infrastructure.

Part B—when should the stimulus come off? What's the trigger? I think both of you talked a little bit about timing. Allen, I heard you say something about maybe triggered by a turn up in the economy or a turndown in unemployment. Would that trigger actually work in practice? Jim, you mentioned one or two years. Maybe you could be a little bit more precise about that.

MR. TOBIN: I would start the phased-in—phasing in of a deficit reduction program after two years, in 1994,—1995–1996, and I think that in the short run, the immediate short run there are opportunities which —many of which were stated already this morning in the very interesting interventions that followed our macrodiscussion about the inner cities, that—where there is a great need, and possibly a way in which spending can be done quite quickly in aid to state and local governments which are strapped financially, as we know, and need funds for good purposes—not completely blank checks to them, but geared particularly to the kinds of problems that were being presented by the team from Chicago this morning. I think that would be a good way of having spending that can occur rather quickly within the next year, and also have its repercussions and further incentives for economic

248

activity fairly quickly—within the year, within 1993. By 1994, you can begin to have larger spending on your own infrastructure and education programs because by that time they will be enacted and you can begin to be administering them.

Mr. Sinai: On timing, Bob, I would say right away, because there is a quarter to two-quarter lag in getting going and having an impact of say, the examples of infrastructure and ITCs. So you should do it right away and retroactive as has been suggested on ITCs to today or what Senator Bentsen has indicated along with Mr. Rostenkowski, to early December.

I think the impacts of those two examples would be the second through the fourth quarter of next year, when the current impulse—up-impulse of the economy may indeed be fading and would come at the right time. If you wait longer, it's dangerous. When—to come off, I would favor an economic trigger, an economy solidly in a growth phase of 3½ percent or a little more for a year-and-a-half and an unemployment rate at 6½ percent, heading lower, and then an economic trigger for fiscal restraint, but also a legislation, if possible—it never has happened before—in advance, right away, coming out of the gate, early next year, that says that when this happens, such-and-such actions are going to take place. And include in those actions some very tough medicine on entitlements and other kinds of measures to reduce the deficit so people understand when times are good, they're going to have to make some payback. All of us are going to have to do our share.

Very quickly, if I could just—a couple of words about Senator Bentsen's comments. I think you have to stay flexible on the number. I used to use 50 billion. I now use 30 billion because the economy has picked up lately and it's easier to underdo fiscal stimulus than to overdo it. What you put into place, if you overdo it, you can't easily dismantle. But if you underdo it, you can always come back to the well and do it a second time and add a little bit more, if the process of fiscal policymaking, which I think it will be, is faster this time around because of the Democratic president and the Democratic Congress.

You have credibility issues on several fronts. One is with the Federal Reserve. They're a significant player in this game. I think $50–60 billion at this time they would think would be too much. I'm not saying you should necessarily listen to that. You should be aware of that.

You also have credibility issues in the financial markets. My judgment is that $50 or $60 billion would send the wrong signal at this time to the financial markets, that $20 or $30 billion, and it's part of why I suggested it, is benign for everybody and also can help some.

And there is an issue as to whether you can spend an additional $50 or $60 billion effectively and efficiently in the time horizon that you have to really get the impact, efficient impact, that you want.

And you do have a credibility issue in the international community as well on these matters because we've run deficits for so long. It is not a good signal to start by too big a dosage early for a new Democratic administration with a Democratic Congress when everyone out there expects this particular pairing to do just that, to return to the perceived old ways of the Democrats. And so, I think it a little better to start earlier. As I say, you can always—once you do it, you can't undo it easily. If you underdo it, you can add to it a little later.

PRESIDENT-ELECT CLINTON: Mr. McEntee and Mr. Cruz. Let me remind you all, we're supposed to—I want to go to the floor, but if you talk longer than you need to, you deprive someone else of the chance to talk at all. So, you might be careful about this. Go ahead.

GERALD McENTEE (AFSCME): Thank you, President-elect Clinton and Vice President-elect Gore. And I will be relatively short.

First, let me say that we do want to thank you for inviting us to this meeting, labor, working men and women. It's the first time that we've been at a table with business and government in a long, long time.

My union represents public workers, public workers from correctional officers at Attica in New York to social workers in San Francisco, hospital workers in Harlem, and we keep the roads open in the winter in Minnesota. They work for cities and they work for states and they work for counties. And for 12 years or four long years, we've felt like we didn't belong at any table at all. What's been happening is that we've had federal aid cut to us in terms of cities and states over a 12-year period of time, a deep and severe recession that has cut into revenues as well.

I heard discussion here this morning about our cities. Our cities are desperate, and I think President-elect Clinton knows as he went around the country. Philadelphia has recently survived bankruptcy. Boston is broke. Bridgeport, Connecticut filed for bankruptcy last summer. Detroit, I guess, is all but closed, unemployment probably around 20 or 21 percent. We heard about Chicago, the city of big shoulders, the last big city that works, and we saw their infrastructure come apart not too many months ago when the Chicago River overflowed in downtown Chicago. In addition, the cities have new and different problems than they had some years ago, AIDS and homeless, crack houses, and now a new tuberculosis.

250

In days gone by, they used to be able to turn to the states for help, but now they turn to the states, as you know, and nobody's home. The states have done some wonderful and imaginative things with the monies available, but no longer, I believe, can they even do those kinds of things. New York state worked hard on their deficit. Their deficit for 1993 will be $4.8 billion. Ohio worked hard. Their deficit, $325 million. The state of Maryland is only three months into their fiscal year and already a $500 million deficit. And you can look at California and Michigan and Massachusetts, and they're all the same kinds of numbers and the same state of affairs.

They're numbers and statistics, but in fact they mean real people. I remember President-elect Clinton, as he would go across the country on the bus trip, and I remember seeing signs that people would carry, "I'll work for food," or signs a child would have around their neck that just said, "Help my daddy get a job." The cities and the states, I think, across the country are literally at the end of the road. And Clinton/Gore have come none too soon.

We believe that there should be a long-term budget deficit reduction program, but we also believe that right now, in terms of the economy, in terms of the commitment to jobs, that we should have a short-term stimulus, something that will put people to work.

We would also like if you would take a look at this tremendous burgeoning cost of Medicaid and how it straps our cities and states, and not just look at it in the long run in terms of answering it vis-a-vis national health care, but see if there is an interim answer, a short-run provision that, as President of the United States, you can put into effect, that will help get this burden at least somewhat off the cities and allow them to move in another direction.

The mayors of the United States came together with an infrastructure program, and they are prepared, as I understand it, with some—and you asked for specifics—they are prepared, as I understand it, to move with 7,252 projects and ready to put people to work in a relatively short period of time. And we're not talking about make-work jobs. We're talking about a public investment but private sector work.

We would certainly agree with the Nobel Laureate, Mr. Tobin, on that long-range program that he talks about, some $50 billion over maybe a two- or three-year period of time. The need is there in terms of this infrastructure. It provides a way to put people to work and put America to work.

And I also would ask the President-elect and Vice President-elect to kind of bring together, through your leadership, business and government and labor. We applaud your selections in terms of Bob Reich and Ron Brown, and we think that that marks a great first step in bridging a gap that has been a very, very deep and long gap between business

251

and labor in America. I think we're prepared to make a shared sacrifice to have America go back to work and make it better, and I think we're ready to do our share of that. And we would ask that the Clinton-Gore team have as one of their goals to make the playing field level for all of us, for government and business and labor.

PRESIDENT-ELECT CLINTON: Thank you.
Mr. Cruz?

MR. FRANK CRUZ (GULF ATLANTIC LIFE INSURANCE): Thank you, Mr. President-elect. I'll make my comments very, very brief and very short. I am the chairman of Gulf Atlantic Life Insurance Company, which so happens to be the nation's first and only Hispanic-owned life insurance company. I mention that simply because I think we, in the spirit of "Rebuild America," have moved our company right into the center of "Rebuild Los Angeles." We are within blocks of the disturbances in the Los Angeles area, and we believe in moving into the inner city area, which I know is something that you strongly advocate with your process of rebuilding America.

I think women- and minority-owned business enterprises of this country will need special assistance from the government. And wearing the hat as the chairman of my company, I strongly call and I urge that you assist and provide assistance to these small and mid-sized businesses in this country. After all, they do hire an enormous amount of people, as the statisticians and economists have told us. And I think the area of ITCs, and in terms of the stimulus that is needed, especially in the realm of the bank loans that the Chicago Group was talking about to make sure that it is made easier for them.

My other hat, Mr. President-elect, I am the chairman also of the California Institute, which is a think tank that has brought together, if you will, the congressional delegation, the 54 members, on a bipartisan basis, to do better work for the state of California and to get that large delegation working better. As you well know, the unemployment rate in the nation is 7.2 percent. California—if the recession has been serious for this country, it has been grave for our state. It is 10.1 percent in that state, and it is extremely difficult.

I would side with professors Tobin and Sinai. And I realize, in all candor, the difficulty of the political decision that you and your administration will have to make in reference to the short-term stimulus, keeping a good policy and tied to good long-range deficit reduction. I argue and I recommend, in all due respect, that we do have an immediate short-range stimulus. It will have a profound effect, especially in the infrastructure in many projects. I would tie it to those options that they have indicated, whether it be an option for time or related to a particular figure, either on the growth factor. But I would certainly give it a period of time. You would send a tremendous message across the country and, in turn, however, it must be coupled—because I see no contradiction in having an immediate, short-term stimulus—coupled with a policy clearly that we will hold down those long-range expenditures to reduce that deficit. And I think that is the—I think it would have a tremendous impact not only across the country but in my state, which is really, really suffering unduly as a result of our relationship with the defense cutbacks. We made this nation, if you will, the global power that it is, and we helped it in the Cold War, and we now ask you to bring us out of the cold.

PRESIDENT-ELECT CLINTON: Ken Brody, and Al and Ron Brown.

MR. KEN BRODY (PETRUS PARTNERS, LTD.): President-elect Clinton, Vice President-elect Gore, thank you all very much for inviting me, and also for having this conference. Listening to everybody last night, I would say that the tour de force that was shown yesterday has made a lot of people more optimistic about what perhaps a government can do than they had been before.

I'm a bit hesitant, in light of economists at the table and the tour de force yesterday, I'm a bit hesitant to give any advice because I find that the more I learn the less I know and the less sure I am of what the solutions may be. Clearly, we've spent 20-plus years getting into our problems. The lists of the challenges is long, and it's clear we're not going to solve them overnight. I think what's important with respect to that is to spend real time in educating the American public about what sort of reasonable expectations they can have. I think that any government today is going to be met with a lot of cynicism, and as a result, people really need to believe that the government can do something for them, and one of the ways of doing that over time is setting out expectations, setting out long-term and short-term goals, and giving the country a sense of whether we're going in the direction that we intend and that the government can make a difference.

I think one of the good news on the economic front right now is we've got a lot of elbow room with respect to inflation, and that elbow room, I think, gives a flexibility that can be used if needed.

I would think that the short-term stimulus that we apply should have a goal, and whether that goal is having a high degree of confidence, of having $3^1/_2$ to 4 percent growth or some other goal, I think to the extent that gets spelled out so that the people and the markets have confidence, that there is a disciplined approach with goals that allows us to see that we're going in a correct direction, I think the better chance you have of not having markets react adversely to you.

Obviously, there's a lot of prioritizing that's needed. I would suggest that it's important to have a number of victories up front, and without spelling out what some of the economic victories are, I think that two victories that can indicate a change in the way business is done and have a significant impact on how Congress can pass legislation would be to have a very serious campaign reform so as to disconnect to some degree special interests and their power from affecting Congress, and to put into effect a modified line item veto so that the sense again is given that there is a new way of conducting business that will have a significant impact.

I think to the extent that the credibility is built up in the government, and part of that credibility may have to be legislation that sets into place a deficit reduction program starting two years out, perhaps, or three years out, but I think that's a judgment that needs to be made, I think we will create—much as Roger said—I think we will be able to create an atmosphere that is very different from what we have had before. Seeing the insurance companies a couple weeks ago come off their stand on health care, listening to Red Poling yesterday talk about his willingness to accept the gasoline tax, I think starts to give a sense that there are things that can be done that we all thought couldn't be done. Discipline, priorities, setting expectations, having understanding —which in this conference, I think, there's a great deal—I think can go a long way to achieving the economic objectives and also dealing with the dilemmas and the terrific trade-offs that are involved.

President-elect Clinton: Al and Ron and then Leon and Elaine.

I just want to say we're going to have to quit in a minute because we've got to start the other program. We have a lot of people here who have a contribution to make, and if everybody talks five minutes, then a lot of people don't get to talk at all.

Vice President-elect Gore: I have just a short question. We heard earlier about other options for stimulating short-term economic growth in addition to a new fiscal package, and one of them, for example, was the easing of bank regulations to free up a lot of money that entrepreneurs could get ahold of to expand and so forth. Another was shifting the Treasury's bond bill strategy.

I don't have a clear idea of how we can talk about those things together. What order of magnitude stimulus would you expect to come from easing those bank regulations, for example? Does it make any sense to quantify it in relation to the size of any short-term stimulus package? Can that be done? How would you do it if you did it, Allen?

Mr. Sinai: First of all, that one's kind of a freebie. To the extent the credit channel works better in the economy because the regulations are, quote-unquote, "eased," that doesn't cost anything in the budget deficit, and I would urge you to look for all the freebies you can get. You want to raise growth without having to raise the deficit—

Vice President-elect Gore: No, I understand.

Mr. Sinai: —because you have to have the—(inaudible)—to get the deficit down. But the people to talk to are the bankers, the ones who say that they are strapped because of regulation. They were in the previous administration. They still say it. I hear it all the time, and I hear what they tell me, and I'm sorry I don't have 10 or 15 of the items that I've heard from them. But I do think if you talk to those who run the banks, they will give you a whole long list of items that are really cramping their style, that they say is from regulation. Some of them are true, some of them are probably false, and out of that you may cull some very worthwhile, useful information.

Vice President-elect Gore: I understand it's a freebie in terms of the deficit, but if you quantified it in terms of the stimulus effect—

Mr. Sinai: I think it's very potent.

Vice President-elect Gore: —compared to how much additional deficit spending, for example? That's what I'm trying to get. Is that possible?

Mr. Sinai: Well, you know, bank lending doesn't necessarily go for some of the things you want to do, like education and infrastructure, rebuilding our capital stock and making us better in the long run. But it certainly can help growth of the economy and provide some more—I think it's very significant. The credit channel, which has kind of broken down over the last three, four years for various reasons—

VICE PRESIDENT-ELECT GORE: (Off mike)—billions of dollars.

MR. SINAI: Oh, the number? The number. That's hard to say. I think that's one one has to study, but I would say it's not trivial. You're talking four or five, ten billion dollars over a year of extra economic activity.

PRESIDENT-ELECT CLINTON: The president of the American Banking Association is over there. Go—let him say.

MR. WILLIAM H. BRANDON, (AMERICAN BANKERS ASSOC.): That's such a fierce battle—can you hear me? If you were to increase lending in the banking system just 4 percent, which we can do, Mr. Sinai, with no effect on safety and soundness, and we can demonstrate that, you would increase the amount of capital coming out $86 billion, which would be a tremendous input back into small business in this country.

You're on the right track, President-elect Clinton. You've already nominated a great Treasury team. What you need to do now is nominate a great team of regulators. They need to understand three things. They need to understand the banking system. They need to understand the regulatory system. They need to understand the legislative system. And they need to be leaders.

There is truly, and I can give you a lot of examples—you asked for three; I could give you three. I'll do it later. I can give you five more for yours, too, and that's a great idea. There is a lot of excessive, over- and redundant regulation and actually superconservatism out there that could be eliminated simply by moving back slightly towards normal. That's all we've got to do. There's no safety and soundness problems under those scenarios. You can do it. After you're president, you ought to pool all your regulators, your Treasury, the Congress, the consumer groups, the home builders and the bankers together in a summit, and you'll be amazed at what you can do.

MR. SINAI (?): Sounds good. If you take one-quarter of that number, it's a big number. (Applause.)

President-elect Clinton: You heard the $86 billion figure. I mean, I've just been sitting here all day thinking this. I went all over the country talking to people who couldn't get any loans from banks anymore. That's still the main source of small business credit. And if you don't do anything about that, you can run the deficit up another 50–60 billion dollars and still have a very restricted impact, I think.

Who was next? Ron, and Elaine.

Ron Brown (Democratic National Committee and Secretary-Designate, Commerce Department): I think Barbara wanted to stay on the banking subjects, so if she can come to me after—

President-elect Clinton: Go ahead.

Audience Member: Well, I just wanted to say one thing. I'm the chief executive officer of a bank in Washington, DC. And you're absolutely right. Banking regulation is holding us back. We're not talking about doing away with prudent banking regulation, but let me give you an example. I think that our loan officers, who are our front-line people, are afraid to give small business loans now because the requirements are such that you have to do the same kind of write-up and work-up that you do for a Fortune 500 $2 billion backup line of credit as for a $50,000 small business loan. So, A, they're afraid to invest their time; B, because they feel that they'd be—they have an inherent risk, they're afraid to go on the line because they're afraid they're going to be rapped up the side of the head by the regulators. And it's true, and these policies affect our cities, our rural areas, and the partially disenfranchised, women, minorities, and people who live in the inner cities and small businesses.

President-elect Clinton: Let's stay on the bank thing a minute.

Audience Member: And it's a freebie.

Mr. Bruce Llewellyn (Attorney, Rubin, Baum, Levin, Constant and Friedman, New York City): First, Governor-elect (sic) Clinton and Vice President Gore, thank you very much for inviting me. And I'm very, very sorry you did invite me because, as I sit here, I begin to feel I'm about 150 years old because in the '60s, I was the regional director of the Small Business Administration for the largest region in the country, and we were trying to put small businessmen into business. And one of the things I learned out of that one was that we cannot lend money to people to go into business without them having some equity in the business, because we had tremendous losses.

Then, in the '70s, I guess, I became the chairman of the largest black bank in the country. It was Freedom National Bank, and we were having difficulties, and we recapitalized. And at that time, Dr. Bremer who was on the Federal Reserve Board, and I met one day, and I said, "Listen, I've got to have some changes." And we changed something called regulation L, which said that a high-income area bank could loan officers and directors to a low-income area bank for up to five years and not be in violation of the anti-trust laws.

And then I became the Commissioner of Housing for the city of New York, and I listened to some of the people from Chicago about the housing. And I guess my advice to you about this is that somehow or other, you've got to make people who live in houses owners or have an equity stake in what goes on, whether it be public housing or what have you. And there are groups in New York—for example, there were some Hispanic housewives who started something called UPACA. You made a connection with the Cornell Hotel School to tell them how to run apartments and how to—and have—reserve the right to inspect apartments. And you can do a lot of things that people begin to think differently about the people they're trying to serve.

Then we get down to inner cities. Inner cities are no better than the services that are available. Nobody wants to live in a house—and I ran the largest minority-owned supermarket chain in New York City—29 stores. And we fed the South Bronx, and we fed Harlem. But we need the conditions in order to survive. And the people need to have a drugstore, a supermarket, and they do not need to travel five miles away, otherwise the neighborhood is not viable.

Then there was a time when the stores tried to open 24 hours a day, and somebody came to me and said, "Well, you going to open 24 hours a day?" I said, "What for? For the benefit of the robbers," I said, "because by 7:00 or 8:00 at night, all of my customers are home. They've locked the doors, and they stay there as prisoners in the neighborhood until they come out in the morning to go to work." So that's another problem.

So it's very, very upsetting to me in a way that here we are in 1992 talking about discrimination in loans and mortgages. The Federal Reserve did a study this year: the data shows that minorities still get discriminated against.

I remember when we had a blackout, and I was in the supermarket business, and then President Carter called me and asked me to take a job as the head of the Overseas Private Investment Corporation for the federal government, and I said, "Well, what do they do?" And he started to tell me. He said, "They provide insurance for American companies doing business overseas against being destroyed by war, insurrection, or nationalized, and they provide insurance for bringing back your profits in case of inconvertibility of the currencies." I said, "No kidding?" I said, "Do you know I had a blackout in the South Bronx?" (Laughter.) "I had $1,200,000 worth of damage. Do you know the next day every insurance carrier I had cancelled my insurance, and I can't get insurance in the United States of America, and you're telling me the government's giving insurance for a guy to go to Senegal?" I mean, it was mind-boggling to me. (Laughter.)

So therefore, Mr. President, I would say to you, there's a chance to do some things here, maybe provide some insurance, because I read the same story again in South Central Los Angeles. And it said that the carriers either one, went bankrupt, took a walk, or cancelled. This is another twenty years later. So I guess the more history changes, the more it repeats. And these are just some of the things, as I sit here and reflected about all this. It's not new. It needs to be looked at once and for all with some commitment about changing the way we go about doing business.

And the final thing I would say to you people is the fact that it might seem very smart to talk about law and order, and we're going to put the bad guys in jail. But in New York City, it costs about $75,000 a year to lock up people and put them in Riker's Island next to LaGuardia field. It would be a hell of a lot cheaper to send them to Harvard. And as you see, there's a lot of Harvard people around here, so it'd be a good investment. (Laughter.) But being a very poor fellow, I went to City College of New York, and I think City College of New York is really what America's all about. And I think if you don't think much of me, I know you'll love my first cousin Colin Powell.

Thank you. (Laughter and applause.)

PRESIDENT-ELECT CLINTON: I wouldn't mind having you in the desert, either. (Laughter.)

Ron, then Elaine, and given the tack we're on, I think Earl, you ought to say something before we quit, too.

Go ahead, Ron.

MR. RON BROWN: I'm glad I deferred to Barbara and Bruce. I just had a point of inquiry of Jim Tobin.

Many in America have, for a long time, relied on unemployment data as a principal measure for how the economy's doing, and we've heard today from the President-elect and others that maybe employment data is a more important guide to focus on. Jim Tobin in his remarks talked about the large number of people in America who are working part-time but who really want and need full-time employment. We also know that there are a large number of people who have dropped out of the labor force. They've just gotten tired of beating their heads against the wall and have stopped looking for jobs, and they don't show up in the data. I would just like to know if Professor Tobin would care to estimate what the unemployment data would be if we counted those who are working part-time and really want full-time employment and those who have just dropped out of the labor market and are no longer counted.

MR. TOBIN: Well, I think you'd get into double-digit rates that way, but you'd also raise the unemployment rates for other periods of time as well. So I think we are capable of analyzing the labor market by a variety of statistics, all of which are relevant: employment, unemployment rate, labor force participation, and so on. But one thing to be said for the unemployment rate, it has been estimated a standard way so that its movement over time does say something. So is the employment figure. So let's—I don't think it's a[n] either/or in those respects.

Could I just say a sentence or two about the deregulation that Vice President-elect Gore asked about of banks? Now, some of these regulations that are hampering the banks now are the result of, perhaps, excessive inattention to regulation in the 1980s which led to some problems in conjunction with deposit insurance that we're all painfully familiar with. And there were—there is a problem of the capital asset ratios of the banks, and we are engaged in trying to meet internationally agreed standards on that. And that may be hard on some banks who are low relative by that standard for some time to come.

I'm not sure that using regulation and the strictness of surveillance by bank supervisors, et cetera is a good tool of economic—macroeconomic stabilization. The banks have gone strongly into government securities relative to ordinary commercial loans because of a rate difference that they find favorable, and if the Federal Reserve would maybe lower interest rates from 3 to 2 percent they wouldn't find that such a good deal as they do now.

PRESIDENT-ELECT CLINTON: It's not just the rate difference, too, the capital requirements are different for the loans. (There's 6 percent difference capital requirement ?).

Elaine, then Leon had his hand up, and I forgot, I apologize, and then Earl.

Go ahead. Then we're going to wrap this up.

Ms. KAMARCK: Mr. President and Mr. Vice President-elect, I would like—as we wrap this part of the discussion up, I'd like to change from the discussion of economic capital to a discussion of political capital, because I think, in fact, that extraordinarily relevant.

There's two topics on the table: short-term stimulus and long-term deficit reduction. The first one requires very little political capital. The second one requires enormous amounts of political capital.

What we know historically is that presidents come in and they have a honeymoon. That honeymoon lasts six months, if they're lucky. Everybody right now in the country, in Washington, loves you guys. Even the Republicans are saying nice things about you. You have a window of opportunity to achieve real progress on the long-term problems that we've heard about in the last two days.

If you look at the four sectors of this budget, you look at non-productive economic subsidies in the budget, you look at entitlement reform, you look at tax expenditures, which are not as progressive as they should be, and you look at the notion of re-inventing government, every single one of them is a political nightmare—(laughs)—that you will have to get through to make honest-to-goodness long-term deficit reduction. Spending money, on the other hand, is quite an easy thing to do. We Democrats do it quite well. We do it quite often.

I would suggest that when you have your maximum political capital is in the first six months of this year. You also have a hundred members of Congress. They have come to Washington. They have heard the concerns—the long-term concerns about the economy. They're concerned about cutting the deficits. They haven't been in Washington long enough yet to know that retaining sugar price supports is really a key to the republic, and all the other things that they learn—that's a joke, folks—and all the other things the members of Congress learn. I think there is an unprecedented opportunity in the first six months of this year to make good on these long-term trends.

If you don't do it, what history tells us is that you can't have that time back. Very few presidents are granted more than one honeymoon. George Bush, ironically, got a second honeymoon, and we know he did absolutely nothing with it, and look where he is today. (Applause.)

261

PRESIDENT-ELECT CLINTON: Leon, Earl, and then the gentleman in the back there.

Go ahead.

REP. PANETTA: She made my speech. (Laughter.)

I think it's—really it's—the only—the caution I wanted to make is from the congressional point of view with regards to a stimulus package, that, recognizing that the larger a stimulus package that you present to the Congress, the longer it's likely to take the Congress to enact the stimulus package. That was the experience in the Carter years when he presented a stimulus package. And by the time it was enacted, by the time it went into place, very frankly, it was too late. And so, that is something I think needs to be taken into consideration, which is the size of that package and how long it takes the Congress to get it through.

The second point I would make is that obviously, with regards to the elements of the package, the more you can link those elements to long-term investments—in other words, to set out your long-term plan, your long-term investments, and then speed up some of those investments in the early period, then you've got a long-term strategy that you're implementing as part of your stimulus package. I think that makes sense.

And the third thing is, obviously, to tie it to deficit reduction as linkage. I think you've got to make it as part of the same package, because if you do a stimulus package first, let me assure you, Congress loves to pass the sugar but hates to deal with the vinegar, which is the deficit part of this. So it does have to be locked into a single package if you're going to be able to get it through.

PRESIDENT-ELECT CLINTON: That's fine. I just want to make one point about this.

We're all talking about this stimulus package of this—in the area of —let's just take the low-side number, $30 billion—as if the whole future of the republic depended on it. You just heard Mr. Brandon say that a 4 percent increase in bank loans is $86 billion. If you go back and look at why that '90 budget deal fell on its face, it's because we didn't control health care costs and reorganize the health care system. And you can gut these entitlements all you want to, but don't forget the Social Security tax is producing a $70 billion surplus. It is a regressive tax.

We're already soaking the middle class and the small business community in this country. And then they're not overspending the Social

Security for the income stream that's going into it. And the truth—I'm just making the point if Elaine is right, and I think she is, then we got six months to do something on health care. We are kidding each other, we are all just sitting here making this up if we think that we can fiddle around with the entitlements and all this other stuff and get control of this budget if you don't do something on health care. It is a joke. It's going to bankrupt the country. And you know—and the stimulus is peanuts compared to increase in bank loans.

So we have to look at—I don't mean we shouldn't do the stimulus. I haven't made the decision about how much and what, but I'm just saying let's don't get fixated on stuff that is not as big as the stuff that's also out there that has to be dealt with. On the spending side it's health care, and on the stimulus side, it has to be something that gets the private sector more active, too. I mean, the rest of this government expenditure is just a part of that, I think. (Applause.)

Earl. Earl is next, the gentleman in the audience, and then Rubin Mark (sp).

MR. EARL GRAVES (BLACK ENTERPRISE MAGAZINE): Thank you, President-elect Clinton and Vice President-elect Gore. As someone who has reported on and experienced first-hand the growth of black-owned businesses for nearly 25 years, it is a pleasure for me to participate in this summit. I appreciate the opportunity to briefly address some key small business and economic development issues which have been ignored or neglected during the past twelve years.

Twenty years ago, minorities, including women, were hoping to get a small business loan. Today, because of you, the officially designated spokesperson for American business is himself a minority. Now without commercializing this, given my business in Washington, I would just say, uh-huh, I believe that a strong support at the federal level for minority business enterprises is central to any discussion of black economic development in the United States. Federal government support of small business initiatives must be included in your administration's immediate short-term efforts to stimulate the economy by rebuilding the infrastructure and creating a job-growth program. As we have reported in Black Enterprise magazines, jobs provided by small businesses and MBEs in particular provide a long-term solution to high unemployment rates in inner city areas. These jobs are more stable in the long term than jobs associated with typical public works programs tied into rebuilding the infrastructure. Minority business enterprises help stabilize the economic base in minority communities, and help improve the overall quality of life in these areas.

There are three policy recommendations I would have and I would want the Clinton administration to address. Number one would be develop policies to stimulate the growth and viability of minority business enterprises. To facilitate this effort, I would suggest establishing a White House initiative for growing minority and women-owned businesses. This initiative should fall under the leadership, I would hope, of Ron Brown.

Further, I would emphasize the importance of identifying an experienced business person to run the Small Business Administration, as well. This individual must be charged to enforce the government loan guarantees for small business now under the Small Business Administration and to enforce greater efforts for private banks to adhere to their obligations under the Community Reinvestment Act. I would ask the executive branch to enforce the federal government's compliance with legislative mandates for minority contracting levels.

My second recommendation is for the federal government to provide economic incentives for state and local municipalities that receive federal funding to establish effective MBE programs. In the wake of the Supreme Court's ruling in the City of Richmond v. Crosin (sp), minority set-aside programs at the state and local levels are suffering greatly. Thirty-three states and subdivisions have abandoned their programs, and 66 others have or are currently reviewing their set-aside policies.

My final recommendation is to establish federally mandated enterprise zones. A federally directed enterprise zone program linked to a national infrastructure redevelopment plan can help revitalize the nation's distressed areas, boost unemployment—boost employment, excuse me, and increase consumer demand. These, gentlemen, should include an MBE program.

In closing, I would remind you that minority-owned and women-owned businesses are not asking for guarantee of results; only guarantee of opportunity. I thank you for the opportunity to share my concerns and recommendations with you and your team of economic advisers.

PRESIDENT-ELECT CLINTON: Thank you. The gentleman in the back there.

MR. MATT SHAFER: I'm Matt Schafer, from Idaho International Trade and Finance Consultants. You mentioned the engine of growth and trying to find some specific ideas. Let me mention three things that could have enormous impact, and ultimately not cost the taxpayer a dime.

The first would be to raise Export-Import Bank lending for exports overseas, especially to richer Third World countries, which are an especially important market if Europe and Japan are in a recession. In the 1970s—you won't believe this statistic, but it's true—US Export-Import Bank financed approximately 20 percent of US manufactured exports overseas, and in 1981 that dropped back to close to 1 percent. Huge impact.

Second, consider venture capital investment in some key technologies from a government point of view and mix that with private sector venture capital as a way of stimulating venture capital. This is already being done through DARPA and the Defense Department, but it could be expanded into some key technologies, and like Ex-Im Bank lending, which can be done at a break-even basis or only a slight profit, both of these steps not only will stimulate exports and the growth of new technologies, but potentially not cost the taxpayer a dime.

And thirdly, it's the idea of some kind of trading company to fill the gap of marketing products overseas. If it's too onerous to capitalize this with some government and private sector money mixed in together with the idea of reselling it to the private sector when it becomes profitable, then at least let's ask the commercial attaches and the State Department attaches up through the level of ambassador who are in charge of selling overseas to be more aggressive than ever before, even with the idea of some government incentives if necessary to make that happen.

Those are three specific ideas that ultimately may not cost the taxpayer a dime.

PRESIDENT-ELECT CLINTON: Let me ask the panelists and maybe some of the people in the audience a question related to the point he just made. One of the things that—one of the words nobody has uttered, I don't think, in the last two days since we've been here—it's a huge portion of our economy—is agriculture. How much of an impact could we have with a stimulus package that included expansion of some of our agricultural export subsidies or guarantees to countries that may be in deep trouble now?

Anybody have an opinion on that? Mr. Tull?

JOHN TULL (J.E. TULL & SONS): Governor, Senators—

PRESIDENT-ELECT CLINTON: We blew off a lot of opportunities in the last couple of years, and I'm interested in it. Go ahead.

MR. TULL: Thank you for finally getting around to agriculture. (Laughter.) As you know, I'm a farmer from Arkansas, and we are almost wholly dependent upon export markets. You spoke yesterday of the need of productivity. Our problem in farming is that we're too productive. We're too efficient. And we have to have the continuation of GSM-102 credits and of P.L. 480 in order to export our products. More importantly, we can compete with anyone in the world in agriculture if we have a level playing field. And I would certainly like to see this administration pursue the GATT and pursue the NAFTA. And that, with agricultural export credits, I think we can bring agriculture back out of its recession. Thank you, sir.

PRESIDENT-ELECT CLINTON: Who was next here? Anybody? We had the gentleman in the back that I also—yes. I tried to recognize you once before.

GRAHAM CLAYTOR (NATIONAL RAILROAD PASSENGERS CORP.): Thank you. I'm Graham Claytor, president of Amtrak. We run the national railroad passenger system.

I want to address a question that's been raised, how long from action to jobs? We have laid off several hundred people around the country, not because we haven't got work for them to do; because we haven't got the financing. Work that's desperately needed. We'd put them to work within weeks. We have 80-year-old facilities that we are using to maintain all of our equipment. We've got detailed plans for making those modern, up-to-date facilities that would provide more productivity. We're ready to start that instantly. We'd get those back to work within weeks and in full force within months.

There's another thing. Where would the money come from? This will take about a billion dollars to do this, get it done, going quickly. Money, we've got $2^1/_2$ cents in the federal fuel tax that's been set aside for eventual reduction of the deficit. We ought to take that money right now and put it to work. That would be about $3 billion right there. We'd like to take a billion dollars of that, and we'd get our national railroad passenger system with people back at work right away in first-class shape.

I would like to talk about high-speed rail, which is coming. High-speed rail, the French TGV and the Japanese bullet train, is down the road quite a piece because that requires building a whole new railroad. We have high-speed rail right now between Washington and New York at 125 miles an hour. We tested a train last week at 150 on the same track. We're ready to put that kind of high-speed rail right away

266

around the country, New York to Boston and in other cities around Chicago.

So, we're ready to roll. All we need is capital improvement, capital money. Thank you. (Applause.)

PRESIDENT-ELECT CLINTON: Now that was a good statement. Mr. Mark.

REUBEN MARK (COLGATE-PALMOLIVE COMPANY): Governor Clinton, a moment ago, you spoke quite strongly about the fact that we were just talking to ourselves unless the longer-term problem of health care costs were addressed. Similarly, the discussion yesterday focused on the investment in people, and that long-term problem, that long-term opportunity, must be addressed also.

And perhaps it's mixing apples and oranges, but could I respectfully request that any short-term economic stimulus package also includes very specific initiatives for early childhood, for elementary education, for the transition, all the things that were discussed yesterday, which will give not only a substantive start, because obviously long-term solutions don't come about unless there is short-term action, but, secondly, provide a real message and a real sense of hope to the tens of millions of people who are counting on your leadership. I mean, if we think about you and every one in this room how we approached school when we were five or six years old, we came reasonably prepared; we came to a building that was functional; and we were welcomed by people who were trained and motivated and respected. And children today, of course, don't face that situation in any of those three areas.

And perhaps that's a reasonable way to break it down. How do we deal with how the children approach? Is there any way in your infrastructure program, understanding there are different kinds of money, that school infrastructure can be treated or stimulus to a school infrastructure can be treated? And is there some mechanism on a federal level that can be used to return the teaching profession to the position that it historically had and should have?

Just as a—I guess I'm probably among the last to speak in this session. I know that I am leaving enormously encouraged, and I think there are 329 or so people who are very excited about the next few months and the next few years. So, that's extraordinary.

PRESIDENT-ELECT CLINTON: Very briefly, the answer to your question is yes, there are some things we can do at the national level on teacher standards and esteem. And I don't know whether we can do anything on school infrastructure. The national government's never done that. Most states don't even do that. Some states do, some states don't. It's a very dicey thing for us to get into in a new way.

I'm going to close with Mr. Corry and Mr. Johnson and Mr. Faux, and ask you to be very brief. We have run way—we started seven minutes early and we've run way over our time, mostly because the only mistake the people putting the program together have shown that no one can speak in five minutes as a presenter. (Laughter.) Go ahead.

MR. ROBERT JOHNSON (BLACK ENTERTAINMENT TELEVISION): Thank you, Governor Clinton.

Very brief. We've heard a lot of statistics, and I just want to sort of caution you about what an old professor at Princeton of mine told me. Many people use statistics the way a drunk uses a street lamp: to hold them up rather than for illumination. (Laughter.)

I want to make a point that—I want to illuminate one point. What we're talking about are people. We're talking about moving this country ahead, and you can't move one society in this country ahead without moving the other. And I think the biggest task that you're going to have to face in your administration is convincing the majority of Americans who are solidly entrenched in the middle class that they must bring along with them millions of Americans who are not part of that same class. That's the fundamental problem that I think this country's going to face.

You see what's happening in Germany, with the resurgence of Nazism because of the competition and the fear for scarce resources and scarce jobs. If that happens in the United States, we have the same potential problem. So I think the fundamental question that we face—I don't there's a debate—we have to create jobs. We have to provide opportunity. The standard of living for everyone in this room is dependent upon the standard of living for every minority American in Washington, DC, in Chicago, in New Orleans, and in Little Rock. That's the only issue that we face, how to move this country ahead together.

Thank you.

PRESIDENT-ELECT CLINTON: Thank you.
Charles?

MR. CHARLES CORRY (USX CORPORATION): Just very briefly again, and to follow up on the same point. I don't think we should overlook the fact that we have the opportunity to stimulate the economy by addressing our prime trade problem, and I'm speaking, of course, of our trade problems with Japan. The fact that our problem is so concentrated with one nation and so concentrated in one sector—that is, automotive—should make it easier to address and correct. This has many redeeming virtues if the new administration can tackle this problem and solve it.

One, we're talking about stimulating the economy and creating jobs in a way that won't require us to impose any new taxes or provide any tax breaks that would diminish government revenues, and it would, of course, not increase the federal deficit. So, many virtues, and it would be a very powerful stimulant because automotive manufacturing cuts across so much of the spectrum of American manufacturing.

PRESIDENT-ELECT CLINTON: Jeff?

MR. JEFF FAUX (ECONOMIC POLICY INSTITUTE): Thank you, Governor. I would like to speak first in support of Jim Tobin's proposal. I think it's the right number, and I think it's the right mix and the right package.

PRESIDENT-ELECT CLINTON: You favor $60 billion over one year or two?

MR. FAUX: Over two. Eighteen months. I would break it out into $30 billion for the rest of fiscal '93, and then $60 billion for fiscal '94. I think we make too much of the immediate economic indicators. We have $300 billion in excess capacity in this economy already. My number for the number of people who are out of work is probably closer to 16 million equivalent in terms of jobs.

The problem here is not to guess, not to rely on guessing what's going to happen in 1993. None of us knows. We don't know whether the growth rate's going to be 3 percent, 3.5 percent, 2 percent, or 1.5. It's a question of risk. And the way I look at it is, supposing the optimists are right, supposing that we're going to grow at 3 percent for the next two years, and then we stimulate the economy, the worst that can happen is by the end of 1994 we have an unemployment rate that's 6 percent rather than 6.5. But supposing the pessimists are right. Supposing we grow at less than 2 percent. A stimulus could be the difference between a rising unemployment rate and a falling unemployment rate. So it's not a question of who's right or wrong about the economy, it's where the risks are.

The last point I'd like to make is to bring us full circle back to the question you raised yesterday. You asked us to think about what constitutes economic security in the new world that we're in. It seems to me that a job for everyone willing and able to work has got to be in that package. If we don't stimulate the economy in one way or another, we are still going to have millions of people in this country without that opportunity, and I think all of our goals on social programs and the social compact gets undercut unless we've got jobs out there for people who want one. If parents aren't working, families don't work. So I think that is the bottom line.

Thank you. (Applause.)

PRESIDENT-ELECT CLINTON: There's not going to be all that much difference in what we talked about now and what we're going to talk about in the next panel, so let's take a five-minute break and get the other folks up here, and I'll just recognize them.

(Five minute recess.)

PRESIDENT-ELECT CLINTON: Let's go on, now. I think we're all here. I want to—we will talk a little more in this session about issues of longer-term investment and deficit reduction, and I want to begin by introducing Felix Rohatyn, the senior partner of Lazard Freres, who is a well-known expert in corporate mergers and acquisitions, chairman of the Municipal Assistance Corporation for New York City, and the gentleman who restructured New York City's debt during the fiscal crisis in the mid-'70s.

I also want to say that Felix went with Senator Bentsen and others to that vaunted and famous meeting of the Perot supporters. And just to prove how persuasive he was—(laughs)—he didn't even get back to New York before Mr. Perot got back in the race for President. (Laughter.) But I heard that he was, nonetheless, brilliant there. (Laughter.) Thank you so much for being here.

MR. FELIX ROHATYN (LAZARD FRERES & COMPANY): Thank you for that introduction, Governor. (Laughter.)

Mr. President-elect, Mr. Vice President-elect, thank you for the opportunity of participating at a truly extraordinary meeting.

The question you're looking at is whether you can have growth, investment, and long-term deficit reduction simultaneously. I believe that the answer is that there is no practical alternative. Without growth, there can be no deficit reduction. Without investment, there

270

can be no growth. I'm not an economic theorist, so I can only speak of the experience and the actions we took to deal with New York City's deficit crisis in the '70s and how we resolved it. I believe there are some valid similarities with our existing national situation.

The City in '75 had a runaway deficit amounting to $1½ billion, or almost 15 percent of its budget, which, incidentally, is smaller than the proportion of the federal budget. It had completely abandoned its capital investment program in order to finance operations. It lost access to the financial markets. It was steadily losing private sector jobs. Debt service reached over 20 percent of the budget when the state effectively took control of the city.

From '75 to '80, we balanced the city's budget through a program of rigid expenditure controls, new revenues, and investment-driven growth. During that period, expenditures grew by 2 percent per annum while revenues grew by 7 to 8 percent per annum. And we have, since 1980, had 12 balanced budgets in a row.

Simultaneously with the onset of our deficit-closing plan, we created a separate financing agency, the Municipal Assistance Corporation, to finance the phase-out of the deficit and to gear up as rapidly as possible the city's capital infrastructure program. This was done by public sales of new bonds, backed by a portion of the city's sales tax. From '75 to '84, New York City's annual infrastructure investment program went from $200 million per annum, which was less than our minimum maintenance requirement, to over $4 billion per annum, the minimum rate required to maintain our facilities.

There is no question in my mind that an ability to gear up our investment program separately but simultaneously with our deficit reduction program reinforced the latter. Slow growth would have required stretching out deficit reduction or mutilating the city with even harsher cuts or tax increases. This would ultimately both be self-defeating by driving taxpayers away and leaving a higher and higher proportion of people requiring government support with insufficient revenues to help them. As it was, taxes were increased. So were university tuitions, transit fares, tolls, wages were frozen, and the public workforce was reduced by 20 percent.

The sacrifice required was considerable, but the investment program mitigated the pain somewhat and provided economic stimulus, employment, and improved quality of life. By 1984, MAC had issued almost $10 billion of bonds before terminating its financing program and beginning to pay down its debt. By now we're down to $6½ billion, and MAC will have totally paid off its debts by the year 2008, which is probably a unique experience for a government agency. We financed the city's capital for ten years, and our debt will be paid off over 32 years, which is the way it should be. The notion that the city would have been required to finance its capital program on a pay-as-you-go basis is totally impractical.

I believe the same principle could apply to a national program. The $80 billion four-year program in your plan could be increased and stretched out and financed separately through a new borrowing agency selling bonds serviced by a dedicated tax, which, as you know, I would urge to be a gasoline tax. The rest of the budget, essentially the expense budget, beginning with health care costs, should then be brought into balance over six to eight years, depending on economic condition.

Let me say, incidentally, that I do not believe there is such a thing as a credible budget deficit closing plan without some kind of a control mechanism to see to it that over time the adjustments inevitably required can be made and can be made on a timely basis.

I do not believe that today's economic risks are mostly inflation. I believe that deflation can be just as deadly, and that there are winds of deflation blowing through the world. A large, predictable public investment program separately financed together with a gradual deficit reduction program, including all of the sacred cows, seems to me more prudent than a one-sided, brutal deficit reduction over a short period of time.

I see nothing on the horizon from the work that I do to indicate potential for large-scale new job creation. On the contrary, business is cutting back, state and local governments are cutting back, cities are in terrible trouble. Public investment is needed both because it is job-creating and because the country is in terrible physical condition.

I believe that private sector stimulus can be done much better by changes on issues such as credit availability and credit regulation. If there is stimulus, it should be, as Senator Bentsen indicated, as part of a G-7 program. And programs such as export guarantee insurance, both for agriculture and in areas where we are facing unfair trade practices such as Airbus sales, should be used in my judgment without hesitation even at the price of subsidizing exports.

None of this is easy or even clear-cut. It will require considerable shared sacrifice fairly distributed. It will require business/labor cooperation and it will require strong political leadership. But I believe it is to be the less risky option. The investment program will give hope to the American people as well as help urban, suburban, and rural areas. On a sufficiently large scale, it can be helpful both in defense conversion and in helping train and employ inner-city youngsters in rebuilding their neighborhoods in CCC-type or other type of activities. I believe this program to be an absolute necessity.

And I think I made my five minutes, Governor.

PRESIDENT-ELECT CLINTON: You did. (Applause.) Give him a hand.

I'm scared to do this because I don't want to blow this string we're on here, but you have written in other places that you also thought we ought to have an investment tax credit. Have you changed your mind about that?

MR. ROHATYN: No, sir, I have not. I believe that a credible deficit reduction plan can include an investment tax credit as one of its components, offset by other cuts.

PRESIDENT-ELECT CLINTON: Thank you.

Henry Aaron is the director of the Economic Studies Program at the Brookings Institution. In the '70s, he was assistant secretary for planning and evaluation for the Department of Health, Education, and Welfare during the Carter presidency. He's a member of the Institute of Medicine and vice president of the National Academy of Social Insurance. And he was an advisor to our campaign, for which I am very grateful. Mr. Aaron.

MR. HENRY AARON (BROOKINGS INSTITUTION): Thank you, Governor Clinton, Senator Gore.

I'd like first to make a couple of brief comments on the recommendations for a quick stimulus package. I believe you have heretofore taken the position that it was wise and prudent to await economic developments as they unfold at the end of the year. Look at fourth quarter GNP, December unemployment, and other indicators. I believe that is the prudent course to adhere to. It may be that stimulus is necessary, but if the economy shows continuing signs of recovery, I think it should be extremely small or possibly shelved.

I'd like to turn and focus most of my attention, however, on long-term deficit reduction, which has been likened to a disease. I think the analogy is apt. It is a slow, wasting disease. The income of each American today is $1,000 on the average, adult and child, lower than it would have been had the deficit not existed for the last ten years. It'll be an additional $1,000 a year less if the deficit persists at its current level. And national wealth, if the deficit persists for another decade, will be $2.5 trillion less than it otherwise would be.

Those are just dry statistics. The real damage is the tangible injury that the deficit inflicts on individual Americans. The federal government now borrows more than half of all private saving generated by businesses and individuals. Business investors and home buyers, therefore, have to compete for a constricted pool of savings, and the result is higher interest rates.

Young couples who would like to buy a first home, but can't afford to do so because of high interest rates, are victims of the federal budget deficit.

Workers whose wages stagnate because their employers can't afford to borrow the funds they need to buy productivity-enhancing capital equipment are also victims of the federal deficit.

And high interest rates increase the exchange value of the US dollar, so automobiles, steel, and machine tool workers who are out of jobs because an overvalued dollar hinders US companies from selling abroad and helps foreign companies sell here are victims of the federal deficit. And so are the businesses who see their profits eroded or their survival threatened because of an overvalued US dollar.

I'm not talking now about economists' abstractions. I'm talking about the daily travail of American workers and businesses. If the federal deficit remains just an abstraction, a number too large for human comprehension, a quantity that floats unconnected with human loss and frustration that it inevitably causes, we are never effectively going to deal with it.

As you know better than I'm sure anybody else around this table, the call for increased spending and for tax breaks—you've heard many of them here—is endless. These claims are tangible and easily understood. And many of them are deserving of approval. But unless the public recognizes that the excessive federal deficits infect the economic hopes and aspirations of US businesses and US workers, the deficit and the pain it inflicts are going to persist indefinitely.

One idea that has surfaced in the course of this conference I believe would not help. A capital budget does not change the central fiscal fact, when the economy is at or near full employment and the government borrows, it diverts private saving from private investment. The US private economy is not now suffering from a glut of private capital, as Mr. Rohatyn just stressed. The United States needs more private investment, not less. That means, I think, that all new government spending should be paid for by either cutting other spending or by raising taxes, not by even more borrowing. If the federal government borrows to pay for infrastructure or anything else, the private economy either has to invest less at home or borrow more abroad. And in either case, American citizens are then deprived of the returns to investment, either because the investment doesn't occur, or because the returns flow to foreign owners.

Setting aside deficit-causing expenditures in a capital budget carries an anesthetizing message: It's capital, so we can borrow to pay for it. To be sure, borrowing is sometimes justified, to stimulate the economy during recession, for example. But it normally is not justified to pay for government activities, unless the evidence is overwhelming that federal investments are vastly more productive than the private investments they would displace. And even then, growth will be enhanced more if the government pays for what it buys.

Experience with state capital budgets may seem to contradict all of this, but state experience in this area, I believe, is badly misleading. Bond rating services quickly and severely punish states that abuse capital budgets. The federal government is subject to no such discipline. The opportunities for abuse at the national level are unlimited and dangerous. I can think of virtually nothing the federal government does that clever advocates could not characterize as investment.

The need to cut the deficit must remain clearly before us because it is important and because it is doable if we all share fairly in the task. Some of the most popular quick fixes are, in my view, delusions. We can and must, as you have stressed, cut the growth of health care costs. But structurally sound cut-backs will take time. And, in my view, you will see meager savings in your first term, but large savings are possible by the year 2000.

Some additional revenue will come spontaneously from increased growth, but the fruits of growth-enhancing measures will be modest and slow in coming. In particular, some advocates, in my view, have grossly exaggerated the growth-enhancing effects of infrastructure investment. These effects are, in many cases, smaller than those of the private investment that they would supplant if financed by borrowing, and I would stress in very few cases, as a practical matter, will it be possible to gin them up fast enough to do much during the current recession.

You earlier asked somebody who said there were a thousand ways to deal with something for three. I'd like to close by listing a few specifics that illustrate the kinds of choices that will be necessary to meet the deficit reduction goals that you have set.

As you have suggested, additional savings can be achieved below the projected defense budget by cutting defense outlays. Agricultural subsidies need to be reduced. Some veterans' pensions should be cut. We need to charge for airways and waterways and for use of the radio spectrum. We are spending money on a NASA space station and an advanced rocket that I think are not of the highest priority. Some reduction in civilian and military retirement is in order. Part B premiums for Medicare have not been raised enough to keep up with rising costs.

Two years ago, I heard Mr. Panetta deliver a no-nonsense pep talk to new members of Congress. It was excellent. He said, in effect, to the members: "You have been elected to cut the budget deficit. Many of you have said that eliminating waste will suffice. Nonsense. Stand with me on the tough votes or don't bother me."

I think I'm hearing that message from the program that you've advanced, Mr. Clinton, because that is the key to delivering on the—meeting the targets for deficit reduction that you have set.

Thank you.

PRESIDENT-ELECT CLINTON: Thank you.

The next speaker is Isabel Sawhill, a senior fellow at the Urban Institute, and director of the Children's Roundtable. She is the former director of a multi-year assessment of the Reagan administration's domestic policy initiatives. I had a great joke about that, but I can't bring myself to do it. (Laughter.) Her publications include, *Challenge to Leadership: Economic and Social Issues for the Next Decade.*

Ms. Sawhill?

Ms. ISABEL SAWHILL (URBAN INSTITUTE): Thank you very much, Mr. President-elect, Mr. Vice President-elect. I hope you'll tell me the joke later. (Laughter.)

Almost everyone who has spoken so far has agreed that even if we recover fully from the current recession there will still be enormous economic problems facing the country. To continue with Henry Aaron's medical metaphor here, economies have always been subject to bouts of the flu, but what we have now is not just a bout of the flu but an underlying cancer that, as you have said, has been eating away at our economy for about two decades now. That cancer, as we learned yesterday, is called slow productivity growth, and virtually everyone agrees that the solution has got to be more investment. The disagreements are not over whether to invest, but rather on how much and where.

Some are going to advise you, Mr. President-elect, to focus most of your attention on the budget deficit as a way of freeing up resources for private investment. The budget deficit is affecting individuals and businesses in all the ways that Henry Aaron has so well described. And although I'm not going to repeat these same points, in the interest of time, I want to associate myself with virtually all of the points that he made. Other people, however, are going to argue that the most important thing we can do is to invest more in education, training, infrastructure, research, programs for children, and other kinds of public investment. We heard a lot of those arguments yesterday. Let me just tick them for you again.

First, in a global economy, capital and technology move very easily across national borders, and the only unique resource that we have are our well-trained workers and our infrastructure.

Secondly, as Marian Wright Edelman, Lee Shore, and others told us, there are investments in our children that would make any venture capitalist drool in terms of the kind of rate of return that we can get on the taxpayer's dollar.

Third, we also heard that wage premiums for well-educated workers have gone through the roof, suggesting to any economist worth his or her salt that investments in people as opposed to machines are going to pay off better in the future.

And finally, as both Bob Solow and Alan Blinder emphasized, poverty, rising inequality, and falling wages for people without a college education are also problems that can be addressed by more attention to investments in people.

So there are good arguments for tackling both deficits, but doing so is going to be extremely expensive, and enacting the kind of spending cuts and tax increases that are going to be sufficient to address both deficits is simply not in the cards. So in the end, you're going to have to make really tough choices about which to make your greatest priority.

And thinking about the choices, I'd like to suggest that you maintain what I call a balanced portfolio of public and private investments. We shouldn't put all of our eggs in the private investment basket, but neither should we put all of our eggs in the public investment basket. I make this argument essentially for two reasons.

First, everything we know suggests that public and private investments are complementary. For example, it doesn't do much good to build new factories and equipment with new machinery if you don't have well-trained workers to operate them.

Second, I don't think it's possible to make any general statements about which type of investment, public or private, will bring a higher rate of return to the nation. The variation in rates of return on projects within each sector is almost certainly far larger than the variation in rate of return between them.

Yesterday, Michael Porter told us, for example, that the private sector overinvests in real estate and acquisitions and underinvests in training, R&D, and other softer forms of investment. Alicia Munnell told us that the public sector overinvests in building new roads and underinvests in maintaining the existing ones in good repair, and you've just heard Henry further, I think, reinforce that point. According to a recent Labor Department evaluation of our job training program, short-term training programs for disadvantaged youth are not as effective as similar programs for adults.

Given the uncertainties—well, I want to add one more point here, which is that making these kinds of distinctions between good invest-ment and bad investment in the public sector and getting Congress to make them isn't always possible. So given this, and given the uncer-tainties, we ought to diversify our portfolio and do the best job we possibly can of selecting projects within each sector with the very best pay-off for our nation.

To make this suggestion more specific, I would advise you to devote more or less half of any new taxes or spending cuts to deficit reduction and about another half to high-priority public investment and some carefully-selected tax incentives for business. And as Mr. Panetta and others at the last session pointed out, by adjusting the timing of both, you should be able to get both some short-run stimulus and some long-run deficit reduction out of it.

I'd like to conclude by thanking you for bringing us together here. You said yesterday that one purpose of these meetings was to recon-nect people to their government. I think we're accomplishing that here. Last night I said on the Larry King Show that I hope and believe this is the beginning of the end of gridlock.

Thank you very much.

President-elect Clinton: Thank you very much. (Applause.) If you were on the Larry King Show, you were reconnected to the people by definition. (Laughter.)

Our final presenter is Bill Gray, the President and CEO of the United Negro College Fund, a former member of the House of Representa-tives, former majority whip, predecessor of Representative Panetta as Chair of the House Budget Committee, and among other things, the pastor of the Bridehope Baptist Church in Philadelphia for more than 20 years, since he was a young 15-year-old minister.

Reverend Gray, the floor is yours.

Mr. Gray: Thank you very much, President-elect Clinton, and Vice President-elect Gore.

Ladies and gentlemen, I'm delighted to join all of you in this distin-guished panel to discuss investment and deficit reduction.

I believe all of us agree that deficits are a major problem facing our economic future. I believe all of us know that a national debt that has been tripled in the last few years and yearly interest payments of $200 billion a year will not help America create new opportunities in a global marketplace. In fact, they hold us back from our full potential and long-term sustainable growth.

Obviously, we must take strong action to curb the growth of deficits.

A package of spending cuts and revenue changes phased in over a four-year period, combined with spending caps and strong enforcement measures, would send, I believe, the best signal to the marketplace and ensure long-term growth. However, as we reduce our deficits, we must be careful that we do not reduce investments in those areas that help long-term economic growth. In the past, we have often made that mistake. Maintaining our fiscal infrastructure is important for future growth. Policies that disinvest for short-term savings in this area ultimately will reduce our growth potential in the future.

Another area that is critical for growth is our human infrastructure, and you heard some talk about that yesterday. Educational opportunity, targeted job training, health care and nutrition programs for our children and for the truly disadvantaged are investment areas that are linked to economic growth and future domestic savings.

Let me illustrate. At UNCF colleges, 53,000 students are being empowered through education, coming from disadvantaged backgrounds. Forty-four percent come from single-parent, female heads of household families. Sixty percent are first in their family to go to college. Fifty percent come from families where the income, combined gross income is under $25,000. They will enter the workforce trained and skilled. That will promote growth in a global marketplace. They will avoid the hopelessness and despair that leads to activities that cost us more. That will promote domestic savings.

However, I've got to give a word of caution. I agree with what Isabel Sawhill said, that any plan that comes forth ought to be directed at both deficit reduction and some investment, whether it's 50-50 or 70-30. Obviously, the investments ought to be up front, and the deficit reduction, particularly if economic growth is just beginning to take place, ought to be timed in such a way that most of it occurs in year two, three, and four. But there's a word of caution. Deficit reduction involves difficult choices. Deficit reduction is not easy. Every spending program has a constituency, and nearly every beneficiary of government spending and tax policy see themselves as national interests and the others as special interests.

We cannot maintain this attitude. We cannot maintain all of the present priorities, reduce the deficit, and make investments that are badly needed. Yet, I believe there is something we can do. I saw it not too long ago when a group of Republicans, Democrats, conservatives, liberals came together under the leadership of Drew Lewis and Bob Strauss and the National Economic Council, and they came up and agreed on a plan, a tough plan. It was real. It called for shared sacrifice. But it also maintained key investments. But, alas, national leadership to support it was lacking.

I believe that all Americans want tough, real deficit reduction, but they also want shared sacrifice around a set of priorities that they can agree with. It will take strong, innovative leadership that is willing to stay involved and build a national consensus for such a plan, that reduces the deficits while at the same time increasing growth and opportunity.

I believe perhaps here this week we are seeing that consensus being built among all Americans as President-elect Clinton and his team listens to all of us talk about the way to do it.

Thank you. (Applause.)

PRESIDENT-ELECT CLINTON: Thank you very much.

Let me compliment all the speakers and, if I might, just make two points to summarize what they have said. Even though they did not, with the exception of Henry, take explicit issue with some of the arguments advanced in the earlier session, I would remind you that if you go back to the formulation that Isabel put out and that Bill Gray supported, and at least the long-term remarks made by Felix, if you take any money you raise in taxes or any money you generate from spending cuts and you divide it 50 percent in deficit reduction and 50 percent to public and private sector investment, that's by definition not a stimulus package that increases the deficit. It may not be the—it may be the right thing to do. And I might say that all during my campaign, actually that's precisely what I tried to do from beginning to end. It wasn't until the last few months that the whole idea of a stimulus even came up, when it looked like this long business cycle recession would just never end.

So that's one issue; you know, should we immediately begin to increase investment and reduce the deficit and forget about the stimulus, or keep it low, which puts some of the remarks here at direct odds with the positions taken by others at the previous session and that will be taken by people here.

The other thing I want to mention, it might have been little noticed, but it's something Mr. Panetta and I have talked a lot about, and that is the comment that Felix Rohatyn made that any multi-year deficit reduction program is not going to have any credibility unless there is some sort of enforcement mechanism. And I would respectfully suggest that the so-called Gramm-Rudman-Hollings enforcement mechanism is not a very good one for us to follow for the future because, number one, it always gets evaded; but, number two, it's based on revenue estimates to some extent; and thirdly, it's based on a firewall between defense and domestic spending that may or may not be relevant depending on rapidly unfolding events abroad and at home. So, we may need a new and different kind of enforcement mechanism, but I want to stand up and support what Felix said. You've got to have some stick in that thing that goes from year to year or it doesn't mean much.

Now, having said that, Mr. Kuttner. We'll just open the floor.

Mr. Robert Kuttner (Syndicated Columnist): Mr. President-elect, Mr. Vice President-elect, there is a meta issue lurking here in this debate and that meta issue is the relationship of chronic slow growth to the deficit. There was a sign on the—

President-elect Clinton: What's the difference in a mega issue and a meta issue? Is it one's big and the other's philosophical?

Mr. Kuttner: I guess. I guess—(laughter)—what I meant was there's an underlying issue behind the ostensible issues here, and it is the relationship of the deficit to chronic slow growth.

I was thinking of that sign, that famous sign, in your campaign office. A lot of people would have preferred that that sign read "It's the deficit, stupid," or "It's entitlements, stupid." But the fellow who ran on that slogan got 19 percent of the vote, and he's not sitting in your chair.

And it seems to me that the issue is slow growth. The issue is long-term strategies and short-term strategies to get to a higher trajectory of growth and then make that growth sustainable. We had a lot of stimulus—we had too much stimulus—in the '80s. It was the wrong kind of stimulus because it did not lead to investment and it did not lead to sustainable growth. Now, a lot of people have concluded from that failure that the remedy is therefore to throw the engine into reverse and to give priority to deficit reduction over and above everything else, beginning with entitlement cuts.

It seems to me that the issues that were talked about yesterday, the structural reforms, are the key to getting to a higher growth path, and the question is how do you get from here to there in the meantime, when a lot of people are losing jobs? And the answer, it seems to me, is that the nature of the stimulus is every bit as important as the degree of stimulus. The nature of the stimulus is investment-led. And then you get on with the business of the structural reforms.

One other thought, a lot of the things that were talked about yesterday, the structural reforms that we need to have a more productive economy, things like lifetime learning and upgrading, things like childcare for working parents, things like universal health insurance access, these are, to use the dirty word, entitlements. And maybe we need another dirty word or a clean word because some of these entitlements will save money and some of these entitlements will make the economy more productive, but they are nonetheless a kind of entitlement.

One last point. I think of World War II. In 1939, the ratio of debt to GDP was 51 percent, the same as it is today. And World War II came along and Franklin Roosevelt quintupled the debt. And we came out of the war with a rebuilt physical plant, a rebuilt human capital plant, new technologies, and 25 years of high growth, which enabled us to work that debt ratio down to 26 percent of GDP. It seems to me if you put the cart before the horse and you put deficit reduction uber alles first, you're going to end up with 2 percent growth as far as the eye can see. You need to get to a higher trajectory of growth, led by investment, and then gradually work the deficit down.

Finally, Mr. President, I—words fail me in describing what an extraordinary event this is. This has to be the defining moment of your presidency. It is the President as teacher, as leader, as explainer, as synthesizer. This is a magical moment, and I thank you for including me and for offering this to the country. (Applause.)

PRESIDENT-ELECT CLINTON: Thank you. I hope that doesn't mean it's all downhill from here. (Laughter.)

If I might, I want to move from you to Mr. Eisner, but I want to set the stage first. This is a very important issue for us here. There is—I would hope we could all agree. We may disagree on whether there ought to be a stimulus and how much it ought to be and, you know, how much we need to bring down the debt, but one of the ideas that I tried to bring to bear in this campaign was that there—all spending is not the same, whether it's in the public or the private sector. And all stimulus is not the same. And that there really is a fundamental difference between investment and consumption.

And I might be wrong about this, but, you know, my friend John Bryant (sp) said yesterday, basically cautioned me against an investment tax credit and said that the kind of so-called—the value-free nature of the '86 Tax Act was a better way to go. But a lot of people took those lower rates in '86 and wasted the living daylights out of that money.

And I—my own view is that if you look at what produces growth, if you look at these massive savings and investment rates that a lot of the developing countries have followed, we can't do that because we don't have the capacity or the desire, and it wouldn't be good policy to depress our own people's standards of living as much as it was depressed, say, in Taiwan or Korea to reach those double digit growth rates.

But there is plainly—I just point that out because there is plainly a difference between spending money and investing it. There are people around this table that have built massive businesses because they saved a lot of the money they earned and reinvested it. And so, I say that just to say that whether we do the stimulus or not and whatever decision we make on the deficit, we have got to change the character of federal spending toward a more investment orientation.

Now, let me introduce Robert Eisner and say this. I don't want to provoke a fight out of this, but I want you all at least to know what the two arguments are. Henry Aaron made a terrific case against having a capital budget. And he's absolutely right. You know, we have a capital budget in my state, but if I get too much debt, the bond markets will blow my brains out, right? So, when I was governor, we didn't have much debt. And that's right. And there is no such discipline on the other side. Robert Eisner, whom I'm about to recognize, is sort of the country's foremost advocate that we have overstated our real debt because we don't take account of capital investments and growth and, as a consequence, we're likely to make very bad policy decisions by not distinguishing between the kinds of debt we have and the real measure of it. So, I would just like to ask him to briefly make the counterpoint argument to Henry and any other point he wants to make, and then we'll go back around the table.

MR. ROBERT EISNER (NORTHWESTERN UNIVERSITY): Thank you very much, Governor Clinton. I would be happy to yield my two minutes to you. You're stating it so well.

I would like to emphasize, to begin with, that deficits can be too large; they can also be too small. You can't tell which unless you measure them right. In fact, the federal budget is measured in a way which would shock any private business or accountant that looks at it. We simply don't do what everybody else does. We don't separate current expenditures from capital expenditures. It's like an individual saying it makes no difference whether he goes into debt to spend his money gambling it away at Las Vegas or spends his money that he borrows to buy a house.

In fact, debt is increasing everywhere. Private debt increases, business debt increases. There is a real question as to whether we should say government debt alone cannot increase. In a growing economy, you expect everything to increase. The economy should be growing perhaps at 7 percent. If it were growing at 7 percent, it means that we could keep the debt-GNP ratio, the debt-GDP ratio, the debt-income ratio, constant at the 50 percent or so it is now. But a 7 percent growth in the debt, which would keep that ratio constant, would mean a $210 billion increase in the debt and the increase in the debt is exactly the deficit. So, it means you could have a deficit of $210 billion a year and still be fiscally responsible in the sense of not letting your debt outgrow your income.

But, as has been said, it is very important what you incur that deficit for. The deficits of the '80s, I'd have to say—and everybody who knows me knows I was no supporter of the Reagan administration, but to keep saying that those deficits dragged down the economy is absurd. Those deficits, badly conceived, badly formulated, were actually a major engine of growth. They gave us growth over the '80s and into the Bush administration.

The point then is that we might well think of balancing the current budget, the expenditures for current things, just as any individual should do, any business might do, but to feel free to borrow for worthwhile, productive investment that will advance us in the future. And that is all we've been talking about now for two days, investment for the future. If you're going to say that we have to hamstring the federal government so that it alone cannot borrow for investment, you're going to prevent us from doing just what we have to do.

Now, I would say a word very quickly on the matter of the current situation. We have lost $100 billion a year of private investment in the last three years of slow economy and recession. The best way to have more private investment is to have a prosperous economy. You can also add, by the way, a very temporary, major, incremental tax—investment tax credit, temporary to give us a big leap now which probably would not cost much on the deficit or over the long run.

On the matter of phasing in measures to see to it that over the long run our debt-GNP ratio does not go up, I would just urge that my colleagues be somewhat bolder and not say, "Well, phase it in at 6½ percent unemployment, something like that." We had under 5½ percent unemployment for three years from 1988 to 1990. There's no reason we can't attain at least that in the Clinton administration and attain it, I hope, rapidly. In fact, I was brought up to believe that 4 percent unemployment was a target. In the Vietnam War, we had 3 percent unemployment. There's no reason we have to have a war to have unemployment that low.

Certainly, in a time of prosperity when we're really booming, you have to be very careful not to have excessive stimulus. At that time, we should take whatever measures we have to either to raise taxes or to cut government spending further if that's what we want to do.

PRESIDENT-ELECT CLINTON: Thank you.

Anybody—Jerry? Jerry Pearlman of Zenith.

MR. JERRY PEARLMAN (ZENITH ELECTRONICS): Just a couple of quick comments, first on the—on short-term stimulus. I certainly would be supportive of a temporary two-year incremental investment tax credit as a timing mechanism and to—[it'll] cost a little bit of money, but to have a real impact on investment. In the long—

PRESIDENT-ELECT CLINTON: Two—two years?

MR. PEARLMAN: Two years. In the long term, the ITC, I believe, has no value in terms of investment because there aren't any corporate projects that are marginal where a 10 percent change in the denominator really makes a bad project into a good project. And so it really is just a change in the overall corporate rate.

I think that there's wide agreement in the—real consensus in the points that have been made about government providing of structural environment to improve the competitive position of business, which will help us in the long term, and that part of that structure has to be education, and part of it has to be breaking the health care cycle. I would offer a couple of other things that I think have got real potential for long-term benefit in three areas: trade, tax, and technology.

In trade, I think that we really have to look, as John Sculley mentioned quickly yesterday, at worldwide best practice, probably starting to look in Germany and Japan, but looking elsewhere in terms of how to coordinate all of our agencies for a concerted trade effort. And that includes all the administrative agencies and the finance agencies.

Second in trade, I think we need tough enforcement of the existing law. I talked to Ron Brown last night, who said he's already heard from Senator Hollings that there's an awful lot of law if enforced would really do a tremendous amount for levelling the playing field that is already there. I'll send you a fair amount of paperwork on that —(laughs)—as I said I would send it to Secretary-designate Brown. I think we have to understand also it's a multi-faceted problem that we talked about the PRC yesterday and MFN as if the trade-off was prison labor and human rights and arms exports alone, but there's also below-cost exports that look good to the consumer in the short run and close our industries down in the long run.

I think we have to be very careful when we analyze trade statistics. You talked about—we've eliminated the deficit with Korea and Taiwan, but that may, in fact, be because the Koreans and the Taiwanese have taken their high-value product and are doing final assembly in Malaysia and Thailand and Indonesia because they also know how— that they need a low labor element in final assembly, and they've simply moved the statistics around, or they've moved them to some places to avoid dumping law.

I think we need to expand NAFTA, as Roger Johnson said. Latin America wants to buy American goods. And as we can roll it out to Chile and Costa Rica and some of the other countries, there's going to be a real increase in US exports. The—I think we need a good GATT— not a GATT, but a good GATT—and there are real problems in the Dunkel draft, particularly in unfair trade practice areas.

In taxes, I would throw one idea out. I don't believe that the taxes— that you're going to be able to collect a lot of taxes from foreign producers by negotiation or by changing their intercompany pricing practices, and I do think that the business transfer tax on imports could raise $30 billion a year and have no cost to companies that have substantial US employment.

In technology, just to finish, I would say more money for dual use technology through DARPA—very low overhead organization, very productive, brings an enormous amount of private money to the party. I'd open it up that foreign companies could play, too, with two caveats: one, they ought to regard it as venture capital, and if they're successfully funded, they ought to pay it back. Everyone at DARPA ought to; and second, they ought to commit, if they're going to play, that they would manufacture over the first five to ten years in the United States.

The end.

PRESIDENT-ELECT CLINTON: Thank you. (Pause—off-mike conversation)

Andrew Brimmer, and then Laura Tyson, then John Young.

MR. ANDREW BRIMMER (THE BRIMMER COMPANY): Thank you very much, Mr. President-elect, Mr. Vice President-elect, in response to the invitation to me to share my views.

With respect to the prospects of a long-term economic growth, I've prepared a piece of paper. I will—I've already given it to your staff, and I will assume that it will be in the record. But what I examined was this.

During your campaign, you recommended that an investment tax credit be adopted as a means of stimulating long-term private investment in the United States. Yet some analysis was suggested that in the absence of some kind of stimulus for long-term investment in the United States, we're likely to have a substantial slow-down in the growth rate over the long term with substantial adverse consequences with respect to output employment and the deficit. Those I summarize there.

I also concluded, which is not in the paper, that I will summarize quickly, that in order to finance that investment, there will need to be a substantial increase in availability of funds not only in the long run, but in the short run. And in that context, there is something which you can do quickly when you get into office: to help increase the availability of funds.

In December of 1991, the Congress adopted and the President signed something called the Federal Deposit Insurance Corporation Improvement Act of 1991. This was, in my judgment, the most Draconian roll-back of ability of financial institutions to lend, especially the commercial banks. You heard some comments earlier about the consequences of the increased regulation on the willingness of banks to lend. I spent a good bit of my time when I was a member of the Federal Reserve Board examining the conditions under which banks lend and supervising those banks.

Currently, and for a number of years now, I've been serving as a director and adviser to one of the largest banks in the country. I see what these regulations and these statutory changes have been doing on the willingness of banks to lend even to customers who would classify for good loans even in bad times. I would hope you would provide some leadership in trying to persuade the Congress to roll back those regulations and to free up the institutions to engage in the necessary lending which we must have if we're to have growth in the long run.

Thank you very much. (Applause.)

PRESIDENT-ELECT CLINTON: Thank you, Mr. Brimmer.

VICE PRESIDENT-ELECT GORE: Could I interject just a brief point?

PRESIDENT-ELECT CLINTON: Yes, Al.

VICE PRESIDENT-ELECT GORE: If I could interject a very brief point here, Cliff Horton was at the last table but is not at this table. During the break, he emphasized that the same issue which we've been discussing in terms of bank lending practices also has an enormous impact on the decisions made by pension fund managers, and that in their case, for example, they went from 14 percent inequities down to 2 percent inequities, and those decisions can come back the other way with deficit-neutral changes in policy that do not enhance the risk of taxpayers in the insurance funds.

PRESIDENT-ELECT CLINTON: Laura, John Young, and Bob Reich.

MS. LAURA D'ANDREA TYSON (CHAIRPERSON-DESIGNATE, COUNCIL OF ECONOMIC ADVISORS): Okay. Just let me make a note. I also had a break conversation on this issue with Marion Sandler, who was on the panel yesterday, and she suggested that she felt there were many people in the industry who would feel that, in fact, we couldn't really go nearly as far as the $86 billion that was suggested in the first panel this morning without really getting into essentially undoing some needed regulation which was advisable. So I think this whole issue really needs to be—this is a key issue for us to examine. And I thought if John Reed wanted to address this issue, that I would cede the floor to him for a minute because I was going to get back to the deficit reduction issue.

PRESIDENT-ELECT CLINTON: Go ahead.

MR. JOHN REED (CITICORP): If I could just for one second on that issue, I had intended to mention it. I believe that there is a need to revise some part of the law that has turned what used to be judgmental regulation into numeric regulation and go back to judgment. The right appointment of people to the regulatory position, particularly the Comptroller of the Currency and the tie with the Fed, can produce a relaxation of the environment fully within appropriate judgmental standards, not walking away from the Basel agreements but getting away from this notion of arithmetic regulation. I do believe if you had stopped when the question first came up before and had asked me, "John, how much?" I would have said $100 billion. So that's, for all practical purposes, the same as 84.

There is a substantial credit crunch as a result of the type of environment within which we are functioning. It is not all or nothing. It's a question of getting regulators who have the self-confidence—and I'm not blaming them as individuals as much as the position they find

288

themselves in—have the self-confidence to make the judgment calls and provide an environment within which banks can do what we should be doing. We have become a brittle part of the economic system and one that is propagating problems as opposed to absorbing problems. We are creating problems with our customers rather than doing the traditional absorption during periods of slowdown. I would broaden my comments to include that to the insurance industry, although I do not know it in anything like the same detail. But they are going through an exactly same situation now. They are also important lenders in this economy.

PRESIDENT-ELECT CLINTON: John?

MR. JOHN YOUNG (HEWLETT PACKARD COMPANY): Governor Clinton, Senator Gore, anyone like I am who has been interested in competitiveness issues for the last decade is delighted to see your campaign and to be invited to this meeting. And the subject of long-term economic growth, I think, really couldn't be complete without talking a little bit about technology. Bob Solow, who opened the session yesterday, got his Nobel prize for sort of showing the relationships between labor and capital and what turns out to be technology. Labor and capital accounted for about half of our productivity growth since World War II, but technology accounted for the other half. So it's one of the really significant factors if we're going to generate the standard of living that we would like to see in the years ahead.

Now, the US has a very different structure about R&D. Half of it is spent by the federal government, and you saw yesterday, if you only looked at private sector R&D, you actually see the Japanese are spending in dollars more than we are today, despite what the total percent of GNP looks like.

Now, the government's half—that is about $70, $75 billion—two-thirds is spent on defense, the rest is spent on a combination of space, NIH, National Science Foundation, and so forth. And how the government spends its money is really very important. Remember, yesterday Roy Vagelos was saying that the NIH expenditure on science that underpins the pharmaceutical industry makes that one of the really strong industries in the world.

The computer companies did an interesting comparison. If you take the twelve computer systems companies and you aggregate their R&D spending, it accounts for more than 20 percent of all the private sector R&D in the United States. If you do a budget cross-cut through the

289

government's half of R&D, the total spending for computers is 2 percent. So it's really a dramatic mismatch.

So what do you do? Well, in the long run, the government has spent about half of its half on defense and the other half on these other things. If you went back to that ratio, you could redeploy $7 billion in commercially relevant R&D. And, in fact, if you decided economic warfare was more important than cold warfare, you might even go 60-40 the other way, which means you could reprogram $15 billion in R&D over the rest of this decade. Big opportunity, no net new dollars, many issues.

How do you do it? Governance issue is certainly at the top of the list. You can like or dislike defense R&D, but you know who's in charge and who's accountable. You start doing it for commercially relevant projects, a whole new set of issues of how to make those judgments. I think there are some models at NIH and NSF on how to do that. There are some very good lists of critical technologies that come from the competitors on things that are going to be relevant to their ability to compete in the years ahead that can be used as a baseline. And there are other excellent kinds of what I think of as driver projects, like the project that Senator Gore has been pushing, the high performance computing and communications initiative, that can take these technologies along simply by doing a project like that and at the same time end up with a great public benefit of putting into place the beginning infrastructure of a 21st century information infrastructure.

So those are all directions that I would certainly commend to you as I think they can have an enormous leverage on getting that trend line productivity growth rate up where we'd all like to see it.

PRESIDENT-ELECT CLINTON: Let me say this. Let me make two quick comments.

Number one, this specific issue will, I think, and should be explored in considerably greater detail in the second half of the next session. But I want to say a word of thanks to John Young and to John Sculley and Babe Brown from Apple and others who are here who helped us put together our technology paper during the campaign. I think it's probably the best single piece of paper we put out.

But I want to ask you a very specific question that has a funny relationship to Mr. Hawkins over there representing the Delta Commission and others here. We talk about these general things and forget that depending on the delivery mechanism and the other things going on in our society here, they may or may not have the specific impact. We talk about increasing investment, increasing R&D, but there may be no delivery mechanism for that investment in the inner cities.

That's like somebody said earlier, you going to put the infrastructure in the suburbs or in the inner cities? There may be no delivery mechanism in south Texas or in the rural parts of the Mississippi delta.

This is a special problem, interestingly enough, in California now more than any other state because of the defense cutbacks and because we don't really know very much about how to do the right kind of defense conversion with at least the minimum dislocation. And so I want to ask you this one specific question.

When I met with the defense leaders who counselled me in the campaign, the number one thing that they said to me that they were worried about, they said, "We know we got to downsize the military. We know we got to cut the military budget. We are worried about how to maintain the necessary technological infrastructure so that if we had to come up with new weapons systems or if we had to gear up defensively, we had to do the things we know we're going to have to do in the future, it will be there." And so, the specific question I wanted to ask is, in this whole idea of redirecting the $15 billion, and you pointed out, it's—you have less control over it, do you think we ought to do it through the Defense Advanced Research Projects Agency, through a new agency to expanding that mission? And how—as a practical matter based on your own experience in this area, how much dual use technology can we really do that will benefit—truly benefit both the commercial sector and the defense sector that we're not doing now?

Mr. Young: Well, my personal view, which is what you asked for, is that I would not do this to the Defense Advanced Research Projects Agency. My personal experiences in business lead me to believe that people focussed on the job they're supposed to be doing end up with the best overall result. They have a clearer mission, a relationship with the Defense Department, and they certainly can do dual use funding—that just makes a lot of sense—as part and parcel of the DARPA job. So I would definitely look to other governance mechanisms rather than trying to confuse a focussed agency like that on something that is terribly important and needs to continue in the future.

President-elect Clinton: Well, I have something to say about the deficit, but we will go back to the crowd. Who else wants to talk? Bob next, and then Bruce Ratner.

Ms. Tyson: I just want to raise a question which I think is actually front and center to this debate about the extent of deficit reduction,

291

the speed, the—and it really is between what Bob Kuttner and Bob Eisner said and what Henry Aaron said, and I guess I'd like to get Henry's response and just raise it for consideration.

On the one hand, you hear people say that we should have—Bob Kuttner made the most complete statement, that we should emphasize the growth as a way to—a path of deficit reductions. But, of course, Henry Aaron was saying that we need to reduce growth—we need to reduce the deficit in order to get growth. It was exactly the opposite notion, that the only way we can get sustainable growth is to reduce the deficit.

Now, I just want to point out that that link between the reduction in the deficit and the rate of growth is really a link which I think needs to be explored. I mean, is the link primarily, Henry, the notion that we're going to get a major reduction in long-run interest rates, and that's going to have a major effect on private investment? Is the link that markets are so concerned about deficit reduction that there would be a major confidence effect if we went for deficit reduction and then growth? I'm trying to sort of unravel this debate here by understanding the argument clearly of deficit reduction leading to growth, rather than growth as a way to deficit reduction.

MR. AARON: Would you like me to respond?

PRESIDENT-ELECT CLINTON: Yes. Give her a brief response, and then—

MR. AARON: I'll try and be brief.

Deficits are good for demand, as Professor Eisner stressed. When the economy is near full employment, they divert private savings. That tends to reduce growth because less domestically-generated savings are available for investment.

Reducing the deficit is not the only thing that's important for economic growth. The kinds of programs that Bill Sawhill stressed are as important, perhaps more important in the long run: technology, improved training, as well as more capital. This is a case where we've got to keep in mind several things at the same time. All are necessary; none alone is sufficient.

PRESIDENT-ELECT CLINTON: Thank you.

Bob Reich, Bruce Ratner, Barbara Wilson, and Wilma Mankiller, and then George Hatsopolous. How's that? I could keep up with that. (Laughter.)

Bob?

MR. REICH: Well, I just wanted to build on that a little bit and also clarify something that I heard. Henry, Bill, the two Bobs over here.

I worry a little bit when we begin framing a conversation around a choice that may not be a choice. What I hear people beginning to frame a conversation around is a supposed choice between deficit reduction and public investment. You know, it's a little bit like that false choice between jobs or the environment. Once you begin thinking that way, suddenly the public dialogue begins being shaped that way.

But, in fact, as far as I can tell, and as far as the studies suggest, only a very tiny proportion of the federal budget actually goes to anything that any of us around this table would call public investment. The General Accounting Office did a study recently. In fact, it was confirmed by the Bush administration's own Office of Management and Budget that only 9 percent—9 percent—of the federal budget went to any of the things we've been talking about: that is, infrastructure, childhood health and education and welfare, training, education—any of the issues we've talked about with regard to building the economy. Only 9 percent. You know, 91 percent of that budget goes to what might be termed consumption.

And so, my question with regard to—clarifying this for all of you is—or, at least getting you to—clarifying it for me, is whether it would be more accurate and more useful for us to think about the challenge over the long term as moving from a society that is overconsuming, both in the public and the private sectors, relative to our—what we're producing, to a society that is investing more, both publicly and privately, relative to what we're producing, and to make that transition in an equitable way. Is that a meaningful—is that something that you could all buy onto?

PRESIDENT-ELECT CLINTON: Well, let me just follow up, then we'll let somebody else talk. That represents more than a 50 percent cut in that number since 1980, too.

Anybody want to say something about that? Yeah, Felix?

MR. ROHATYN: I think that point that Bob made is very important. The reason that I feel that public investment is so important isn't necessarily to stimulate the economy; it's because we're about $2 trillion underinvested in the public sector. And most of the public investment is done at the state and local government level, and those state and local governments are tapped out in terms of debt service. And I think people are underestimating the drag on the economy of the state of the cities and the state of the states and what it would do to the economy to recreate the investment ability of state and local governments to build the things they have to build, in addition to recognizing that living conditions in many of our cities is a disgrace to civilized society. But the reason we have to have public investment is because we have to have it, because without having it, we are in terrible shape.

PRESIDENT-ELECT CLINTON: Bruce.

MR. RATNER: If we're going around, I can wait, probably.

PRESIDENT-ELECT CLINTON: What?

MR. RATNER: Are we going around, or—

PRESIDENT-ELECT CLINTON: No, you're next.

MR. BRUCE RATNER (FOREST CITY RATNER COMPANIES): Okay, I'm next. Okay. Well, actually I'd like to follow up, Mr. President-elect and Vice President-elect, on Mr. Rohatyn's point, which is that investment comes in many forms. And as we all know from yesterday, when a rising tide rises, it does not lift all boats. And the boat that it has not lifted over a period of 20 and 30 years, of course, is the boat of urban poverty in our cities. And we have ignored, really, the extent to which urban poverty really drags our economy down. And that's very important.

As the President-elect said, health care draws us down, but so do— so does the urban poverty in our cities. I think if we were to add up the total cost of Medicaid, welfare, public housing, food stamps, crime, we would find that the total drag to our economy between state, city, and federal governments probably exceeds $200 billion. And my guess is that it should be up there with health care as a drag on our economy.

So my first suggestion or comment would be that we've got to analyze, as we have with health care, how much poverty in our inner cities really drags our economy down. And that's an analysis I've never seen done. Maybe Brookings has done it. Maybe the Policy Institute has done it. but I haven't seen it, and I think that's very important.

The second comment is, and the second suggestion is, that we must do economic development in our cities, in our inner cities, and bring the jobs back to the cities. They left after—in the '60s and '70s and '80s. They were brought there after the war. Our urban—our poor went to the cities to get jobs. Now the jobs have left, and we have to bring them back.

How do we bring them back? Again, a disciplined approach. Two things: One, you need to do a strategic economic plan for our inner cities which really isolates the areas where we can have job growth, whether it be biotechnical sciences or our hospital-related facilities in a place like the Bronx, of all places; whether it be retail, which I could write a paper on—the importance of retail and its role in economic development in cities, and it must be—arts is another area. We talk about infrastructure. I don't know if anybody really knows what the so-called multiplier effect is of infrastructure. It's about $1^1/_4$, $1^1/_2$. Do you know that the arts economic development in cities—arts have always remained in cities—is about $2^1/_2$ times—for every dollar spent on arts, we get a $2^1/_2$ time economic increase for every dollar spent. So I suggest that we look at our cities not so much in terms of—as a moral imperative, but as an economic imperative, and what we will find, I think, Mr. Panetta, if we did the work on it, we'd find that it's revenue neutral to do economic development in our inner cities.

And I suggest that that should be our agenda. Two things, really: analyze exactly the cost of our cities and how much they drag us down, and second, the notion of doing a strategic plan.

And one last comment. For the first time, there is a study that shows that cities drag suburbs down. The Federal Reserve Bank of Philadelphia has done the first study of that sort. We've always thought that, in fact, when cities went down, suburbs grew. On the contrary. I would even suggest that it's possible that the decline of our cities somehow parallels the decline in our economy. And there may really be an economic reason for that. It's called deglomeration economics, and one would look at that. I'm not an economist. But thank you very much.

PRESIDENT-ELECT CLINTON: Before I recognize Barbara Wilson, let me just say that one way to measure what Bruce said in terms of the cost of this is you could measure the different spending patterns of state and local government over the last 12 years, and I think what you would see is—just based on my own experience—is except for the fact that the states are spending much, much more on education, thanks largely to support from the business community and people at large, and have taken up more than the federal government has cut—except for that, you will find that state and local government are spending more on problems and less on opportunities than they were 12 years ago. And I think that's one way to measure what your loss is—how much are you spending on things after you make a mess of it as opposed to what you're spending on building and keeping bad things from happening, and we're spending more on problems and less on opportunities than we were a dozen years ago.

Barbara?

Ms. Barbara Wilson (U.S. West Communications): Thank you. One thing I wanted to do was to emphasize a point that John Young brought up, and that's dealing with the importance of an information infrastructure. I think that there are things that the government can do to encourage the investment and the building of that information infrastructure that do not require dollars from the government, but require leadership from the government. I firmly believe that as we look to the future that an information highway is going to be, in the '90s and beyond, what waterways, railroads and highway systems were in the past for economic growth and vitality. You also get added benefits of—an information highway can do such things for rural America as improve quality, cost and accessibility to health care services, improve learning experiences through distance learning, not just productivity and economic development.

I have several specific things I'd like to suggest that the government do in this area. First is that—to advocate a free-market approach to this area. We have some very historical and antiquated boundaries that were based on technologies that no longer exist, between, say, cable and telecommunications. The technologies have merged, we need to recognize that.

Second, I would say where there is outdated and kind of industrial structures in places from public policy reasons in the past like the modified final judgment, that I believe are no longer valid, we need to eliminate those.

The third thing I would suggest is that the regulatory area needs to be looked at to be streamlined. I think we can streamline regulations, still protect consumers, but not stifle the inventiveness of new products and capabilities or prevent some participants who are more than capable of bringing dollars, investment and jobs to different areas from participating.

The last thing is that I believe that we can advocate that private network being done with private dollars, but with very strong leadership, and I would like to strongly suggest that Vice President-elect Gore be named to a presidential commission that really looks at how we can bring our resources together to get our communications policy in place in this United States and bring those type of information capabilities to all Americans. The old adage says information is power. We need to deliver that power to everyone, be they urban, rural, no matter what the economic status. And I know my industry and my company would love to participate.

Thank you very much.

PRESIDENT-ELECT CLINTON: Thank you.
Wilma?

CHIEF WILMA MANKILLER (CHEROKEE NATION): Thank you very much for inviting me. I have taken a fair amount of teasing about my name during this conference, and I finally got a little tired of it. Last night on the elevator when a man again teased me about my name, which is Mankiller, he asked me about the origin of it, and I told him it was a nickname and I had earned it. (Laughter.)

I have some written comments about the issues that I think are important, so I'm not going to take a lot of time. We've already talked, President Zoh yesterday talked about high unemployment on Indian reservations and about our decision as tribal governments to help ourselves. For several hundred years, the United States government has been trying to figure out what to do with the, quote, "Indian problem," unquote, and basically we have some ideas about how to do that ourselves, and I'd like to talk about those briefly.

Unemployment. The national average—just briefly—the national average unemployment on Indian reservations is around 54 percent. During the Great Depression, unemployment in this nation was between 20 and 30 percent. So it's a significant problem. As a social worker, I think that the best social program that we can provide to people is a job, and with that in mind, there are some specific things that I'd like to recommend.

First of all, I, myself, and President Zoh, who are here today, represent only two of more than 500 tribes and Alaska native villages that possess about 100 million acres of land. That sounds like a lot of land, but it's only a fraction, obviously, of the land holdings that we originally had on this continent. I have several recommendations that I'll run through very quickly that would help us.

One is that we would like to have investment tax credits and wage credits for private investors in Indian country similar to those approved

297

by Congress last year in H.R. 11 and then vetoed by President Bush. Those should be enacted. In addition, we also would like to have eligibility for loans and political risk insurance coverage through OPIC, which was talked about again this morning, and also that that be made available for people to invest in tribal communities.

We also would like a review of the Tribal Governmental Tax Status Act so that we can issue bonds to rebuild our own communities. And we also would like the ability to issue mortgage revenue bonds so that we could build our own houses. One of the things that's most difficult for me to deal with is seeing homeless native people in our own homelands. In essence, we're exiled in our own homelands, and I think the ability to build our own houses rather than going to HUD every year and trying to beg for an appropriation from HUD is the best approach to that.

We also would like you to exercise some leadership in trying to resolve the issue of double taxation on businesses that are in Indian country. Both the state taxes our businesses and then the tribe taxes them. We've issued taxes, levied taxes so that we can solve our own problems, and we'd like to continue to do that.

I also—finally and, I guess, more of a proprietary problem is that I'm concerned about the Fair Trade Agreement and its impact on companies like our company. We have a small manufacturing company, and we also have a small distributing company. And while I understand the importance of moving forward with that and I'm told that it's inevitable that it will move forward, what I'd like to ask for, then, is some consideration for small businesses of our size—200 employees or so—and how that's going to impact us. We've already lost a significant amount of work to the federal prison industries. Most people think they make license tags and that sort of thing. They've taken almost the wire and cable harness work in the country, which is the kind of work that we do, and are manufacturing furniture and many other kinds of things. We're competitive, we have a good quality company, we produce good work; we can't compete with labor that's paying people—I don't know what they're paying them, 40 or 50 cents an hour.

So those are some of the issues that we're concerned about that would help us.

And I agree totally, and finally, with the gentleman this morning that said that there needs to be a new view, a new way of looking at poor people. I think that there has got to be a change in thinking. Before I came over here, I had lunch with a 19-year old Indian, young woman, who we put through a vocational program through a Job Corps center that we operate, and she had three children, all under four years old. And yet, rather than she could have done better by simply going on AFDC, she wanted a job. So she left her children in the care of her mother, came to our vocational education center, and got trained for a job.

So I think that's what we want to do. We're here to help you in any way we can, and we would like your assistance in developing the economies of our communities.

Thank you for the opportunity to be here. (Applause.)

PRESIDENT-ELECT CLINTON: Thank you. George?

MR. GEORGE HATSOPOULOS (THERMOELECTRON CORP.): Mr. President-elect, I would like to make my comments in response to a question that Laura Tyson posed as to the relationship between deficit reduction and economic growth. I have been studying the issue of economic growth in our industry for the last 10 years, and that has helped me put in practice a number of things I learned, to maintain very high growth for our own company. So, I have learned from the academic exercise I've gone through and put things—some things to work, and they do work.

The point is that there are some fundamental problems that US industry is facing that can be illustrated by the following empirical findings.

First of all, the rate of return that US non-financial corporate sectors have earned the last 10 or 20 years has been about double that of Japan, and not nearly double that of Germany. In other words, US industry is the most profitable industry in the whole world. Yet, US corporations have been—felt compelled to put a lot of cash in the hands of their stockholders.

In the last five years of the '80s, they were—US corporations paid half a trillion dollars of dividends and repurchased shares another half a trillion dollars, which makes a total of one trillion dollars of negative cash flow. At the same time, Japanese corporations, which are still a small fraction of the total of the United States, had an infusion of equity capital of about $200 billion, including whatever they—net of what they paid on dividends.

So, you find yourself in a situation where the US industry is caught in a dilemma of trying to satisfy their short-term investors, which Michael Porter so well spoke of, and at the same time trying to compete with international giants that have enormous access to—easy access to capital. And the reaction is essentially downsizing. And this is basically one of our major growth problems, and we see it across the board.

Our industry, as Professor Solow said, is the most efficient in the world, more productive. I want to add that it produces per unit of capital, our corporations produce twice the gross national product than the Japanese do. Yet, we're downsizing because we are in a capital squeeze and a squeeze of ownership of very short-term oriented intermediaries or traders. And Mr. President-elect, this is the basic problem of growth.

What we need is, first of all, national savings. And the only reason—there is no reason to have a budget deficit reduction if we have sufficient private savings to counteract it. Japan could run a much bigger budget deficit without being hurt at all, because they have an enormous pool of private saving. We don't have that. So, the issue is not deficit, not even public debt that was discussed. The issue is national savings, which could go into our businesses to produce jobs. That is the problem. And that's why, I think, one of the highest priorities is to have a tough, credible program of deficit reduction.

PRESIDENT-ELECT CLINTON: Don, do you want to say? Do you agree with that? Ann? Either one of you. Ann Kaplan and then Don Tyson.

MS. ANN KAPLAN (GOLDMAN SACHS & COMPANY): I was going to start a new topic, so I'll let him respond to that.

PRESIDENT-ELECT CLINTON: He didn't have his hand up. Go ahead, Carol.

CAROL BARTZ (AUTODISK): I'd like to respond to that. I feel like I'm representing the sort of forgotten middle here. As a CEO of a mid-sized company, $350 million, I neither have the influence of my colleagues, Mr. Young and Mr. Sculley, nor the empathy of the small business people here. Nonetheless, in ten years, we have created 1,500 jobs and $350 million, very profitably I would say, the good news being it's in the software industry, which is one of the industries that we still dominate in this global economy.

The bad news, and I really thank you very much, George, is that we're facing a lot of pressures, one of which I would call the patient capital pressure. We must have investors that stay with us to stop the insidious lawsuits that are facing us as companies. After ten years of continued quarterly growth in my company, we had one down quarter and just settled a lawsuit for $5 million that would have cost us up to $100 million if we had gone to court. And we had the cleanest case

300

that has ever been seen by a very prominent law firm. We had no choice but to handle it in that manner.

A second thing that really hurts this industry that we still lead in is an issue around piracy or, if you will, protection of intellectual property. We lose $10 to $12 billion a year on pirated copies of our products, $10 to $12 billion that could turn into more jobs, more R&D, and more growth. And that, by the way, is not only in terrible places such as the former Soviet Union or Thailand, where 97 percent of copies are pirated, but even in our own august, lawful land, and the economies and countries such as Germany and Japan and so forth. We really need some help in this arena.

The last thing I would say is as a medium-sized business leader, I applaud the factfinding that you're doing. I do that in my own business. But then I get on with it. If I don't get on with it, I'd be out of business. And so, so much for consensus, you are a very smart man; get on with making decisions as fast and quickly as you can. Also, use the quality standards that many of us in business have put on our own companies to judge the federal government. Use the concept of profit, or results, which is probably more applicable, to judge the federal government, and then you can't help but get reelected next time. Thank you. (Laughter, applause.)

PRESIDENT-ELECT CLINTON: I wonder if maybe we ought not to take a call or two from the radio show? Let me say, too, we've done something—you've probably all figured this out, since you're all so smart. There are sandwiches outside this door and up the stairs, and they'll tell you where it is, and you can go get one if you want, but I'm not going to have a break for lunch. Go get one and eat and come back if you want. But this is too interesting and the morning session ran too long. So let's take a call or two from our radio audience.

MODERATOR: Mr. Clinton, this is a call from Kendra Bradley, who called in from Brighton, Massachusetts.

CALLER: Hi. I have a question about—I hear all these people talking about people who have lost jobs. I'm 26. I have a masters degree in mass communications. I've been looking for a job for three years, since May of '90. I've held freelance positions. I've done internships for free without school credit.

I'm wondering if all these employers have forgotten about people like us. We can be molded into what they're looking for in somebody.

And I keep looking for jobs. I go on interviews and somebody goes and they look—they end up choosing somebody who has more experience. How is somebody like me supposed to get the experience, and what do we do next? I feel like we're kind of being pushed to the side.

I went to school for six years and didn't get government help. I can't even collect unemployment at this point because I've never held a full-time position. And I'm starting to get frustrated. And I know there are a lot of people out there like me, and we're taking jobs in restaurants to get money in some way, shape or form. But I'm 26. I want to start my career. I'm very smart and I'm ready to get moving in the direction that I want to go in in advertising, and it's just absolutely impossible right now, especially in Boston, it seems like.

President-elect Clinton: Anybody else want to answer her question before I do?

One real problem you have is that it's hard for a company—one of the first things that a company will do is cut back on its advertising budget if the economy is down. And, of course, the New England region has been devastated. You could tell that in the last election when the states of New Hampshire, Vermont and Maine, which almost always go Republican, voted for the Clinton-Gore ticket. Part of it was just the pure collapse of the economy of New England. And Boston is, as you know, a magnet for activities in the nearby states as well. So I think that in the last two years, for you to have found a job in your area, you might have had to go some place else, which I know you don't want to do.

So the best thing I can do for you is to try to do what Carol said; make the right decisions and go on and adopt an economic program that will help to revitalize the economy of Massachusetts and New England.

And let me say that one of the reasons that I think it's important for us not to just pretend that this recession is over and everything is going to be hunky-dory is that in the last year or two, you might be interested to know that for the first time in over a dozen years, college students began—graduates began to have almost equal amount of difficulty with high school graduates in finding new jobs for the very reason that you said. So your problem is that we have not generated any new jobs in your—particularly in your region of the country, and until we do, we can't.

Now, the flip side of that is that you have a skill that will be highly marketable in a growing economy, and that's what we're here talking about.

I think Bob Reich wanted to have—say something on this.

302

Mr. Reich: I just wanted to both empathize with my fellow New Englander, but also suggest that we have to maintain an important distinction here between the business cycle and the long term—what we call the structural problems of the economy, Kendra. It's not very much consolation to you, I know, but people who have good college educations, people who have degrees, particularly advanced degrees, but even college educations, as we saw yesterday, they are going to do pretty well in this new economy, this new global economy, over the longer term.

The business cycle—recessions come and go. Recessions are always—take a lot out of everybody. This is a very painful recession, particularly for white collar employees for the first time. I remember, you know, when I got to Boston for the first time in 1981, we were in a recession—'81, '82—and one of the taxi drivers I had had just got his PhD from MIT just a couple of months before. But then he went on—I saw him a few years later, he went on into the computer business, and he was doing extremely well. In fact, he was doing far better than anybody who was teaching at Harvard University or MIT, but then he fell on hard times again. Business cycles do come and go, they're awful, and there are an awful lot of things that the government and the private sector ought to do to mediate the effects of business cycles. But again, just bear in mind that there is this long-term issue, and anybody who is listening who wants long-term income guarantee ought to be worried first and foremost about education and training.

Moderator: Kendra Bradley, are you satisfied?

Caller: Yeah, well, I was just hoping that things turn around, and I'm keeping my fingers crossed. And—

President-elect Clinton: If you look at the advertising industry, people expand in the advertising industry when they think they're going to get more customers. They do more advertising. So we have to restore—what you do will be almost certainly affected in a very positive way if we can restore growth. And what Bob told you is the truth. You're still way better off with a college education than you would be without one, and way better off with your graduate degree. But I hope we don't reach a point in this country where we're going to have to go back to what happened in this state. We had more people living in my state at the end of World War II than we did at the beginning of the '60s because everybody had to leave here to make a decent living, and

I hope we don't have to have huge migrations across America. I think New England is—will be able to make a recovery, and if we do, I think you will have a lot better chance at a job.

Can we take one more question?

MODERATOR: Okay, this is from Edward Howden who is on the line from San Francisco. Mr. Howden, go ahead. You're up.

PRESIDENT-ELECT CLINTON: We can hear you, Edward.

CALLER: Is—are you ready for Edward Howden?

PRESIDENT-ELECT CLINTON: Yes.

MODERATOR: Yes, you're on the air right now. (Pause.) I think there may be an infrastructure problem.

CALLER: Congratulations to the President-elect on a brilliantly conceived and beautifully executed meeting. I'm one of your so-called senior constituents—middle class, my wife and I are retirees in our middle and late 70s, modest income, modest pension, some Social Security. I've long felt that we Americans should get accustomed to paying our way better than we are doing for the services that we want our society to give us, so I have some rather serious doubts about giving me a break on a middle-class tax cut. I'm not at all sure that we really ought to go that way. I would have no objection to some paring of my limited income in the way in which it is now pared by the tax on part of my Social Security income. I would have no objection to a gas tax on myself. I would like to see some provision made for low-income folks who have to have that gasoline, out West and where they go long distances, where they have to depend on cars—there ought to be some provision for them not to be hit hard by a gas tax. But I think we need a gasoline tax.

We need housing for low-income people—desperately need—and I hope we can go in that direction. And finally, just I'll touch on mass transit—Amtrak and other environmental matters that need us. I think if you were to challenge us with a program laid out that would include such elements, it seems to me that the otherwise politically difficult, as

304

it's called, subject of tax increases and so on, could be handled, and I think you could take us along the direction we need to go.

PRESIDENT-ELECT CLINTON: Thank you very much. (Applause.) Give him a hand, wasn't he great? Thank you very much.

There are some things that can be done with the income tax code rather inexpensively to deal with the problems of cost of consumption for low-income working people. And the—in terms of the middle class, the most severe problems we have now are basically with middle-class earners with young children because they have been affected by the six increases in the Social Security tax in the last decade which have basically had the cumulative impact of realiy socking it to small business and middle-class people, essentially to cover the deficit because, as I said, Social Security tax now is no longer just a direct transfer into Social Security, it produces a $70 billion surplus, and we're not saving that against the day when the baby boomers retire to keep the tax down there, we're just spending it to cover the debt so that my real concern is with that group of people who have a far smaller percentage of their income to spend raising their children than their counterparts did a generation ago. That's the one place where our tax system is just way, way out of whack compared to the way it has always been.

And I really appreciate what you said. It was a very statesman-like thing to say, and for the last seven years, for the first time in our history, our retiree population is less poor than the rest of the population. It had never happened before, and that's because of, as Mr. Kuttner said, some of those entitlements—Social Security, Medicare, SSI, and I think some adjustments may be in order, particularly for upper-income people who are getting a lot more out of it than they ever paid in. And I really appreciate what you said.

Anything else around the table here?

In the back, yes, sir? No, no, right there.

AUDIENCE MEMBER: President-elect Clinton and Vice President-elect Gore, you know, the point here in this session after one and a half days of conferring together, and I think both you and we as an audience and as participants could have good reason to be discouraged and overwhelmed and intimidated by this parade of concerns and difficulties around the world. But I think instead we're feeling quite differently and quite oppositely that we are encouraged, and that we are thinking optimistically about the future.

I suppose there's an argument to go back to the perspective and remember that George Washington, as he crossed the Delaware, this

President-to-be had even greater problems than we do today. Certainly President-elect Roosevelt, as he looked at the nation in shambles in the times of the Depression, would have every reason to be overwhelmed and concerned. And perhaps President-to-be Eisenhower would have had greater cause than we today to be concerned about the future as he looked to the prospects of a Normandy invasion. America has gone through tougher times, greater wars, more overwhelming concerns than we're experiencing today.

But nevertheless, these are big problems and big concerns. And to you, Mr. Clinton and Mr. Gore, we as your participants want you to know, don't be afraid to ask America for further sacrifice, for further help, just as you've heard from the man over the radio just a few minutes ago. More important than that, know that along the way, along this journey you and we are taking together, that you have proven today that your leadership, your brand of presidency is deserving of our support, and you're going to have a nation gathered together perhaps unlike that of any other time in history. We are looking forward to your presidency, and today is the beginning of that affair.

PRESIDENT-ELECT CLINTON: Thank you very much. (Applause.)

In—let's see, in order, we have John Reed and John Sweeney, and then Fred Bergsten, and a gentleman there, then—Roy, did you have your hand up? Okay. John, John, then we'll go to Fred, and then the gentleman there, and then Roy.

Go ahead.

MR. REED: Mr. President-elect, Mr. Vice President-elect, we've said most everything that we're going to want to say in terms of how to form a package, so I'd like simply to add two points that have not been said that might be useful.

First, in preparation for coming here, I tried to get an estimate of how much the interest rate structure is distorted by the presence of the deficit. It clearly can only be a guess. I came up with the notion there's probably $100 billion there, $30 billion of which is paid for directly by the government in terms of excess payment on the debt of the government, which, of course, leaks partially overseas, the rest paid primarily by those who have outstanding mortgages, a little bit beyond that. But I would say to you just as a number that there's $100 billion there for a credible deficit reduction package. In other words, the markets believe that there is an interest rate benefit that could accrue to you of about $100 billion a year.

The second thing I would say, which has also not been mentioned and might prove to be useful, because this could be a tough crafting-together, there has been no growth in M2 in real terms in six years. It's lower today than it was six years ago. I believe that your administration can work with the Fed—

PRESIDENT-ELECT CLINTON: John, tell a non-economist what M2 is.

MR. REED: This is the basic money supply as it's measured by the pros who think that this definition of money, which is basically checking accounts and savings accounts, is the sort of key linkage to the growth rate of the economy. And if you run an economy as we have—and I would say the Japanese and Germans have, also—where you have no real growth in M2, you virtually assure yourself that you are eventually going to have no real growth in the economy. And this is something that we have seen. The Fed obviously did this to fight inflation. They've been very successful, but there is an opportunity here now, I believe.

If the Fed believes that you and your administration—I have every reason to believe that they will—have a credible antideficit program, they have room to give you. Free of charge. It need not cost the economy anything. There is room by simply getting the growth rate of real M2 up to 2 percent a year, $2^1/_2$, well within their own targets—if you get that growth rate sustained for two or three years, it will give you some space to take it back through taxes or cutting the medical programs back or whatever is the necessary anti-inflationary package.

So both with regard to the premium that the marketplace can give you for a coherent antideficit package and good coordination with the Fed, there is good reason to believe that you could put together a package that has stimulus—which I think you need—but also allows you to address the deficit problem in ways that don't make it 100 percent effective—costly to you. And I simply wanted to toss that out.

PRESIDENT-ELECT CLINTON: Brenda, you want to make a comment before I go back over here to John? You had your hand up.

MS. BRENDA SHOCKLEY (COMMUNITY BUILD, INC.): But I wanted to talk about—it wasn't on this issue.

PRESIDENT-ELECT CLINTON: Okay.

John Sweeney.

MR. JOHN SWEENEY (SEIU): Thank you, Governor, Senator Gore. As a representative of service workers both in the private sector and the public sector, I'd just like to make two quick points.

First, with regard to Governor Clinton's reminder about short-term investment and—with long-term goals, I believe that increased aid to states and cities is the best method of short-term stimulus. Despite recent evidence that there have been—has been an upturn in the economy, there is still a need for a short-term stimulus package to aid fiscally stripped (sic) states and cities all across the country. California and New England have been hit particularly hard by the recession and could benefit enormously from some kind of direct federal assistance.

Mr. President-elect, this morning you pinpointed the long-term economic policy—as you said, nothing is possible without health care cost containment. Your economic program over the next four years cannot be successful unless there is a comprehensive health care reform that shows cost savings, and cost savings soon.

There's a lot of talent in this room, a lot of people who have been working on these issues, both in business and in labor and academia. But we didn't have anybody in the White House with the political will to put it all before the country and to solve the health care crisis and to see the benefits in terms of the economy.

We now have that person—a man who has espoused all of the complex issues of health care, and not only the costs but access and quality as well, during the campaign, who has articulated the desires of so many working people all across this country who are a substantial part of those who have no health care.

And if we can focus on cost containment, if we can come up with the means and the ways to reduce our health care costs, to stabilize our health care costs, the health care reform dividend, under a spending cap, is potentially larger than the peace dividend. Managed competition, without cap, promises cost savings in the long run, but we cannot afford to wait that long. We must resist the temptation to put the lid on government health spending because this will only shift even more cost to the private sector. The cap must cover all health care spending. We can do this and we can do it in the short term.

We need affordable quality health care for all. We need comprehensive, systemic health care reform. We need it now. And thank God we've elected the man who can do it.

Thank you.

308

PRESIDENT-ELECT CLINTON: Thank you.

We've got to tie this up pretty quickly. Let's see, I want to have—Dr. —(name inaudible)—wants to say something about health care, so I'm going to recognize him. Then we'll go back to Fred.

But please, everybody, be as brief as possible. We've got to go on to Senator Gore's session now.

AUDIENCE MEMBER: Thank you, sir. I came here with the idea of being thrilled to hear you gentlemen—and ladies and gentlemen, speak about our economy. I did not realize I'd have an opportunity to address you.

Clearly, health care and health care issues are going to be a major problem in the next four years. As we learned yesterday, 13.5 percent of our GDP is consumed by health care and it's on the way up. Other industrialized countries consume around 8 percent. The difference between 13.5 percent and 8 percent is somewhere between $50 billion and $60 billion.

It is also true that there are 37 million people in this country that have no insurance. There are 60 million people in this country that in the last two years have been without insurance at some time. The cost of these people's health care is amortized by those of us who can pay. And that is a reality with which we have to live.

The cost of health care goes up because technology improves, drugs improve, and the cost of equipment. Insurance costs, as we were told yesterday, are passed on to consumer products. The cost of cars in this country goes up about $1,400 for every new car produced because of health care expenditures. But the greatest cost of health care is not because of drugs, it's not because of equipment, it is the bureaucracy that is out of control. The bureaucracy of health care is the fastest growing component of health care in this country right now.

The access to health care is also a major problem. We have enough doctors, we have enough hospitals, they're just not located in the correct place. They're not utilizing any kind of control form, any kind of managed form of health care process.

But another issue which is very difficult, and it is intangible, that has to be addressed are the expectations of the American people with health care. If I had to summarize what the expectations are, it is: Spare no expense. Most people in this country want as much done for their loved ones for as long as possible, and spare no expense. That is a problem that we have to deal with. Either we're going to continue to embrace that policy or we're going to have to think about health care allocation of resources and funds.

What are the options? Universal coverage. Universal coverage is a very real option. It's an idea whose time has come. But—and we heard about universal coverage all through the campaign. But I have not heard anybody address the speed in which universal coverage will be implemented. Is it a four-year plan? Is it an eight-year plan? The cost of universal coverage is probably about $25 billion to $40 billion. Today you were discussing the infusion of $30 billion into the economy in one year. Universal coverage will consume this very rapidly.

Then it comes down to a promise made during the presidential race about health care being a right or a privilege. We're going to have to have a basic health care package, but who will decide what's in that package? And more importantly, who will pay for that package?

A national health care budget, a cap on spending. What will that do? Clearly, it will bring fiscal responsibility to an industry that has been without fiscal responsibility for some time. But it also runs the risk of cutting quality, because by putting an emphasis on cost, we must also keep the focus on the quality of health care that is provided in this country.

The types of coverage that are provided. What will be a national mandate as far as insurance coverage? Will it be managed care? Managed care has to encompass managed competition, because once again, without competition you run the risk of sacrificing quality.

We also have to look at community rating systems, as done in the City of Rochester, New York, and the State of Hawaii. This will be something that will be fought by the insurance industry, but it's something that could bring great cost savings to health care.

During the presidential race, the Republican position was that malpractice reform would save $20 billion. That's probably an overestimation. But defensive medicine and malpractice reform may save as much as $5 billion, and this is another issue which needs to be looked at. My recommendation would be that we look at health care reform. We need to look at health care where there is no sacred cow; that we look at health care with the idea of reforming the entire health care delivery system. But at the same time, we need to remember that we are blessed with good doctors, good nurses, good hospitals, good nursing homes, and a wonderful pharmaceutical and equipment industry that develops state of the art equipment for health care diagnosis and treatment. And we need to defend ourselves and make sure that, to borrow a phrase, we don't throw the baby out with the bathwater when we reform the health care system.

Thank you.

PRESIDENT-ELECT CLINTON: Brenda is next, and then—oh, you want to talk about this? Kathleen, and then Brenda, and then we'll go back to the crowd.

MS. KATHLEEN STAFFORD (AMGEN, INC.): Actually, I just want to add to what he said. We actually agree with most of that. As Dr. Vagelos pointed out yesterday, containment of costs can best be met by innovative medicines that help to avoid hospitals, surgery and nursing homes—by the way, I'm a biotechnology representative here—which are the most expensive aspects of our health care system. The most important incentive for the biotechnology industry, which is one of our fastest-growing and most important industries, is the hope that when a new medical treatment is developed, the system will allow for patient access to these new treatments. A budgeting system must exist where the newest medical technologies are evaluated on the basis of cost savings they provide in the areas of health care system as well as patient benefits.

I would like to say one thing. We talked a lot about the Canadian system yesterday. While the Canadian system has been very, very successful with respect to cost containment and patient access, those who are really familiar with the system will know that access to new technologies is, at best, limited and sometimes shut off completely. So the Canadian system isn't the panacea for us, and we want to preserve the good things that are in our system, such as access to wonderful pharmaceuticals that can save lives.

Thank you.

PRESIDENT-ELECT CLINTON: Thank you. Brenda?

MS. BRENDA SHOCKLEY (COMMUNITY BUILDERS): Thank you. President-elect Clinton, Vice President-elect Gore, I'd like to share with you my pleasure and honor at being here, but it doesn't seem like a good way to spend my two minutes. I'd rather thank you for the opportunity to represent a nontraditional economic sector, the persistently poor, or you may want to translate that to the long-term poor.

I'd also urge you to continue with your commitment to put people first by adopting a long-term economic strategy which recognizes the economic value and importance of developing human capital, a natural resource which also cannot be replaced. And long-term, as was pointed out yesterday, begins at birth.

I'd ask you to also emphasize the persistently poor. In short, the

311

persistently poor, for our economic purposes today, can be defined as those persons for whom the traditional economic models do not work. Those were the people who systematically became poorer even during times of national prosperity. These people, as Larry Farmer reminded us yesterday, reside in both urban and rural communities. I am most familiar with the profile of the resident of the urban community: an individual, a male between the ages of 18 and 30, who faces unemployment rates of over 50 percent; a family, most often single female with children under the age of five, earning less than 50 percent of her county's medium income—median income. In short, the parents of the children that Marian Wright Edelman discussed yesterday.

For these individuals, families and communities, the label "at risk" describes almost every aspect of their existence. Who can comfortably make a choice between a start for a child and a job for her parent? For that reason, I propose a long-term strategy which expands the framework of enterprise zones to include all of the proposals in Putting People First into a White House-coordinated multiagency initiative which would bring to bear all of your proposals at the same time in many of these communities.

I also propose that the community-based strategies which you've heard from many of the others and you will hear from some of my other colleagues be used to implement this. I, along with they, are committed to empowerment as well as the revitalization of these communities. I will present the details of this proposal in my three-to-four page paper; however, by way of example, each targeted zone would likely include employment readiness programs, basic literacy education, stipends, counseling, skills training, job placement, mentorship, and follow-up. Business incentives would be expanded to include job creation and redefining of jobs in a manner which puts more people to work with fewer skills, to work sooner, with the opportunity to learn and advance on the job.

Both community, capital formation models, including the Community Development Bank, but also to include creative enforcement of the CRA requirements as well as some tradeoffs in terms of regulations with the conventional banks. Special allocations of low income tax credits, micro and small business loan funds, and coordinated programs around child care, families, health, drugs, and violence.

This proposal, I believe, can be implemented, at least at the demonstration level, by reallocating and targeting existing resources. I strongly agree with Vince Lane that, given the opportunity, the money is there and can be identified if used wisely. I also believe that, properly developed, this proposal will garner private sector and foundation support.

You have sparked a glimmer of hope in a sector of the economy which has long been neglected and known it. That hope is fragile and needs a long-term economic strategy now. Thank you for including the interests of these stakeholders, these Americans, in this conference. Thank you. (Applause.)

PRESIDENT-ELECT CLINTON: Mr. Hawkins.

WILBUR HAWKINS (TENNESSEE VALLEY AUTHORITY): President-elect Clinton, Vice President-elect Gore, I'd like to again spin off on what Brenda was echoing in terms of the need to remember the forgotten poor.

As you served as chairman of the Lower Mississippi Delta Development Commission, Governor Clinton, you knew and found out that the problems facing rural America and many of the metropolitan communities was, in fact, devastating. For those of you here who do not know of the work of the Delta Commission, it was a presidential commission that spent almost two years looking at the problems and needs of 219 counties, stemming along the Mississippi River from Carbondale, Illinois to the Gulf of Mexico, an area impacting over 11 million Americans, both urban and rural.

Time will not allow me to go into detail in terms of the recommendations, but Mr. President-elect, I can tell you that I have not heard anything here today or in the last couple of days that was not covered in our Delta initiatives, everything from Vince Lane's initiative with the public housing residents in Chicago for incentives, for saving, for private home ownership, to what we're talking about in terms of infrastructural incentives for the private sector. But beyond that, I would encourage each of you here today to receive a copy of the Delta Commission report because we outlined recommendations for not only the federal, the state, and the local governments, but also for the private sector, foundations, and individuals alike.

So, I'd like to thank you, Mr. Clinton, again. And I'd also like to commend you on one other item, and that is the diversity in this conference. We tried with the Delta Commission to always have EGG in everything that we did and not in our faces, and I must say that this is one heck of an omelette. And through EGG, we mean ethnicity, geography, and gender. Thank you. (Laughter.)

PRESIDENT-ELECT CLINTON: I'm going to let Ann Kaplan have the last word because we've stayed way too long on this, and we've got to go on with Senator Gore's program. Everybody that's out there in the audience, just raise your hand at the end of that, and we'll try to get to everybody. Go ahead.

ANN KAPLAN (GOLDMAN SACHS): Thank you. I'll try to be brief.

I wanted to make the point that states and localities are very important players in economic development, even though there's been much said about the financial constraints that they're under. It should also be recognized that states and localities have independent agencies that have viable programs where they can finance many projects that pay for themselves, and can thus contribute to the growth of infrastructure.

An example that was mentioned earlier is the efficiency of the low-income tax credit, which finances virtually every new low-income apartment unit, as well as the single-family, first-time homebuyer program. Neither of these programs exist at the moment. They were popular in Congress. They were passed by Congress, but they were vetoed, and one of the things you could do early in 1993 is to pass this legislation.

Second, existing authorizations such as that of ISTEA can be fully funded because they've already been authorized.

Third, the constraints on local and state government in terms of what can be financed can be eased. Universities now can only finance up to $150 million, and we know of multiple projects of research facilities and other higher educational facilities that could be financed if that were lifted.

And, finally, it's absurd that pollution control projects, housing projects, economic development projects have to fight with each other in order to be able to issue debt based on federally imposed caps on what states can issue.

Thank you.

PRESIDENT-ELECT CLINTON: I wasn't for that when it was done. I appreciate that.

Tony.

TONY SANCHEZ (SANCHEZ, O'BRIEN OIL & GAS CORP.): Thank you, Mr. President-elect Clinton, Vice President-elect Gore. Thank you very much for the opportunity to be on this panel.

I have not heard very much about an energy policy, so I want to speak to you about an area in which I participate, which is the oil and gas industry where we have lost in the last ten years 440,000 jobs,

314

which is equivalent to closing 40 GM plants, and where 75 percent of our oil and gas independent operators have been eliminated. Currently, we as a nation are spending $55 billion annually to import oil, relying on imports to supply 50 percent of our domestic needs.

With this in mind and all of its very serious implications, I would recommend to you an energy policy to encourage domestic exploration and development for the following main reasons: to maintain the integrity of our national security; to replenish in some measure current production; to assist in addressing our trade deficit; finally, and perhaps just as important, to help restore some of these jobs to this very vital industry and all its parallel and support industries.

To achieve these objectives and goals, I would urge you to consider the following as part of an overall energy policy. Incentives to encourage increased exploration and development drilling. Such incentives could be graduated as the risk increases. A change in the passive law rules, which currently limit deductions of oil and gas expenditures, to encourage more investment into the oil and gas industry and bring badly needed capital into the industry.

Three, through incentives, encourage the use of high technology tools and very expensive exploration methods, such as three dimensional seismic, to fully identify and exploit known oil and gas reserves and develop new ones.

I have a picture that I will leave with you which is very recent, and you'll see the recent technology advances.

And lastly, to increase the depletion allowance from the current 15 percent to 27.5 percent, which at this level the industry has shown is very attractive to the investors.

The fact is, if we continue to import ever-increasing percentages of our energy needs, we will place our national security in jeopardy. Further, the cost of these imports will have a negative effect on the goals and objectives which you support for this country.

Governor, we've sat here for a day and half, and we have listened to some very noble and some very compassionate ideas and suggestions. However, if we have another energy crisis, all of your efforts and all of our efforts will most probably be derailed.

Thank you very much.

PRESIDENT-ELECT CLINTON: We'll adjourn for about five minutes.

Senator Gore, do you want to bring your panel up here?

Thank you all very much. This was very good.

(Afternoon recess.)

ECONOMIC CONFERENCE AFTERNOON SESSION TUESDAY, DECEMBER 15, 1992

VICE PRESIDENT-ELECT GORE: Well, ladies and gentlemen, President-elect Clinton has asked me to moderate this session. I'm very much looking forward to it. We're going to talk about the relationship between the environment, technology and economic growth.

The environment and technology are obviously related, but because there are some differences between the two subjects, we're going to try to do this in two parts and also discuss the relationship between the two parts during both parts of the session.

First of all, let me say that there are obvious reasons why so many people have an increasing interest in protecting the environment, but the one reason we are going to emphasize during this discussion here today is that it represents a tremendous business opportunity. The stakes are very high. The Japanese and the Germans, among others, are now investing heavily in the new technologies and products that foster economic progress without environmental destruction.

They and some U.S. corporations are finding that these investments result in brand new efficiencies and productivity gains that in most cases would not have been found except for the initial commitment to improve environmental efficiency.

The other side of the coin is that in areas like Eastern Europe, we find consistently that those countries that have paid the least attention to environmental quality, their economies have suffered the most.

President-elect Clinton and I have found in traveling around this country so many examples of men and women in the business community who are putting people to work and earning enhanced profits by making a commitment to be a part of this new movement.

A company in Maine recycling newspapers into superior packaging, the company converting vehicles to use natural gas in Colorado and opening up fueling stations throughout their market area, the oil recyclers in California removing lead from used oil and in the process from the air, children teaching their parents to recycle—all are partners with us in this new effort, as are many of the men and women around this table.

We're honored to have such a distinguished and thoughtful group of Americans here today to talk about how environmental concerns and technological development interact with the economic issues of this conference. Each one of you brings your special perspective to this discussion. We look forward to gaining insights from the experiences and knowledge that you will share with us.

Let me begin by asking John Bryson, who is the CEO of the second largest utility in the United States of America, Southern California Edison, to make the first presentation.

JOHN BRYSON (CEO, SOUTHERN CALIFORNIA EDISON): Thank you very much, President-elect Clinton, Vice President-elect Gore. At our company, Southern California Edison, we have concluded that our continuing business success requires environmental leadership. By establishing this objective, we have put the skill and the ingenuity of our employees to work for environmental improvement, and we have found that the best economic plan and best economic practices can also be the best for the environment.

Specifically, we have put this idea into action with such steps as a no-regrets pledge to reduce emissions of carbon dioxide, the primary greenhouse gas, by 20 percent in the next two decades, while still cost-effectively meeting the needs of a rapidly growing southern California population; support for the tightest air quality requirements in the world for our power plants in the Los Angeles area; and a program to help our customers reduce their energy needs by eight to ten billion kilowatt hours annually by the year 2000. That eight to ten billion kilowatt hours is equal to serving up to 1.5 million people, new customers, without building new power plants.

And we have been able to make these commitments by relying on new energy-efficiency, environmental and power generation technologies.

In the brief time available, I want to make four points.

Point one, this conference has emphasized that as a nation, we must invest now in the infrastructure for the 21st century. An important choice in that investment is between energy-intensive or efficiency-intensive infrastructure. In the global marketplace, competitors like Germany and Japan can produce a unit of economic output for roughly half the energy we use.

Energy efficiency will lead not only to technological development, but to economic growth and environmental improvement. It will provide the basis for producing the next generation of globally competitive U.S. products and services.

Point two, most of the technologies we need to build for tomorrow are already at hand. Energy-efficient technologies, such as lasers, ultraviolet coatings curing, infrared heating, various microwave applications, and induction furnaces can address simultaneously the environmental and economic problems we face. Superefficient lighting, for example, can save money and cut energy use by up to 75 percent.

An important case is electric transportation. Today's cars are the main source of urban air pollution worldwide. Urban air cannot be cleaned to healthy levels without greatly reducing auto emissions. Seventy to 90 percent cuts are needed, for example, in Los Angeles.

Electric vehicles have no tailpipe emissions, and even counting associated power plant use, they are more than 90 percent cleaner than current gasoline engines. They are also, and this is worth underscoring, twice as energy-efficient as internal combustion vehicles.

Now, today in the U.S., we lead in electric vehicle technology, but we may lose our competitive advantage if we do not provide vehicle manufacturers an early market while battery technology is advanced. We need fleet purchase commitments by major buyers, including the federal government, and emission offsets for electric vehicles.

Point three, public utilities and public/private partnerships offer valuable means for building the new energy-efficient infrastructure. The nation's investor-owned utilities invest more than $60 billion each year in technologically sophisticated infrastructure. These regulated utilities, which bridge between the public and private sector, can play a crucial role in creating the new energy-efficient infrastructure.

Nationally, electric utilities become the leading providers of technical know-how and financial assistance for business, particularly for medium-sized and small businesses seeking to save money by applying cost-effective, energy-efficient technologies.

Last week, recognizing the special public service role of public utilities, the Progressive Policy Institute suggested that the nation's electric utilities could play a role in the development of a national fiber optics communications system. That is an idea worth investigating.

And then one partnership example. Southern California Edison has helped to jumpstart electric vehicle technology by leading the formation of a public/private consortium to assist aerospace companies in retooling to build electric vehicle components. The EV industry, with requirements for many high technology components, is estimated to have the potential for creation of more than 50,000 jobs and billions of dollars of economic development.

Point four. As we rebuild our infrastructure with energy-efficient technologies, we will create skills and products that can be marketed worldwide. For example, our company's independent power subsidiary, Mission Energy, is beginning to succeed very significantly internationally because it is recognized for an ability to build and operate clean and highly efficient power plants.

Many countries are privatizing state-owned electric production systems, and they are doing that in the face of a huge worldwide demand for clean energy. This translates into an estimated need for new electric generation capacity over the next two decades worth $2.5 trillion. Success in that market could mean tens of thousands of new U.S. jobs while enhancing economic and environmental interest worldwide.

It would greatly assist U.S. participation in this vast new market to have expanded financing opportunities provided by the Export-Import Bank and the World Bank to put the U.S. companies on an equal financial footing with their international competitors.

321

Lastly, as a southern California business executive, I wish to speak briefly about our region's special issues. Southern California is, I think, on the front lines of America's future.

We have the nation's poorest air quality and among the most congested transportation systems; the nation's largest pool of technologically advanced workers displaced by defense and aerospace spending cuts; the largest influx of immigrants from diverse cultures around the world; plus the intense problems of all major urban areas in the U.S.

In developing the plan for national investment in education, and in infrastructure, I hope this administration will pay special heed to the special opportunities and pressing demands of southern California.

Thank you.

VICE PRESIDENT-ELECT GORE: Thank you very much, and thanks for compressing your remarks so well. Let me ask one brief question before we go to the next presenter.

So many of the investments you describe are so obviously cost-effective, and others, like Dick Clark is here from PG&E, have had exactly the same experience.

Why is it in your view that there is still so much reluctance and/or resistance on the part of some of your competitors to make these same kinds of investments, if they consistently seem to pay off?

MR. BRYSON: Well, I think part of the answer may have to do with conventional thinking. That is, when we set out to ask ourselves whether we could reduce carbon dioxide emissions in the face of growing demand, our initial thought was we could not, and we simply had to meet the additional demand.

But we had set out this environmental objective and we pressed our employees, our planners, to look at alternative means of meeting demand, and to their surprise we came to the conclusion that we could establish this unique undertaking among electric utilities, without adding any extra costs at all to the customer bill over the next two decades.

So some of it is new thinking, and some of it is simply being aware of the technologies that are out there. We need to provide markets for these best technologies.

VICE PRESIDENT-ELECT GORE: Well, thank you. In introducing our next presenter, I want to use the thought you just expressed as a bridge to describing the experience that Frank Popoff has had.

There was another time in American business history where a new way of thinking challenged the prevailing set of activities, and it was when the quality revolution came in.

There was a prevailing consensus in American industry that the level of product quality in the early 1960s was pretty well established by the forces of supply and demand, and couldn't be dramatically improved unless jobs were cut or profits were cut.

But then the Japanese, listening to some American experts, like W. Edwards Deming and others, reexamined the entire production process, to reintroduce new levels of quality at every step along the way, and they found just what you described a moment ago.

They found they could introduce new levels of quality without any extra cost. And all of a sudden we started walking into our stores and finding consumer electronics products, for example, that certainly seem to be simultaneously better and cheaper. And then many American companies began to absorb the lessons of that quality revolution to their advantage.

The environmental efficiency revolution is now confronting us with almost the same set of lessons all over again in that the prevailing assumption is we cannot improve the existing level of environmental efficiency except at additional cost, which might cost jobs and/or profits. And yet once again some of our competitors, by reexamining the entire production process, and introducing new attention to environmental efficiency at every step along the way, are finding they can simultaneously improve environmental efficiency as well as productivity and profits.

Frank Popoff, the CEO of Dow Chemical, has taken this one step further, and integrated into your company's activities financial mechanisms for pushing in that direction.

Thank you for joining us.

FRANK POPOFF (CEO, DOW CHEMICAL): Thank you very much, Vice President-elect Gore. And thanks to you and President-elect Clinton for a special event, one that in the best tradition of quality exceeds expectations, both in the concept and the yield. And thanks also for the chance to talk about the economy and the environment.

At one time conventional wisdom said that the economy and the environment were irreconcilably opposed. Today, there's a growing recognition that pollution prevention and waste reduction are not just societal imperatives but make doggone good business sense.

Like the rationalization and the realization that total quality management is not a cost, but a competitive advantage, I think we're learning today that environmental reform can be the genesis of jobs and create its own competitive advantage if—and I repeat if—we strike the right balance between environmental reform and economic development.

That balance was the essence of the Earth Summit in Rio. It's the core of sustainable development, a concept that says there can be no environmental reform without economic development, and no economic development without environmental reform. Sustainable development recognizes that poverty is the ultimate polluter and that hunger has no environmental conscience.

The theory of sustainable development is relatively easy and the search for the balance, that balance that creates jobs and a viable economy, is hard.

But clear examples exist and principles are beginning to become evident. The examples have some common features. They're based on absorbing and not passing on or postponing environmental costs; on funding investment in technology development here at home and in technology cooperation abroad; and, on managing environmental issues with market incentives in mind consistent with the best practices in trade and in taxation.

Time limits me to just a few examples of how sustainable development's working. My first example deals with the management of waste.

My industry, the chemical industry, like many others, has programs to reduce waste. We call ours WRAP, waste reduction always pays; 3M calls theirs Pollution Prevention Pays. But whatever name you give them, they have literally taken hundreds of millions of dollars of costs out of our structure, if not billions of dollars of cost.

But you don't just need to point to industry. An equally impressive example is at the municipality level, where progressive municipalities have shown, for example, that free trash service is very expensive in terms of siting new landfills and filling up existing ones.

Now they charge by the individual bag when picking up trash, and surprise, surprise, there's a lot less trash to pick up and a lot less tax to pay.

Recycling has proven to be a real success story, first in aluminum, and subsequently now in plastics and paper and glass. Both in-process and post-consumption recycling are very impressive. But the concept really works when coupled with a total waste management hierarchy, and in our business we call it reduce, re-use, recycle and recover. And it deals with the reduction of waste through efficient processes; the re-use of scrap and of products that we produce; the recycle in terms of process and post-consumption; and of course ultimately as, through new technology we now can, the recovery of energy through efficient waste energy technologies.

324

This is part of a program called responsible care in our business. And it's got real teeth. It's a condition of membership in the CMA and it's audited annually, and no one wants to be drummed out of their favorite trade association.

But we put teeth in responsible care. Indeed we have to to gain the credibility we need. There are lots of other examples—new technologies with higher conversion rates, with lower scrap rates, with lower energy consumption.

And there are substitute materials, materials in transportation, in insulation, in construction that conserve energy, that reduce waste, that save weight and size, and generally prevent pollution.

These examples are underpinned by some key principles to my mind. And let me quickly share a few.

Item. We must set environmental priorities. All issues are not created equal. Those that help people and serve the environment happen to be my favorites, but regardless of what your favorite issue may be, be it population or energy or climate or biodiversity or solid waste, clean air, clean water, wetlands or urban sprawl, regardless, we need priorities and we need focus.

To fix priorities we'll need to build a broad-based consensus, the broadest possible base, with real partners around the common table, partners that include industry and labor, academia, the environmental community, just to mention a few. Panels that can dump their single issue and self-interest orientation of the past, and the acrimony that goes with it.

We'll need to harness good science and risk assessment in our review. And maybe we'll need a national environmental forum to link up with its international counterparts.

Item. We must make pollution prevention versus end-of-pipe treatment our ultimate goal. To do this we must ensure that the polluter pays, be they private citizens, be they businesses large and small, be they government agencies—they must pay rather than pass on, postpone or try to duck the environmental impact of their actions, and in so doing create the superfunds and the sons of superfunds for the future.

We must begin to develop and employ full-cost accounting and full-cost pricing of our products based on complete life cycle analysis, ensuring that the full product costs, including the environmental cost, is incorporated in our products, and then pass on that full cost to an ultimate consumer so that they can decide to consume or not consume your product, based on full information and freedom from hidden costs and subsidies.

We must use market mechanisms as the locomotive for environmental reform. To do this we must espouse global and international environmental standards based on solid U.S. leadership and example.

If an economy is to be global, the rules by which it plays must be more and more global and less and less national, or the globalization process will surely be reversed in the name of unfair competition.

Post-Rio vacuums developed. The world's waiting to see what Agenda 21 initiatives will be put forward and how they'll be achieved. The choice will be between, on one hand, more legislation and regulation—and certainly we need good legislation and regulation. But we don't need an excess of control and command which really hasn't worked all that well. Check Eastern Europe as a case in point.

Do we trust industry and government and all the other constituencies to work together in pro-active, pre-emptive initiatives using the realities of the market? I certainly hope so.

We need to level the environmental playing field by demanding environmental stewardship of our trading partners, and by cleaning up our own act. We must put an end to our own subsidies and incentives and, by all means, our disincentives—disincentives such as an inability to get the best agricultural products to our farmers, the safest, most efficacious grams-per-acre new products through an arduous regulatory process, to deal with the disincentives in product liability and tort reform, a subject that was only mentioned recently in this session.

In other areas, I submit the cost of capital, accounting standards, regulatory administrative costs, to mention just a few. Clearly government has a leadership role. It must set and enforce standards, levy fees. And I think it must use taxes, but only as a last resort, and then tax consumption rather than production in this ever more global economy.

So where are we now and where do we go from here?

The U.S. spends two and a half percent of its GDP on its environment. That's environmental compliance when you get right down to it, while that number in Germany is 1.8 percent, in Japan it's 1.2 percent.

As that number goes up and collides with the 7 to 8 percent of GDP we spend on education and the 12 to 13 percent we now spend on medical care, all of which are gaining and growing in multiples of the economy, we all stand to lose. Environment, education, and medical care must not be competing issues. While we must achieve their goals, all of their goals, we must control their costs or face a competition where nobody wins.

Thank you very much.

VICE PRESIDENT-ELECT GORE: Thank you very much. I thought that was an excellent presentation. And somebody who had not listened to

326

this debate for the last five years and suddenly turned on his or her television set and heard the CEO of Dow Chemical giving that talk might have been surprised. I'm not. I know the leadership role that you have been playing. In the discussion that will follow shortly we'll get into some of these issues.

Before asking Lynn Williams to give the perspective of labor on this issue, I want to ask a couple of people to jump into this discussion first. I want to ask Carol Browner, President-elect Clinton's nominee to head the EPA, to talk about how government can work with industry to achieve environmental objectives and realize the balance that Mr. Popoff is talking about. And then Alice Rivlin, who is to be the number two at OMB, to talk about the implications for macroeconomic policy options. And then maybe a couple of other business people—Dick Clarke and Paul O'Neill. And then we'll come back to the formal presentations. Carol.

CAROL BROWNER (EPA ADMINISTRATOR-DESIGNATE): Senator Gore and Governor Clinton, thank you. I want to talk briefly about my perspective from having run for the past several years the third largest environmental agency in the country. I want to focus on the regulatory scheme and what I think is the need to bring rationality and efficiency to that regulatory scheme.

Mr. Popoff made some I think very eloquent comments about this, and I would like to add to those. It is time to move away from the adversarial process that has developed both in terms of the development of the rules that are implemented by the environmental agencies, but also in what I think is often a too abusive permitting process. There are many bites at the apple, no one really knows when it's done. There are far too many permits for the same project.

I want to give two examples in Florida that I think have worked well and that I think can be used nationally. The first one involves Walt Disney World. As many of you know, we are home to Walt Disney World, and Walt Disney World came to us about a year ago, a year and a half ago, and they were interested in doing their last build-out, a 20-year program to I think almost double the size and add lots of new resorts that you all can come and visit.

They needed a wetland permit. They would impact approximately 400 acres of wetlands in that process. We began a discussion prior to the permit even being filed with the agency about how we could best, one, minimize the impacts to the eco-system, and, two, mitigate, as most states have a mitigation program for wetlands impact. Where we finally ended, less than a year after the permit was filed—and, again, this was for a 20-year build-out, a very large permit—is that they were able to decrease their wetlands impact to approximately 300 acres, a 25-percent reduction in impacts. And they have agreed to purchase 8,000 acres of an eco-system that we have long wanted preserved in Florida but no one really had the cash resources in state government or local government to preserve. They have put up an endowment to manage that and restore that over about a 10-year period and then it will transfer into a not-for-profit ownership.

The reason I bring this example up is traditionally what we do in regulatory schemes involving wetland permits is we allow people to go out and create a wetland—they scrape down an upland and they build another wetland where one didn't previously exist. We've had tremendous failures because of this type of permitting program.

And so what we've done in Florida is we've moved beyond that. We've moved to eco-system restoration and preservation. Disney is happy. The environmental community is happy. The local community is happy. And the state environmental agency is happy. We did this because we all came to the table in a non-adversarial manner. We talked about our differences. We talked about how to resolve those differences. We made concessions, and we moved forward in a timely manner so that Disney can begin their development in a timely manner.

The second example I'd like to talk about deals with developing legislation. Most of you are aware, under the Federal Clear Air Act, there are opportunities for states to pass their own legislation so that they can run in essence the federal clean air program. There are time frames in the federal law, you have about three years if you want to do this.

I went to the utility companies and the other affected industries in Florida, and I asked them if they would be willing to sit down in advance, three years in advance, to develop a legislative package that we could take to the legislature and pass the program early so we could actually do the type of planning that we need to do and that they could do the type of planning that they need to do to come into compliance.

Not only did all of the major utilities and industries in the state ultimately support the legislative package, they also supported the adoption of fees in advance of the federal mandate, so that the state agency would actually have the money to do the program. This was a first in Florida. It's easy to give state agencies and federal agencies, even local government, mandates, but it's frequently done so without any sort of adequate funding. So we now have the funding in advance of what the federal law requires and we will slowly move up to what the federal law requires so that we can effectively put in place a program—and business will be working with us in the development of that program.

Again, that was done through a consensus-building process, a non-adversarial process. There are a number of other examples I could give you, but I wanted to share those two with you. I think it is extremely important that we move in that direction, and I am confident that in this administration that that will be possible, that there will be opportunities as reflected by this conference that has been put together over the last two days to develop an important, rich, and ongoing dialogue between all of the affected interests.

Thank you.

Vice President-elect Gore: The elimination of an adversarial approach obviously takes a change in perspective on the part of both participants in that dialogue, and if that change does take place the opportunities for our country to move forward are really tremendous, and it's an exciting possibility.

Alice Rivlin has written and spoken a great deal about the use of market incentives. A lot of the ideas are controversial even as options. But in following on what Frank Popoff said about the advantages of market approaches to command and control approaches, I wonder if you have any thoughts.

Alice Rivlin (Deputy Director-Designate, OMB): Yes. I think there has been a remarkable convergence over the last few years between what the environmental community was saying and what the business community was saying, and it's reflected here today. And the business community has realized that what we all want to achieve is not just a higher per capita gross domestic product, but a higher level of living for everyone, and that includes the quality of the air and the quality of the water and the quality of the landscape.

The environmental community has also recognized that the way to go about achieving improvements in the environment has been too costly, that we have relied on very expensive and detailed command and control regulations. And as Frank Popoff has said, we need to get the prices right, we need to make sure that the costs to the environment of the products that are being produced are fully reflected in the price and that the polluters pay.

Now, that sounds terrific, but when budgeteers translate that, I think they tend to use this ugly word "taxes" and "subsidies." But this discussion does tie in to the discussion earlier about the deficit. There is an opportunity as we look ahead, to the extent that we must increase government revenues, to reduce the deficit. And I believe we have to face that.

We should be looking at taxing the things that we don't want to have happen, pollution and excessive use of energy. That means perhaps gas taxes, perhaps carbon taxes. And we should look at that as an alternative to producing—to taxing the things we do want to have happen, such as more jobs and more income.

And on balance, we need to think about how to use the opportunities that most of the people around the table agree on in reducing the deficit and increasing our economic growth.

VICE PRESIDENT-ELECT GORE: Thank you, Alice. Now let me call on Dick Clarke. I said earlier that John has the second largest utility. You've got the largest utility in the country in PG&E. And I wanted to ask you what improving environmental performance does for the bottom line of not just your company but your customers.

RICHARD CLARKE (PACIFIC GAS AND ELECTRIC): Well, I think the energy efficiency programs that John alluded to provide tremendous benefits to consumers, to our customers. They also provide enormous benefits for the environment, and they certainly help America's movement toward greater energy security.

To give you some sense of the order of magnitude, if we applied nationally the kinds of energy efficiency programs that John referred to—and they are being done in parts of New England—we could save 32 to 120 billion dollars a year in people's electric bills. The 32 billion [dollars] is the estimate of our energy group, the Electric Power Research Institute, and the 120 billion is the Rocky Mountain Institute's estimate. So there's a wide range, but there's enormous numbers with the savings that can be achieved to getting our energy use more efficient than it currently is.

It also helps our businesses be more competitive as they compete in the global economy. And another very positive aspect to this is that there is enormous job creation that flows from an energy system in which instead of just building new power plants we are installing energy-efficient appliances, heating systems, cooling systems, lighting systems, putting in variable speed-dry motors in factories, insulating the miles and miles and miles of pipes that are uninsulated—(audio break)—putting in thermal pane windows.

There are so many things that people can do. We estimate a half a million new jobs could be created in this sector of energy efficiency in the next five or six years, and a million jobs out through the year 2010. And the environment benefits—and of course all consumers, as people who live in the environment, get this benefit as well—because if we could again have on a national basis the kinds of programs we're talking about, we could hold CO2 emissions at 1990 levels. And we could have gone to Rio this last time and indicated that we could sign an agreement that CO2 emissions could be held at 1990 levels.

And you can add even more to that through the utilization of clean-air vehicles, the electrical vehicle John referred to, the natural gas vehicle that I use, that I drive, which of course brings about enormous reductions in air emissions, and uses an American fuel at 70 cents a gallon by comparison. So there are tremendous benefits that can be achieved through these energy efficiency and clean-air vehicle programs. And the environment wins, the consumer wins, and the economy wins.

Vice President-elect Gore: Thanks. I'll just interject this comment—that the Big Three have just entered into a new cooperative venture on an American electric vehicle initiative that bears further discussion in the next section of our panel here.

But before going to Lynn Williams, there's one other person, Paul O'Neill, a CEO of Alcoa.

Paul O'Neil (CEO, Alcoa): Thank you very much. If you don't mind, I'm going to talk in headlines in the interest of time, because there are several things I would like to say. First of all, do not lag in your commitment to the idea of sustainable development. It is in my judgment no doubt that we can have sustainable development, and that the idea of sustainable development is consistent with a prosperous economy, more prosperous than anything we've ever done. And if you're interested in some examples to illustrate the point, I'll give those to you later.

There are some problems. The problems are associated with cleaning up the costs of some things that were very well intentioned, for example the use of PCBs to reduce the danger of combustion in electrical systems for example, that we have now determined is not good for human health. There is a very great problem, though, because I believe trying to reduce the PCB contamination to nondetectable levels is frankly a travesty in the context of a world economy and a world environment, where for example, as we have been investigating opportunities in the former Soviet Union, we are finding people are dying at the age of 47 on average because of their pollution. And at the same time, companies here in America are spending billions of dollars to achieve nondetectability—it seems to me it doesn't make any sense

331

if you assume that your responsibility is for civilization and not to achieving some glossy goal that is not supported by scientific evidence.

I think it should be clear—it certainly has been clear to me, and has been for a long time, that we need a gasoline tax. There should be no doubt that we can accommodate a gasoline tax. In effect, we had one during the Gulf War: our gasoline prices went up 40 or 50 cents a gallon and, yes, there were some distortive effects, but as a society we handled it. Yes, we should take care of the low-income population—they need help in this area. But there should be no doubt that we can help ourselves a lot—the environment—we can raise some revenue for Mr. Panetta and Alice who are need of it a lot if you listen to this conversation—in the process. There should be no doubt we are ready. When the chairman of one of the largest automobile companies in the country says we're ready for it, we're ready.

We should also look very hard at a carbon tax. I know you've been beat up for that. Listen to the science; don't listen to the emotion.

On the issue of technology, I would offer you this. I believe our future depends on technology. But I would also say to you I am very wary of the federal government's ability to induce technology in the right order. I'll give you one illustration to make the point. Not too long ago my people came to me and said, "Here's an $18 million project, and we want to do it, and the government is going to pay for $12 million of the 18 [million dollars]." And I said, "Would you do it if it was all our own money?" And they said, "Of course not." (Laughter) Okay? I think that's not an isolated question, and you all—your administration I think needs to work on the idea of maybe a discounted-cash-flow model that says if society is not likely in our broad distribution to get an economic benefit out of this over some 20-year period of time, we shouldn't do it. Now, that doesn't mean we shouldn't do undifferentiated, uncertain research. But it ought to be done in universities with a very clear-headed view of what it is we're doing, and not confuse budget lines in making improvements in our economy, because technology becomes the talisman that we hold ourselves up to, and so we spend a lot of money, and Alice and Leon will have to fight off the crowds who want to get their apple under their tent.

I was struck by a conversation this morning. Twenty years ago President Nixon said we're all Keynesians now. I don't think it was true then. But if you listened to the conversation this morning, it sounded like we're all Keynesian. I've got to tell you I don't believe the world is Keynesian any more in this sense. I think Keynes was right in his analysis of our ability to stimulate the economy, when economies were much more isolated than they are today. We are not isolated.

If you look at what's happening in the oft-cited experience in Los

Angeles with the aerospace industry coming down, it's a direct consequence of what's happened in the Soviet Union and Central Europe. And we haven't even talked about the secondary consequence of what's going on in the Soviet Union and Central Europe, which is also impacting our domestic economy close to the—closed down now. As a consequence of what happened in the Soviet Union and Central Europe, there has effectively been added to the world aluminum supply 20 percent more capacity. And it's not just aluminum. This is not a narrow, self-interest question. A lot of what's happened in the Soviet Union and Central Europe is gravitating toward us, across the oceans, and it impacts in Asia. And therefore I am really wary of believing that the Keynesian models will work any more.

That's not to say I'm against $30 billion worth of stimulus if you want to do it—it's probably good political Keynesianism. It may not be good economic Keynesianism. But I wouldn't count on $30 billion solving problems which are really a wrap around the world. We're no longer an island economy, and I think you sir, gentlemen, you need to disabuse people of the idea that you can solve the problems that have been laid before you, and that somehow we can do the stimulus that worked in the Eisenhower period and somehow things are going to be wonderful.

One more quick point. I promised Marian Wright Edelman yesterday at lunch, because I disagreed with what she said to you about full funding for Head Start. Let me tell you why, and let me use it to make a very important general point. I think you need to conceive your roles as society's leaders, not as the managers of the federal government. And in that regard what Marian said to you I think is really critically important. Yes, as a society we have an obligation to take care of those who can't help themselves to get an early childhood education. But the 14 million children that are represented by that notion are only a third, or maybe a fourth, of the total number of children in this country under the age of 18 that should have had, and in the future need to have, early childhood education. And I think you need to hold the feet of the middle class and the upper class to the fire of making this society work. It isn't good enough to take care of only the low-income children. You need to hold up the banner that every child in this country gets early childhood education, and that doesn't mean sending all the money to Washington so that you can send it back to us. I think you have got to call us to our responsibilities. It's an important thing that has been lacking.

One more point. It goes to a point of regulation and taxes. We've talked a lot about regulatory impact. We now have 7,000 pages in the Federal Tax Code, and we've got 100,000 pages of regulations to implement—Senator Bentsen and Mr. Panetta know this very well. If there was one radical, bold move you wanted to make, in addition to dealing with the health care cost problem, which I think is a worthy problem, we really ought to go to a consumption tax. And I mean one that has no deductions and no credits. And I tell you I'd be very happy if all I had to do was have two accountants at the end of the year write the government a check related to our gross revenue, and let every individual in this society do the same thing, because at the moment we're spending $250 billion a year to administer the Federal Tax Code. And now, if you think about it in the context of the world economy, it adds no value whatsoever to our ability to compete in the world, because customers don't pay you for that. There is no satisfaction in administrative cost of a tax system. So I would submit to you, if you want a big hit in freeing resources—we'll put H&R Block out of business, forgive me—we'll create $250 billion worth of accountants and lawyers that can be retrained as engineers and contributors. (Laughter/applause) Thank you.

VICE PRESIDENT-ELECT GORE: We can't have a full discussion of all the points that you touched on there. I want to try to bring the focus back to the principal subject of this part of our discussion. We'll get into some of the technology points you raised in just a moment, but I want to ask Lynn Williams, head of the steel workers, to address this issue of environment and economic growth from labor's point of view.

LYNN WILLIAMS (UNITED STEELWORKERS OF AMERICA): Well, thank you very much, Vice President-elect Gore and President-elect Clinton. I'd first like to express my appreciation quickly for the opportunity to participate in this historic conference. And I would like to compliment you on your wisdom and your courage in calling this conference, and particularly on the intensity with which you pursue the goals here— without food, without sleep. (Laughter) It's been a dramatic—it provides dramatic evidence of your concern about the conference, and much more importantly about the country, and we appreciate that very much.

It is a truism that oil and water don't mix. In that same vein, there has been the constant refrain that environmental protection and industrial production don't mix, and by extrapolation jobs and the environment are in conflict with one another. Fortunately, today, after 22 years of experience under the Clean Air Act, another environmental and occupational safety and health act, I believe we are able to refute that claim. Between 1973 and 1986, we reduced pollution, decreased CO_2 emissions, and expanded the economy by almost 40 percent, while at the same time maintaining the same level of energy consumption.

That observation leads me to the first comment which I would like to make: environmental attentiveness should not be a job loser; it should be a job creator. While I am not advocating the promotion of pollution abatement and/or prevention, solely because of its positive impact upon the job market, that aspect of our environmental laws has only recently emerged. At a time in which we are keenly sensitive to the need of developing and expanding new job opportunities, environment-oriented jobs are a positive contribution, and can be part of an economic stimulation program. Clean-up of Super Fund sites, construction of sewage-treatment facilities, and clean water rehabilitation efforts are labor-intensive activities that also have a social objective.

The environmental goods and services industry has been a fast-growing one. By some calculations, the abatement and prevention industry comprises 70,000 businesses, employing over one million workers, with a 1991 income level of $130 billion. According to an article by Senator Wirth, and I quote, "Using a standard multiplier effect, to gauge the full impact of this sector in our economy, economists suggest that there is a 3.5 million jobs flow," end quote.

The second point relates to the trade aspect of this growing market. The OECD projects that the global market is expanding at the rate of five to six percent per year, and will reach $300 billion in seven years. The International Finance Corporation projects an even larger market by the year 2000, namely $600 billion. These figures indicate a global market greater than the aerospace and chemical industry. Our interest in job creation is advanced if we can remain in the forefront of the commitment to environmental controls. Otherwise our trading partners will seize the environmental goods and services markets through exports, resulting in a loss of US jobs and future job opportunities. Actually this disadvantageous trend is already underway. US firms have lost the edge to Western Europe and Japan in air pollution control technology, due to the lax enforcement of our environmental laws during the Reagan and Bush years.

End of the pipeline pollution abatement investments have often been resisted by many of our corporations. Now, however, environmental awareness has taken on a new characteristic, namely pollution prevention. Pollution prevention has an economic value for the company. It makes the company cost competitive and more productive, precisely because pollution is in reality waste—both in terms of a loss of a resource and in terms of abatement. There is a direct relationship between pollution prevention and manufacturing modernization, which focuses on continuous improvement to eliminate waste as inefficient. Some of our companies are now engaged in a review of their

335

production processes. Such a review, stimulated through environmental intervention to prevent pollution rather than treat it, can put firms on the cutting edge of technology. The drive for technologic advancement is an important aspect, both of sustainable development and a key factor in job security, especially in global market competition.

Jobs in the environment have a dual linkage. Not only are jobs enhanced by environmental measures, but environmental objectives are achieved through a healthy economy. As we all know, poverty is a major factor in ecological catastrophes. According to a recent ILO report, quote, "Employment alleviates poverty. In the process, the concept of sustainable livelihoods in forged. The labor market is boosted by the introduction of social pollution abatement techniques, and cleaner process techniques. It follows that the prevention of environmental degradation is conducive to the promotion and safeguarding of employment," end quote. In other words, sustainable development and sustainable livelihood promote one another.

Furthermore, there is an inherent linkage between occupational health and environmental health. The advancement of the quality of a worker's life on the job has had an immediate connection with the rising awareness of the environmental quality of community life. Environmental health and occupational health both relate to the same industrial processes which must be controlled. The 1970 OSHA legislation was enacted after years of development of the public's awareness of environmental hazards, and was preceded by the passage of the Clean Air Act, which provided the statutory precedents for a work force and environmental regime. Throughout the history of the implementation of both acts, environmental protection and occupational safety and health from time to time have been confronted by the same opposition: environmental blackmail. In addition, we had to insist that the systematic policy of deregulation of environmental laws or safety laws did not in any way substitute for an aggressive macroeconomic policy.

While the plant gates may devise a regulatory responsibility over environmental health hazards, it is the emissions from the same industrial processes for which abatement or prevention measures are required. Community health and worker health are linked in a continuum, and ultimately both are advanced together.

While oil and water don't mix, economic progress is increasingly involved with environmental protection. Environmental technologies, while directed at pollution abatement and prevention, also contribute to the competitiveness and efficiency required for survival in a global economy. For the labor movement, this translates into more secure jobs and, equally important, more safe and healthy jobs. As we stated in our steel workers convention report, entitled, "Our Children's

World," in the long run the real choice is not jobs or environment, it's both or neither.

VICE PRESIDENT-ELECT GORE: Boy, that was a terrific statement, Lynn. Thank you very much. I want to open this part of the discussion up to the panel, and then we're going to shift to Craig Fields' presentation.

I want to make one point on the comment you made about the relationship between eliminating waste in the form of pollution and eliminating economic waste. If you're going into the woods hunting for a bear, and you don't see the bear, you look for the bear's tracks, or you get a dog that can follow its scent. If you're an industrialist looking for inefficiency to eliminate, and you walk on the factory floor and you don't see it, you have to follow its track. And what a lot of innovators, like some of the people around this table, are finding, is that the tracks that are easiest to follow are the pollution, the pollution markers that can lead to the elimination of invisible deficiencies. Let me—Yes?

JOHN CORRENTI (NUCOR CORP.): Yes, I would like to make a comment—

VICE PRESIDENT-ELECT GORE: John Correnti.

MR. CORRENTI: —about investment in new technology, and how it relates to the environment. In Nucor Corporation, the investment in new technology has created the sixth largest steel company in America, and currently one of the most profitable, if not the most profitable steel company in America.

Today I am here on behalf of our 6,000 employees, who I believe are the most dedicated, loyal, most productive, and some of the most highly-paid manufacturing workers in America. They have a message for you: Do not write the obituary of the American steel industry. It is alive, well, and profitable in places like Darlington, South Carolina; Norfolk, Nebraska; Jewett, Texas; Plymouth, Utah; Blytheville, Arkansas; Crawfordsville, Indiana; and Hickman, Arkansas. By the expressions on your face, you're saying, "Where the heck are those places?" Where they are, ladies and gentlemen, that's rural America. And in my behalf, or in my belief, I think it's the greatest untapped resource for productivity and labor in America.

I want to talk about one of those places today—Blytheville, Arkansas. You heard about it yesterday—it's about 180 miles east of here, in the Mississippi Delta—in the Mississippi Delta. I ran into a governor in the State of Arkansas about five years ago who believed in the investment in new technology, and he believed in the people in the Mississippi Delta, and he convinced us to spend $250 million. That investment turned out to be our most profitable steel company. After that, we invested another $300 million, and that steel mill just started up. And we're currently investing another $200 million to create the largest structural steel company in the world, located in Blytheville, Arkansas.

And I want to tell you where most of that steel goes. Most of that steel is sold in the United States. But listen to where some of it is exported to: Indonesia, Singapore, the UK, Hong Kong, and last, but not least, we ship steel to Japan. Why do they buy that steel from us? Not because they like us or because they want to help us out—a quality producer and a low-cost producer. It's cheaper than the steel they can buy at home.

Now, why are we able to do this low cost and quality? Well, we empower our work force. The average W-2 wage in the Mississippi Delta this year, in Blytheville, Arkansas, will be $49,000. And if you just take the factory workers, it's going to $55,000. That's the average. There are some foremen this year who will make $70,- or $80,000. How do we do it? Invest in new technologies and modernize. These new technologies are environmentally friendly. For instance, the steel industry in these new technologies recycle 50 million tons of iron and steel scrap annually. Last year, America's steel-making furnaces recycled nine million junk cars. That's double that of paper, aluminum, cooper, lead, zinc, glass and plastics combined. The amount of steel recycled each year in this manner is equivalent to one-third of the municipal solid waste that is landfilled annually in the United States. That's a savings of two million bucks per year in waste disposal costs.

Number two is you have to educate and train your employees. Not only do we educate our employees, we educate their sons and daughters. And I challenge everybody here in corporate America. In our company, we provide $2,000 per year per child for every employee to go on to college—higher education—every child of every employee. That's the greatest investment, not only in the employee's family, but also in our business, and that's a great investment in America. I wish more companies would do that.

The other thing we do—and I'm going to end here in a minute—is when we empower those employees, there's an easy way to do it. What empowerment means to me is if you're a management leader, get out of your employees' way. If you're a union leader, get out of your members' way. If you are a government leader, we have to get the rules and the regulations out of our employees so that they can produce efficiently and effectively. And I believe that the American manufacturing worker will out-produce, out-think, out-work anyone anywhere in this world if we adhere to those principles. I'm optimistic about America. We can compete today, we can compete tomorrow. Thank you very much. (Applause)

VICE PRESIDENT-ELECT GORE: Let me just take three more, and then we're going to turn to Craig Fields. And those of you who did not have a chance to speak during this part of the roundtable discussion are invited to do so in the last part of the roundtable discussion. But I want to call on Gus Speth, and then Drew Lewis, and then Mary Ann Mills. Gus?

GUS SPETH (WORLD RESOURCES INST.): President-elect Clinton, Vice President-elect Gore, I want to begin by commending you for moving the country beyond the sterile debate between jobs and the environment. You started that in the campaign, and you've continued it here today, and you've already performed a great public service by doing that. I think you have a great opportunity in your administration to bring the environment and the economy together in a way that we have never seen before, to develop policies that support our environment, its protection, and our economic growth simultaneously. I don't think we will achieve our objectives by compromising always between the two, although some of that will always be necessary. What we really have to do is transcend the debate between them by finding those strategies which promote both economic strength and environmental protection simultaneously. And they do exist. You are absolutely right to have said that in the campaign.

I would urge you to begin this process by incorporating these strategies into your early economic plan. I think it will strengthen that plan both substantively and politically in the country.

Two things just jump immediately to mind. There has been a lot of discussion about infrastructure investments which could be what we might think of as green infrastructure—in sewage, in water, in energy and transportation. These are things that are well worth considering, and I believe I would urge you to consider them as part of your plan.

The second element that just jumps out is this question of revenue generation. Whether it's to reduce the deficit or to pay for other aspects of the plan, or to pay for the reduction of other taxes, green fees —gasoline tax, an energy pollution fee, a tax on the emission of certain of the ozone-depleting chemicals, of toxic pollutants, of water pollutants. There's a long list of possible green fees that are available which could generate anywhere from 30 to 50 billion dollars a year when fully introduced, that could both clean up the environment and provide the revenues needed for the kind of economic plan that we have been discussing here for the last two days. And I would encourage you to consider that.

Looking a little bit down the road for the longer term, I don't think we will succeed in bringing our economic and our environmental objectives together with the current set of approaches. As Frank Popoff was saying earlier, and as others have pointed out, our current model or paradigm of environmental governance in the country was brought together in the early 1970s in a very different climate and in a very different period to meet very different needs. We need to move beyond that now to a new model or a new paradigm of environmental governance. And the elements of that have come out in the discussion that we've had here already. We need to focus on technological change, on the rapid introduction and infusion of new technologies that are designed with environmental realities in mind. And we need to review our regulatory policies and our tax policies, and our spending and R&D policies in order to get these new technologies on the line. And if we do we can not only clean up the environment, but we will have those technologies available for international markets and for competition.

A second element of this new model would be the rapid introduction of market-based approaches, of revenue-neutral market-based approaches, of income-generating market-based approaches, as Alice Rivlin said, that can make the price of products in the marketplace reflect their real environmental cost as well as the cost to produce them. And when it becomes cheaper to do the right thing for the environment on the part of the consumer, then we'll see our environment cleaned up very quickly.

We need to look for solutions outside of traditional environmental laws and outside of traditional environmental approaches. Some of the highest pay-off opportunities are in other sectors or in new agricultural policies, new energy policies, new transportation policies. And so we need to find these high pay-off opportunities and sector strategies in other areas.

And, lastly, as I think Frank Popoff said, we need to move beyond this severely adversarial system that we've created, and to find the trust that will allow us to introduce new flexibility that will allow us to empower companies to do the best possible, that will allow us to go back through these 20 years of environmental rules and regulations that have accumulated, and make them more consistent, and make them more user-friendly, and make them more efficient and effective. But we can't do that unless we bury this hatchet and get beyond the adversarial relationships of the past. Thank you very much.

340

Vice President-elect Gore: Thank you, Gus. Drew?

Drew Lewis (Union Pacific Corp.): Okay. Thank you very much, President-elect Clinton and Vice President-elect Gore. As a partisan Republican, I am very glad that Cliff Wharton mentioned diversity yesterday. Without that I wouldn't be here. And I respect your tolerance, and also I have great respect for the clear ability you have to reach out. So thank you for permitting me to be here. I'm going to be very brief.

First, one issue I'd like to talk about applies to both the deficit and the environment, and it really comes up to the point that Paul made. I think the easiest way for you to impose a tax that helps both the environment, the infrastructure, and the deficit, is a gasoline tax. And I believe you should do that. We're the largest consumer of the fuel you're going to tax in the world. I think we burn about 600 million gallons a year on the railroad and our trucking companies. So we'll be paying more tax than anybody else in the country. We still think you should impose a tax, and hope you'll do it.

On the environment, and this is really I guess addressed more to you, Carol, than anyone in the room. We got into this business feeling we were part of the solution. And in dealing with local, state, and federal government, you turn out to be the problem and not the solution. And I hope, and I've dealt with EPA going back to Administrator Ruckleshaus, and at that point we weren't in the business. I think what we need are four things that would help us a great deal. One, uniformity in interpretation of the regulations. And we have found there are interpretations different throughout the regions in this country—a very difficult way to operate your business.

Second, I think there needs to be acceleration of the paperwork in the EPA. We had one petition on an administrative law judge's desk for nine months before we got an answer, and the only way we got that is we went to Mr. Reilly, and he worked it out by getting an answer for us.

Third, I think we need a simplification of paperwork. It's very expensive, very time consuming, and I believe in many cases superfluous. And I hope you would look at that.

And, fourthly, and this I guess is addressed more to you, Mr. President-elect, if you do support the Super Fund Number Two, I hope that somehow we'll see that some of the money gets to the purpose for which it was intended, not be consumed by paper shufflers and lawyers—and that's where the money went. And we really should address that issue. I think Super Fund makes sense, but we've wasted all the money. Thank you.

341

PRESIDENT-ELECT CLINTON: Could I—I wasn't going to say anything during this panel, but Drew has provoked me here in a very positive way.

I think Madeleine Kunin and I are the only two people here who have been governors the last 10 years and—I think we are—and one of the main reasons I asked Carol Browner to be the EPA administrator is that if you've been in state government it's as close to being in private industry to know what it's like to be governed by the federal government in this area. There are all kinds of things I'd like to say in that regard, but I agree with the uniform interpretation of regulations. I also don't like it when the EPA basically tries to have it both ways, as they did with the paper companies on docks and emissions into the water. They let the states set a high standard, and then had a scientific report saying of course everybody will die if you do that. They didn't quite say that, but it wasn't right what they did.

But let me say that all this rhetoric we're using, which I deeply believe in—you know, ending the adversarial relationship and going to a more market-oriented mechanism and less command and control— that's all good when you're looking at modifying processes to reduce pollution. But one of our biggest problems is the problem represented by the Super Fund, and some other areas where you've got to fix something bad that's already happened, where we spend too much money on lawyers, too much money on consultants. The endless decisions. It's almost impossible to get anybody at the local level to agree what the best solution is. And I'm saying all this by way of making a personal plea which is that—to Drew Lewis and everybody else in this audience—if you have specific ideas about what we could do to make the whole management of waste issue better handled by us, in a responsible way—not only in terms of getting to decision, but also in bringing all the affected parties along, I would very much like to have it. I am just appalled by the paralysis and the political divisions, and the fact that the money is being blown. And we really need—whoever is writing—all of you I hope will write us something—but anybody who has any personal experience and knowledge or opinion on this, this is something that I think we are duty bound to do a much better job on, and we need all the ideas we can get. Thank you.

VICE PRESIDENT-ELECT GORE: I certainly agree with that. And when that law was passed in December 1980, it was first implemented in January of 1981 by folks who were essentially hostile to the intent and purpose of the law when it was first put in place. And I think at least some of the problems can be traced to that.

But Mary Ann Mills brings a unique small business perspective to this dialogue.

MARY ANN MILLS (SOAPBOX TRADING CO.): Thank you, that's true. My 60 employees in DC right now are bursting with pride. Because I'm here, they feel they're here. So we all thank you very much for including us.

I am dazzled by what is happening in the utility industry. I think if business worked collectively together to start doing business more environmentally responsibly, we could have a huge impact on what happens in this country. There are companies existing in this country that have proven environmental responsibility and profitability are not mutually exclusive. Although I have a small company, I am associated with a global company, a retail organization, that has long-standing environmentally sound policies that we've practiced since our inception. I thought it might be a good idea to share a few of those that we engage in, hopefully to initiate some discussion and hopefully ideas for other companies in what they could do in this field.

Our products are packaged minimally. We offer refilling and recycling services in our stores. We source our ingredients responsibly. And, for an example, as part of our trade-not-aid program, we work with the Caiopo Indians in Brazil. They collect Brazil nuts for us and produce Brazil nut oil that we use in one of our hair conditioners. Not only does that give us a good product, but it also helps teach the Caiopo Indians in Brazil that it is more profitable to harvest sustainably from the rain forest than cut it down. We're also working with the Sanana Pueblo Native Americans in New Mexico, sourcing our blue corn for a range of skin care products in our stores. We also are planning to build a wind farm in the UK, which is where our international headquarters is located. And that will hopefully give back to the energy source what we take out to manufacture our products.

We also recently did a very extensive environmental audit, which we call our green book, that looks at every aspect of our business, from the product life cycle to environmental management. We would like to see other companies measuring their success by other things than their financial abilities. And an environmental account like this would be one step in that direction. We would also like to see other companies join us. We don't want to be considered an unusual company; we want to be considered a business that does business as usual.

And one thing that we would love to see happen in the near future is to see governments start using their powerful dollars to buy more responsibly. Think what could happen if you all decided to move towards recycled paper. That one move alone could have a dramatic

343

impact on rewarding those companies that are doing socially and environmentally responsible positive things.

I have one more point that I'd like to bring up, and that is I continue to see that we are undervaluing our natural resources in this country, that we are not placing a replacement cost on the values of these natural resources. How much does it cost to replace the eroded topsoil of Missouri? How much does it cost to replace our old growth forest? I know that—Ms. Rivlin, you may remember in the Carter administration Arthur Andersen did a balance sheet for the US, which, although it was incomplete, at least attempted to start putting a proper price-tag on our natural resources and public lands, and I hope that in the future we can pull that out, dust it off, and build on that further. Thank you.

VICE PRESIDENT-ELECT GORE: You mentioned your employees were bursting with pride. A lot of businesses—Frank Popoff was saying this earlier—have found that an unexpected benefit of adopting an environmental goal, like the ones that you've adopted, is that employee morale and participation in the company's efforts can change overnight dramatically.

MS. MILLS: There's no doubt about it.

VICE PRESIDENT-ELECT GORE: Anybody else had that experience? Yes?

AUDIENCE MEMBER: Definitely. In our company we have volunteer programs in the community. We get our employees out. We are very involved in many different situations. And it's created—it's just like having a great new team. We used to have ski teams and get out and do more active, sporty things, and now we're finding that we're getting out in the community, outreaching, and finding that it's really, really building a great spirit in our company.

VICE PRESIDENT-ELECT GORE: Thank you. I know I said I was going to go straight to Craig Fields. But Lilia Clemente has asked to say a word before we shift gears. And please do.

Lilia Clemente (Clemente Capital, Inc.): President-elect Clinton, Vice President-elect Gore, thank you for this opportunity to participate in this conference. As a portfolio manager who seeks production investments around the world, I welcome this opportunity to take part in the economic conference, where conference and industry leaders explore the competitive challenge and likely to make—investment responses likely to make. Recognizing the intensely global character of our industries, and reaffirming Mr. Popoff's points, today's environmental challenges and investment opportunities are indeed global. And our country, as one of the world's waste and polluter generators, is viewed as being—having special responsibility to find solutions.

Environmental degradation, first seen as a problem of rich nations, has become a survival issue for developing nations, which faces the double-edged sword of poverty and ecological degradation. This status quo is not an acceptable option. Therefore a strong need exists for partnership and cooperation before our stock holders to meet this environmental challenge.

Let's take some glaring examples. Mexico City's air is fouled up by one and a half pounds of pollutants every day for each citizen. For Mexican children, it's like smoking cigarettes from birth. The average lead level in the Mexican citizen's blood is supposed to be four times that of Tokyo residents. Worldwide deforestation is destroying habitat at the rate of 50 acres a minute. And against an annual population growth of more than 86 million per year, there is an annual worldwide loss of, as Mary Ann said, of about 25 billion tons of topsoil. The list could go on and on.

And I think another point I would like to make—worldwide ecological degradation poses exciting, significant opportunities for American challenges and companies. In our business, we have seen a lot more environmental funds come in, so I am bullish for this new industry which could rival, you know, there were related manufacturing facilities we should have—the growth of the clean-up industry worldwide. We have about more than 50,000 companies in the environmental industry, generating 140 billion [dollars] income per year. And this door, as—(inaudible)—has said, from Southern Pacific, we are in the leading edge of this technology. And this door to lead to a host of possible growth industries, such as exotic new technologies of full production and in your own—(inaudible)—methods, et cetera. So I am bullish on a lot of our companies—it provides wonderful opportunities.

Another point. Businesses and all its managements cannot afford to wait for improving environmental standards to be forced upon them by government officials, concerned investors, demanding public. Sustainable development, sustainable economic growth, sustainable energy policy, has to become part of business as usual. There has been—profit-maximizing corporations have often been accused of ignoring the environmental consequences. But we see now an increasing trend where CEOs believe that environmental performance makes good business sense, and some companies have adopted environmental management systems and audits.

Far from being an impediment to sustainable development, the financial services industry, where I come from, can act as a catalyst for change in day-to-day practices. We see emerging trends, expansions in our investment decision-making processes, incorporating environmental, social, and ethical concerns.

Finally, another political objective for us is to get environmental concerns on current and future GATT rounds. International trade needs a level playing field, not a level rain forest, in an economic sense of the produce. In other words, our GATT negotiators must not permit environmental scoundrels to compete unfairly with those who honor pledges of sustainable development.

Again, thank you, President-elect Clinton, thank you, Vice President-elect Gore. Yes, we can—oh, yes, we can accept the challenges facing the future. The future of the environment is people, machines and nature working together, without doing each other harm. This conference, under your leadership, exists as a foothold toward a goal. And, as we say on Wall Street, I'm bullish on America. (Laughter) Thank you.

VICE PRESIDENT-ELECT GORE: Thank you very much. That was a terrific presentation.

We're going to shift gears now and talk about the role of technology in promoting and enhancing economic growth. And, as we have already heard, some of the technologies that are most promising are directly relevant to the topic of the environment; some of them are not. But the person who will give a presentation now is eminently qualified to discuss the subject. Craig Fields is the Chairman and CEO of the Micro Electronics and Computer Technology Corporation, an Austin-based R&D consortium of over 50 US and Canadian information technology corporations. And of course Craig joined MCC two years ago after a much publicized removal as director of DARPA, for doing what I thought was the right thing. And it is a great pleasure to hear your thoughts on this, Craig. Please proceed.

CRAIG FIELDS (MICRO AND COMPUTER TECH. CORP.): Thank you, Senator Gore. In the last session, John Young established, I think quite clearly, the importance of technology for productivity. I would like to add, in introduction, that all companies are basically becoming high-technology companies. This is not something that just touches a few of us. If you work in an auto factory, you're producing a high-technology product that is about 30 percent electronics. And if you work in a food-processing plant, your product may not be high technology, but the process behind it is. And if you work as a travel agent, it may look like you're providing a warm, personal service—and you are—but behind you is a high-technology system for reservations, for credit checking, for billing, for advertising, so on and so forth. If you work in a turban factory that I know, then you are getting about a factory and a half out of your single factory by just better scheduling of tools, thus using technology in place of some investments. There are a lot of other examples like this.

So we all have a stake in technology, and that stake is actually going up. It is going up because we've entered a time of a very intense and new kind of competition. You heard a little about this from John Scully yesterday—tremendously rapid obsolescence—products that go out of date in a year. Customers that demand not only the lowest price and the highest quality, but enough variety in the products you offer that they can get almost a custom piece of goods, as if it was just in mass production. And then, to make it even more difficult, the small advantages that you get in time-to-market price and quality and variety can translate into very large market-share advantages, sort of like the racehorse that may be only a fraction of a second faster but gets most of the prize money. And then, to make it even harder, there is no company that I know now that is getting a product out based on their efforts. It's always their efforts, their supplier, their supplier's suppliers, and a variety of partners and allies. So multi-company linkages in what we call virtual companies is now part of the norm. We won't be able to compete in this kind of world without technology, above and beyond what we have today.

What I wanted to address in part was in this rather pressure-cooker-like environment what can the government and your administration do in order to help in competitiveness, help in productivity. And, given the time is short, I wanted to address only three things. One is technology development. Secondly, technology commercialization. Thirdly, information infrastructure. So I am going to leave out topics like high-technology trade and intellectual property protection and so on.

Much of what I have to say will be quite familiar to you. In my office in Austin I have four cubic feet of reports that have been written since 1985, all saying about the same thing, recommending how we can do better with technology policy in competitiveness and productivity. But, nevertheless, it's worth going through some of the highlights.

First, on technology development. It would be easy—in fact almost irresistible—to list important technologies that are worthy of federal assistance, or to discuss management or bureaucratic organizations who are doing technology development in the federal government. In fact, I'd like to talk about something that is more difficult and more important. Since the end of World War II—or even during—the Defense Department has had a paradigm for deciding what to invest in in technology, which is fairly straightforward—backtracking from threats to the missions needed to counter the threats, to the systems needed to accomplish those missions, to the technology. You need to have a paradigm for civilian technology investment. With such a paradigm, problems such as the ones you raise—the one you raise as an anecdote—really would be very infrequent. That has to be a consensus, a consensus with industry. It has to address economic growth.

If you start with even a simple statement, like giving priority to technologies that lead to the most good jobs for Americans, you start down a very complicated road of reasoning, which really no one has worked through. It probably means more investment in the traditional areas of information technology, like software and semiconductors, materials technology and biotechnology. It probably means getting input from the industries that produce large numbers of high value-added jobs for Americans—automobiles, electronics, the process industries of chemicals and pharmaceuticals and food processing, and aerospace. But it probably includes a lot more as well. Getting that paradigm down seems to me a very high priority thing for you to do early in the administration, so that you are guided by some reason rather than the sort of wheeler(?) fashion at the moment.

If you have such a paradigm, I really urge you to embrace what I'm going to term accountability—namely to look at the output, not just the input. There's an incredible temptation in the government to view a success things like increased R&D spending. In fact that's not the success; the success is the effect on Americans of whatever you do.

I've spoken with a few of your soon-to-be employees about this. They said accountability is too hard. I think it's very hard, but I don't think it's too hard. There are some natural consequences of accountability. One is that there will be more emphasis on manufacturing and production technology, since we have to not only invent but also produce. And then, as you heard earlier and to close the loop, there will be more emphasis on environmentally-correct manufacturing, because, as you heard, pollution is waste, and no one wants wasteful manufacturing.

Topic Number Two: Commercialization. Without commercialization and diffusion and dissemination, then you're not going to get business value from technology and hence value for Americans. I won't repeat the topics that were discussed the last day and a half that really are right for all businesses, large and small, but just say that there are some tremendous opportunities for helping small entrepreneurial high-tech companies, the growth companies that Allen Patrikov talked about. Better use of the small business innovative research program, better use of the small business administration linking small company suppliers with large company customers for the comparative advantage of both, the manufacturing extension centers, trying to use the talent in the federal laboratories, perhaps by spinning out small entrepreneurial firms. And I can go on with a number of ideas associated with small companies.

And then the other area I wanted to raise vis-a-vis commercialization was for the government to try to work with industry to expand markets or even create new ones. One thing to do there is to work on standards—standards to reduce market risks. The area of multi-media is an area that's just ripe for that right now.

And then, secondly, you also heard before, having the government act as a smart first customer, an early adopter. We have in high technology a chicken-egg problem of initially low volume equaling high price, equally low volume. The government can help as a smart customer in breaking out of that. You have a particular opportunity that is arising in your investment in infrastructure because there, if you are demanding a smart customer for physical infrastructure, it can help for example advance materials technology and information infrastructure, telecommunications, and information technology. This is dual-use investment.

The third and last topic I wanted to raise was information infrastructure. Information infrastructure imparts to allow companies to work together—what we call either enterprise integration or agile manufacturing, linking suppliers and customers to address those things—those topics of time to market and price and quality and variety I mentioned earlier.

I brought with me today an American industry-led plan of what we want in the United States, and I have a translation of the Japanese plan of what they want in Japan for agile manufacturing. Both plans say the same thing. The real question is who's going to do it, do it best, and do it first.

In order to get there from here, there are three kinds of things you have to pursue. One is going on quite nicely now, namely the R&D. You have been instrumental, Senator Gore, in getting that going, it's going well, and it should continue.

There are two other things that are important. The second one is that you have inherited just an incredible mess in the legal and regula-

349

tory area. RBOCs, other telephone companies, cable companies, broadcasters—

VICE PRESIDENT-ELECT GORE: RBOCs?

MR. FIELDS: Regional Bell—

VICE PRESIDENT-ELECT GORE: Regional Bell Operating Companies. Excuse me for—

MR. FIELDS: No, please—spectrum allocation, the modified final judgment—it goes on and on, and with no direct dollar cost to the taxpayer. If you can just untie that knot, I think you can free up a lot of private investment, and that's important.

And then the third and last thing that I think needs to go on is to realize that information infrastructure is much more than telecommunications. If we had gigabytes today going from every point in this country to every other point—

VICE PRESIDENT-ELECT GORE: Gigabytes are a billion bits of information per second, the equivalent of transmitting an entire Encyclopedia Britannica per second. Excuse me, go ahead. (Laughter)

MR. FIELDS: Thank you. I actually worked on this issue with your staff —not quite well enough. (Laughter) If we had what you just said, we wouldn't—(laughter)—we would not have information infrastructure. We need standards, databases, libraries, security, user authentication, payment mechanisms—I can go on and on. And we can get a lot of that today with our current telecommunications. We can get some of that 21st infrastructure in the 20th century. And I think that we should do that. And that, again, is something we should get going.

What you have is an opportunity with a Clinton-Gore technology policy to have an impact over the next 50 years that has been as much as we've seen with Vannevar Bush's proposition for science policy that he gave to Harry Truman in 1945. And what I'm happy about is that we now seem to have a team that not only has the skills to get elected to public office, but actually to perform in public office. And so I am very optimistic. Thank you. (Applause)

Vice President-elect Gore: Thank you very much. We have an awful time problem, because we have to end the entire conference at a quarter till, regardless. And we have another panel. And out of courtesy to them, we are going to have to bring them on. At the suggestion of President-elect Clinton, I am going to ask if anybody has a summary comment, and I apologize—we apologize to everybody who has not had a chance to speak. But a summary comment of 30 seconds or so around the table. Those who haven't spoken, it does you an injustice, but—Yes?

John Glendenin (Bell South Corp.): Vice President Gore, President Clinton, this is not a summary comment in the strictest sense, but I think it underscores the point that Craig just made about the need for a national technology policy, and I applaud the fact that you have embarked on that.

Let me read you a November 6, 1990 quote from the *Wall Street Journal* to underscore the absolute necessity for what this technology policy proposes. Quote: "There were signs from the start that the robot industry was doomed in America. Inventor Joseph Engleberger appeared on the Tonight Show with a robot that opened a can of Budweiser and led the band. The audience laughed, and talent agents booked the act. The Japanese government, meanwhile, flew Mr. Engleberger first class to Tokyo to address 700 industrialists and field questions for six hours. Americans saw the robot as a novelty. The Japanese saw it as a solution." The fact is we have not had a technology policy recently. Of all the materials that were sent to us during the campaign, I found your September 21st issuance of this technology policy document to be absolutely the most critical of all. You titled it "Technology, the Engine of Economic Growth." In the information age, technology is the engine of economic growth, and I would just go back to what Paul O'Neill said: I hope that you do not flag in your commitment to this technology policy. It is critical for our future.

Vice President-elect Gore: We mean it. We mean it. Now, that was more than 30 seconds though, and we're in such trouble. Thank you so much. Yes?

Pam Linton (Pollution Solutions of Vermont): I have a few brief comments. I am a small business, and I'm also in the environmental business, and one that is mandated to operate by today's best-known technologies. And I was very pleased with Carol Browner's and Gus

351

Speth's comments, and a few other of the panelists, about government and private sector working together. I completely advocate this partnership, and am trying myself to model myself on a small scale by doing intensive internal audits with the cooperation of government officials. And I hope that I am successful.

Following Mr. Fields' comments, there are a few questions that I think need to be on the table for this administration. One is: What technological and management interventions can you offer? Currently technology-based standards and environmental laws do not jibe. We need some flexibility so that we can make some advancements technologically without violating environmental laws. I think this is doable, but I would ask you to address that in this administration.

Second, what provisions are being made, not just for mandated but voluntary environmental investments and innovations? I would suggest a tax credit. I am a reasonable woman—I can wait until January 22nd. Another place that you might look at this area is for instance if you have innovative environmental compliance and impeccable records that you might influence the insurers to reduce insurance premiums for pollution legal liability.

And then last: What can government do to enhance public and private sector cooperation in the area of training? Government is a very large employer. I think as a small business and a taxpayer that we contribute to the salaries of government workers, and we would like to see you give some of that expertise back to the private sector. Thank you.

VICE PRESIDENT-ELECT GORE: Bill Wiley?

BILL WILEY (BATTELLE-PACIFIC NORTHWEST LAB): Yes, sir. Thank you very much, Vice President-elect. And I am very pleased to be here. I will say one thing: that you have the opportunity to make a paradigm change in the way we fund and develop scientific and technological activities in this country. The seven or eight areas that Vice—President-elect Clinton mentioned the other day can be incorporated into the structure that has given rise to technological innovation since 1950—the Vannevar Bush and the Manhattan Project efforts need only a little tweak, and integration with some kind of an industrial policy which gives rise to cooperation between the investments on the part of the federal government and the investments on the part of industry.

VICE PRESIDENT-ELECT GORE: Thank you. Ed Lewis.

EDWARD LEWIS (ESSENCE COMMUNICATIONS): Thank you, Mr. Vice President, and President-elect Clinton. I just have very short comments to say this. I know the power of television. I represent the print media. And, as a board member of the Magazine Publisher's Association, you have a standing ovation, standing invitation, to come and speak to us with regard to the environmental concerns and economic development. And I urge you, as an American citizen, to continue to include all of us, because that's the way we're going to solve our problems. Thank you.

VICE PRESIDENT-ELECT GORE: Thank you. Ed Romero.

ED ROMERO (ADVANCED SCIENCES, INC.): Thank you, Vice President-elect Gore. I think—(inaudible)—I would encourage you to look at reestablishing the tax credits for energy savings and environmental remediation activities. And, secondly, look at creating a closely-knit dynamic team effort by uniting our laboratories, such as our laboratories in New Mexico, our universities, and the private business sector, in the highly focused joint ventures to meet our environmental challenges.

VICE PRESIDENT-ELECT GORE: Let me say in closing—Well, one more. Yes?

KATHERINE HAMMER (EVOLUTIONARY TECH, INC.): One real quick one. And this—I'm not going to talk about this topic, but bring something up from yesterday. You have the potential to be an outstanding leader. And in that capacity I think you need to help the American worker examine its own soul—his own soul, her own soul. I see a very underdeveloped sense of consequence when people smoke for 20 years and then sue a tobacco company. That is an underdeveloped sense of consequence. When a defense contractor's employee is surprised that they're laid off, that's an underdeveloped sense of consequence. And we are not taking responsibility as workers for helping this become a stronger country. And I think you need to help with health care, you need to help with training. But you also need to turn it back on us. We're failing here.

VICE PRESIDENT-ELECT GORE: Thank you. Maria Torano.

Maria Elena Torano (META): Just a brief comment. First of all, I would like to congratulate both of you for electing—for appointing Carol Browner to your Cabinet. She was an outstanding woman in Florida's government, and just by the comments you made we know that she'll carry the message of our state and our country in her new position.

One second comment is that we're thankful because you have had four Cuban Americans as panelists today. And that we just cannot wait to get back home and mention to our community that this administration is opened to people like us.

One last comment is that we need—(inaudible)—environmental companies which I represent need to start penetrating the international market. And we need the support of organizations such as the World Bank, the IDB, OPIC, the Ex-Im Bank to help us. We can't succeed alone. The competition is a little too strong. So anything you can do to facilitate our path in the international arena, we will appreciate it.

Vice President-elect Gore: Alfonso Fanjul, last comment.

Alfonso Fanjul (Flo-Sun): Thank you. I came from Cuba as a political exile 30 years ago. Castro took everything I had. The United States has given me everything I have. My business is agriculture. My comments were going to be primarily on the environment, and I think Secretary Browner covered them well. We need cooperation, we're spending too much time and effort just on not getting anything done.

The second area I wanted to talk about is that we oppose NAFTA as currently negotiated. We think that has to be renegotiated. It is unfair to the American farmer, it is unfair to the American laborer, and it is unfair to the American consumer. And we believe that in the context of trade negotiations we need to bring in the issue of environmental sensitivity. Thank you very much.

Vice President-elect Gore: Let me say in closing, this panel—the discussion has just started. We've identified some exciting opportunities. We are raring to go, to exploit these opportunities on behalf of our country. And to those who didn't get a chance to speak, our apologies, but we have got to move on to the next panel. I'm going to turn it back over to President-elect Clinton, with thanks to all of you who have spoken. (Applause)

354

PRESIDENT-ELECT CLINTON: Thank you all very much. While the panelists are changing seats, let me say that we are going to have to leave here at about a quarter till four, maybe a couple of minutes later, because we have to walk over to the Old State House next door to be at a press conference which will be at 4:00 our time, but is about as late as we can start and have any hope of getting on the evening news apparently—I would think they have enough for the evening news. I'd rather stay here till 6:00. But, anyway, that's what our handlers say we should do. Please take your seats as quickly as possible so we can begin.
(Break)

PRESIDENT-ELECT CLINTON: All right. If we go a little over it's not going to be the end of the world. This is an important panel. We're going to be on the evening news whether we have a press conference or not. (Applause) On the other hand, we may not be on the evening news, which may even be better. (Laughter)

Let me say by way of introduction to this panel that I want to try to focus this last discussion a little bit and then, without in any way undermining the freedom of speech of the people around the table, I do want to at least begin by asking everyone to focus on the topic, which is the connection between economic growth and changing the way government does its business. There has been a lot of discussion lately around the whole jargon of—at least it's been—David Osborne wrote a book called *Reinventing Government,* and another book called *Laboratories of Democracy.* And he is part of a group of people, including Doug Ross who is here, who have been interested in the whole notion of whether you could not only make taxpayers happy, but actually improve the performance of government and the productivity of an economy by changing the whole way a government does its business. Now some of this is as simple as the old-fashioned slogans of reducing paperwork and eliminating waste, fraud and abuse, and privatizing certain things or not, or stopping certain subsidies or not. But some of it involves changing the way government does its business. You heard a little talk in the last—in Senator Gore's panel about changing the nature of environmental regulations from a command-and-control regulatory model to one in which we set goals, get market incentives, and then evaluate results, rather than just trying to micromanage the process.

There is also in government today, in various parts and places across the country, a serious attempt to literally restructure the way government bureaucracies themselves operate through this sort of total quality management approach which our state government here has begun

355

to implement, and which Donna Shalala had great success with at the University of Wisconsin.

So there are a lot of different concepts in the air here. But I did want to just sort of set the stage by saying that I think that one of the things that—it's obvious, if you listened to everybody who talked today, whether they were Republicans or Democrats, or somewhere in between, and everybody who talked yesterday, there is a virtual unanimous consensus that even when we disagree about what we should do, everybody acknowledges there will be a very active and aggressive national government in our future, and that if we are going to have the kind of economy we want there will be some sort of partnership, for good or ill, between the public and private sector.

So today we have three panelists, whom I'll ask to be fairly brief. Two of them, David Osborne and Doug Ross, whom I will introduce, will talk a little about the whole notion of reinventing government, what that means in its various manifestations. And the other, Ernesto Cortes, will talk a little bit, I hope, about what it would mean to empower citizens and how important it is to have citizens themselves be empowered. If you're going to have government function properly, the government has to be able to hear from the poor as well as the rich, and those in between. And the way government relates to people —does it—does government promote independence, or does it promote dependence? This is a big issue for Native Americans. We have two of the heads of our major tribes here in America—they may want to say something if they're still here.

David Osborne is the co-author of *Reinventing Government,* and the author of a book called *Laboratories of Democracy,* which featured, among other things, some things we tried to do in our state, which I appreciated. He lectures widely to business, government, and academic audiences. He's a fellow at the Progressive Policy Institute, and a consultant to state and local government, and a columnist for *Governing* magazine. In *Reinventing Government,* he argues we must change the nature of government to keep up with rapid social and economic change. That book hit the New York *Times* Best Seller List within two months of its release, even though it apparently dealt with a fairly arcane topic, I think showing how desperate people are to believe that growth can change and work for them.

Doug Ross is the president of Michigan Future Incorporated, a citizen organization which seeks to apply rebuilding—to work on rebuilding Michigan's economy, and a visiting lecturer for the Institute of Public Policy Studies at the University of Michigan. He was in former Governor Blanchard's Cabinet. He has been a friend of mine and an associate over the past decade, in which he has always been a leader nationally among state government circles in the effort to reinvent government. In 1988, he won our National Governors Association's Award for Public Service Excellence.

Ernesto Cortes is the regional director of the Industrial Areas Foundation for Southwestern United States. He created community organizations such as UNO in Los Angeles, COPS in San Antonio, EPSISO in El Paso, and TMO in Houston. If any of you have had any contact with any of those organizations, you know what a remarkable achievement Mr. Cortes has to his credit.

I think Doug and David are going to do their presentation together, and I'll recognize them at this time.

Doug Ross (Michigan Futures, Inc.): David and I together think that in order for you and the federal government to succeed with the kind of agenda that has been talked about over the last couple of days, that both governance and leadership will have to change in fundamental ways. As you know well, the governors over the past decade tried to deal with many of these same problems of how it is you become a partner to companies in your own state and to workers in your own state that are trying to increase their productivity. And while they had a relatively easy time coming to a consensus about what they ought to do—which is to try to provide the skilled workers the technology and the patient capital their companies needed to be competitive, I think what really surprised them during the 80s was that when they turned to the bureaucratic programs and agencies that they had always used to get things done they didn't work any more. The industrial age organizations in an information age economy had become obsolete.

And it became evident in a series of ways rather quickly. The first and most obvious was they were way too slow. We were talking increasingly about companies that had to change very quickly, needed rapid decisions in order to be competitive, and these were centrally-run, hierarchical, rule-driven monopolies that simply could not respond quickly.

Secondly, the scale was never adequate. Because they used only the public dollars put into them with appropriations, if they trained 10,000 workers, it was always in a state that needed to train 200,000. If they counseled 300 firms on how to improve their technology use, there were 5,000 firms that needed it. If they put $20 million in capital out there, it was usually in the context of a $40 billion economy, and it just didn't make any difference. And the quality was always inferior. They were not customer driven. They were not set up to be that way. They didn't know what their customers wanted, and even if they could find out they generally had very little incentive to do anything about it.

So what the governors found pretty quickly was that traditional public programs designed to deliver services to businesses and workers were dinosaurs. So the governors, who were—including the one from Arkansas—a pretty creative bunch, went out to look for a third way. Laissez-faire wasn't an alternative, because their states were in big trouble. Bureaucracy simply didn't work any more.

So they came up with a different solution, and it was essentially to use government to build markets rather than to deliver public services. And to explain the principles and give you an example, let me turn it at this point to David Osborne.

DAVID OSBORNE (PROGRESSIVE POLICY INSTITUTE): Thank you, Doug. And I also want to thank you, Mr. President-elect, for the privilege of being here today.

As Doug said, if you look at the innovations in state government— and I would add in local government—in the last decade, you can begin to see some patterns, some fundamental principles around which this new kind of governance, this kind of seat-of-the-pants in- novation has taken place. And they are principles that are fairly similar to those of you familiar with the restructuring that has gone on in the business world in the last decade. I just want to run through a few of them very briefly.

Our old industrial age bureaucracies focused almost exclusively on delivering services. They were set up to row the boat. Our new more entrepreneurial public organizations act more as catalysts: they spend more energy steering than rowing, because the traditional service de- livery mode, using civil servants to deliver some public services, is extremely expensive, and every government in America today is under tremendous fiscal pressure. So entrepreneurial organizations have be- gun to act as catalysts and partners and facilitators, creating public- private partnerships, using their leverage to change what happens in the business community, what happens among community organiza- tions, what happens out of the neighborhoods.

Secondly, our old industrial age bureaucracies were, in most cases, monopolies, whether they were schools or welfare departments or public works departments, they were monopolies. And today our more entrepreneurial public organizations are learning how to inject compe- tition into public service delivery to drive excellence.

Third, our old industrial era bureaucracies focused accountability on inputs: Did you follow the rules? Did you spend according to the line items? Our new more entrepreneurial public organizations are focus- ing the accountability on outcomes, on results: Did you achieve the results that were intended? And, if so, we'll award you. Craig Fields touched on this in the last session.

Fourth, our old bureaucratic organizations organized themselves according to the convenience of the bureaucracy, the convenience of the providers. Entrepreneurial organizations try to organize themselves according to the convenience of the customer. They speak to the customer driven. They try to give customers choices, for example, of different service providers, and force the providers to compete to please the customers.

I just want to give you an example of what I am talking about, which I think every American can relate to. Probably the single most successful social program in the history of the United States was the GI bill—it's everybody's favorite program. We brought a generation of men home from World War II. We educated them. We turned them into the backbone of a 30-year economic boom. And we did not do it by building veterans universities. We basically gave people a voucher. We said, "Choose your college. Choose your university. Choose your technical school. We'll pay for it." In health care, we did go the traditional route: We built veterans hospitals, and we assigned veterans to hospitals. The hospitals were monopolies, they had captive customers. And if you know anything about the difference in quality and impact, between the veterans hospital system and the GI bill, you can begin to appreciate the power of putting the customer in the driver's seat.

Finally, our old more bureaucratic governments tended to use administrative programs to do everything. You know, people in government have what I call "programitis." If there's a problem there must be a program to solve it. It's a little bit like ham and eggs—government and programs, they just go together. But we all understand that programs are not always the best way to solve a problem. Sometimes it's more effective to restructure what happens in the private marketplace to address the problem. In the last session you discussed market-based environmental policy, creating different market incentives for companies and individuals to solve environmental problems—perfect example.

Now I wanted to briefly bring this home to the subject of this conference, which is how we build a high-performing economy. Let me give you an example. One of our greatest challenges is that of increasing the skill level of our work force. It is really probably the single fundamental key to economic growth in our future. The problem is we don't have a system to do that. What we have are dozens of tiny adult education and job training programs. My state, Massachusetts, has 42 at last count; Michigan had 70 at last count; New York State had 85. They are very difficult to access. You don't know where to go if you want to use one of them. There is no user-friendly front door. It's very hard to get information on which ones work and which ones don't work, on which ones are in demand in the marketplace and which ones are not in demand. And it is aimed primarily at one small slice—primarily one small slice of the work force, which is the poor. We do not have a job training system for the majority of our work force in this country. Our competitors do. The Germans do. The Japanese do. And it's a tremendous problem. This is as big a challenge as education reform.

Now, the conventional response in the 1980s was, Okay, we've got a mess on our hands, let's create another program. Let's create the 71st job training program. The problem is that doesn't do anything about the first 70. Secondly, we'll never have enough money to create big enough programs to deal with this problem. Somehow we have to figure out how to change the American marketplace so that we create incentives for firms to provide training, and individuals to buy training.

Now, there are a number of things that need to happen to create that marketplace. We need information. Customers, businesses and individuals, need good information about where to buy training, what training is of most value, which providers do the best job, which are placing people in the best jobs. Secondly, we need more demand in the system. And your proposal to require companies to spend 1.5 percent of payroll on training, or if they do that pay some form of tax, will increase that demand by pushing businesses to spend more to buy more training. We also have to increase demand by empowering low- and moderate-income people to buy more training.

And finally, in a marketplace that works you need brokers. You need some place—when we go to buy a house we don't just look at houses, we go to a real estate broker. When we go to buy stocks we go to a stockbroker. Markets need a place where buyers can find sellers and get good information about the quality of what they are selling.

Now the State of Michigan in the 1980s figured all this out and came up with an approach, which I don't have time to outline completely, but the heart of it was a voucher in the form of a smart credit card which every person in the work force would carry—called an opportunity card. That person could walk into something called an opportunity store, sit down with a counselor, learn about what was available, which providers did the best job, which—how much they cost. And if that person had a low income, money would come with that opportunity card, and that person could use that as a voucher to go buy training. That was an effort to create a market-driven, customer-driven performance-based job training system. Unfortunately, the governor who sponsored it, Governor Blanchard, right in the middle of this complex process of building such a system, lost an election, and his successor eliminated the initiative, which means if you want to do it in

Washington we're going to have to invent it anew rather than follow a proven model that's already developed at the state level.

With that, let me just turn it back over to Doug.

MR. ROSS: To conclude, if we could, we would like to close with a point that Paul O'Neill made, we thought very effectively, and that is that this kind of governance requires a different kind of leadership. We think that for this to work, for such a diverse decentralized fast-changing nation, to have its energies freed to move in a common direction, we need you to operate first as the leader of the American people before even you are CEO of the government. Unless we have a vision —and by vision we don't mean a vision statement about we need to be a prosperous country with good-paying jobs. We think we actually need pictures. You need to show us what these new high-wage, high-skill middle-class jobs look like. Otherwise we think you're talking about doing the same work with maybe a little more technology or working a little harder. We need to see what these classrooms look like, which are structured like the new work where kids do the work of instructing their knowledges and teachers coach them. We need to see new pictures of parents and community responsibility. So we need from you to make this work the painting of a very pictorial, concrete vision with values that help us figure out ourselves which are the right ways to pursue it, and finally, á la Max Dupre, we need you to measure the right things. We need the measures such that we can tell if we are making progress from where we are to this vision that you will and already have begun to paint for us. Thank you very much.

PRESIDENT-ELECT CLINTON: Thank you. Yeah, you can clap for that. (Applause) Max Dupre had to leave, I think, and go home. But let me say I regret that very much. He has written two books. One is called *Leadership Is an Art*, and the other is called *Leadership Jazz*, and I highly commend them to all of you. They are briefer than some of us have been here—(laughter)—but they are very well done, and very much worth the cost of the books. Astonishing.

Before I go on to Ernesto, I want to just drive home the dimensions of the problems that they are discussing here. If you were to unpack— let's just take the job training issue—if you were to unpack the pattern of publicly-funded job training programs in America, you look at what —the programs that state money goes into, the programs that federal money goes into, and you start it at the source, namely the federal taxpayer paying into the federal tax till and then paying into the state tax till, and then the money comes down through this incredible proliferation of programs—rule makers in Washington, rule makers at the state level, people checking on the rule makers at the state level to make sure they didn't mess up. And then you're supposed to figure out where your little box is. There's an incredible rake-off of money—not in any criminal way. I mean you just lose a lot of the money. And it is, in my judgment, there are many, many programs like this. I could go through the way the Medicaid program is run and administered, and a lot of other programs. This whole business—this is a very serious business—how much money we lose from the time the taxpayers part with it until it gets back to the beneficiary, because of the incredible overlap between federal, state and local jurisdiction, and because of the manner of regulation, and because the way these programs are divided up—balkanized. It's very, very important. It's something we ought to give some thought to.

I'm going to let you talk now for a minute, and then when we go back I'd like to—and for Ernesto to talk—I'd like for Donna Shalala to talk just a couple of minutes about her experience at the University of Wisconsin on these issues. Go ahead.

ERNESTO CORTES (INDUSTRIAL AREAS FOUNDATION): Thank you, Governor Clinton, Senator Gore. As obvious from what you've heard today, that the quality of life in our cities and our rural areas have seriously deteriorated the last 20 years. Mr. Reich's book, *The Work of Nations*, Professor Wilson's book, *The Truly Disadvantaged*, as well as many other scholarly works, have documented the successful distance of the wealthy and fortunate from the fate of those who are less fortunate in the war zones in the centers of despair that have become urban and rural America.

At the same time, far too many of our adult population feel that politics and public life are largely irrelevant to them. And, as a result, our public discourse has become impoverished and the sense of disillusionment seriously inhibits our ability to collaboratively work together.

Now, the forces affecting our cities originating from changes in national and world economies that we have heard the past few days, and dealing with these forces, will require some of the major shifts in economic policy that you propose. I hope that as we talk about investment we recognize the importance of investment in our cities and impoverished rural communities. The Industrial Areas Foundation believes that the revitalization of our cities depends upon two things: first, resources and technical competence and the kind of reorganization of government that Mr. Osborne has so eloquently spoken and written about. We think secondly, and equally important, is the capacity of our citizens to do politics. Not just electioneering, not just participate in our

362

what I—pardon me—call our quadrennial electronic plebiscite, which has unfortunately more to do with marketing and direct mailing and ads than real politics. But I mean the ability and opportunity of our citizens to engage in public discourse, debate, argue, negotiate, and compromise, which will culminate in initiator and collaborative action. Not just taking part, but working together to improve local schools, to bring about health care to a community, to give students access to job training or higher education. We need citizens and neighbors, and not just customers and clients.

Now, this kind of entrepreneurial political activity, upon which the revitalization of our cities and communities depends, is as important I think as business entrepreneurship. It is a social capital of our communities. The government can facilitate, encourage, recognize and reward it; but it cannot create it. Government cannot create local initiatives, but it can recognize the way in which local collaborative initiatives develop confidence and competence in ordinary people who are thereby able to do extraordinary things. But it must understand the importance of these initiatives, that they should have an institutional base which is rooted in people's imagination, curiosity, values, and our search for meaning.

As a result, we think we need a strategy for rebuilding our communities which aids and abets local initiatives. Our hope is that such a strategy would structure a federal match and leverage the commitments of local municipalities and communities. Working upon the concept of a hopefully augmented Community Development Block Grant, which have been very successful in communities like San Antonio, the federal government could increase that amount based upon serious and indigenous local participation and planning.

It is important that these efforts be part of an overall strategy of state and local initiatives, corporate and private sector investments, to make resources available to match the local capital of local community institutions. The federal contribution would encourage and reward substantive commitments from the corporate community, just as evident for example with the Commonwealth effort in Baltimore, which you have spoken eloquently about, Governor, or the jobs training program initiative with Governor Ann Richards and former Mayor Henry Cisneros help the COPS organization structure in San Antonio, which is based upon a concept of individual training accounts and choice in the job training effort.

Such federal effort would need to be coordinated with authenticately locally-based institutions which would be involved in planning and holding such efforts accountable. Those institutions must be non-governmental, financially self-sufficient, have a demonstrated track record and constituency, so that they can be part of the partnership that is so needed if we are going to hold our public efforts accountable. If local communities would have a serious commitment of local resources to deal with basic infrastructure needs, the kind we have talked about, and these efforts would be targeted to inner-city and poor areas, and involve hopefully those residents in the reconstruction of the cities, then cities would get augmented grants.

The strategy should also involve an effort for first-time home-buyers, such as the Nehemiah Homes Project, which has already constructed over 3,000 housing units for single-family homeowners, and which you have talked eloquently about in the past.

There are thousands of efforts which I could talk about, but we don't have time, and I want to try to honor as best I can the commitment that you've asked us all to make. I'm reminded that Gary Wells said that a fellow named Edward Everett talked for two hours at the—celebrating the Battle of Gettysburg, and not one person remembers what he said, but Lincoln talked for three minutes, and all of us—most of us—remember every word he said.

So I would like to end by saying to you that I'd like to talk about these efforts. But, more importantly, I hope that you will recognize the role that you can play, the bully pulpit that you have, the ability that you are able to put people back to work in rebuilding our communities. Senator Bentsen, Governor Richards, former Lieutenant Governor Hobby, and a number of state officials demonstrated this effort in South Texas when they helped us get local federal—national federal dollars to match $250 million that the State of Texas put for water and sewer projects along the border. That would frankly never have occurred if people in the—(inaudible)—had not organized themselves to put together to the social capital and the moral vision to try and force and get the national and the state government to make a commitment to that kind of effort. Thank you very much. (Applause)

President-elect Clinton: Thank you. Let me say that, before we get into the roundtable conversation, you've heard two different points of view that in my view both have to be represented in our efforts to create the government we need for the 21st century. I—the most impressive things I've seen traveling around this country in the last seven or eight years fall into two categories, I would say. First the effort to restructure public organizations in ways that make them work along the lines that David and Doug discussed—whether schools or other public organizations.

And, second, the effort to empower people at the grass-roots levels to have community organizations. And when you see the two forces merge it's really stunning. And we didn't get a chance to talk about it today, but Vince Lane was here, the head of the Chicago Housing Authority. He used to be the director—he's now the head of the board. When he was the director—this is a guy that had never been elected to anything, right? He was an appointed public servant. We went to some of these housing projects in Chicago where they swept the housing projects of drug dealers and weapons and cleaned them up and made them safe and sanitary. And the little kids poured out of the housing project, and grabbed onto him and hardly let him walk. It was like he was the Pied Piper, because he had given them power over their lives, not because he had sent them a check or given them anything; he had given them power over their lives.

And Mary Holton was here from the South Shore Development Bank. That bank made money all during the 80s. They didn't go broke. And all they did was loan money to poor people and small-business people in their own neighborhood. But they knew how to do it. So I think that these two points of view we have heard here are very important to whether we can succeed in—and I would just go back to the comment—the last person who talked over here in the panel of the next to last, saying that I had to put some of this back on the American people—I had to hold the American people responsible for the consequences of their actions or inactions and tell the rest of the people in this country what they had to do to get this country going again, and I think that you heard two points of view that are quite important in that regard.

Donna, would you talk a couple of minutes about the University of Wisconsin?

DONNA SHALALA (SECRETARY-DESIGNATE, HHS): Just a couple of minutes. I believe that it's a myth that complex bureaucracies that are heavily regulated can't improve the services that they're responsible for. And working in a heavily regulatory environment of a large public institution, we have been able to take the principles of total quality management, working on everything from long lines in the bursar's office, which everybody remembers from their college years—cutting them down from an hour and a half to 15 minutes, by setting up teams that thought through the systems and the processes—teams of part-time workers and full-time workers, managers participating as peers, empowering the people responsible for those areas, to see if they could think through what was going on so they could cut down the time the students had to stand in line.

The impressive thing about total quality management, whether we have empowered people, cutting graduate school admissions time from 45 days to three, or our bursar's lines, is that it's not a fix-it strategy. It's changing the culture of an organization so everyone is empowered into a continuous improvement mode. And so that you're always raising the bar, you're always making certain that the service you're trying to improve is in a mode where you are never finished with it. And it's exciting for the people that are working in the bureaucracy. But, more importantly, there are measurable results in terms of saving money as well as improving the quality of the services.

I would suggest that while we are fundamentally restructuring, and thinking about the appropriate role of government, and the levels of government, there are things that we can do that will empower the people who now work in government, and simultaneously improve services as well as save money. A lot of this has to do with being clear about the mission, clear about the customers of the particular services, and sensitive to them. We've even used total quality management in the classroom, where students put together their own quality teams and give the professor feedback after every class. And we have fancy faculty members who have learned everything from improving the quality and strength of the chalk that they use on the blackboards to making their lectures and the materials they present more clear. And then the students have passed down those recommendations to the next group of students coming into the classroom.

So there are things that we can do without huge investments of resources, but rather by investing our faith in people, that I think will make a difference in big, complex bureaucracies. And since you've given me the biggest one, I intend to improve on what we can do at HHS.

PRESIDENT-ELECT CLINTON: We will find out. If anybody can do it, you can.

Let me just give you an example of the kind of problems she has to face. The Health Care Financing Authority, which is the instrument of the government's micromanagement of the public side of health care costs in America, which is supposed to be in charge of helping us make America a healthier country at a lower cost, has told all the states that are going broke over Medicaid costs that they cannot change their nursing home rules to say that prospectively people who are now minimum-care nursing home patients, if they want to get Medicaid, will have to be cared for in the home with home health care or in boarding homes, both of which are cheaper, unless we do it retroactively, and go back and kick everybody out of the nursing homes that fall in the same category. Now, that's the sort of thing we're dealing with out here. So you've got state governments spending millions of dollars of your tax money today, because nobody wants to go kick a bunch of people out of nursing homes, for whom we may not have positions. But that is the sort of thing that goes on that for all I know the Secretary of HHS doesn't even know about. Because somebody way down there decided that's what made sense.

Ms. Shalala: The new one does.

President-elect Clinton: Paul—What did you say?

Ms. Shalala: I said the new one does.

President-elect Clinton: The new one does. (Laughter.) That's the third time she's heard this—she's getting sick of it.
Paul?

Paul Miller (Loyola Law School): Thank you. I'm happy to speak to this issue of government empowering people and people empowering government. Over 26 percent of working-age Americans with a disability live below the poverty level in this country, and people with disabilities have the highest rate of unemployment of any group. There is this tremendous under-utilization of a great human resource in this country, namely persons with mental and physical disabilities.

We heard yesterday about how investment today saves money in the future. It thus pays to invest in people with disabilities. It's simply, as you just said, more expensive to keep people dependent than to keep them independent and working. And this, I believe, includes investing in education, job training, architectural and communications access and accessible housing. In order for disabled persons to live independent lives with dignity, to go from lives of dependence to independence, they must have government support. Disabled persons want to participate in the economy, not just be subject to its charity.

And let me give you three quick examples of how I see this working. First, you talk about investments in infrastructure. By investments in infrastructure, I think we should look to not only sewers and bridges, but to create curb cuts, to create accessible town halls and accessible courthouses. That will be a tremendous benefit to local governments to create access to people with disabilities.

Second, the enforcement of the Americans With Disabilities Act regulations to remove discrimination in the workplace, government and public accommodations to free up this untapped workforce and consumer base that is now excluded from society.

John Sculley spoke yesterday of the need to reorganize how work gets done in America. In other words I think what he was talking about was the support of reasonable accommodation mandated by the Americans With Disabilities Act.

Lastly, the development of personal assistance services necessary for many persons with severe disabilities to live independently outside of nursing homes, working and paying taxes.

Lastly let me just mention, government reform means removing disincentives to work. For example, in the SSDI and SSI programs, developed based upon presumptions that disabled people can't work. It creates disincentives that disabled people can't enter the work force for fear of losing their health care benefits.

These disincentives must be removed.

In conclusion let us make our work force, our consumer base and your administration reflect the diversity and talents of all persons. This country has been trying to eliminate the glass ceiling. Let us begin to address and eliminate the glass curb. (Applause.)

PRESIDENT-ELECT CLINTON: Good for you.

I'd like to call on one more person who's here to speak perhaps for the community of the disabled Americans, Beverly Chapman from Orlando, who's been very active for years, who's sat patiently through this whole session, hasn't missed a single moment of it and she's behind me.

I think there's someone back there with a microphone.

BEVERLY CHAPMAN, ORLANDO, FLORIDA: Hello. I'm—I've lived with the disability of muscular dystrophy for 38 years. That results in the fact that I can't walk, I can't lift my arms and I also can't breathe without the help of a machine.

We talked about technology today. Thanks to technology I drove my van 1,000 miles from Orlando, Florida to Little Rock, Arkansas to help. I'm here to help in the rebuilding of America.

Paul Miller talked about tapping untapped resources. People who might hear of what my physical limitations are would think maybe that person can't do anything.

Well, by God, I can do a lot and there are millions of other disabled people just like me who can also contribute to this world. People like Franklin Delano Roosevelt set the pace.

We all want a part of the American dream. We all want to help share the responsibility. Yes we have rights but yes we also have responsibilities to be the best human beings we can be, to develop ourselves fully and, with the help of government and—I believe very strongly—in partnership with industry, some of the best minds in our country, we need to put people back to work. And almost everything we've talked about in terms of disadvantaged individuals; people of color, people of size, people of ethnic backgrounds.

The disabled minority is the one minority that any one of you can become part of at any moment due to an accident or illness. Disabled people are your people. They are us and we, together, can help make a better world for not only them but they'll turn around and make a better world for us too.

Thank you. (Applause.)

PRESIDENT-ELECT CLINTON: All right. That's good.

Let me just make one point that I hope will tie the message that Paul and Beverly and Ernesto have made to the arguments that Doug and David have made. Most of you know, if you've just been hanging around here and watching the newspapers, that my state is in the—now having a special session of the legislature to deal with a terrible crisis in Medicaid funding. This is happening all over the country.

We don't have enough money to pay for all the things that are happening because more and more people have lost their medical insurance and they're using Medicaid bills.

Well, the federal government has told the states, who administer the Medicaid program under federal rules—so the states and the federal government pay for it together—that, here's a long list of things you have to do and here's some things you can do if you want.

When we had to make Medicaid cuts I would like to have brought in the Paul Millers and Beverly Chapmans of my state along with all the other affected people and said, "Okay, here's how much money we've got. Now what—it's," your—you know, not just the upside, doing something good. How are we going to manage this pain? How are we going to make these decisions?

And I can tell you that at least for the disabled community what they would have said is, "Let's keep the in-home services, let's promote as much independence as possible." "We can serve more people at lower costs even if we have to cut back a little bit on some of the things we're doing institutionally."

But because the federal government has decided that people like you don't have enough sense to make decisions like that they say, "You've got to provide these institutional services at this level, with this amount of money even if you can't serve a single living soul in their home."

So, we wind up spending more money on few people and frustrating the very constituencies we're trying to help because we don't have a community-based, grass roots oriented flexible, efficient delivery system.

Another problem Donna has to deal with but I mean I just want to give you—that's a very specific example. There are people like—going through this decision in more than half the states in the United States as we sit here today. That is a concrete manifestation of the issue we are here to discuss today.

Derrick, would you like to say something?

DERRICK CEPHAS (NEW YORK STATE BANKING DEPARTMENT): Thank you very much.

I think I may, in fact, be the only bank regulator here today and I heard a good deal of discussion earlier today about the credit crunch and I'd like just to make a couple of points about that and some other points, quickly, about bank regulation.

It is true that there is a credit crunch and it is true that the recent bill passed last December by the Congress is partly responsible for that. But I don't want anyone to think that repeal of FDICIA or amendment of FDICIA, the bill of 1991, will all of a sudden cause a great rush of new credit. I think there are a great number of issues.

The bank regulatory system is in need of substantial repair generally and one's a short term issues (sic) and others are long term issues.

Short term, the S&L crisis, I think, and the BCCI scandal both caused Congress to overreact in certain ways last year in the regulation of banks. We heard John Reed and others talk about some of the difficult issues.

Short term issues I think that ought to be addressed: One, we ought to do something to alleviate the credit crunch. We ought to provide incentives for banks to lend. We ought to remove some of the legislative and statutory and regulatory disincentives to bank lending.

We ought to repeal some of the onerous provisions of FDICIA of last year, we ought to reduce regulatory burden and here I'm talking about two things; both the cost and the inefficiencies of regulatory burden as well as a great lack of flexibility and the rigidity.

Interstate branching; if that were passed that would be a way for banks to provide credit across state lines, collect deposits across state lines, again providing more services and more credit to a larger number of people at a cheaper cost to the banking system.

In the foreign bank area foreign banks provide a tremendous

amount of credit and lending in the United States and I think we need to encourage foreign banks to come. We need to encourage foreign banks to stay here and reduce some of the excessive regulation on foreign banks.

One of the main things here is I think there is a proposal that's being considered now at the Federal Reserve and the US Treasury to require all foreign banks to operate in the United States in the form of a subsidiary as opposed to a branch and I think that is a very detrimental proposal and if passed, I think, would have a negative effect on all Americans.

Finally, the last thing we ought to look at is a substantial revision of the Community Reinvestment Act. Here, I think, in terms of both enforcement and participation we ought to make community reinvestment an ongoing obligation of banks and an ongoing obligation of community groups to be very much involved in it and get away from having CRA solely an issue to be addressed in the context of an application.

Those are the short term issues.

Long term issues, quickly, have to do with basic restructuring of the financial system. The Treasury proposal of 1991 contained a lot of risk diversification points that I think ought to be considered again. But unless we attack both the short term and the long term issues in bank regulation we will continually have, from time to time, these periodic problems of a lack of lending. So the credit crunch which we have now, I think, we might very well see again or some other difficulties in the banking system unless we attack these things systematically.

PRESIDENT-ELECT CLINTON: Is Charles Stitt still here? Are you here in the room?

Jim, you want to say anything?

JAMES JONES (AMERICAN STOCK EXCHANGE): Well, first of all, President-elect Clinton, Vice President-elect Gore, it's a great pleasure to participate in this national classroom and you're both master teachers. We appreciate it.

I would like to underscore very much the points that have been made about a customer concept and total quality program for the federal government.

The American Stock Exchange is an institution that has certain characteristics of a government agency. We have done that. It has not only been fulfilling and rewarding for the employees but clearly for our customers. And in a global competition we think that's the key to it.

371

The one caution on this as well as things we've discussed in fiscal policy is not to promise or expect too many returns too soon. And I think one of your great challenges of your leadership will be—and the monument of your presidency will be that the pay-off of your program will probably occur after your two terms in office because that's what we were facing for the last two decades—an expectation of instant gratification. And now we have to fundamentally rebuild this society.

In terms of some of the Government reform and how that can accomplish it I would also like to underscore what's been said about job training. Going back to my days—White House days in the 1960's, some very well intentioned job training programs were put into effect, many duplicating each other. And probably there have been more failures, from the standpoint of the customers, in those programs than anything else.

You talked yesterday about employment security, a new definition of it.

One suggestion I would like to make is that the concept of the national service corps, which is intended for young people now, might be expanded and tied in to the whole unemployment compensation system as a way to tell folks who have had fulfilling work and for reasons, various reasons, are no longer able to work that they can continue to be fulfilled by having a voucher, by having unemployment benefits, by having job training and by committing themselves to improving their local communities in an area of community service.

Also, in this whole quality program are the employees of the federal government—the civil service. It's been fashionable until recently to sort of kick around the civil servants and they offer a great potential of service to this country, using the quality programs to help them.

They can, I would even suggest, exchange programs in a way that they can learn about the industries, the businesses, the sector of society more closely that they're supposed to either administer or manage the programs.

Also, it seems you might want to work with the congressional leaders to basically reform some of the Budget Act to go for things like biennial budgeting so that at least one year out of two the Congress will devote most of its attention to seeing how these programs work and how they can work better for our mutual customers, namely the citizens of the United States.

Also, enhanced rescission or some sort of line-item veto would, I think, strengthen your hand and strengthen the administration of government.

Other departments that need to be reformed—Department of Commerce. That has tremendous potential for developing the economic potential, particularly of emerging growth and mid-size businesses and

372

for managing, or better, enhancing the trade potential we have. We've —it's been tried before. It was tried in the 1960's, it was abandoned. I think that conditions are substantially different now and that ought to occupy a top priority of the administration.

You have great opportunities. I think what we're seeing in this conference today is a seed change in the way national leadership communicates and involves and includes the country at large and I commend you for it.

PRESIDENT-ELECT CLINTON: Thank you very much.

Daphne Sloan and then Daniel Tully.

DAPHNE SLOAN (WALNUT HILLS REDEVELOPMENT FOUNDATION, INC.): Thank you.

Mr. President-elect and Mr. Vice President-elect, I thank you for the opportunity to probably introduce to some and reintroduce to others the whole notion of community-based development corporations of which one I head in Cincinnati, Ohio.

And I'd like to further state that it is pleasing to me to be on this panel in particular, especially with Secretary Shalala because that's where one of the two departments where community-based development corporations utilize funding. And I'd like to cite a couple of examples of same and then I'd like to talk with you further about what I think is not so much a reforming but probably a streamlining of those two departments; one of course, is the Department of Health and Human Services and the other one, of course, is the Department of HUD.

Community Development Corporation of Kansas City—this premier agency created, if you will, in excess of 250 jobs through a $500,000 seed grant that came from the Department of Health and Human Services through its discretionary funds.

Let me share with you a little bit about that particular project as well as one other.

The CDC of Kansas City has a shopping center entitled Lenwood. It transformed a blighted abandoned hospital site into a modern, 80,000 square foot retail complex. A total of $5.5 million was raised from the following sources: the Department of Health and Human Services Office of Community Services Discretionary Grant Program, Prudential Life Insurance Company, the Baptist Ministers' Union, the City of Kansas City, the Whole Family Foundation and the Syndicated Limited Partnership. The center opened in 1986 and is 100 percent occupied.

The shopping center provides 331 permanent jobs and created 250 temporary jobs during construction. Don Maxwell heads that organization in Kansas City.

New Community Corporation—this is a Newark-based community development corporation—built the first new shopping center with a supermarket in the city in over 20 years. The Pathmark Shopping Center was opened in 1990. Financial assistance for this project was received from: the New Jersey State Enterprise Zone, the Depart of Economic Development with a $1.38 million loan at four percent interest, the City of Newark provided a tax abatement and assistance with demolition, Prudential Insurance added a below market-rate mortgage, First Federal Fidelity Bank contributed the construction loan, an Urban Redevelopment Action Grant of $1.5 million came in with the state condemning the land.

These are two examples, if you will, of, in my opinion, already a partnership that has been proven and does work.

Moving these examples a little bit close to home in Cincinnati—I certainly will not sit here and boast of my colleagues without boasting of myself—the last HHS grant that we received was a $300,000 OCS grant where we were successfully able—and I share this one because it's replicible—we were successfully able to renovate a 120-plus year old abandoned school building. It now is 42,000 square feet of commercial office space, of which our executive offices are there. It brought in 80 new jobs, it brought in another 50 temporary jobs. Seed money coming from the Department of Health and Human Services created a leveraging of some $3.2 million on a $300,000 grant.

I think these are examples of how community-based organizations, as a small business entrepreneur is using, if you will, those departments to create opportunities in our neighborhoods.

What's unique about our small business is that our small businesses are run by people who live in that community. Usually the leadership is small businesses within that community.

The programs work because the community tells us, if you will, what it is they would like to have us do and then we go about the business of doing it.

I'd just like to say to you that if we ever get past the red tape—the bureaucratic red tape—to be able to make these types of statements as examples of what is working in this communities (sic) I think you have already, with community-based development organizations, that particular entity to move your program of putting people first in place.

Thank you very much.

President-elect Clinton: Thank you.

Daniel Tully, then John Sandner and Gary Lamb.

374

DANIEL TULLY (MERRILL LYNCH AND COMPANY, INC.): Okay. Our firm, as you may know, is known as We the People so it's not surprising that we would applaud your concept of putting people first. I think it's a very powerful one.

I'm delighted, in reading your book, that this is not a slogan or a 30-minute to a 30-second sound bite but a philosophical belief and value system that you're putting into our government. And I'm delighted to hear that it's going to be the driving force in a value system that your administration will have. I think it's very, very powerful.

As for the topic of reinventing the government, I would say let's do it. It's long overdue, it seems to me. Earlier today and yesterday a number of the speakers said that we are at a turning point. I think that we are. I agree.

I think that it is now the time for a new approach to evaluate how we will commit the tax dollars of our taxpayers. I have a number of ideas that we have successfully implemented in the securities industry that I'll be delighted to share with Leon Panetta as it relates to some of the programs that we call burden of proof.

As far as the economic growth is concerned, on the savings and investment side I would just quickly say that we are for the investment tax credit, we would be for the research and development credit, we would be for a renewal of the IRA along the lines that Senator Bentsen has recommended. We would be for a capital gains tax cut and we are for the deficit reduction.

And I will end by saying that the last couple of days have been excellent. Many of the speakers—yesterday we had David Glass and Cheryl Handler. They both ended by saying there are no real short term fixes. There are long term points of view, that we have to create a new alliance, we have to have a shared vision, we have to set common goals. I think that you are doing that.

I'm delighted that I'm one of the last speakers because we spent the first day talking about strategy and assessing the environment. I'm sure you will put your team together now to develop the plan and the strategy. And the difference between good companies and great companies—that last part of it—and that is to have the intestinal fortitude to go ahead and implement the plan. And by observing you, Senator— President-elect and Vice President-elect, I think we are very, very confident that we will be able to do that.

And I wouldn't want to end with a commercial but I will recall that earlier in the panel Lilia Clemente did say that she was bullish on America and I am too. (Laughter.)

Thank you.

PRESIDENT-ELECT CLINTON: Good for you.
John Sandner, Gary Lamb and Elena Hangii.

JOHN SANDNER (CHICAGO MERCANTILE EXCHANGE): Thank you, President-elect Clinton.

It's really unfortunate. It's nice to be the last speaker, Dan, but it's unfortunate because our time is so short. And I believe that this particular panel is probably the most critical of all panels; dealing with the government structure, government reform and economic growth.

I'm reminded of something someone said in an earlier panel that eastern Europe has more Ph.D.'s than anywhere in the world and they have more natural resources than anywhere in the world and they're one-eighth the standard of living of us here in the United States. Why?

Because they don't have a delivery system. They don't have—they do not have a system that is efficient and neither do we. And that's what you're trying to change and I commend you for that.

But I think any system—and that's what we're talking about—in government has to be built on incentives.

Incentives are what drive business and we ought to use that model.

When I think about what someone said about Apple Computers starting in a garage can you imagine where Apple Computer would be today if you had the types of incentives that government is thriving on today? There wouldn't be an Apple Computer.

I think of our own case of the Chicago Mercantile Exchange where we started as a butter and egg exchange on a street corner years ago. And today we are the risk manager for the world.

Tonight we'll carry in the books of the Chicago Mercantile Exchange, forming in 300,000 positions representing almost $4 trillion in risk management positions for the world economy and the global economy. That came because of incentives and a model that works.

Government doesn't have that model. And it's got to be driven by incentives. I listened to Dave Osburn and that's exactly what he says, that government should be driven by a business mile of incentives and proficiency and driven by consumer demand and not provider demand.

But there's another part to that mile that we haven't really talked about, and I'll only take one more minute or two. And that is there are parts of government that are not involved in acting like a business but they should be involved in the incentive to make business succeed rather than being involved in the business of protecutus gluteus maximus—(laughter)—or being involved of (sic) "Let's not be—we can't be too careful."

Well, the truth is you can be too careful and you can stifle productiv-

376

ity and growth in business and you must shed yourself from unnecessary regulation and create a model and an incentive that before I draft a rule, before I promulgate legislation, before I do a tax initiative I must first see, does this help business. Because without business success there can be no government success and if there's no government success we can't enable the people. And that's what we're talking about today is empowering the people.

And President-elect Clinton, the people have empowered you for one reason: to re-empower them. And this conference is a manifestation, for the first time in decades, that the people are beginning to feel empowered. And I thank you for that. (Applause.)

PRESIDENT-ELECT CLINTON: Thank you.

GARY LAMB (IOWA FARMERS UNION): Thank you, President-elect Clinton.

During your campaign you spoke frequently of a place called Hope, using your home town in Arkansas as a metaphor for restoring the confidence of the American people that things can change for the better.

Many people identified with that but I especially did because for the last 40 years I've worked a 400 acre farm in the heart of the heartland near a place called Chelsea, Iowa.

In Iowa it's been said that agriculture creates somewhere between 60 and 70 percent of all of our jobs. And we were reminded, rather painfully during the decade of the 80's, that agriculture was indeed much more than the farms that dotted out countryside.

We have approximately 96,000 farmers in Iowa. But only an estimated 3,000 under the age of 32.

Professor Neil Harrol, who you have met and know, estimates that in the next five years nearly one-third of those 96,000 Iowa farmers will be retirement age.

He also estimates that somewhere between 12 and 15 percent of the Iowa farmers may face foreclosure in the next few months while they've produced the best crop they've ever produced in their lifetime.

And I say that because a tremendous change is about to take place not only in our system of agriculture but also in the economic and social infrastructure that surrounds us.

For two days now we have heard the words and the infinite wisdom of some of our nation's most brilliant minds and most brilliant thinkers and it's clear that the message and the challenge is to increase the productivity of our nation's industries and our nation's workers in all sectors of our economy.

Yet no industry has increased its efficiency and productivity—even close—to that of American agriculture. But it hasn't stabilized our farms, our rural communities. It hasn't created more well paid jobs for our people, it hasn't lessened the pressure on our land and water resources. In fact, just the opposite. It's torn the literal heart out of our family farm system of food production in our rural communities.

It's the very same system that has been the model and the envy of the world for decades. And it's the very same system that today Russia and other CIS republics are trying to move toward.

Mr. Clinton, give us a rural policy that includes a long-vision farm policy, yes, that creates safety nets but a rural policy that addresses the needs of all of rural America—all that's there and all that it encompasses; a policy that addresses not only hunger in this country but hunger globally as well; a rural policy not separate from urban or inner city policy within our national agenda, but a rural policy that compliments our inner city policy within that same national agenda.

Continuing to pursue public policy that encourages or economically forces human resources off of our farms and rural communities into the cities not only has a negative impact on rural America, it undoubtedly contributes to the growing unemployment, homelessness, hunger, crime and drug problems within our inner cities as well.

Give us a rural policy, Mr. Clinton, that may be the key connection between reforming and changing government, and real economic growth.

Our nation, the state of Iowa or my farm can neither tax nor borrow its way to prosperity. We must earn our way.

Give us a rural policy that will allocate the research dollars to create value-added products, both edible and non-edible, like soy ink, soy diesel, ethanol, which would clean up our environment, reduce our dependency on foreign oil and stimulate our rural communities. The potential is endless.

Those value-added agriculture products will, in turn, create more jobs and more revenue and contribute to a growing, broad-based economic recovery both in urban and rural America.

Give us a rural policy that does not focus on the weaknesses and vulnerabilities of rural America, but rather on our assets and our strengths.

Give us a rural policy that recognizes our nation's most precious and valuable resources. Our land and our water must not be utilized—or must be utilized for the good of many, not exploited for the greed of a few.

And last and not least, Mr. Clinton, give us a rural policy so those of

378

us whose heritage and roots run deep in the American soil may once again dare to hope and dream that someday, if they so desire, our sons and daughters can return with their families to the Hope, Arkansas and to the Chelsea, Iowa's.

It is absolutely essential that a new public policy for agriculture and rural America must be part of the national agenda in your administration.

I thank you for your time and your patience and your concern. I thank you for this conference and the diversity of the people you have invited. But most of all, President-elect Clinton, I thank you for restoring hope and faith in the American people and in the American system.

Thank you. (Applause.)

President-elect Clinton: Elena.

Elena Hanggi (ACORN): My name is Elena Hanggi and I am a member of and past president of an organization called ACORN. We're a national grass roots community organization of low and moderate income people. We are a multi-issue, multi-racial organization that has led the way for affordable housing and credit availability for low and moderate income areas of this country.

I want to publicly and strongly commend President-elect Clinton and Vice President-elect Gore for understanding and appreciating the diversity of our country, our nation; understanding that America is made up of polyester and patches just as it's made up of worsted wool and silk.

In President-elect Clinton's "Putting People First," if I could just quote directly you say, "We will reach our goals only if we focus on our county's greatest resource. That is why 'Putting People First' is the heart and soul of my national economic strategy and the key to the American future."

ACORN motto is, "The People Shall Rule," which is also the motto of my and President-elect Clinton's home state of Arkansas.

We think that the single most important thing the new administration can do is to make that motto a reality for the federal government.

Government reform isn't just what, it's who and what. It's expanding our democracy to include all the people in constituencies who have been left out.

This weekend we've heard a lot of initials, a lot of acronyms; GNP, GDP, RBOTs and so on and so forth. The initials that we're most familiar with in everyday America are BOHICA. Now, in DC-ese that's pronounced BOHICA. And it means, Bend Over, Here It Comes Again. (Laughter.)

PRESIDENT-ELECT CLINTON: I'm speechless.

MS. HANGGI: We believe that now, for the first time in a long time, we have an opportunity for that to not mean here comes a swift kick in the britches but in fact for that to mean here comes someone—a government and administration—that is interested in including all of America in the process and the substance.

Here in America we have a huge untapped reservoir of experience and commitment of organized low and moderate income people who have been fixing up abandoned houses, signing CRA agreements with banks that bring money into our neighborhoods, creating and restructuring their public schools and registering their neighbors to vote and getting them involved in the political process.

And if I could just do a sidebar quickly here, President-elect Clinton, to add—to give you the third incentive that we couldn't think of yesterday and the thousand incentives for banks to loan to low and moderate income folks. That incentive is the incentive that drives business in general and that is profit.

As someone else mentioned, these are not giveaway programs. These are profitable, loan-making programs for banks. They make money. I just want to—I felt it was important to mention that.

The new administration should tap these resources by setting up partnerships with these community organizations and seeking out leaders from these organizations and neighborhoods to fill policy making and regulatory positions in the federal government.

Some years ago it would have been unheard of for a black woman to be elected to the United States Senate. But now that is a reality and it's high time.

Similarly, why should we not, for the next opening on the Federal Reserve Board—why should that not be filled with a low income person? Let's not forget that when the economy catches a cold, low and moderate income America gets pneumonia. We need that voice in perspective on the Federal Reserve Board and in all government structures.

To paraphrase President-elect Clinton, our federal government needs to not just look like America but come from the conditions that all classes of America face.

Everyday people are worried, everyday people are watching, and

380

everyday people want to work on your team. You can make empowerment complete by including us.

Thank you. (Applause.)

PRESIDENT-ELECT CLINTON: I'd like to now call on Ron Carey, the Teamsters President and then Doctor Ruth Ono.

RON CAREY (INTERNATIONAL BROTHERHOOD OF TEAMSTERS): Reinvesting or reinventing government means more. It means being effective in serving the people. It demands of us a reexamination of the role that government plays, or should play, in serving the people.

For example, and from a labor perspective, labor and management have now arrived at a new consensus. And that is that only government can deal with the runaway health care costs.

We need to look at how government affects the quality of life for America's working people. And in many other areas workers must have a chance to win, not just a choice of how to lose.

Government has to play a role in training workers for good jobs.

If we're to look at our trading partners, we see that countries with the most successful economies are the countries that invest in their workers and provide a level playing field for labor unions.

We've talked a great deal. I've heard a great deal about productivity. But the fact of the matter is, American workers are the most productive workers in the world. So when we hear the words, "work harder, increase productivity," I'm not sure I know what that means.

The problem is not productivity. The problem is that we must expand our pool of good jobs and prepare our people to do these jobs.

Ron Brown, this morning, asked a very important question—increase jobs. Ron Brown said, how many part time jobs, how many temporary workers are looking for good paying full time jobs.

And that phone call that we heard the first day—I think we have to look at that very carefully. A laid off worker, single with six children—how will he be able to embrace the great American Dream.

As you move forward from discussions to concrete proposals and specific actions, the government we re-invent should be the one that should keep faith with all of its people by being fair to them, by giving them a chance to win—not replacing them, and by understanding that for America's working families nothing is as important and as critical to their futures and their children's futures as good jobs and that they are prepared to perform those jobs. Thank you very much. (Applause.)

PRESIDENT-ELECT CLINTON: Thank you. I want to recognize Dr. Ono and then William Donaldson, but before I do let me say that—I hate to sound like a Johnny one note here, but I think its important to note how all these things affect one another.

One of the reasons there is such an increased preference today for both part time workers and having your existing workers work overtime, which is something no one has talked about (since?) here. Both of those things give you the same economic benefit, which is, you don't have to hire somebody new and pay the health costs.

And there are other—of course, there are other—there's Social Security and all of that stuff. But I think that the structure of the American economy has basically operated toward more under-employed people, more over-worked people who are fully employed, and more people who wind up being unemployed completely just because of external factors. And if we could find a way to reorganize the other stuff, you might wind up with people working fewer hours a week who are fully employed and more full time as opposed to part time employees. But I think it's worth focusing on that a little bit.

Dr. Ono and then Mr. Donaldson.

RUTH ONO (QUEENS HEALTH SERVICE): Thank you, Mr. President-elect, Mr. Vice President-elect. You made reference earlier to the last speaker who mentioned the fact that you brought us together as a family. In Hawaii, we refer to that as an (Ohana?). I feel so proud to be a part of your American (Ohana?), your family. And you have a very special brand of Aloha in the spirit of caring for the future of America. We thank you.

I shared with Dr. Shalala earlier that after what we've heard articulated the last two days, I'm almost afraid to let on that I've been with the health care industry for 30 years.

But seriously, it is with a sense of pride that I share with you that I am affiliated with the parent company which owns the oldest, largest, private medical center in Honolulu, Hawaii—the Queen's Medical Center.

As a matter of fact it was founded in 1859 by King Kamehameha IV and Queen Imma. And we had the pleasure of hosting Mrs. Clinton when she was there five months ago, and Senator Benson's staff just a couple of weeks ago, as a matter of fact.

In the interest of time, I will not go into the model health care system which you were so kind to speak about during your campaign. I will share this with Dr. Shalala and include some pertinent information in the report that I will be submitting to the President-elect.

I should also like to include recommendations with regard to the contributions Hawaii can make to US penetration of Asia, not only in health and fitness, tourism development, education, and research and development—particularly in the areas of ocean science, astronomy, and alternate energy—but especially in reshaping the global economic landscape of the Asia-Pacific countries. For, like it or not, Asia-Pacific is becoming the most productive economic region, as well as its largest creditor. And yes, I hope that we can still keep agriculture on Hawaii's agenda.

John White indicated yesterday that 75 percent of the federal debt occurred during the last 12 years. Today, Dr. Tobin referred to the recession as one of the past four years. And, in addition to that, Mr. McMillion had indicated that this recession is the worst we've suffered in the past 50 years.

Americans must be survivors because during those 12 years, we've experienced the worst of times.

Hawaii can play an important role in bridging the gap. America has a Pacific destiny. Hawaii, with its strategic location and its multi-ethnic, multi-cultural legacy, can serve as America's bridge between the forces that border the Pacific. Hawaii looks forward, President Clinton, to the best of times under your administration. Thank you.

PRESIDENT-ELECT CLINTON: Thank you. Let me make a point here. I think it's been made before, but in Hawaii, which is the only state in the country which has had a required universal health program since 1974—which even self-employed people have to buy into. And it is in theory a "Play or Pay" system, although hardly anybody pays to the government. Everybody buys private health insurance because they have community rating and large pools for small business and self-employed people.

The cost is approximately two-thirds of the national average—significantly cheaper. And you might say, well, it's just because everybody's so healthy out there—which is partly true, but you should also know that that system has to absorb about 20 percent of its case-load who are native islanders who come from surrounding islands around the islands which make up the state of Hawaii, and they are quite poor people.

So, they do load on to that system some uncompensated care and still manage to provide health care to almost 100 percent of the people at a cost way, way below the national average with a combination of mandated insurance reforms; aggressive, aggressive primary and preventive care; and a good delivery system for it; and a good management system in the private sector. It's a very impressive thing, indeed.

Mr. Donaldson.

WILLIAM DONALDSON (NEW YORK STOCK EXCHANGE): Thank you very much, Governor, Senator. I wish I had the time and the authority to speak for the 51 million Americans and some $4 billion worth of market value listed on the US Stock exchange, but I don't.

I'd just like to make two or three simple points which interest me. And that is that we've spent the last day and a half or two days looking at facts and figures, talking about strategy, talking about budgets. We've had a lot to do with the why government should be doing certain things and the what government should be doing, and yet today at this moment, we're reaching into the implementation phase—How should government be structured to get this done?

I think anybody that has run an organization would say that the ideas are plentiful, it's the implementation that's tough. And I would agree with Jack Sandner when he says that the subject matter of this panel, I believe, is extremely important. I hope it's not prophetic that it comes at the end of the day.

I'd just like to make two thoughts. One is, I'd like to define this word entrepreneurship to go beyond what we all think of it as. We think of it as somebody who starts a company, or somebody who starts something. I would say that there are characteristics of entrepreneurs that extend beyond small organizations. There are entrepreneurs in large organizations. There are men and women who are able to pick up large organizations and move them.

These entrepreneurs have a concept of self-excellence, if you will, that drives them. They also have an ability to see things slightly differently than other people see them.

I would submit that what we've got to do is create an organizational structure that allows the entrepreneurs at the top—the leaders at the top—to be met by a force coming up from the bottom.

I would submit that leadership from the top is going to get diluted and frustrated as it attempts to move down through the bureaucracy. And the only way that that leadership is going to have an effect is if we engage and empower and incent (sic) and reward the people at the bottom—a force coming up to meet. That has to do with organizational structure.

Leon Panetta, you've got a huge job ahead of you, but I'd just like to remind you and to suggest to the President-elect that your middle name, OMB, is management. And budgets are important, but it seems to me that the implementation phase is extremely important.

We haven't taken a look at the way this government is managed for a long, long time. And I would hope that you or a commission—I don't want to foist off more on you but there would be some sort of an organized way of looking at and imbuing the entire federal bureaucracy with this concept of releasing entrepreneurship.

My last statement is to say that this is a entrepreneurial meeting. You have taken a risk, you've taken a chance. I believe you succeeded. It's the first time it's happened. I thank you for having us all here and I thank you personally. (Applause.)

PRESIDENT-ELECT CLINTON: Thank you.

Now, I'd like to thank you for your very perceptive statement. I—we did take something of a risk. A lot of people thought there was no point in doing this. But I did and still—I feel more strongly now than I did before you all showed up.

Let me also say—and Mr. Panetta may want to take a moment to respond. We can only stay about five or six more minutes but—if you look at the budget of OMB there's obviously more B than M in it. And there needs to be at one level—I know, all of you here who have children are now smiling. (Laughter.)

Anyway, I didn't mean it that way. Maybe a lot of both. I know what you mean.

If—and there's plenty of work to be done there too. One of the things that we haven't had time to talk about today that Leon and I have talked about extensively is how dysfunctional the budgets are.

The budgeting process is somewhat dysfunctional because it's based on estimated revenues, which is a bad way to start with a base. And then the budgets themselves don't tell you a lot about how the organizations function. Now, that's often true in the private sector too but it's certainly true in the government.

But if you look at the way OMB is organized there is an insufficient recognition that the federal government needs to go through the same searching reevaluation. And I don't mean throwing people in the street. I'm against that.

But just a reorganization of how we do business, how these departments are set up, how we can be more responsive to the taxpayers as customers. That whole function has been largely ignored probably for a generation, since the civil service reorganization that Herbert Hoover oversaw in the 50's. And we very much want to bring to bear the best insights of everything that everybody has learned from the grass roots up in the 1980's as well as running organizations in difficult times.

So, again, I want to issue a specific invitation on this point to those of you who will be writing your little memos after this is over to respond to that. We are going to do our best to put the M back in OMB in a way that empowers the federal employees, makes the taxpayers prouder and makes a lot of sense in terms of how this government works.

And in the end, even if we put the commission together, the mechanism through which we do that will be the departments themselves and how they're set up and what we're able to achieve at OMB.

Leon, you want to say anything in that—

Rep. Panetta: I was thinking. You've said it all. As a matter of fact, in this last session of Congress I introduced a proposal to basically separate out the management function because I was so disgruntled with the way OMB was implementing their management function.

It's all—

President-elect Clinton: You don't like that anymore, do you?

Rep. Panetta: No, no. It's not a good proposal anymore. (Laughter.)

President-elect Clinton: I've been meaning to ask you about that.

Rep. Panetta: The whole thrust has been on the numbers. It's all been through the budget and they've forgotten about the management side and we've paid a hell of a price as a result of that.

We've estimated that something like $75 to $100 billion has really been lost by poor management in government. And you've all felt it on the other end. We felt it and the taxpayers have felt it so management has be strengthened.

President-elect Clinton: Who was next? Mr. Cizik?

Robert Cizik (Cooper Industries): Governor,—President-elect Clinton, on behalf of the 12,000 members of the National Association of Manufacturers I'd like to thank you for riveting the attention of the American people on the domestic economy and the problems of competition.

We've discussed, over these last two days, several arcane subjects—demand, supply, competition, productivity.

The study of economics has always been viewed as a dismal science. Perhaps over these past few days we've proven that designation to be totally accurate.

But it's a dismal science that I think the events of early November tell us can only be ignored at your own risk. It is a very important area and you've established, by your interest in this subject, that only profitable and productive companies can afford to pay higher wages and that you can't finance the American Dream on the minimum wage.

If we are not a strong domestic economy we won't be, as we have always been proud of being, a superpower. In fact, we won't be a super anything.

Now, in the area of reinventing government it seems to me that high on the list has to be regulatory reform. Now, I realize that's an easy subject to pick. The US Treasury estimates that we spend, in the area of regulatory compliance, some $350 to some $500 billion.

I'm always amazed by the wide range of these figures but I guess when you're working in billions of dollars it's relatively easy to go from 300 billion to 500 billion.

Now, I don't know how you operate as a chief executive but I suspect I do. A figure of that size, as a CEO of a large company, would attract my attention and I suspect it should and will attract your attention.

There is the area of legal system reform. We live in a very litigious society. Legal costs are running amuck. Among the industrial companies (sic) we spend in excess of $100 billion a year for outside legal counsel. That compares to the total after-tax profits of the manufacturing companies of only $80 some billion.

In my company alone we sell about 30 percent of our products outside the United States. We have 100 percent of our lawsuits within the United States. This is an area that I think has to be looked at by your administration.

I'll end by saying something about the investment tax credit. I would be disowned by my members if I didn't mention that. I heard it mentioned today that it would not mean anything.

Our studies, our models would indicate that a 10 percent targeted investment tax credit, within five years, would add $120 billion in gross domestic product to this economy a year and it would add 1,200,000 jobs. I think that is something that should be of interest to you administration.

Thank you very much.

President-elect Clinton: You know, first of all let me support what you said there. I—we had a study done by a nonpartisan group during the campaign. It had nothing to do with my campaign, we had no idea what they were going to come up with.

They said that the—even an incremental investment tax credit, properly drawn, would add a half a million jobs to this economy in the first year.

Now I agree with the statement that was made earlier, in one of the earlier panels, that a good—a bad project won't be made into a good project by putting another ten percent incentive in there. I agree with that.

But it's more complex than that. If you have competition for corporate money, for example, that's between—you're going to turn it back to the shareholders in dividends, you're going to give it to the government in taxes or will you go ahead now and make this investment that you ought to make now and try to be as modern as you can.

I think a lot of investments will be made. I also think it's important to understand that investment tax credit, in this context, would benefit a lot of people buying plant and equipment in smaller operations who don't have shareholders for whom the ten percent credit may make a lot of difference just on the tax liability side alone. So I'm inclined to agree with you.

MR. CIZIK: I was talking to the management of Tootsie-Roll last night —a small company. They have the same interests in an investment tax credit that we as manufacturers do. And of our 12,000 members, two-thirds of them are small manufacturers.

PRESIDENT-ELECT CLINTON: Let me say, all I know is in 1985 we put one in here and I got lacerated for it, saying it was a big tax giveaway to business and everything. And four years later, for four years in a row, we were in the top ten states in the country in growth of manufacturing jobs. And it also extended to environmental pollution equipment and our big paper companies here had achieved a standard of dioxin emission into the water which was less than half of what the EPA was permitting.

So I do think you can make a pretty compelling argument that there's some relationship between the tax system and investment patterns.

Let me ask you one specific question. We have under 17 percent of our workforce in manufacturing.

MR. CIZIK: Correct.

PRESIDENT-ELECT CLINTON: Our major competitors have 28 and 33 percent respectively. That's probably because they have—they do a lot of things we don't do and—it's not because they freeze people in the specific manufacturing jobs that they have but it is because when people lose manufacturing jobs in one sector they tend to go on to other manufacturing jobs. But there's an overall pro-manufacturing policy.

Now, I don't think that our economy can be or should be as closed as the Japanese economy or even in some ways that can recreate the culture that exists in Germany where one in three workers is a manufacturing worker.

But I do think that it is unrealistic to expect us to maintain both high productivity and high income levels unless we have a certain percentage of the workforce in manufacturing.

And I was wondering whether the National Association of Manufacturing had done any kind of studies which would indicate where the bottom is on this or if we had a good economic policy which dealt with your health care costs, retiree health care costs, the litigation issues—all the things you outlined.

Do you think there's any possibility that we might, for example, return to 20 percent of our workforce in manufacturing? Now, do you have any sense of where the bottom is or where the top is? Because it's a big issue for the American economy and whether I should, as President, strive to return us to 20 percent or is that an unusual and unwarranted interruption in the way everything's going to happen anyway?

MR. CIZIK: I think it's a very doable goal and I commend you for thinking that way.

We have done some studies which would indicate—well, first of all, about 20 percent of our gross domestic product comes from manufacturers. We feel we can, with the proper policies and with us doing our job too—and we have to do our job—we have to train, we have to invest, and we have to introduce the latest technology in manufacturing. Many of us are doing that.

But we could easily move that—not easily, but we can move that percent of the gross domestic product from 20 percent to 25 percent. At 25 percent we would be adding some four million jobs to this economy. Four million high paying, value added jobs.

Again, we cannot finance the American dream, as I said earlier, on the minimum wage. We do not pay them minimum wage. I think we would be able to accomplish this.

PRESIDENT-ELECT CLINTON: Senator Gore.

Vice President-elect Gore: Listening to this discussion on reforming government, I was struck by how similar many of the concepts are to the ones presented in the very first session yesterday by John Scully (ph) when, as part of the assessment of the changes in the world economy he described the qualities necessary for success in the new economy of today. And he mentioned time-to-market, flexibility, quality, decentralization, lower costs and customization, among other qualities.

And at the beginning of this session President-elect Clinton noted that the total quality management revolution, which swept through American business and industry over the last 15 years, has somehow bypassed government.

And it seems to me our challenge is very clearly to take those principles and apply them to the management of government in order to establish the kinds of qualities that are necessary for success in government as well as in business.

A part of it, it seems to me, has to do with the new capacities we have to deal with information because just as it would have been impossible and unthinkable to pull together a conference like this one 20 years ago, with the technologies that existed at that time—without computers, without C-SPAN, without the abilities that have made this whole national conversation possible. So in the time when the New Deal was introduced, it would have been impossible and unthinkable to imagine government services being delivered in a way that tailored to each individual and each individual family exactly the cluster of services that were needed and no more.

Someone in manufacturing was telling me recently about an innovation in the garment business which will, he said, soon make it possible for someone to go to a tailor shop or a dressmaker and have measurements taken in a new and more sophisticated way, and have those measurements automatically fed upstream into the automatic cutters that measure the cloth, and, in any event, the very next day have the garment, tailored in the chosen color, delivered to the person's home.

In just that same way, government has to stop mass producing a package of services to individuals in completely different circumstances, often giving them more than they need, deserve, or want, and, in the process, dulling initiative and preventing the kind of creative behavior that they ought to come to on their own initiative, and often giving them far too little of what they need in order to empower them to compete and have the kinds of opportunities that are necessary for success.

We have the capacity, in our country now, available to government to tailor the kinds of empowering services at low cost with flexibility and high quality and no more, in order to help our citizens succeed in the marketplace of tomorrow.

390

And I don't think there is any more important task that we can undertake in this new administration than in implementing the kinds of ideas we've heard in this session. I've really been excited by it.

PRESIDENT-ELECT CLINTON: Anyone else have a closing comment before we pack it in?

AUDREY RICE OLIVER (INTEGRATED BUSINESS SOLUTIONS, INC.): Yes, I do.

PRESIDENT-ELECT CLINTON: Audrey.

MS. OLIVER: I would be amiss if I did not acknowledge my feelings about African-Americans, minorities, women. It's very interesting to me that the ethnic and minority people, women, in this country have never been in charge of this government. So, the demise in the economy concerns me because sometimes I believe it is not at our hands.

There are many programs in place that were designed to assist us—to help us get through to equal opportunity, to participate in the economic mainstream of this country. The very programs that were put in place to assist us are now turning into monsters.

We are constantly completing paperwork, processing paper. And for those of us who are just trying to make a living, trying to participate as small businesses, we do not have the time nor the resources to complete the incredible amount of paperwork that the federal government requires, that the states require. I think big business would echo this also because it is absolutely a maze.

We need to look at streamlining forms—(audio break)—make it somewhat easier for the small businesses to make large businesses recognize that doing business with us—we're not a thorn in their side because each time they have to complete that paperwork, they—(audio break).

They talk about how much we cost to do business with. I do not believe that it is so—(audio break)—Earl Graves today, and how we need a program that is empowered, an administrator who can make decisions on the spot.

We have to ask Peter about Paul to get our processes done as far as our work. We need someone that can make a decision on the spot.

You heard Vince talk about Chicago and the innovation that was happening there when they were given the right and the power to

391

make something happen. That is what minorities and women are looking for—an opportunity to participate, to be empowered, to contribute back to this economy which we do so well as small businesses.

President-elect Clinton, Vice President-elect Gore, you are challenged here today by all the businesses that have come here—the small businesses that fuel this economy. We are here from many walks of life talking about the issues that are germane to this society today.

My company, Integrated Business Solutions, Incorporated—located in San Ramon—is a high-tech firm. Small and growing.

But we've done all the things that were discussed here today. We've had controlled growth. We employ people—I have 50 people working for me. We train people each summer, students who come in to learn how to be technicians. We send our employees to school. We pay benefits and the benefits that we pay, we do not ever want to stop paying because we think that's an incentive for them to work with us. We believe that health benefits are very important to our employees livelihood—child care.

And because of this they are very loyal to us. They work for me seven days a week, if need be, 24 hours a day. I don't have to ask for more. We are interested in research and development money. And I listened to John Young talk about the Defense Advanced Technology money in research and development and some going to the 12 computer systems companies. Do not forget the small businesses who are on the verge, who are interested in the same things that big businesses are interested in.

We can partner with big business. We can do many things together, but they have to recognize that small companies—you can learn from us because we have a lot to give.

We have an opportunity today to lead in unity as a united front, to make a difference for America. Contrary to what the television has said, has been reporting, about this being a PR show—dog-and-pony show—it is not.

This surrounding has reached the very souls of our heart. I do not think I could tell you the emotion that runs in the room, in the hallways, as we go back and talk. We are energized.

We believe in this opportunity for a new America, a united America, putting America back to work. All these things are representative in this room today. And we thank you for your vision because you are truly visionaries and we hope that we can meet the challenge. Thank you. (Applause.)

PRESIDENT-ELECT CLINTON: Thank you.

Bob Friedman, Patricia Cloherty, Bob Reich, and Ernesto in that order. We got to hurry though, we're running real late. Go ahead. (Laughter)

Bob Friedman (Corp. for Enterprise Development): Okay. Thank you. Thank you both for two of the most extraordinary days of my—

President-elect Clinton: I'll stay here till dawn. I don't care.

Mr. Friedman: I think one of the ways to build this economy is to open the doors—to make sure that all people have access to the marketplace. It is one of the themes that runs through putting people first and I just want to underscore it.

There are tens of thousands of people on the margins of this economy in depressed rural and urban centers—unemployed people, people on welfare—who want nothing more than the chance, a reasonable chance, to try and start a business to support themselves.

Your initiatives, a thousand micro-enterprise programs, a hundred community development banks, offer to open that opportunity and I think in doing so to expand the economy.

I think it marks a significant shift from spending on the poor to investing in the poor in a way that will grow the economy.

There is another initiative that you have talked about that I think is important to at least mention here which is the Individual Development Account Demonstration Program. A third of American households have no or negative investable assets when the cost of entry to the American mainstream has gone up, whether through the price of an education, the price of business capitalization, the price of a home.

We have pursued a bifurcated asset development policy in this country. We subsidize asset acquisition by the non-poor to the tune of $100 billion a year and we penalize it for the poor.

A welfare mother who seeks to escape poverty by starting a business and acquires, for example, a sewing machine to run an upholstery business and thereby exceeds the $1,000 asset limitation, or who saves some money for her or her children's education, becomes ineligible for benefits.

You have called for removing the asset limitations—the barriers in our income maintenance programs—to asset acquisition. You have called for a way to help build asset base.

I think, when I look at our history at the economic policies that have resulted in long term significant, widely shared economic growth they are democratic—small "d"—investments in the common genius of the American people—like the Homestead Act and the GI Bill.

I think what the Homestead Act was to the 19th Century and the GI Bill was to the 20th, the Individual Development Account can be to the 21st.

Thank you very much for leading us to the future.

PATRICIA CLOHERTY (PATRICOF & COMPANY): Governor Clinton, Senator Gore, everyone has to run. I'll be quick.

In general, I'm of the view that government actions affect the economy only at the margin. Business has enormous ability to accept regulatory pummeling and to, in effect, through its pricing mechanism adjust to the world.

On the other hand, I think that the—for better or for worse—Oh, also I am skeptical—end of the day—at the issue of reform. I mean, for some reason, in our—of this, my political adulthood, reform has always proved more complicated and more costly—remember tax simplification!

And so, I look at this issue of economic growth and government reform and what affects—influences me today is that I think, unfortunately, the goose is ill and the golden eggs are not being laid.

So that while one can be comfortable in fat times that government will go on and do what it does and somehow the international economy, and your own, will help you struggle through.

I think today anything that the government does becomes a moment. We simply have borrowed our way through a consumption oriented couple of dozen years and the need is imperative to build up the country's net worth. So, anything that the federal, state, and local governments can do to move that along becomes very important.

Now, my own particular beat is not government, it's entrepreneurial small business. I'm in the venture capital business. Now, the margin of which I speak, where government actions, in fact, matter is in entrepreneurial small business because the ones who can, in fact, handle the regulatory burden and the zigs and zags of policy better are the larger companies.

I think the small ones don't have sufficient capital cushion to be able to get through the protracted regulatory and policy debates. So that I think at the moment the need is very, very great to begin to articulate a—in fact, I have recommendations really in two areas.

One is programmatic within the current government structure and the second is more policy. I do think, Bill Donaldson, that the issue of how you organize yourself to do a task is made simpler when you know what the task is. And it does occur to me today that after several years of re-distributive policies that if we make the shift toward the investment part of the equation that you then have to re-align your thinking—your leadership and your thinking and your political compromises all down the line that guide the government, the executive agencies—align them in that direction.

And I think it would be quite bold—business also has tended to fall into a pattern of establishing, sort of, battle lines around little fronts. In our industry it's the reduction in the rate of capital gains tax. And that has become like the India-Pakistan to be. It's very refined. We have a whole series of those that we study with a microscope and then work through it.

Now, it occurs to me that in this day and age, a rather bolder approach would really be to take the reality at hand—which is re-building the nation's net worth—the agency at hand, which at first blush is SBA—and the fabric of policies at hand and examine them, government-wide, to see what, in fact, can work to optimize the nation's formula for releasing entrepreneurial energies toward building valuable companies that create jobs, wealth, and yes, taxes.

So, just first, because it is late, my own view right now is that it would be quite a dramatic and unexpected, but productive and cheap, step to take would be to rename SBA.

Make it embrace not only small business—which has come to reflect a stable, almost permanently small sector of the population, and call it, I don't know, Agency for Enterprise Development. And have it embrace, in addition to traditional small business—which are very numerous in the country—embrace also the smaller universe of potentially very high value companies that contain the seeds of the future Federal Expresses, Apples, Staples, whatever, Office Depot. I mean, you name it. They are small and they are in that universe and they should be included as one of the constituencies, certainly, of that agency.

And then the third constituency is what I call emerging entrepreneurs. And it consists—I don't care if it's immigrants, the minority groups, the women, and yes, some of those old white men who are trying to begin to take the first steps toward building new businesses.

I mean, it could be renamed. It's mandate can be broadened. And it's programs, particularly some of them are especially serviceable in today's financial structures, particularly where the banks debts that we've discussed—the bank issues—what bank debts are required.

In any event, it seems to me that that agency warrants some attention and furthermore could be used for a couple of points of emphasis at no additional cost, including the technology transfer issues that we've been talking about as part of the defense wind-down—not unlike that which happened in demobilization after the Second World

War, as well as second point of emphasis would be the international issues.

I mean, the irony of the situation is that the romance of our nation involves entrepreneurship profoundly. I mean, we're raised on Horatio Algier. Unfortunately, the reality is pretty tattered because entrepreneurs can't get money and once they get it they have some—the cost of getting into business has been made effectively higher by the costs—the regulatory burden.

So, in any event, I think that the agency warrants some attention. It could be very interesting as a vehicle.

Secondly, also, though, I do think that government-wide, apart from the particular agency, there should be a—I don't know whether the White House—at what level—but a government-wide effort to look at what—how can the conditions which cause entrepreneurship to flourish in the United States, and to continue to be a major path of social mobility for our people—how can that be articulated clearly, maintained rigorously, and nurtured? And it seems to me that those are two challenges that need attention.

Thank you.

PRESIDENT-ELECT CLINTON: Thank you.

UNIDENTIFIED PANELIST: Thank you, President-elect Clinton, Vice President-elect Gore.

I just want to thank you for allowing me to be part of such a historic conference. At first it was somewhat overwhelming for me—a Hispanic woman, small business owner—to be among such diverse and distinguished individuals. I commend you for daring to seek out ideas and recommendations from the group that you've brought together.

As a small business owner, I have many ideas for reform in government and an even longer wish list for changes. But in the essence of time, I will submit all my recommendations in writing, except for one point—women.

Don't overlook women as another important resource. Women have so many—so much to offer as business people. I would really like to see some preference given to women in business.

It's time for change. It's the right time. It's the right place. And I believe, like all the Americans who voted for you, President-elect Clinton, that you and your administration can implement these changes.

This conference is, indeed, a bold and refreshing start.

Thank you very much.

PRESIDENT-ELECT CLINTON: Thank you. Kathleen.

KATHLEEN PIPER (PIED PIPER FLOWER SHOP): Thank you, President-elect Clinton.

PRESIDENT-ELECT CLINTON: Kathleen, you know, became our signature small business person. She was on every television program.

MS. PIPER: Thank you, President-elect Clinton, for seeking to include ordinary people like myself, a florist from South Dakota.

I would like to pick up on your cue that we have not discussed agriculture and rural issues nearly enough this week.

The conversations in the cafes and the grain elevators around the Midwest frequently turned to the subject of the role of the USDA in communities such as mine.

During the last 12 years, the USDA seems to have become a tool of the multinational agricultural conglomerates. Let's put people first in the USDA. Let's put rural small business people first. Let's refocus the USDA to put people, like young farmers, first—people who want to maintain their family farms and to keep our communities alive.

The mechanism is already in place, as you are well aware, through the state rural development councils. They need your help to stay funded. They're not operating in all states but they really do work. South Dakota is proof of that.

We, in rural America, were delighted yesterday when you talked about the need for the new energy policy in this country. It is our belief that the best renewable energy source is corn ethanol.

Further ethanol development would do two critical things in rural America—or all of America. It would provide a constant market for our corn production and it would move the country towards one of your goals, which is less dependence on imported oil.

A direct link between economic development and a stable corn price will do more for rural America than any new pilot program. Perhaps re-invention of government is not really what we need. We need a realignment of programs already in place. Let's just use, as our priority, those programs that put people first.

Thank you.

PRESIDENT-ELECT CLINTON: Bob. Ernesto.

ROBERT REICH (SECRETARY DESIGNATE OF LABOR): I've been sitting here for a couple of days with uncharacteristic quietude.

But let me just say that as the clock runs out, unlike the typical academic conference that I very often attend, where participants walk away remembering less about what they heard than what they said,— (laughter)—this is a remarkable gathering and I for one want to thank all the participants, at least, who are remaining here for an extraordinary array of ideas—challenges are absolutely enormous before us.

We've gone through lower earnings, health care crisis, the nation's poor, American competitiveness, and on top of that a $4 trillion deficit, and also a great deal of cynicism about the capacity of government.

But, on the other hand, Mr. President-elect, Vice President-elect, this gives me enormous, enormous hope—much more than I've had before about the capacity of Americans to come together, come up with solutions and get on with the job.

PRESIDENT-ELECT CLINTON: Me too.

Ernesto.

MR. CORTES: Mr. President-elect, I've heard a lot of discussion about how we ought to re-invent government, and I think all of it is very interesting and useful and some of it is even elegant.

However, I'd like to put—make one minor disclaimer. I think Arthur Oakland once wrote in a book, called it, *The Market Has Its Place.*

The market is a very powerful institution for producing and allocating resources, but the market also has to be kept in its place. And the only institution that can reinforce and support and hold a market accountable sometimes is society—what some people call mediating institutions: families, churches, labor unions, social organizations, community organizations.

And I would urge us to think about the role that they ought to play in initiating entrepreneurial activity and making government work.

A very wise politician once said, all politics is local, and I think you of all people would I think agree to that and understand that. And I hope that as the leader of this country, you forego your role as CEO for a while and recognize the way in which local communities can make local governments and municipal governments work if they're led correctly and if they're provided the proper resources. Entrepreneurship requires resources.

And I want to, again, urge you—us all to think about the logic of public investment which will make the market system productive. In-

398

vestment in things like elementary and secondary education, nutrition, immunization.

In basic economics, I once learned that there was a thing as a public good and that public goods do not lend themselves so easily, okay, to market activities.

For those reasons, you know, when we had a polio epidemic in this country, we made a decision under an Eisenhower administration to give away the vaccine, not to try to sell it to people, because there was some logic to it. And I think we need to remember those kind of examples from our history to make our market system more productive and more useful through public investment, elementary and secondary education, infrastructure, targeted particularly for our cities which are in despair and hopefully giving our people who are working people an opportunity to rebuild our communities.

Thank you.

PRESIDENT-ELECT CLINTON: Thank you very much. I think both your points are very well made. Let me just make one remark about mediating institutions. You mentioned a few and we had community organizations and non-profits and labor unions and some others represented here.

One of the things that's really bothered me about the whole kind of adversarial climate of the '80's is I think it's clear to everybody that all these organizations—government, management, labor, everybody—had to change, and sometimes change in very profound ways.

But if you don't change or if you don't have a place at the table then, you know, time will pass you by but the need for the mediating institution doesn't go away. Somebody still needs to be out there sticking up for the little guys. And I think that that's a very important point you made and I very much appreciate it.

Yvonne.

Ms. YVONNE: We have a saying in our company about states—If we are all thinking the same, we are all not thinking. So, I'm not going to sit here going through what we have been going through the last two days.

The only thing that I have to say is—America, the world is watching. Mine is short and sweet.

399

PRESIDENT-ELECT CLINTON: Is Steve Wolfe still here? He wanted to say something. Did he leave?
(Response inaudible.)

PRESIDENT-ELECT CLINTON: Excuse me?
(Response inaudible.)

PRESIDENT-ELECT CLINTON: This man has been trying to talk all day. I'm going to let him speak before we go.

ALAN BILDNER (SME COMPANY, INC.): Thank you, Mr. President-elect and Mr. Vice President-elect. I want to talk for a moment about the supermarket business which hasn't been discussed.

My name is Alan Bildner. I'm from New Jersey, a businessman there. My family and I owned a moderate size supermarket company until a few years ago, which I chaired. And I'm here as a representative also of Food Market Institute, which I chaired, and I'm currently chairing an urban initiatives committee of FMI, which has as its task encouraging job development in the urban areas, training and education, and job creation.

Food Market Institute is made up of—represents about $180 billion at retail. Of our membership, 80 percent are made up of operators of 10 stores or less and half are single store operators.

Our Food Market Institute and our membership, our food industry —retail food industry—sees no evidence that the recession is winding down nor do we see increased consumer confidence.

We would encourage you, Mr. President-elect and Mr. Vice President, while you're considering the structural changes that have to be made in our economy, that you also move quickly on your programs for job stimulus in the short term. And we would encourage you, when considering the investment incentives of investment credit, research and development, job training incentives to make certain that these are applied to the retail sector, which, after all, in the past decades has been instrumental in creating jobs.

My wife says that I can't say hello in less than five minutes, but I'm going to do it tonight and I just want to wrap up my own remarks and add in my thanks to those expressed for the extraordinary vision you've had in putting this summit together.

I think that in addition to everything else that you've accomplished you've created a model for the potential for coalitions of businessmen and the not-for-profit sector and government working hand-in-hand

400

to help solve our problems, and we're grateful for that. Thank you. (Applause.)

President-elect Clinton: Thank you very much. I'd like to say, before we go, we ought to all give Mickey Kantor, John Emerson, and all the people who put this wonderful meeting together a big hand. (Applause.)

I want to thank all of you for being here today and for being here yesterday, and to assure you that we have kept detailed notes.

But I want to again say for those who are still here, I want every participant in this conference to give us between one and three pages of specific suggestions of things you think we ought to do. And we will definitely take them into account.

I'm glad we're ending on this. I hope that the taxpayers who watched this and who are going to pay for all these things we do, for good or ill, feel that they're going to get their money's worth.

I certainly think they got their money's worth out of the last two days and I'm very, very proud just to be a citizen of this country after listening to all of you. And stick with us, work with us. We'll follow-up on this. We'll get back together and we'll do our best to make good decisions.

Thank you very much. (Applause.)

END OF CONFERENCE

PRESIDENT-ELECT CLINTON'S POST-ECONOMIC CONFERENCE NEWS CONFERENCE

President-elect Clinton: Well, I'd like to read a brief statement and then let Senator Gore make a remark or two and then we'll be glad to answer some questions.

First of all, I have to tell you I found this last two days to be productive, positive and provocative. Full of ideas and experiences and perspectives that represent the length and breadth of our country. People from every walk of life, every conceivable background.

They represented, in sum, what is very best about America. This kind of participation, itself, is very important to me and it will continue throughout my administration. And I don't mean just the people who were here, but also those who took the time to call from across the country.

This is all a part of the effort we have to continue to make to reconnect the American people to their government. We heard a lot of serious questions raised and some significant differences among the people who were here on what the best answers to those questions are.

But what I found most striking was the fundamental agreement on several critical points.

First there was absolute consensus on the need to substantially increase our level of investment to get this economy going again and to develop the abilities of our people. We can't hope to rebuild our economy simply by paving roads and building factories. We also have to have the best educated and best trained work force in the world.

Second, there was a remarkable degree of consensus that we have to increase access to capital if we expect small business—the real job generating engine of this economy—to flourish and if we expect our entrepreneurs to have the opportunities they need to innovate and to compete.

Third, while probably no two participants agreed on all the details of our budget dilemma and what ought to be done about it, there was, after all, a remarkable level of consensus about the need for a balanced approach between a new investment agenda and a long term commitment to deficit reduction that will be credible, public and specific in the short run.

Fourth, despite the enormous range of solutions offered, every speaker who touched the subject reflected the emerging consensus that reducing health care costs and providing a basic system of health care to all Americans is a national imperative. We can't do anything else on the deficit if we fail to curb the monster of spiraling health care costs.

Now we must take the beginnings of the consensuses forged here and move forward. Our work didn't begin here, it won't end here. And

405

I'll need the advice and support of other Americans as we move forward to make the tough choices that lie now in the very near future.

We have to build a legislative package, craft its details, get it through and make it work in the real lives of our country.

This conference didn't answer every question or give us the solution to every problem. No single conference can do that. But the American people should be certain of this: I'm not going to stop working and our team is not going to stop working until the economic challenges have been faced and tackled. Until we have given it our best shot and our best response.

As long as people are out of work and children are left behind, as long as families struggle, as long as the potential of this country is not being fulfilled, we will not rest. We'll explore every idea and challenge every prejudice. We won't stop looking or pushing or trying until our job is done.

I think that what happened in the last two days at least demonstrated to the people who were here—and I hope to the rest of the American people—that while our administration doesn't have all the answers and maybe never will, we're working hard on the problems.

We're going to take what came out of this meeting and what I think will be a virtually unanimous participation by the principles in writing back their one to three page document of suggestions, put it with the rest of the work our team is doing and proceed to put together the budget and the legislative package for January 20th.

Senator Gore.

Vice President-elect Gore: I'd like to make three additional points, briefly.

Number one: there was an impressive agreement among the participants at this conference that the pursuit of environmental efficiency represents an enormous business opportunity for our nation. And an important challenge which we can and must address successfully.

Number two: a better national approach to developing and implementing new technologies—especially to those which by common agreement are likely to have a tremendous leverage over the future—can bring great improvements to our economic performance.

Third and finally: there was a certain magic to the diversity of this conference. And I just want to make this point. That didn't happen by accident. It was intentional and we worked at it.

Everyone who participated in this conference—and I daresay, most who watched the conference—came to feel an extra quality that was a part of the dialogue because of the richness of the diversity at that conference.

406

Every institution in our society has the opportunity to tap into that same richness and diversity if they don't leave it to accident. If they work at it. If we as a nation work at it we can become much greater than the sum of our parts.

Q: Governor, you seemed to be somewhat skeptical in your comments today about the effect of a short term stimulus package. You said it paled compared to reforming health care.

In your remarks just now, you didn't mention short term stimulus. Are you backing away from having a job creation package when you go into the office? A short term package?

PRESIDENT-ELECT CLINTON: No. I think—no. If you go back and look at my—the plan that I started with 13 months ago and the way we modified it, we always paid for all of the things that we were proposing to spend. The argument for the stimulus: I think you create jobs through increasing investment.

I belong to the crowd that believes that we'll create a lot of jobs over the long run if we change the tax system away from consumption toward investment.

If you raise rates on upper income people, but you have an investment tax credit, you have a long—you have a long term capital gains, you have a housing tax credit—you lower your taxes not through lower rates from—and consumption, but through investment. That's what I believe.

So, the whole focus of my economic program will be job generation.

When the deficit became particularly prolonged, the issue then was: should we actually—I mean, the deficit—the recession—the issue then was: should we actually add to the deficit in, let's say, this fiscal year to the tune of somewhere between 20 to 30 to $60 billion—that was the range of numbers discussed today. And I've just simply not reached the final decision on that.

I believe that we'll generate more jobs over the long run—and there was pretty good consensus on that today, too—by increasing investment in the public and private sector, and that our ability to stimulate the economy by simply adding $30 billion more to the deficit over the long run will not be as important as our shift from investment—to investment from consumption.

Q: Are you looking more now toward the lower range though—the 20 rather than the 60—is that fair to say?

PRESIDENT-ELECT CLINTON: Well, first of all, I have to say—I've got to reach a decision about what to do about it. And I'm going to—in terms of the dollars, if we decide to go for a stimulus package to modify this fiscal year's budget, I will make the decision on how much as late as I can based on the latest available evidence.

Andrea?

Q: You said that everything that you had proposed during the last 13 months were paid for. But, a lot was paid for by your suggesting 80 to $100 billion in health cost controls which now Henry Aaron among others told you today that's not going to happen—

PRESIDENT-ELECT CLINTON: No.

Q: —as quickly as you suggested. He said, in fact, that if—you will see meager results in your first term.

PRESIDENT-ELECT CLINTON: No, but—no. Wait a minute. If you go back and look at the—Putting People First, we treated healthcare costs as deficit neutral which I don't necessarily agree with.

But, in other words, we—the assumption behind the other proposals in Putting People First is that for four years it will, in tax dollars, cost as much money to provide universal coverage to those who will have to be paid for by the government, as you can save off the present budget projections.

Q: (Inaudible)—pay for extending your coverage.

PRESIDENT-ELECT CLINTON: That's right. That was going to be—

Q: How are you going to beat that?

PRESIDENT-ELECT CLINTON: That's how we were going to do it. Well, that's not what he was talking about. He was talking about how you couldn't use healthcare cost controls to lower other spending. And I—I had calculated that in all along.

Q: He also claimed that you won't get the savings that you had envisioned from healthcare cost controls in the near term; that—

PRESIDENT-ELECT CLINTON: Well, I didn't—

Q: —you won't have that money to advance toward universal access.

PRESIDENT-ELECT CLINTON: I thought the argument he was making is that it would take that money to pay for universal access. I concede that in the near term.

Ron?

Q: Before—(inaudible)—the consensus that you cited were primarily things that you have been talking about throughout the campaign really: investing more in infrastructure and education, controlling healthcare costs, long term versus short term on the deficit, and so forth.

Was there anything that you heard in the last two days that caused you to change your views about ideas that you have been skeptical about such as the gasoline tax, carbon tax, cap on entitlements? Any of those ideas now look better to you than they did before as a result of what you've heard?

PRESIDENT-ELECT CLINTON: Well, let me answer you in this way. There were a number of things which were brought up repeatedly by people from different walks of life that caused me to think they ought to be considered, at least within some framework.

And let me—on the entitlements issue, you know my position is always those people who can be demonstrated to be getting more out of the entitlement package than they paid in may be asked to pay more for their entitlements.

I am reluctant to say that truly middle class Social Security recipients —people with incomes of between 25 and $30,000 a year—should have those things cut when they are, after all, in a system which is producing a surplus because of the regressivity of our tax system.

I mean, Social Security tax is very unfair. It's unfair to small business because you pay it whether you make any money or not just based on your employees; it's unfair to people with incomes below $51,000 a year as compared with incomes above $100,000 a year because of where the cap is on the Social Security tax.

So, I have been very reluctant on that. But, I think there will plainly be some entitlement reform, and I think the issue is: who is really getting more than they put into it so that it's inter-generationally unfair.

We know, for example, that Medicare recipients with incomes of above $125,000 or so, by and large, could pay more. We know that Social Security recipients at high levels of income are going to draw benefits out of proportion to what they paid in and, therefore, more of that income should be subject to taxation. Those are two things we know. We're looking at the rest.

On the gas tax issue, you know, I never—I mean, we've raised the gas tax here at home. The point I made from the South Dakota primary forward about the gas tax was that I was not in favor of a huge gas tax increase on top of the present tax system because it's already unfair to the middle class.

And that I thought—there were a lot of good arguments made for the gas tax today, and for consumption taxes generally. But, I don't think that we should be doing anything to aggravate the inequalities of the last decade.

So, from my point of view, if somebody came to me with a gas tax proposal, I would say: how are you going to fold it into other proposals to make it fairer because you have: number one, increasing income inequality in the 1980s; and number two, increasing taxation inequality in the 1980s.

And you put those two things together, you don't want a—no matter what other merits of the gas tax are, you don't want to load it onto the inequality we already have.

So, there would have to be some sort of offset, from my point of view, for me to entertain that seriously from my policy folks.

Yes?

Q: (Inaudible)—concern expressed about slow money slide growth. And I would like to know how you plan on shaping your relationship with the Federal Reserve and Chairman Greenspan. Will you plan to meet with him once a month?

And also in relation to that, if the economy begins to grow, will you fight a raise—a rise in interest rates?

PRESIDENT-ELECT CLINTON: Let me answer the first question first.

As you know, I invited Chairman Greenspan down here, and I had a very good talk with him that lasted more than two hours, as I remember. I asked him to stay for lunch, and we talked about a whole wide range of things. And I was immensely impressed by the range and scope of the conversation. It was a good conversation.

I don't know that we will agree always on what the money supply targets ought to be. You should know that there is now some debate—and this is a subject that did not come up, interestingly enough—the whole money supply target thing only came up one time, as I remember, the last two days—but the relationship of the growth of the money supplies is now defined given how hard it is to define what it is to the growth of the economy is more debatable now that it used to be.

So, one of the things that we're going to try to decide on, I think, in the next couple of weeks in our economic team, is what our definition of the money supply is, how much we think it has to grow, what our policy is, and at least I would discuss that with Mr. Greenspan.

You know, under our system, the Federal Reserve is separate from the Executive Branch; not under the political control of the Executive Branch. But, I think—Senator Bentsen and I expect to have—both of us—a good relationship with the Federal Reserve, and to work with them to share information and research, and to do things in the public interest. And if we have disagreements, we'll have them and they'll be public, I think, eventually.

But, it's an important relationship, and I will do what I can to work on it.

Q: (Inaudible)—it becomes necessary because the economy is growing. Will you fight that?

President-elect Clinton: Well, I will until—I would be—I would be opposed to that unless there was serious evidence of a return to inflation. If you go back over all the charts of the first day, and then the two discussions earlier in the day—the first two discussions—there was a general consensus, even among those who were fighting—if you go back—remember this?—there was the Henry Aaron position that said: we probably don't need any stimulus. Sure don't decide on one now.

And then there was the position taken by Tobin supported by Eisner and Faux that, you know, do a $60 billion one. And then they argued one year, two years, year and-a-half. Remember that? Those were the extremes.

But, they all still seemed to be more or less in agreement on the other questions. So, I just—you know—we're just going to have to see.

Q: Governor, could you tell us if you heard anything over these past two days that would lead you to believe that the US economy is, indeed, coming out of the recession, and that the structural problems that you've been concerned about repeatedly over these past few

411

weeks have been resolved? The thought being, of course, that if you do go ahead—as you appear to be indicating—with some sort of economic stimulus program—20 billion or 40 billion or 60 billion—the fear among some, like Henry Aaron, is that you will overheat the economy and you will generate a lot of inflation which could be real painful to many Americans.

PRESIDENT-ELECT CLINTON: Well, that's what I was going to—I didn't make myself clear in response.

He did not imply today that he thought inflation was a serious, imminent threat. What he thought was that if we didn't go after the deficit, that long term interest rates would be high, and that the economy would never fully recover. I'm sorry I wasn't as clear as I should have.

But, there was a big consensus among those folks that there was a huge undercapacity in this economy, and that, therefore, inflation didn't seem to be a serious, immediate threat.

And that's—to answer your question—why I wouldn't favor raising interests if the economy looks like it's picking up, because the number was used by one of the people today that there was a $300 billion undercapacity in the economy. I don't think that's what the worry is.

I think the fight here is between—deficit reduction and stimulus—is whether or not a short term bump in the economy—in the absence of long term deficit reduction—will get you—may heat the economy up now, but you'll be right back in a recession within two years or three years because long term interest rates will remain high, and the American economic system won't have the discipline it needs. And I think that is a serious problem.

There was—I think there was a pretty good consensus here. And I can tell you there's a pretty good consensus among our advisors that, whatever we do in the short run—that is, should there be a stimulus, and if so, how big—there's a consensus on two things: whether you increase the deficit or not in the first year, you must increase investment in the first year and every year thereafter.

And there must be a credible multi-year deficit reduction program; perhaps one which would run well into—beyond the next four years.

Q: Can I—(inaudible)—

PRESIDENT-ELECT CLINTON: Sure.

412

Q: Does that mean you are emerging from this conference convinced that there does, in fact, have to be at least some stimulus to the economy?

PRESIDENT-ELECT CLINTON: Well, it means—

Q: (Inaudible).

PRESIDENT-ELECT CLINTON: If you define stimulus as a substantial increase in investment incentives, public and private, the answer to that is yes. If you define stimulus as meaning am I going to deliberately increase the deficit in this budget year, the answer to that is I haven't made up my mind yet.

And, you know, you asked—you know—you asked two other questions. Are we coming out of this recession? I don't think the evidence is in.

Am I convinced there's been any progress on the structural problems of the economy that we started out with? Absolutely not.

VICE PRESIDENT-ELECT GORE: Can I add something to that?

PRESIDENT-ELECT CLINTON: Yes.

VICE PRESIDENT-ELECT GORE: I'd like to add briefly that I think there was a clear consensus in favor of an additional tool for adding stimulus to the economy, and that is: carefully, in a sensitive way, changing the regulatory system to get more investment capital out of the banks and insurance companies and pension funds, into small businesses for expansion, and into other business for expansion.

And as Laura Tyson said, it needs to be studied and handled very carefully. But, I think there was a real consensus that that can be done, and must be done.

PRESIDENT-ELECT CLINTON: Let me just reinforce that. And again, I don't want to minimize any of these other issues that we are always talking about—you know, should there be a stimulus, how much should it be, and all that.

But, you heard the President of the American Banking Association say that a 4 percent increase in lending would free up $86 billion a

413

year. The credit crunch is what I saw all over New England, I saw in South Florida, I saw in California.

It is one of the great, sort of, dysfunctional parts of the economy that the engine of our job growth over the last few years has been small business, and there has been a real absence of available investment capital for small businesses.

The other thing—let me just say one other thing that I neglected to say in my opening statement. There was an astonishing consensus among people who were there that there wasn't enough government money—whether you think there should be a stimulus or not—that there's not going to be enough taxpayer dollars to revitalize the cities—in the absence of a dramatic increase in the environment which gets private sector dollars in there.

And that—that—everybody talked about that. They said: you ought to leverage public dollars with private dollars.

If you remember, the business person from Chicago who sounded the most aggressive yesterday in terms of telling me: you've got to challenge the business people. He didn't say: you've got to write a bigger check for my city. He said: you've got to get people to put business into my area. You've got to give us a chance to participate in that.

And I think, again, I would say that's one of those areas where there's a huge amount of under-utilized capacity. You could put a lot of investment, and put a lot of people to work in a lot of these cities, and have no impact on inflation at all.

Yes?

Q: Mr. Alvarez Machain was acquitted yesterday. Has the United States learned anything from this experience? And are you prepared to renegotiate the extradition agreement with Mexico?

PRESIDENT-ELECT CLINTON: I—what was the first part of your question? I'm sorry.

Q: Mr. Alvarez Machain, the Mexican doctor who was—

PRESIDENT-ELECT CLINTON: Who was taken out of the United States.

Q: Was acquitted yesterday. And did you think—I mean, the United States, has it learned anything from this experience? And are you—

414

PRESIDENT-ELECT CLINTON: Well—

Q: —prepared to renegotiate the—

PRESIDENT-ELECT CLINTON: I would like—I'll tell you what I think. I think we should review our position. And I know what the Supreme Court ruled in this case.

You know—basically, I know that the Supreme Court ruled that unless the treaty explicitly forbids it, the country—our country was free to go into Mexico, or into any other country that we had a similar treaty with, and take someone out. That was the ruling of the Supreme Court.

My own view is that that is too broad a policy for our country to have. I think that goes too far.

I wouldn't waive all rights under any circumstances for the representatives of my country to go into another country to extradite someone or take them out, but I would say that we should not even think about that unless the other government had either deliberately refused to honor extradition—you know, in trying to undermine what we did —or not lifted a hand to try to implement the law.

I think in the absence of some evidence that the government was actually taking a dive or trying to thwart us, that the principle that the Supreme Court articulated was way too broad. And I—so I will review that in the hope of maybe working out a slightly different arrangement between the United States and Mexico that now exists in that treaty.

Q: In view of repeatedly warning people not to expect any quick fixes for the economy, now that you have your team in place and you've had this conference, do you have a focus on some specific targets and goals over 6 months, 12 months, people can expect in terms of new job creation, gross domestic product, some specific going forths?

PRESIDENT-ELECT CLINTON: Well, I'm going to ask for that when we get down to the specifics, but we haven't had that—the meeting—any meeting in which those kinds of things might come out, have not occurred yet.

Yes?

Q: Will you call an early meeting of the G-7 ministers?

415

PRESIDENT-ELECT CLINTON: An early meeting?

Q: Yes. An early summit meeting of the G-7 as was suggested?

PRESIDENT-ELECT CLINTON: Well, let me say this. I'm going to—I attempted to make contact with all of them, and I think I have talked to them all—all my counterparts.

And I've talked to Senator Bentsen about it extensively—about—and you heard him mention it. He understands that a big part of his work will be engaging the finance ministers and the central bankers of the other countries.

And so, I think we will be involved with them from day one. Whether I will call an early meeting or seek an early meeting with them as a group, I have not determined yet.

Thanks.

HOWARD COUNTY
LIBRARY

Keep this card in the book pocket.
Book is due on the last date stamped.